*The Organization
of Behavior*
A NEUROPSYCHOLOGICAL THEORY

The Organization of Behavior

A NEUROPSYCHOLOGICAL THEORY

D. O. HEBB
McGill University

LEA LAWRENCE ERLBAUM ASSOCIATES, PUBLISHERS
Mahwah, New Jersey   London

Lawrence Erlbaum Associates, Inc., Publishers
10 Industrial Avenue
Mahwah, NJ 07430

Cover design by Kathryn Houghtaling Lacey

Library of Congress Cataloging-in-Publication Data

Hebb, D. O. (Donald Olding)
The organization of behavior : a neuropsychological theory /
   D. O. Hebb.
      p. cm.
Originally published: New York : Wiley, 1949. (A Wiley
   book in clinical psychology). With new foreword.
      Includes bibliographical references and index.
ISBN 0-8058-4300-0 (paper : alk. paper)
1. Neuropsychology. I. Title.
BF181 .H4   2002
150.19'8—dc21   2002018867
                                                       CIP

Printed in the United States of America
10 9 8 7 6 5 4 3 2

To
G. C. H., C. O. H.
and
A. M. H.

DONALD OLDING HEBB

Photograph by Richard E. Brown, April 1979.

Foreword

Richard E. Brown
Dalhousie University

Peter M. Milner
McGill University

Since the publication of *The Organization of Behavior* in 1949, it has become one of the most influential books in Psychology and Neuroscience (over 4100 SCI citations since 1989). According to Adams (1998, p. 419): "Two of the most influential books in the history of biology are Darwin's *On the Origin of Species* (1859) and Hebb's *Organization of Behavior* (1949). The books are famous because of the simple but powerful ideas that they contain." While Darwin's book can be purchased in any bookshop, Hebb's book has been out of print since 1966, ensuring that Hebb's comment that a classic normally means "cited but not read" (Fentress, 1987, p. 105) would be true in his case. One of us (REB) found this situation intolerable and decided to organize a reprinting of this book. This new edition of *The Organization of Behavior*, therefore, rectifies a long-standing problem for behavioral neuroscientists—the inability to obtain one of the most cited publications in the field. A complete list of Hebb's publications from 1925 to 1987 is also included.

The Organization of Behavior played a significant part in the development of physiological psychology; the investigation of the neural foundations of behavior (Fentress, 1999; Milner 1999). It introduced the idea of the "Hebb synapse" and the "Hebbian cell assembly." The more frequently cited of these two ideas is the Hebb synapse, but, as pointed out by Seung (2000, p. 1166): "Hebb's synapse is not his only legacy. Even after half a century, his theory as a whole is still inspiring, because it is a general framework for relating behavior to synaptic organization through the dynamics of neural networks." Hebb was amused that as a result of his neurophysiological postulate, learning synapses had acquired his name—"because this postulate is one of the few aspects of the theory he did not consider completely original. Something like it had been proposed by many psychologists before him, including Freud in his early years as a neurobiologist." (Milner, 1993, p.127).

1. A Short Biography of Donald O. Hebb

Donald Olding Hebb was born on July 22nd, 1904 in the village of Chester, Nova Scotia, Canada. Both of his parents were physicians and his mother was the third woman to obtain an M.D. from the medical school of Dalhousie University in Halifax, Nova Scotia. His earliest ambition was to write a successful novel so he studied English and Philosophy at Dalhousie University, graduating in 1925. Although his degree was in Arts, he also took classes in chemistry, physics and mathematics, obtaining a second-class distinction in mathematics and a first class distinction in physics. He spent the next year teaching at the high-school he had attended in Chester. During this time he discovered Freud and James and began to study psychology. He then moved to Montreal and in 1929 became a part-time graduate student at McGill University, taking a graduate seminar in systematic psychology (Dalhousie University had no Department of Psychology at the time). To support himself he took a job as a teacher and after a year he was promoted to principal of an elementary school in Montreal. During the next few years he became an enthusiastic reformer of teaching methods [1; numbers refer to Hebb's publication list], but his reforms were not always appreciated and he became a full-time graduate student in psychology at McGill in 1931. He completed an MA thesis, entitled "Conditioned and Unconditioned Reflexes and Inhibition" in April 1932. Although Hebb [112, p. 283], in the light of subsequent work, dismissed this MA thesis as nonsense, it does contain original ideas and was passed "cum laude" by two examiners. As the thesis was theoretical, Hebb was encouraged to do experimental work, which he started under the supervision of one of his examiners, Dr. Boris Babkin, a former student of Pavlov.

During the writing of his MA thesis, Hebb was bedridden with a tubercular hip, and his experimental work ended when his wife was killed in a car accident. He became depressed and disenchanted with the direction of his research and the McGill psychology department. Encouraged by Professor Babkin, Hebb wrote to Karl Lashley at the University of Chicago and was accepted there as a PhD student in July 1934. Lashley was an eminent and respected physiological psychologist. In fact, during the 1920's his laboratory was almost the only one in America where genuine research on the neural bases of behavior was being done. He was at the peak of his career when Hebb became his student. Hebb learned a great deal during the year he spent in Chicago, with lectures from such giants as Thurstone, Köhler, Herrick, and Lashley.

The next year Lashley was offered a professorship at Harvard and Hebb obtained permission to accompany him, so his PhD was awarded by Harvard University. His PhD thesis (Hebb, 1936) examined the innate organization of visual perception in the rat and the results of this research were published in a series of three papers [2, 3, 4]. In these papers, Hebb concluded that some aspects of rat vision are innate, though by the time he wrote this book he had reverted to a more empiricist position. Hebb remained at Harvard for another year as a teaching assistant and to complete research on place learning in rats that he had started in Chicago.

His first appointment after leaving Harvard (1937) was a two-year fellowship with the neurosurgeon Wilder Penfield, director of the newly established Montreal Neurological Institute. His responsibility was to investigate intellectual deficits in patients with cortical lesions, mostly those resulting from operations performed for the relief of epilepsy. He was particularly intrigued by the finding that patients with large frontal-lobe lesions had normal intelligence-test scores, some even improved after operation. He also detected visual impairment in a patient after right temporal lobectomy, a cortical region not previously associated with vision. Hebb's work with Penfield at the Montreal Neurological Institute developed his interest in human brain function and the behavioral effects of neurological damage [9], especially with respect to intelligence [7, 8, 13] and initiated a long-term collaboration between the two men. Indeed, Hebb's student, Brenda Milner, began her work with Penfield and went on to study H. M., surely one of the most famous patients in the history of neuropsychology.

At the end of his Fellowship Hebb accepted a position at Queen's University in Kingston, Ontario and studied the effect of cortical lesions on rat learning. He wrote a paper in which he made the unheard of proposal that early experience could permanently influence intelligence [18], a theme that runs through much of Hebb's later writing, including this book. He also developed the Hebb-Williams maze during this time, although the paper was not published until much later [34]. This work arose from Hebb's interest in intelligence testing and he was attempting to develop a Stanford-Binet test for rats.

In the meantime, Lashley had been appointed Director of the Yerkes Laboratories of Primate Biology in Orange Park, Florida. In 1942 he persuaded Hebb to join him in an investigation of the effects of brain lesions on intelligence and emotion in chimpanzees. During the five years he spent in Florida, Hebb devised tests of chimpanzee emotion as well as making some pioneer observations of dolphin behavior [38]. His work with chimpanzees developed his interest in emotionality [28] and led him to compare emotional problems in chimpanzees and humans [35]. Concerning his time working with chimpanzees, Hebb said that he "learned more about human beings during that time than in any other five-year period of my life, except the first." [112, p. 293]. It was during this period with Lashley and his colleagues that Hebb wrote most of *The Organization of Behavior*.

In 1947 Hebb returned to McGill [at a salary of $5500 per year, plus $500 moving expenses] as one of four new professors recruited to revive a psychology department that had all but ceased to exist during the war. The Chairman, Robert MacLeod, moved to Cornell the next year and Hebb occupied the Chair for the next ten years. When *The Organization of Behavior* was published in 1949, it was, to Hebb's astonishment, an immediate success, but he was in no position to sit back and enjoy the acclaim. After the rather sedate pace of life in Orange Park he was now teaching three undergraduate courses, including the large introductory course, plus an evening graduate seminar, setting up animal labs and arranging funding for research on the effects of rearing on perception and intelligence in rats and dogs. He was also preparing an introductory textbook for his course [61]. This left him with little time, or incentive, to tinker with his neural theory or to revise it in the light of the revolutionary developments in neuroanatomy, neurophysiology and information theory that were taking place.

Under Hebb, McGill was at the forefront of the physiological approach to psychology. McGill graduates of that era were in demand in all parts of the world. Hebb's textbook, published in 1958, was distinctly physiological in scope and further contributed to the dissemination of his neural theories of mental processes. For the next 25 years he taught his notoriously rigorous graduate seminar (mandatory for every graduate student) and Introductory Psychology to classes of more than a thousand students. In 1970 he was appointed to a four-year term as Chancellor of McGill. He was successively elected President of the Canadian Psychological Association and the American Psychological Associations; he was also elected a Fellow of both the Royal Society of London and the American Academy of Arts and Sciences. He received many other honors, including innumerable honorary degrees. In 1976 he retired to his family home in Nova Scotia and was appointed honorary Professor at Dalhousie University in 1977. He died in 1985 following a hip replacement operation.

2. The Organization of Behavior

When did Hebb develop the ideas that went into *The Organization of Behavior*? The idea for the Hebb synapse first appeared in 1932 in his MA thesis, where he discussed the functioning of the synapse in conditioned reflexes. Hebb opens his introduction by stating that: "The purpose of this paper is to present a theory of the functioning of the synapse based on the experimental work of Sherrington and Pavlov, on reflexes and inhibitions. The implications of these things for psychological theory, in some aspects, has been far from clear. In looking for a firm basis for psychology in physiology, there are some peculiarities about the results of both investigators which demand serious consideration and suggest another interpretation of their work" (Hebb, 1932, p. 2).

In Figure 1 of his thesis, Hebb makes his first attempt to illustrate the synaptic changes associated with conditioning. The figure shows branches of a stimulus input going to two unconditioned reflex arcs. Pavlov's experiments show that if one of the

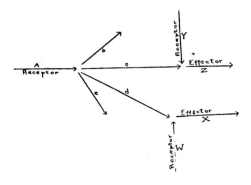

FIG. I

$\left.\begin{array}{l}W-X \\ Y-Z\end{array}\right\}$ reflex arcs.

A is another receptor.

b,c,d,e, connecting neurons.

(Arrowhead gives direction in which impulses
  are transmitted.)

FIGURE 1.

reflex arcs is active when a stimulus is applied to the input, the
branch going to that reflex becomes more potent; branches going to inactive effectors do not. Hebb went further, assuming
that the potency of other branches declines. He summarized the
first section of his thesis as follows: "An excited neuron tends to
decrease its discharge to inactive neurons, and increase this discharge to any active neuron, and therefore to form a route to it,
whether there are intervening neurons between the two or not.
With repetition this tendency is prepotent in the formation of
neural routes" (Hebb, 1932, p. 13).

This may be seen as the emergence of the Hebb synapse idea.
Hebb underlined it (the typewriter code for italics) as he later
italicized the corresponding postulate in his book.

On November 24th 1934, Hebb submitted a revised version of
his MA thesis as a term paper for Anatomy 316 (Elementary Neu-

rology), which he took as a PhD student at the University of Chicago. This paper, entitled "The interpretation of experimental data on neural action" was noted as "A very thoughtful paper" by C. J. Herrick. In this paper, Hebb shows two diagrams of possible synaptic activity during conditioning and states that: "There is as yet no understanding theoretically of the process of conditioning, and when this is understood, it may throw light on the reflex activity of the [spinal] cord, and perhaps account for the existence of some of the apparently rigidly inherited patterns. The conception of block and facilitation at the synapse postulates a process which can strengthen and perpetuate a route once formed, but none whatever to account for the establishment of the route in the first place—a most important weakness in the whole theory" (Hebb, 1934, p.15).

Hebb's first use of the term "Organization of Behavior" was in the title of two papers published in 1938 [5, 6] on the field orientation of the rat. In these papers Hebb examined the effects of cortical lesions on learning visual discriminations. Although these papers have the mark of Lashley on them, Hebb's focus was to develop a better behavioral test for the study of the effects of cerebral destruction. He states that: "It is clear that the success of the physiological analysis depends on the adequacy of the behavioral tests used. Much of the difficulty found in the evaluation of the effects of cerebral destruction, both clinically and with animal experimentation, is due to the fundamental difficulty of the analysis of behavior and to the unsatisfactory available accounts of it." [5, p. 333]. In light of recent research on context conditioning, it is interesting that these studies discussed the importance of room cues on the discrimination of objects in an open field.

During the years between 1934 and 1946, Hebb continued to work on his ideas about the organization of behavior. While still in Chicago in 1934, he wrote five chapters (90 pages) of a first draft of a book entitled "Scientific methods in psychology: A theory of epistemology based on objective methods in psychology." Parts of this book were to be included as a final chapter in *The Organization of Behavior* but were deleted during the editorial process.

In Feburary, 1944 Hebb discovered that Lorente de Nó had recently shown that closed circuits were to be found throughout the brain, and "that one neuron by itself may not be able to excite a second neuron at the synapse, but can do so if supported by simultaneous action from another neuron" [112, p. 295]. It was these ideas (of neural loops) of Lorente de Nó that Hebb realized "were just what he needed to develop a more realistic theory of the mind" (Milner, 1993, p. 127). On 28 April, 1944, Hebb wrote to Lorente de Nó to ask if he could spend a month at the Rockefeller Institute to "become familiar with your work." When Lorente de Nó replied on 1 May 1944 that "At present my work is concerned with the relationship between the production of the nerve impulse and the metabolism of the nerve, a problem that is of little immediate interest to a psychologist," Hebb decided to delay his study trip to Rockefeller and wrote to Lorente de Nó (4 May 1944) that "I am profoundly convinced that psychological progress will depend on research such as yours ... that psychological theory can go no farther without a more detailed basis in neurophysiological fact."

Hebb first outlined his ideas for *The Organization of Behavior* in five pages of typed notes in June 1944. These notes contain his early thoughts on the term "organization." In this definition, he considered both behavioral and physiological organization and considered the "concept of *set*," which he used to denote the pre-existing state of the nervous system encountered by an incoming stimulus. The second draft of *The Organization of Behavior* was developed in March-July 1945 and written under the title "Precis: The structure of a set of neuropsychological speculations." A complete draft of *The Organization of Behavior* was finished in 1946 and sent to Lashley, who wrote two pages of comments on the manuscript in February 1947. In June 1947, the book was submitted to Charles Thomas publishers. Henry Nissen received the manuscript from Thomas on 21 June 1947. It was 150 pages long and insured for $300.00.

Nissen edited this manuscript from June 1947 to September 1948, sending Hebb numerous comments and suggestions for changes. On 22 September, 1948, Hebb sent the final draft of the manuscript to the publishers. However, in January, 1949, Thomas decided not to publish the book, citing "circumstances beyond their control" and returned it to Hebb. After consulting with Beach, who suggested Hoeber (the publishers of his 1948 book, *Hormones and Behavior*), and considering Appleton-Century as publishers, Hebb sent the book to John Wiley and Sons, who accepted it with great praise on 18 March 1949 and published it in the fall of 1949.

On April 26, 1949, Hebb wrote to Lorente de Nó that "I believe that my book will be able to show that modern ideas in neurophysiology, and particularly some of those that you have developed, have a revolutionary significance for psychological theory."

3. The Cell Assembly: Conception.

Ever since his observations of patients at the Montreal Neurological Institute, Hebb had puzzled over the nature of thought and the way ideas might be represented in the brain. The relevance to his problem of Lorente de Nó's recurrent loops struck home to him in 1944, as mentioned earlier, and provided the key to his theory. Lashley (1942), in a paper written before Hebb arrived in Orange Park, raised the possibility that reverberations of Lorente de Nó's loops might play a role in vision. His use of the loops as oscillators for his wave-interference theory was more limited and very different from Hebb's grand scheme to represent concepts with them, but Hebb never refers to it in his book, which may be one reason for Lashley's less than enthusiastic reception of it.

In the absence of evidence to the contrary, Hebb assumed that before they became cell assemblies, Lorente de Nó's loops were randomly connected to sensory input. When a stimulus was impressed on the system some loops would receive more input than others, depending on the pattern of the connections, and they would therefore reverberate more intensely and persistently. After a number of such episodes the connections within the most vigorously reverberating group of cells would be strengthened to such an extent that partial input, or even remote associations, would subsequently activate the whole assembly.

Hebb postulated that when an assembly was firing as a result of sensory input, its activity represented the perception of the stimulus; when it fired in the absence of the corresponding sensory input the activity represented the concept of the stimulus. When a sequence of stimuli occurred frequently, Hebb assumed that the aroused assemblies would become associated with each other via strengthened cross-linkages, to establish what he called *phase sequences.*

Having established the physical reality of ideas and their mode of association, Hebb was able to discuss expectancies, attention, attitudes, intelligence, even mental illness, in the rest of the book with a freedom not permitted to a serious psychologist in America for almost half a century. It is probable that this contributed to the popularity of the book among psychologists who had been deprived of such rich fare for too long. The earlier, more speculative chapters, on the other hand, attracted the attention of computer scientists, engineers, philosophers and biologists of all persuasions. Before its publication, Hebb used a manuscript of the book in his graduate seminar at McGill and it fell into the hands of one of us (PMM, who had spent the war working on radar and atomic energy). After reading a few chapters he applied to do graduate work with Hebb and was accepted.

Hebb's neurophysiological postulate (p. 62) was of particular interest to physiologists. Psychologists have always assumed that association requires contiguity of two or more events, but many physiologists thought that learning occurred when a connection was used repeatedly. As Hebb pointed out in his MA thesis, if such a synapse is initially ineffective it can never increase in strength, however often it fires. The implication of Hebb's postulate is that synapses increase in strength only if the post-synaptic neuron is fired by some other input at about the same time as a pre-synaptic impulse occurs. When synapses that behaved in this way were found, neurophysiologists called them "Hebb synapses" and the name has stuck.

Learning synapses in computer models of the brain are also often referred to as Hebb synapses, though usually they do not adhere strictly to Hebb's definition. In order to prevent all synapses from increasing indefinitely in strength, it is additionally postulated that synaptic effectiveness is reduced when pre- and post-synaptic elements fire at separate times. It is interesting that in his 1932 MA thesis, the synaptic learning process described by Hebb (see page *xi* above) included a process by which synaptic strength was reduced when the post-synaptic membrane did not fire at the same time as the incoming impulse.

4. The Cell Assembly: Half a century later.

Hebb's notes indicate that the chapters in which the cell assembly and phase sequence are developed cost Hebb much time and effort, and he was aware that too often speculation had to be substituted for vital neurological and anatomical information that was not available. On page *xl* of the Introduction he gives the reader permission to skip those chapters. He argues strongly in defense of his neural speculation, but on page 80 he tells us that he expects the model to be amended in the future, as better information about the nervous system becomes available. The future is now with us, and it is possible to see that Hebb was not fortunate in his timing relative to the state of neurophysiological knowledge.

As the book was being published, information was coming to light concerning the importance of the reticular system of the brainstem for arousal. During the next few years the relevance to behavior of subcortical structures such as the amygdala, septal area and hippocampus began to be evident. Furthermore, as he worked on the book, Hebb accepted the widespread belief of most physiologists and avoided incorporating synaptic inhibition (though a theory to account for it was advanced in his MA thesis), only to have J. C. Eccles (Eccles et al., 1954), previously the most vociferous opponent of the idea, conclusively demonstrate its existence a year or two later.

Somewhat more recently, new genetic, histological and brain imaging techniques have fueled the rise of a modern phrenology, quite at variance with the anti-localization sentiment prevailing when this book was being written. Even if the present trend toward nativism is sometimes exaggerated there seems little doubt that Hebb's assumption that cortical connections are initially random was overcautious. His argument that vision developed very slowly in human babies was based on two very dubious observations. The impaired vision of chimpanzees reared in the dark turned out to be caused by irreversible damage to the retina, and von Senden's reports of the difficulties of people given sight as adults after being born blind could be plausibly explained as damage to innate connections due to lack of normal stimulation during development.

Even the simple purity of Hebb's neurophysiological learning postulate has proved illusory. We now know that synaptic activity gives rise to a complex sequence of molecular changes, some brief, others lasting for hours, days, and sometimes permanently, that change the characteristics of both sides of the synaptic junction (e.g. Greengard, 2001). The inelegant reverberating loops of the cell assembly, almost as impervious to research as the mental activity they were meant to replace, are no longer needed to explain the persistence of thoughts. The stimulated neurons may continue to fire because of a persisting intrinsic change rather than by recurrent restimulation.

Without Hebb's speculation many of these discoveries might not have been made, or only after a longer delay. The biological speculations in chapters 4 and 5 of this book are interesting from a historical point of view, though as neuroscience they have now been largely superceded. Many of the later chapters, being based mainly on more reliable behavioral observations, continue to be valid and to the new reader they frequently bring the tingle of encountering a brilliant, and often witty, insight into a problem.

When he embarked upon the book, Hebb's original purpose was to explain in neural terms the processes whereby early experiences build the concepts required for subsequent intelligent behavior. He made some progress towards that end and pioneered the way for the vast armies of neuroscientists presently engaged in the task. What he succeeded in doing was to engineer a change in the philosophical outlook of behavioral scientists. Traditionally psychologists were dualists, believing that mental processes take place in an incorporeal mind; a "black box" whose workings could only be inferred by introspection or by observations of the behavior it produced. Hebb offered a more direct window to the mind, investigation of its neural machinery. His monograph held the promise of a genuinely monist psychology.

5. Why Hebb remains important today

It is difficult to read a paper in the neurobiology of learning and memory today that does not mention its debt to Hebb. To cite but one example, Döbrössy and Dunnett (2001, p. 871) state that "The mechanisms by which environment and experience can influence brain structure and function first received direct experimental attention after Hebb's observations and theoretical proposals that learning is represented in the brain by synaptic changes in response to repeated concurrent activation." The reviews of Hebb's ideas by Fentress (1999) and Milner (1999) show how Hebb has influenced research in many areas of psychology and neuroscience and how our findings have now gone beyond Hebb's wildest speculations. Hebb's cell assembly theory is becoming more important for guiding research (Sakurai, 1999) while the Hebb synapse remains a central component of molecular biological (Tsien, 2000) and computational (Klemm et al, 2000) models of learning. As stated by Ray Klein (1999, p. 3), "In the scientific literature, references to Hebb, the Hebbian cell assembly, the Hebb synapse and the Hebb rule increase each year. These forceful ideas of 1949 are now applied in engineering, robotics, and computer science as well as neurophysiology, neuroscience and psychology—a tribute to Hebb's scientific acumen, foresight and courage to put forth a foundational neuropsychological theory of the organization of behaviour."

Acknowledgements

We would like to thank the McGill University Archives and, in particular, Gordon Burr, Senior Archivist, for his help in obtaining copies of archival material.

References

Adams, P. (1998). Hebb and Darwin. *Journal of Theoretical Biology, 195*: 419–438.

Döbrössy, M. D., & Dunnett, S. B. (2001). The influence of environment and experience on neural grafts. *Nature Reviews Neuroscience, 2*: 871–879.

Eccles, J. C., Fatt, P., & Landgren, S. (1954). The 'direct' inhibitory pathway in the spinal cord. *Australian Journal of Science, 16*: 130—134.

Fentress, J. C. (1987). D. O. Hebb and the developmental organization of behavior. *Developmental Psychobiology, 20*: 103–109.

Fentress, J. C. (1999). The organization of behaviour revisited. *Canadian Journal of Experimental Psychology, 53*: 8–19.

Greengard, P. (2001). The neurobiology of slow synaptic transmission. *Science 294*: 1024–1030.

Hebb, D. O. (1932). Conditioned and unconditioned reflexes and inhibition. Unpublished MA Thesis, McGill University, Montreal, Quebec, April 1932.

Hebb, D. O. (1934). The interpretation of experimental data on neural action. Unpublished manuscript, University of Chicago, Nov 24, 1934.

Hebb, D. O. (1936). The innate organization of visual perception in the rat. Unpublished PhD Thesis, Harvard University, March, 1936.

Klein, R. M. (1999). The Hebb legacy. *Canadian Journal of Experimental Psychology, 53*: 1–3.

Klemm, K., Bornholdt, S., & Schuster, H. G. (2000). Beyond Hebb: Exclusive-OR and biological learning. *Physical Review Letters, 84*: 3013–3016.

Milner, P. M. (1993). The mind and Donald O. Hebb. *Scientific American, 268*(1), 124–129.

Milner, P. M. (1999). *The Autonomous Brain*. Lawrence Erlbaum Associates, Mahwah, NJ.

Sakurai, Y. (1999). How do cell assemblies encode information in the brain? *Neuroscience and Biobehavioral Reviews, 23*: 785–796.

Seung, H. S. (2000). Half a century of Hebb. *Nature Neuroscience, supplement, 3*, 1166.

Tsien, J. Z. (2000). Linking Hebb's coincidence-detection to memory formation. *Current Opinion in Neurobiology, 10*: 266–273.

Donald Olding Hebb: Publications in Chronological Order: 1925–1987.

Numbering system based on: Milner, P. M. & Milner, B. (1996). Donald Olding Hebb: 22 July 1904—20 August 1985. *Biographical memoirs of the Royal Society of London 42*: 193–204.

__. Hebb, D. O. (1925). 25 class history. *Dalhousie Gazette*, 25–29.

1. Hebb, D. O. (1930). Elementary school methods. *Teacher's magazine* 12(51): 23–26.

2. Hebb, D. O. (1937). The innate organization of visual activity: I. Perception of figures by rats reared in total darkness. *Journal of Genetic Psychology* 51: 101–126.

3. Hebb, D. O. (1937). The innate organization of visual activity. II. Transfer of response in the discrimination of brightness and size by rats reared in total darkness. *Journal of Comparative Psychology* 24: 277–299.

4. Hebb, D. O. (1938). The innate organization of visual activity. III. Discrimination of brightness after removal of the striate cortex in the rat. *Journal of Comparative Psychology* 25: 427–437.

5. Hebb, D. O. (1938). Studies of the organization of behavior. I. Behavior of the rat in a field orientation. *Journal of Comparative Psychology* 25: 333–353.

6. Hebb, D. O. (1938). Studies of the organization of behavior. II. Changes in the field orientation of the rat after cortical destruction. *Journal of Comparative Psychology* 26: 427–441.

7. Hebb, D. O. (1939). Intelligence in man after large removals of cerebral tissue: Defects following right temporal lobectomy. *Journal of General Psychology* 21: 437–446.

8. Hebb, D. O. (1939). Intelligence in man after large removals of cerebral tissue: Report of four left frontal lobe cases. *Journal of General Psychology* 21: 73–87.

9. Hebb, D. O., & Penfield, W. (1940). Human behavior after extensive bilateral remov,al from the frontal lobes. *Archives of Neurology & Psychiatry (Chicago)* 43: 421–438.

10. Hebb, D. O. (1940). Clinical tests of adult intelligence. *Psychological Bulletin* 37: 513–514.

11. Hebb, D. O. (1941). Clinical evidence concerning the nature of normal adult test performance. *Psychological Bulletin* 38: 593 (Abstract).

12. Hebb, D. O. (1941, April). Higher level difficulty in verbal test material. *Bulletin of the Canadian Psychological Association* 1: 29 (Abstract).

13. Hebb, D. O. (1941). Human intelligence after removal of cerebral tissue from the right frontal lobe. *Journal of General Psychology* 25: 257–265.

14. Hebb, D. O. (1941). *The McGill Picture Anomaly Series*. Kingston, Ontario, Author.

15. Hebb, D. O. (1941). The McGill Picture Anomaly Series: Data on 100 unsophisticated adults. *Bulletin of the Canadian Psychological Association* 1: 47–49.

16. Hebb, D. O. & Williams, K. (1941, February). Experimental control of cues determining the rat's orientation. *Bulletin of the Canadian Psychological Association* 1: 22–23 (Abstract)

17. Hebb, D. O. (1942). Observations on cerebral dysfunction. *Psychological Bulletin* 39: 491– 492 (Abstract).

18. Hebb, D. O. (1942). The effect of early and late brain injury upon test scores, and the nature of normal adult intelligence. *Proceedings of the American Philosophical Society* 85: 275–292.

19. Hebb, D. O. (1942). *The McGill Picture Anomaly Series, M and N*. Orange Park, Fla.: Yerkes Laboratories. 34 pp.

20. Hebb, D. O., & Morton, N. W. (1942). The McGill verbal situation series. *Bulletin of the Canadian Psychological Association* 2: 26 (Abstract).

21. Hebb, D. O. (1942). Verbal test material independent of special vocabulary difficulty. *Journal of Educational Psychology* 33: 691–696.

22. Hebb, D. O., & Morton, N. W. (1942). *The McGill Verbal Situation: Series A and B*. Montreal: McGill University. 19 pp. [Book]

23. Hebb, D. O. (1942). *Directions for the use of the McGill Picture Anomaly Series, M and N*. Montreal: McGill University.

24. Hebb, D. O., & Morton, N. W. (1943). The McGill Adult Comprehension Examination: Verbal Situation and Picture Anomaly Series. *Journal of Educational Psychology* 34: 16–25.

25. Hebb, D. O., & Riesen, A. H. (1943). The genesis of irrational fears. *Bulletin of the Canadian Psychological Association* 3: 49–50.

26. Hebb, D. O., & Morton, N. W. (1944). Note on the measurement of adult intelligence. *Journal of General Psychology* 30: 217–223.

27. Hebb, D. O. (1945). Man's frontal lobes:A critical view. *Archives of Neurology & Psychiatry (Chicago)* 54: 10–24.

28. Hebb, D. O. (1945). The forms and conditions of chimpanzee anger. *Bulletin of the Canadian Psychological Association* 5: 32–35.
29. Hebb, D. O., & Foord, E. N. (1945). Errors of visual recognition and the nature of the trace. *Journal of Experimental Psychology* 35: 335–348.
30. Hebb, D. O. (1946). Behavioral differences between male and female chimpanzees. *Bulletin of the Canadian Psychological Association* 6: 56–58.
31. Hebb, D. O. (1946). Emotion in man and animal: an analysis of the intuitive processes of recognition. *Psychological Review* 53: 88–106.
32. Hebb, D. O. (1946). On the nature of fear. *Psychological Review* 53: 259–276.
33. Hebb, D. O. (1946). The objective description of temperament. *American Psychologist* 1: 275–276 (Abstract).
34. Hebb, D. O., & Williams, K. (1946). A method of rating animal intelligence. *Journal of General Psychology* 34: 59–65.
35. Hebb, D. O. (1947). Spontaneous neurosis in chimpanzees; theoretical relations with clinical and experimental phenomena. *Psychosomatic Medicine* 9: 3–19.
36. Hebb, D. O. (1947). The effects of early experience on problem solving at maturity. *American Psychologist* 2: 306–307 (Abstract).
37. Hebb, D. O. (1948). Research planning in the Canadian Psychological Association. I. Report on experimental, physiological, and comparative psychology. *Canadian Journal of Psychology* 2: 13–14.
38. McBride, A. F., & Hebb, D. O. (1948). Behavior of the captive bottle-nose dolphin, *Tursiops truncatus*. *Journal of Comparative & Physiological Psychology* 41:111–123.
39. Hebb, D. O. (1949). Temperament in chimpanzees: I. Method of analysis. *Journal of Comparative & Physiological Psychology* 42: 192–206.
40. Hebb, D. O. (1949). *The organization of behavior: a neuropsychological theory.* NY: Wiley. xix, 335 pp.
41. Hebb, D. O. (1950). Animal and physiological psychology. *Annual Review of Psychology* 1: 173–188.
42. Clarke, R. S., Heron, W., Fetherstonhaugh, M. L., Forgays, D. G., & Hebb, D. O. (1951). Individual differences in dogs: Preliminary report on the effects of early experience. *Canadian Journal of Psychology* 5: 150–156.
43. Hebb, D. O. (1951). The role of neurological ideas in psychology. *Journal of Personality* 20: 39–55.
44. Hoyt, R., Elliott, H., & Hebb, D.O. (1951). The intelligence of schizophrenic patients following lobotomy. *Treatment Service Bulletin: Department of Veteran's Affairs, Canada* 6: 553–557.
45. Hebb, D. O., & Bindra, D. (1952). Scientific writing and the general problem of communication. *American Psychologist* 7: 569–573.
46. Hebb, D. O., Heron, W., & Bexton, W. H. (1952). The effect of isolation upon attitude, motivation, and thought. In *Fourth Symposium, Military medicine 1, in cooperation with McGill University.* Ottawa: Defense Research Board.

47. Hebb, D. O. (1953). Heredity and environment in mammalian behaviour. *British Journal of Animal Behaviour* 1: 43–47.
48. Hebb, D. O. (1953). On human thought. *Canadian Journal of Psychology* 7: 99–110.
49. Hebb, D. O. (1953). On motivation and thought. *Contributions a Etude des Sciences de l'Homme* 2: 41–47.
50. Hebb, D. O., Heron, W., & Bexton, W. H. (1953). Cognitive effects of a decreased variation to the sensory environment. *American Psychologist* 8: 366.
51. Hebb, D. O. (1954). The problem of consciousness and introspection. In: J. F. Delafresnaye (Ed.) *Brain mechanisms of consciousness*, pp. 402–421. Oxford: Blackwell.
52. Hebb, D. O., Heath, E. S., & Stuart, E. A. (1954). Experimental deafness. *Canadian Journal of Psychology* 8: 152–156.
53. Hebb, D. O., & Thompson, W. R. (1954). The social significance of animal studies. In: G. Lindzey (Ed.). *Handbook of social psychology, Vol. 1*, pp.532–561. Cambridge Mass: Addison-Wesley.
54. Hebb, D. O. (1955). Drives and the C. N. S. (conceptual nervous system). *Psychological Review* 62: 243–254.
55. Hebb, D. O. (1955). The mammal and his environment. *American Journal of Psychiatry* 111: 826–831.
56. Hebb, D. O., & Heron, W. (1955). Effects of radical isolation upon intellectual function and the manipulation of attitudes. In *Terminal report on conditions of attitude change in individuals*. Ottawa: Defense Research Board.
57. Hebb, D. O., & Mahut, H. (1955). Motivation et recherche du changement perceptif chez le rat et chez l'homme [Motivation and search for perceptual change in rat and man.] *Journal de Psychologie Normale et Pathologique* 52: 209–221.
58. Hebb, D. O., Murphy, C. W., Kurlents, E., & Cleghorn, R. A. (1955). Absence of increased corticoid excretion with the stress of perceptual deprivation. *Canadian Journal of Biochemistry and Physiology* 33: 1062–1063.
59. Hebb, D. O. (1956). The distinction between "classical" and "instrumental." *Canadian Journal of Psychology* 10: 165–166.
60. Bloch, V., & Hebb, D. O. (1956). Étude des phenomènes d'enrayement et d'activation du comportement par stimulation thalamique et réticulaire chez le rat non anesthésié. [Phenomena of cessation and initiation of behavior by thalamic and reticular stimulation in the non-anesthetized rat.] *Psychologie Française* 1: 8–9.
61. Hebb, D. O. (1958). *A textbook of psychology*. Philadelphia: Saunders. x, 276 pp.
62. Hebb, D. O. (1958). Alice in Wonderland or Psychology among the biological sciences. In: H. F. Harlow & C. N. Woolsey (Eds.) *Biological and biochemical bases of behavior*, pp. 451–467. Madison: University of Wisconsin Press [Symposium on interdisciplinary research, University of Wisconsin, 1955]

63. Hebb, D. O. (1958). The motivating effects of exteroceptive stimulation. *American Psychologist* 13: 109–113.
64. Hebb, D. O. (1959). A neuropsychological theory. In: S. Koch (Ed.) *Psychology: A study of a science, Vol. 1*, pp. 622–643. New York: McGraw Hill.
65. Hebb, D. O. (1959). Intelligence, brain function and the theory of mind. *Brain*, 82, 260–275. [23rd Hughlings Jackson Memorial Lecture, Montreal Neurological Institute, 1958]
66. Hebb, D. O. (1959). Karl Spencer Lashley: 1890–1958. *American Journal of Psychology* 72:142–150.
67. Hebb, D. O. (1959, Apr.). Motivation and thought. *Bulletin of the Maritime Psychological Association* 8: 4–9.
68. Beach, F. A., Hebb, D. O., Morgan, C. T., & Nissen, H. W. (Eds.) (1960). *The Neuropsychology of Lashley*. New York: McGraw-Hill. xx, 564 pp.
69. Hebb, D. O. (1960). The American revolution. *American Psychologist* 15: 735–745. [APA Presidential Address]
70. Pritchard, R. M., Heron, W., & Hebb, D. O. (1960). Visual perception approached by the method of stabilized images. *Canadian Journal of Psychology* 14: 67–77.
71. Hebb, D. O. (1961). Call for Dr. Finagle. [review of *Plans and the structure of behavior*] *Contemporary Psychology* 5: 209–211.
72. Hebb, D. O. (1961). Distinctive features of learning in the higher animal. In: J. F. Delafresnay (Ed.). *Brain mechanisms and learning*, pp. 42–53. Oxford: Blackwell.
73. Hebb, D. O. (1961). On the meaning of objective psychology. *Transactions of the Royal Society of Canada* 55: 81–86.
74. Hebb, D. O. (1961). Sensory deprivation: Facts in search of a theory. *Journal of Nervous & Mental Disease* 132: 40–43. [Discussion of symposium presentation]
75. Hebb, D. O. (1961). The role of experience. In: S. M. Farber and R. H. L. Wison (Eds.). *Man and civilization: Control of the mind*, pp.37–51. New York: McGraw Hill.
76. Hebb, D. O. (1962). Auditory-oculomotor reflexes at birth. *Science* 135: 998–999.
77. Hebb. D. O. (1962) John Davidson Ketchum. *Transactions of the Royal Society of Canada*, 56, 197–198.
78. Hebb, D. O. (1962). The mind of man. *McGill News* 44:34–35. [Text of symposium presentation]
79. Hebb, D.O. (1963). Introduction to Dover reprint. K.S. Lashley, *Brain mechanisms and intelligence*, pp. v–xiii. New York: Dover.
80. Hebb, D. O. (1963). The semiautonomous process: Its nature and nurture. *American Psychologist* 18: 16–27.
81. Hebb, D. O. & Milner, P. (1963). Aktivitätsformen der Gehirns und Verhaltensorganisation. *Naturwissenschaftliche Rundschau* 16: 258–262.
82. Hebb, D.O. (1965). The evolution of mind. *Proceedings of the Royal Society, B*. 161, 376–383.

83. Hebb, D. O. (1966). *A textbook of psychology.* (2nd ed.). Philadelphia: W. B. Saunders. xvi, 353 pp.
84. Hebb, D. O. (1967). Cerebral organization and consciousness. *Research Publication of the Association for Research in Nervous and Mental Diseases* 45: 1-7.
85. Hebb, D. O. (1966, January). Education for research. *Canadian Federation News* 8: 53-57.
86. Hebb, D. O. (1968). Concerning imagery. *Psychological Review* 75: 466-477.
87. Hebb, D. O., & Thompson, W. R. (1968). The social significance of animal studies. In: G. Lindzey & E. Aronson (Eds.). *Handbook of social psychology. Vol. 2* (2nd edition), pp.729-774. New York: Addison-Wesley.
88. Pribram, K. H., Hebb, D., & Macdonald, G. (1968, Sept.). The ghost in the machine. *Psychological Scene* 2: 28-43.
89. Hebb, D. O. (1969, May) The mind's eye. *Psychology Today* 2 (12): 54-57, 67-68.
__. Hall, E. (1969, November). Hebb on hocus-pocus: A conversation with Elizabeth Hall. *Psychology Today* 3 (6): 21-28.
90. Hebb, D. O., & Favreau O. (1969). The mechanism of perception. *Radiology Clinics of North America* 7: 393-401.
91. Hebb, D. O. (1970). A return to Jensen and his social science critics. *American Psychologist* 25: 568.
92. Hebb, D. O., & Krebs, D. (1971). Comment on altruism: The comparative evidence: Infrahuman altruism. *Psychological Bulletin* 76: 409-414.
93. Hebb, D. O. (1971). Concerning Hebb's criticism of Jensen and the heredity—environment argument: Response to Gordon by Hebb. *American Psychologist* 26: 665.
94. Hebb, D. O. (1971). The nature of a university education. *McGill Journal of Education* 6: 5-14.
95. Hebb, D. O. (1971). Whose confusion? *American Psychologist* 26: 736.
96. Hebb, D. O., Lambert, W. E., & Tucker, G. R. (1971). Language, thought, and experience. *Modern Language Journal* 55: 212-222.
97. Hebb, D.O. (1972). *A textbook of psychology.* (3rd ed.). Philadelphia: W. B. Saunders.
98. Hebb, D. O. (1972). Possible test for Hebb's hypothesis concerning imagery—Reply. *Psychology Review* 79: 368.
99. Hebb, D. O., Lambert, W. E., & Tucker, R. (1973, April). A DMZ in the language war. *Psychology Today* 5, 55-58, 60, 62.
100. Hebb, D. O. (1974). What psychology is about. *American Psychologist* 29: 71-79.
101. Hebb, D. O. (1975). Psychological aspects of imagery. In *The Brain mechanisms. A collection of papers dedicated to the 90th birthday of Ivan Beritashvili*, pp. 64-68. Georgian Academy of Sciences, Tiflis.
102. Hebb, D. O. (1975). Science and the world of imagination. *Canadian Psychological Review* 16: 4-11.

103. Hebb, D. O. (1976). Physiological learning theory. *Journal of Abnormal Child Psychology* 4: 309–314.
104. Hebb, D. O. (1977). The frontal lobe. In W. Feindel (Ed.) Wilder Penfield: His legacy to neurology,. *Canadian Medical Association Journal* 116: 1373–1374.
105. Hebb, D.O. (1977). To know your own mind. In: John M. Nicholas (Ed.) *Images, perception and knowledge.* pp. 213–219. D. Reidel Publishing Co., Dordrecht-Holland.
106. Hebb, D. O. (1977). What he gives with one hand.. *Contemporary Psychology* 22: 849. [Comment on Jerison's overview of Bindra, *Contemporary Psychology* 22: 417–419].
107. Hebb, D. O. (1978). A problem of localization. *Behavioral and Brain Sciences* 1: 357.
108. Hebb, D. O. (1978). Behavioral evidence of thought and consciousness. *Behavioral and Brain Sciences* 1: 577.
109. Hebb, D. O. (1978, November). On watching myself get old. *Psychology Today* 12(6): 15–23.
110. Hebb, D. O. (1978). Open letter: To a friend who thinks IQ is a social evil. *American Psychologist* 33: 1143–1144.
111. Hebb, D. O. (1978). Review of *Divided consciousness: Multiple controls in human thought and action. American Journal of Psychology* 91: 545—547.
112. Hebb, D. O. (1980). D. O. Hebb. In: G. Lindzey (Ed.). *A history of psychology in autobiography.* Vol.VII. pp. 273–309. San Francisco: W.H. Freeman.
113. Hebb, D. O. (1980). *Essay on mind.* Hillsdale NJ: Erlbaum.
114. Hebb, D. O. (1980). The structure of thought. In P. W. Juscyzk & R. M. Klein (Eds.) *The nature of thought: Essays in honour of D. O. Hebb*, pp. 19–35. Hillsdale, N.J.: Lawrence Erlbaum Associates.
115. Hebb, D. O. (1980). The view from without. *Philosophy of Social Science* 10: 309–315. [Review of *The self and its brain*].
116. Hebb, D. O. (1980, November). An inside look at ageing. *American Psychological Association Monitor*, 4–5.
117. Hebb, D. O. (1981). Consider mind as a biological problem. *Neuroscience* 6: 2419–2422.
118. Hebb, D. O. (1981). Open letter in response to D. O. Hebb: Reply irrelevant? *American Psychologist* 36: 423–424.
119. Hebb, D. O. (1982). Comment on a commentary—*Introspicere ergo esse?*—Reply. *Neuroscience* 7: 2300.
120. Hebb, D. O. (1982, May). Hilgard's discovery brings hypnosis closer to everyday experience. *Psychology Today.* 16(5): 52–54.
121. Hebb, D. O. (1983) Neuropsychology: Retrospect and prospect. *Canadian Journal of Psychology* 37: 4–7.
122. Hebb, D. O. (1984). Clinical psychology training in Canada: Its development, current status, and the prospects for accreditation: Response to Conway. *Canadian Psychology* 25: 192.

___ . Hebb, D. O., & Donderi, D. C.(1987). *Textbook of psychology* (4th ed.). Hillsdale, NJ, USA: Lawrence Erlbaum Associates, xii, 384 pp.
Note: Buchtel, H. A., Editor. (1982). *The Conceptual Nervous System.* Oxford: Pergamon Press. [An edited volume containing 21 of Hebb's publications from 1951 to 1977. These are publications 43, 47, 49, 51, 54, 62, 65, 69, 72, 73, 75, 80, 82, 84, 86, 90, 96, 100, 102, 103, 105. But they are not in their original published format]

Donald Olding Hebb: Biographies/Obituaries

Fentress, J. C. (1987). D. O. Hebb and the developmental organization of behavior. *Developmental Psychobiology* 20: 103–109.
Fentress, J. C., & Klein, R. M. editors. (1999). Special issue: The Hebb legacy. *Canadian Journal of Experimental Psychology* 53: 1–131. [contains 10 papers]
Harnad, S. (1985). D. O. Hebb: father of cognitive psychobiology: 1904–1985. *Behavioral and Brain Sciences* 8: opp. p.529.
Klein, R. M. (1981). D. O. Hebb: An appreciation. In: P. W. Jusczyk & R. M. Klein (Eds.). *The nature of thought: Essays in honour of D.O.Hebb*, pp. 1–18. Hillsdale N.J.: Lawrence Erlbaum Associates.
Milner, P. (1985). Donald Olding Hebb: 1904–1985. *Proceedings of the Royal Society of Canada, Series IV* 23: 93–96.
Milner, P. (1986). Donald Olding Hebb (1904–1985). Obituary. *Trends in Neuroscience* 9: 347–351.
Milner, P. M. (1993). The mind and Donald O. Hebb. *Scientific American* 268 (1): 124–129.
Milner, P. M. and Milner, B. (1996). Donald Olding Hebb: 22 July 1904–20 August 1985. *Biographical memoirs of the Royal Society of London* 42: 193–204.
Mogenson, G. J. (1988). Obituaries. Donald Olding Hebb:1904–1985. *Canadian Psychology* 29: 315–316.

Preface

In this book I have tried to bring together a number of different lines of research, in a general theory of behavior that attempts to bridge the gap between neurophysiology and psychology, as well as that between laboratory psychology and the problems of the clinic.

The book is written, consequently, with the hope that it will be intelligible to the clinician and the physiologist as well as to psychologists. The development of psychological theory can be a cooperative affair, and has often been so in the past: witness Helmholtz, Jackson, Pavlov, Freud. The clinician and the physiologist frequently have direct access to data of first importance for psychology, sometimes without recognizing the fact. Though I have done my best, it may be chimerical to hope that my discussion is extensive and clear enough to stand on its own feet, for the nonpsychological reader. The reader who needs it will find more of the details of psychological theory in Morgan (1943) on physiological psychology, Hilgard and Marquis (1940) on the theory of learning, Woodworth (1938) on "experimental" (normal human adult) psychology, and Moss (1942) or Maier and Schneirla (1935) on animal psychology. Of these, Morgan is most directly relevant, and in several places I have assumed a knowledge of fact to the extent provided by his text.

It is a pleasure to record my indebtedness to the colleagues who have read and improved the contents of this book. I owe much to students in a seminar at Harvard University in the summer of 1947, and in another at McGill University in the following winter. Part or all of the manuscript was read by Professor Harlow W. Ades, Professor Frank A. Beach, Dr. J. G. Beebe-Center, Professor R. B. MacLeod, Dr. Francis McNaughton, Dr. G. A. Miller, Dr. Karl Pribram, Professor H. E. Rosvold, and Professor R. W. Sperry, and their help is gratefully acknowledged. I am much indebted to Professor Edwin G. Boring, Professor George Clark, Professor K. S. Lashley, and Dr. J. C. R. Licklider for their painstaking and detailed criticism of a large part of the manuscript, improving both matter and style. My greatest debt, perhaps, is to the weekly colloquium and the persistent theoretical debate at the Yerkes Laboratories of Primate Biology between 1942 and 1947; and to a small group taking part therein who have also read the entire manuscript and have contributed greatly to it—Professor Henry W. Nissen, Mr. and Mrs. Robt. Blum, and Dr. Austin Riesen. This board of critics should also include my wife; and to it, for the positive contributions made as well as for some of the changes and deletions forced on me, both the reader and I owe much.

Finally I should like to express my gratitude to those who have helped with clerical work in the preparation of this book, in its various stages: particularly, Alice Sellers, Therese Mahoney, and Margaret Halliday. The McGill University Research Fund supported some of the experimental work that is briefly reported here, and also made it possible to secure additional clerical assistance.

D. O. HEBB

Montreal
April, 1949

Contents

Introduction

It might be argued that the task of the psychologist, the task of understanding behavior and reducing the vagaries of human thought to a mechanical process of cause and effect, is a more difficult one than that of any other scientist. Certainly the problem is enormously complex; and though it could also be argued that the progress made by psychology in the century following the death of James Mill, with his crude theory of association, is an achievement scarcely less than that of the physical sciences in the same period, it is nevertheless true that psychological theory is still in its infancy. There is a long way to go before we can speak of understanding the principles of behavior to the degree that we understand the principles of chemical reaction.

In an undertaking of such difficulty, the psychologist presumably must seek help wherever he can find it. There have been an increasing number of attempts to develop new mathematical methods of analysis. With these, in general, I do not attempt to deal. The method of factor analysis developed by Spearman (1927) and greatly elaborated by Thurstone (1935) is well established as a powerful tool for handling certain kinds of data, though the range of its use has been limited by dependence on tests that can be conveniently given to large groups of subjects. Another method is the application of mathematics more directly to the interaction of populations of neurons, by Rashevsky, Pitts, Householder, Landahl, McCulloch, and others.*
Bishop (1946) has discussed the work from the point of view of neurophysiology, and his remarks are fully concurred with here. The preliminary studies made with this method so far have been obliged to simplify the psychological problem almost out of

---

* Two papers by Culbertson (*Bull. Math. Biophys.*, 1948, *10*, 31–40 and 97–102), and Bishop's review article, list some of the more important of the actual titles in this field.

existence. This is not a criticism, since the attempt is to develop methods that can later be extended to deal with more complex data; but as matters stand at present one must wait for further results before being sure that the attempt will succeed. Undoubtedly there is great potential value in such work, and if the right set of initial assumptions can be found it will presumably become, like factor analysis, a powerful ally of other methods of study.

However, psychology has an intimate relation with the other biological sciences, and may also look for help there. There is a considerable overlap between the problems of psychology and those of neurophysiology, hence the possibility (or necessity) of reciprocal assistance. The first object of this book is to present a theory of behavior for the consideration of psychologists; but another is to seek a common ground with the anatomist, physiologist, and neurologist, to show them how psychological theory relates to their problems and at the same time to make it more possible for them to contribute to that theory.

Psychology is no more static than any other science. Physiologists and clinicians who wish to get a theoretical orientation cannot depend only on the writings of Pavlov or Freud. These were great men, and they have contributed greatly to psychological thought. But their contribution was rather in formulating and developing problems than in providing final answers. Pavlov himself seems to have thought of his theory of conditioned reflexes as something in continual need of revision, and experimental results have continued to make revisions necessary: the theory, that is, is still developing. Again, if one were to regard Freud's theory as needing change only in its details, the main value of his work would be stultified. Theorizing at this stage is like skating on thin ice—keep moving, or drown. Ego, Id, and Superego are conceptions that help one to see and state important facts of behavior, but they are also dangerously easy to treat as ghostly realities: as anthropomorphic agents that *want* this or *disapprove* of that, *overcoming* one another by force or guile, and *punishing* or *being punished*. Freud has left us the task of developing these provisional formulations of his to the point where such a danger no longer exists. When theory becomes static it is apt to become dogma; and psychological theory has the further danger, as long as so many of its problems are unresolved, of inviting a relapse into the vitalism and indeterminism of traditional thought.

It is only too easy, no matter what formal theory of behavior one espouses, to entertain a concealed mysticism in one's thinking about that large segment of behavior which theory does not handle adequately. To deal with behavior at present, one must oversimplify. The risk, on the one hand, is of forgetting that one has oversimplified the problem; one may forget or even deny those inconvenient facts that one's theory does not subsume. On the other hand is the risk of accepting the weak-kneed discouragement of the vitalist, of being content to show that existing theories are imperfect without seeking to improve them. We can take for granted that any theory of behavior at present must be inadequate and incomplete. But it is never enough to say, because *we* have not yet found out how to reduce behavior to the control of the brain, that no one in the future will be able to do so.

Modern psychology takes completely for granted that behavior and neural function are perfectly correlated, that one is completely caused by the other. There is no separate soul or life-force to stick a finger into the brain now and then and make neural cells do what they would not otherwise. Actually, of course, this is a working assumption only—as long as there are unexplained aspects of behavior. It is quite conceivable that some day the assumption will have to be rejected. But it is important also to see that we have not reached that day yet: the working assumption is a necessary one, and there is no real evidence opposed to it. Our failure to solve a problem so far does not make it insoluble. One cannot logically be a determinist in physics and chemistry and biology, and a mystic in psychology.

All one can know about another's feelings and awarenesses is an inference from what he *does*—from his muscular contractions and glandular secretions. These observable events are determined by electrical and chemical events in nerve cells. If one is to be consistent, there is no room here for a mysterious agent that is defined as not physical and yet has physical effects (especially since many of the entities of physics are known only through their effects). "Mind" can only be regarded, for scientific purposes, as the activity of the brain, and this should be mystery enough for anyone: besides the appalling number of cells (some nine billion, according to Herrick) and even more appalling number of possible connections between them, the matter out of which cells are made is being itself reduced by the physicist to something quite unlike the inert stick or stone with which mind is traditionally contrasted. After all, it is that contrast that is at the bottom of the vitalist's objection to a mechanistic biology, and the contrast has lost its force (Herrick, 1929). The mystic might well concentrate on the electron and let behavior alone. A philosophical parallelism or idealism, whatever one may think of such conceptions on other grounds, is quite consistent with the scientific method, but interactionism seems not to be.

Psychologist and neurophysiologist thus chart the same bay—working perhaps from opposite shores, sometimes overlapping and duplicating one another, but using some of the same fixed points and continually with the opportunity of contributing to each other's results. The problem of understanding behavior is the problem of understanding the total action of the nervous system, and *vice versa*. This has not always been a welcome proposition, either to psychologist or to physiologist.

A vigorous movement has appeared both in psychology and psychiatry to be rid of "physiologizing," that is, to stop using physiological hypotheses. This point of view has been clearly and effectively put by Skinner (1938), and it does not by any means represent a relapse into vitalism. The argument is related to modern positivism, emphasizes a method of correlating observable stimuli with observable response, and, recognizing that "explanation" is ultimately a statement of relationships between observed phenomena, proposes to go to the heart of the matter and have psychology confine itself to such statements *now*. This point of view has been criticized by Pratt (1939) and Köhler (1940). The present book is written in profound disagreement with such a program for psychology. Disagreement is on the grounds that this arises from a misconception of the scientific method as it operates in the earlier stages. Those apparently naïve features of older scientific thought may have had more to do with hitting on fertile assumptions and hypotheses than seems necessary in retrospect. The anti-physiological position, thus, in urging that psychology proceed now as it may be able to proceed when it is more highly developed, seems to be in short a counsel of perfection, disregarding the limitations of the human intellect. However, it is logically defensible and may yet show by its fertility of results that it is indeed the proper approach to achieving prediction and control of behavior.

If some psychologists jib at the physiologist for a bedfellow, many physiologists agree with them heartily. One must sympathize with those who want nothing of the psychologist's hairsplitting or the indefiniteness of psychological theory. There is much more certainty in the study of the electrical activity of a well-defined tract in the brain. The only question is whether a physiology of the human brain as a whole can be achieved by such studies alone. One can discover the properties of its various parts more or less in isolation; but it is a truism by now that the part may have properties that are not evident in isolation, and these are to be discovered only by study of the whole intact brain. The method then calls for learning as much as one can about what the parts of the brain do (primarily the physiologist's field), and relating behavior as far as possible to this knowledge (primarily for the psychologist); then seeing what further information is to be had about how the total brain works, from the discrepancy between (1) actual behavior and (2) the behavior that would be predicted from adding up what is known about the action of the various parts.

This does not make the psychologist a physiologist, for precisely the same reason that the physiologist need not become a cytologist or biochemist, though he is intimately concerned with the information that cytology and biochemistry provide. The difficulties of finding order in behavior are great enough to require all one's attention, and the psychologist is interested in physiology to the extent that it contributes to his own task.

The great argument of the positivists who object to "physiologizing" is that physiology has not helped psychological theory. But, even if this is true (there is some basis for denying it), one has to add the words *so far*. There has been a great access of knowledge in neurophysiology since the twenties. The work of

Berger, Dusser de Barenne, and Lorente de Nó (as examples) has a profound effect on the physiological conceptions utilized by psychology, and psychology has not yet assimilated these results fully.

The central problem with which we must find a way to deal can be put in two different ways. Psychologically, it is the problem of thought: some sort of process that is not fully controlled by environmental stimulation and yet cooperates closely with that stimulation. From another point of view, physiologically, the problem is that of the transmission of excitation from sensory to motor cortex. This statement may not be as much oversimplified as it seems, especially when one recognizes that the "transmission" may be a very complex process indeed, with a considerable time lag between sensory stimulation and the final motor response. The failure of psychology to handle thought adequately (or the failure of neurophysiology to tell us how to conceive of cortical transmission) has been the essential weakness of modern psychological theory and the reason for persistent difficulties in dealing with a wide range of experimental and clinical data, as the following chapters will try to show, from the data of perception and learning to those of hunger, sleep, and neurosis.

In mammals even as low as the rat it has turned out to be impossible to describe behavior as an interaction directly between sensory and motor processes. Something like *thinking,* that is, intervenes. "Thought" undoubtedly has the connotation of a human degree of complexity in cerebral function and may mean too much to be applied to lower animals. But even in the rat there is evidence that behavior is not completely controlled by immediate sensory events: there are central processes operating also.

What is the nature of such relatively autonomous activities in the cerebrum? Not even a tentative answer is available. We know a good deal about the afferent pathways to the cortex, about the efferent pathways from it, and about many structures linking the two. But the links are complex, and we know practically nothing about what goes on between the arrival of an excitation at a sensory projection area and its later departure from the motor area of the cortex. Psychology has had to find, in hypothesis, a way of bridging this gap in its physiological foundation. In general the bridge can be described as some comparatively simple formula of cortical transmission.* The particular formula chosen mainly determines the nature of the psychological theory that results, and the need of choosing is the major source of theoretical schism.

Two kinds of formula have been used, leading at two extremes to (1) switchboard theory, and sensori-motor connections; and (2) field theory. (Either of these terms may be regarded as opprobrium; they are not so used here.) (1) In the first type of theory, at one extreme, cells in the sensory system acquire connections with cells in the motor system; the function of the cortex is that of a telephone exchange. Connections rigidly determine what animal or human being does, and their acquisition constitutes learning. Current forms of the theory tend to be vaguer than formerly, because of effective criticism of the theory in its earlier and simpler forms, but the fundamental idea is still maintained. (2) Theory at the opposite extreme denies that learning depends on connections at all, and attempts to utilize instead the field conception that physics has found so useful. The cortex is regarded as made up of so many cells that it can be treated as a statistically homogeneous medium. The sensory control of motor centers depends, accordingly, on the distribution of the sensory excitation and on ratios of excitation, not on locus or the action of any specific cells.

Despite their differences, however, both theoretical approaches seem to imply a prompt transmission of sensory excitation to the motor side, if only by failing to specify that this is not so. No one, at any rate, has made any serious attempt to elaborate ideas of a central neural mechanism to account for the delay, between stimulation and response, that seems so characteristic of thought. There have indeed been neural theories of "motor" thought, but they amount essentially to a continual interplay of proprioception and minimal muscular action, and do not provide for any prolonged sequence of intracerebral events as such.

But the recalcitrant data of animal behavior have been draw-

---

* The simplicity possibly accounts for the opinion expressed by an anatomist who claimed that psychologists think of the brain as having all the finer structure of a bowlful of porridge.

ing attention more and more insistently to the need of some better account of central processes. This is what Morgan (1943) has recognized in saying that "mental" variables, repeatedly thrown out because there was no place for them in a stimulus-response psychology, repeatedly find their way back in again in one form or another. The image has been a forbidden notion for twenty years, particularly in animal psychology; but the fiend was hardly exorcised before "expectancy" had appeared instead. What is the neural basis of expectancy, or of attention, or interest? Older theory could use these words freely, for it made no serious attempt to avoid an interactionist philosophy. In modern psychology such terms are an embarrassment; they cannot be escaped if one is to give a full account of behavior, but they still have the smell of animism: and must have, until a theory of thought is developed to show how "expectancy" or the like can be a physiologically intelligible process.

In the chapters that follow this introduction I have tried to lay a foundation for such a theory. It is, on the one hand and from the physiologist's point of view, quite speculative. On the other hand, it achieves some synthesis of psychological knowledge, and it attempts to hold as strictly as possible to the psychological evidence in those long stretches where the guidance of anatomy and physiology is lacking. The desideratum is a conceptual tool for dealing with expectancy, attention, and so on, and with a temporally organized intracerebral process. But this would have little value if it did not also comprise the main facts of perception, and of learning. To achieve something of the kind, the limitations of a schema are accepted with the purpose of developing certain conceptions of neural action. This is attempted in Chapters 4 and 5; Chapters 1 to 3 try to clear the ground for this undertaking. From Chapter 6 onward the conceptions derived from schematizing are applied to the problems of learning, volition, emotion, hunger, and so on. (In general, the reader may regard Chapters 1 to 5 as mainly preparatory, unless he is particularly interested in the neurological details, or in the treatment of perception; to get the gist of the theory that is presented here one should read the two following paragraphs, and turn directly to Chapter 6.) In outline, the conceptual structure is as follows:

Any frequently repeated, particular stimulation will lead to the slow development of a "cell-assembly," a diffuse structure comprising cells in the cortex and diencephalon (and also, perhaps, in the basal ganglia of the cerebrum), capable of acting briefly as a closed system, delivering facilitation to other such systems and usually having a specific motor facilitation. A series of such events constitutes a "phase sequence"—the thought process. Each assembly action may be aroused by a preceding assembly, by a sensory event, or—normally—by both. The central facilitation from one of these activities on the next is the prototype of "attention." The theory proposes that in this central facilitation, and its varied relationship to sensory processes, lies the answer to an issue that is made inescapable by Humphrey's (1940) penetrating review of the problem of the direction of thought.

The kind of cortical organization discussed in the preceding paragraph is what is regarded as essential to adult waking behavior. It is proposed also that there is an alternate, "intrinsic" organization, occurring in sleep and in infancy, which consists of hypersynchrony in the firing of cortical cells. But besides these two forms of cortical organization there may be disorganization. It is assumed that the assembly depends completely on a very delicate timing which might be disturbed by metabolic changes as well as by sensory events that do not accord with the pre-existent central process. When this is transient, it is called emotional disturbance; when chronic, neurosis or psychosis.

The theory is evidently a form of connectionism, one of the switchboard variety, though it does not deal in direct connections between afferent and efferent pathways: not an "S-R" psychology, if R means a *muscular* response. The connections serve rather to establish autonomous central activities, which then are the basis of further learning. In accordance with modern physiological ideas, the theory also utilizes local field processes and gradients, following the lead particularly of Marshall and Talbot (1942). It does not, further, make any single nerve cell or pathway essential to any habit or perception. Modern physiology has presented psychology with new opportunities for the synthesis of divergent theories and previously unrelated data, and it is my intent to take such advantage of these opportunities as I can.

1. *The Problem and the Line of Attack*

This book presents a theory of behavior that is based as far as possible on the physiology of the nervous system, and makes a sedulous attempt to find some community of neurological and psychological conceptions.

The purpose of this first chapter is to define the major difficulties in the way of such an undertaking and to show how these difficulties determine the line it must take. The great need, as I have tried to make clear in the Introduction, is for a physiological theory of thought (or some equivalent term that can be applied to animals as well as to man).

Let us look first at the specific problem from which the present speculations began, to see why the discussion is oriented as it is.

The problem lay in certain puzzling effects of operation on the human brain. The effect of a clearcut removal of cortex outside the speech area is often astonishingly small; at times no effect whatever can be found (Hebb, 1942a, 1945b). It is possible that there is always a loss of intelligence in aphasia, when the "speech area" is seriously damaged, but this does not, of course, explain why damage elsewhere should have no effect. It would be unreasonable to suppose that most of the cortex has nothing to do with intelligence, and there are in fact definite indications that this is not true. Intelligence must be affected by any large brain injury—yet sometimes it seems not to be.

A final touch is added to the puzzle when we find that it is tests of the Binet type that least show the effect of injuries outside the speech area. The Binet is the measure of intelligence that is most sensitive and accurate with normal subjects. How can it be possible for a man to have an IQ of 160 or higher, after a prefrontal lobe has been removed (Hebb, 1939), or for a woman (described by Rowe, 1937) to have an IQ of 115, a better score than two-thirds of the normal population could make, after losing the entire right half of the cortex? Those two are perhaps the most striking cases, but high scores after brain operation have been reported by nearly everyone who has used standard tests as a method of study, and they have to be explained.. Most investigators have preferred to forget them, and to search only for intellectual defects. The defects certainly must exist, and it is important to find them; but it is just as important to learn why Binet-type tests, the most valid and sensitive indices of normal ability, should often show no effect of injury to the brain.

The only explanation that has been proposed, and perhaps the only feasible one, has to do with perceptual learning and with concepts as distinct from conditioned responses or motor learning (Hebb, 1942a). The explanation, roughly, is this. The level of intelligence-test performance is a function of the concepts a patient has already developed. Once developed, a concept is retained, despite brain damage that, if it had occurred earlier, would have prevented the development. The patient with brain injury at maturity may continue to think and solve problems normally (in familiar fields), although his intelligence would have been far from normal if a similar injury had happened at birth. The explanation meets the clinical facts and, moreover, is supported by the way in which some intellectual capacities are retained in old age when others are disappearing.

But now we come to the crux of the matter. As an explanation, this is only a good start. What is a concept, physiologically and *à propos* of the loss of neural cells? Though it has been tried before now, an explanation cannot be half neural anatomy and half consciousness. They are different levels in a logical hierarchy. A problem recognized at one level can be solved by recourse to a more fundamental set of conceptions, but an hypothesis cannot well comprise two levels, take in two universes of discourse at the same time. We want to explain certain clinical facts. To really do so, we must find an anatomical and physiological understanding of what is known psychologically as a concept; and we must be able to deal with its relation to perception and to learning.

And with *that*, we land right in the middle of the generalized problem of explaining mammalian behavior. What is a concept, if it is not a conditioned response? What is perceptual learning? And so on. Before such questions can be answered, psychological theory must have a new base of operations. As an illustration, a particular problem has been cited; but the difficulty is really general, as the following section will try to show, and there is no phase of psychological theory in which the same central weakness does not appear.

It has already been suggested that the essential need is to find out how to handle thought, and related processes, more adequately. The difficulty in doing so goes back to fundamental assumptions. If this discussion is to rest on solid ground, it must start with certain ideas with which every psychologist is concerned but which have been confused, vague, or ill defined.

This first chapter, accordingly, will dot some *i*'s and cross some *t*'s, so that we can get down to business in what follows. There are two fundamental assumptions to be dealt with. One of them must be rejected, one accepted. The rest of this chapter will show how they determine a point of attack for the revision of theory.

REJECTING THE ASSUMPTION OF A COMPLETE SENSORY CONTROL

The first to be discussed is what can be called the assumption of a sensory dominance of behavior. It is the idea that behavior is a series of *reactions* (instead of actions), each of which is determined by the immediately preceding events in the sensory systems. The idea is not altogether consistent with recognizing the existence of set, attitude, or attention; and an implicit inconsistency of this sort is at the root of the current confusion in psychological theory.

It may be noted in passing that the assumption of a sensory dominance of behavior is not the property of any particular theory. Theories differ as to how a sensory event has its effect, but not as to its all-important role. *Gestalt* psychology avoids words like "stimulus" and "sensation" but as a system is not less preoccupied with stimulus configurations than other systems are with their stimuli (p. 23).

Now for the source of confusion.

In the simplest terms, "attention" refers to a selectivity of response. Man or animal is continuously responding to some events in the environment, and not to others that could be responded to (or "noticed") just as well. When an experimental result makes it necessary to refer to "set" or "attention," the reference means, precisely, that the activity that controls the form, speed, strength, or duration of response is not the immediately preceding excitation of receptor cells alone. The fact that a response is not so controlled may be hard to explain, theoretically; but it is not mystical, and "attention" is not necessarily anthropomorphic, or animistic, or undefinable.

Now the tradition in psychology has long been a search for the property of the stimulus which by itself determines the ensuing response, at any given stage of learning. This approach seems partly a consequence of psychology's persistent fight against animism * and deserves respect for that reason; but it is no longer satisfactory as theory. Almost without exception psychologists have recognized the existence of the selective central factor that reinforces now one response, now another. The problem is to carry out to its logical conclusion an incomplete line of thought that starts out preoccupied with stimulus or stimulus configuration as the source and control of action, eventually runs into the facts of attention and so on, and then simply

---

* And partly, as we shall see, the product of antiquated physiological conceptions. Fighting animism meant that psychological phenomena had to be reduced to a pattern of cause and effect. The only means at hand was a physiology of the nervous system in which a knowledge of sense organs and peripheral nerve was the main content. As a result, it is still easy to feel that psychology becomes part of a larger demonology with any retreat from the stimulus-response formula. As for "insight," "purpose," "attention"— any one of these may still be an invocation of the devil, to the occasional psychologist. However, this attitude should not be too much made fun of. It cannot be emphasized too strongly that there is continual danger of slipping momentarily into animistic thinking; and consistent use of the S-R formula does at least avoid that danger effectively. It behooves those of us who wish to use other terms to see that they are clearly defined.

agrees that attention is an important fact, without recognizing that this is inconsistent with one's earlier assumptions. To complete this process, we must go back and make a change in the basis of the theory.

There are three points here: one is that psychologists have generally recognized the existence of attention or the like; another that they have done so reluctantly and sparingly, and have never recognized the fact in setting up theories. The third point is obvious enough, that we need to find some way of dealing with the facts consistently. Since everyone knows that attention and set exist, we had better get the skeleton out of the closet and see what can be done with it.

The first two of these points have been pretty clearly established by Gibson (1941). His review needs some clarification in one respect, since he declined to attempt any definition of "set" or any other of the long list of terms with a similar meaning that he gathered together, although he evidently recognized, in classifying them so, that they have something in common. This common meaning has already been defined. When one considers the problem in the light of the implicit assumption of a sensory dominance of behavior it becomes clear at once that the notions of set, attention, attitude, expectancy, hypothesis, intention, vector, need, perseveration, and preoccupation (Gibson, 1941, pp. 781–782) have a common element, and one only. That element is the recognition that responses are determined by something else besides the immediately preceding sensory stimulation. It does not deny the importance of the immediate stimulus; it does deny that sensory stimulation is everything in behavior.

All such terms, then, are a reference to the "central process which seems relatively independent of afferent stimuli," defined by Hilgard and Marquis (1940), which I shall call here the *autonomous central process.* Gibson's review shows in effect that the process is ubiquitous, that it crops up in every sort of psychological investigation—and that almost everyone has recognized its existence, in one form or another. To Gibson's list can be added Pavlov's (1928) and Hull's (1943) stimulus trace— a lasting cerebral state, set up it is true by a specific stimulus but not transmitted and dissipated at once; Beach's (1942) central excitatory mechanism; Morgan's (1943) central motive state; and Kleitman's (1939) "interest"—a factor in wakefulness. All these things have the same property of an activity that has a selective effect on behavior without being part of the present afferent excitation.

Everyone has had such ideas about the control of behavior; and yet, as Gibson noted, "The meaning [of the term "set"] is felt to be unsatisfactory, and the concept is employed reluctantly and only because the facts make it absolutely unavoidable." The reluctance is partly no doubt because of a feeling that the concept is animistic, in some obscure way. But why animism, if the facts of behavior make it unavoidable? The trouble really seems to have been in finding how to make an essential idea intelligible.

Hilgard and Marquis' central process, and Beach's central excitatory mechanism, are hypothetical entities, but they certainly have no flavor of animism about them. "Attention" and "set" are now seen to fall in the same class: it may well be that their connotations are misleading and that we shall have to look for new terms, but the idea itself is respectable, and such language need no longer risk starting a witchhunt.

THE NEUROLOGICAL PROBLEM OF ATTENTION

There is a further hazard on the course. This is the apparent lack of a theoretical rationale for the autonomous central process. Actually, modern neurophysiology has already removed this difficulty.

Here again the situation can only be understood historically. A main function of the neural cell is of course to transmit excitations, and earlier ideas of anatomy and physiology made the central nervous system appear, in principle, a collection of routes, some longer, some shorter, leading without reversal from receptors to effectors—a mass of conductors that lies inactive until a sense organ is excited, and then conducts the excitation promptly to some muscle or gland. We know now that this is not so, but the older idea still has a profound effect on psychological thought—demonstrated, for example, in the assumption of sensory dominance, discussed above.

The lack of a rationale for nonsensory influences on behavior that seemed to exist in 1920 certainly exists no more. Psychologists have long had to recognize (since the days of the Würzburg school at least) the existence of a determining tendency, whether physiology made it comprehensible or not. Modern electrophysiology has more than caught up with psychology and now provides abundant evidence to support the same idea. When the detailed evidence of neurophysiology and histology are considered, the conclusion becomes inevitable that the nonsensory factor in cerebral action must be more consistently present and of more dominating importance than reluctant psychological theory has ever recognized. Instead of a joker to occasionally confuse the student of behavior, nonsensory activities appear in every fall of the cards and must make up a large share of the deck. Neurophysiologically, it may even become a problem to account for *any* consistent effect of a specific stimulus (pp. 121, 126).

Electrophysiology of the central nervous system indicates in brief that the brain is continuously active, in all its parts, and an afferent excitation must be superimposed on an already existent excitation. It is therefore impossible that the consequence of a sensory event should often be uninfluenced by the pre-existent activity. If we recognize in that activity the psychologically known factor of set and the like (as Denny-Brown, 1932, suggested some time ago), the problem for psychology is no longer to account for the existence of set but to find out how it acts and above all to learn how it has the property of a consistent, selective action instead of producing the random-error distribution postulated by Hull (1943) in his "oscillation principle."

So there really is a rational basis for postulating a central neural factor that modifies the action of a stimulus. The theoretical problem now is to discover the rules by which it operates. At first glance this is a problem for the neurophysiologist only. But look closer; much of the evidence, from which these rules must be worked out, is psychological, or behavioral. The problem is after all the problem of attention, and seen best in the activity of the whole animal. It is in the highest degree unlikely that it can be solved either from the physiological evidence alone or from the behavioral evidence alone. What we need, evidently, is some synthesis of both kinds of datum. The psychological data have been reviewed briefly (for a fuller account, see Hilgard and Marquis, 1940; Gibson, 1941; Morgan, 1943—under such headings as *attitude, expectancy,* and *set*). Let us turn now, again briefly, to the anatomical and physiological evidence that has made a drastic change in the theoretical problems of behavior.

For our purposes, the physiological evidence can be treated under two heads, as bearing on (1) the existence and properties of a continuous cerebral activity, and (2) the nature of synaptic transmission in the central nervous system.

1. The studies reviewed by Jasper (1937), beginning with Berger's work and its confirmation by Adrian, have shown with practical certainty that the central nervous system is continuously active, in all its parts, whether exposed to afferent stimulation or not. It appears that the EEG, or electroencephalogram, must be at least in part a summation of action potentials, an index of actual cellular firing. There are changes of cell potential without active transmission of impulses (Gibbs, 1945), and it is quite possible that these are the source of much of the EEG. However, there is a considerable body of evidence to show that neural tissue is persistently active; and presumably the EEG includes a record of that activity. *It is taken here as a working assumption that the EEG is correlated with neural firing*—that large potentials indicate a local synchrony of firing, even though other factors contribute to the size of the potential. The psychological usefulness of this assumption will perhaps become evident in the following chapters.

The evidence concerning persistent activity consists first of a number of studies showing directly that the neural cell fires spontaneously, *i.e.,* under no stimulation except that of the nutrient fluids bathing it (Fessard, cited by Jasper, 1937; Prosser, 1934; Lehmann, 1937*a*, 1937*b*; Bronk, 1939; Dubner and Gerard, 1939; Libet and Gerard, 1939). Secondly, a very important paper for the theory of behavior, by Weiss (1941*a*), reports spontaneous, almost incessant motor activity in a transplanted amphibian limb innervated from a pool without afferent fibers. The activity of the limb was not normally coordinated, which agrees with the general idea that sensory activity is essential to the regulation of central neural firing but not essential to initiating it. Finally, the work of Adrian and his collaborators: Adrian and Matthews (1934) rejected the earlier opinion of Adrian (1931) and Adrian and Buytendijk (1931), and concluded definitely that the EEG is the summation of single sharp potentials, the result of actual cellular firing. They concluded further that the activity is not necessarily maintained by sensory activity. Elsewhere Adrian (1934, p. 1126) has stated his general conclusions: "There are cell mechanisms in the brain which are set so that a periodic discharge is bound to take place. The moment at which it occurs can be greatly altered by afferent influences, but it cannot be postponed indefinitely."

Several comments may be made on these conclusions. Spontaneity of firing by central neural cells is not philosophic indeterminacy, as some writers have thought; the "spontaneity" means only that synaptic stimulation is not the sole cause of firing. As Adrian pointed out, also, the cell that is capable of firing spontaneously is also open to synaptic control. If it is left undisturbed the processes of metabolism will lead in the end to firing, but obviously an afferent stimulation could always catch the cell in the period between the absolute refractory state and the time of spontaneous discharge. With a frequent arrival of impulses at the synapse, therefore, the cell can never reach the point of spontaneous action but must remain under afferent control.

A very interesting relationship exists between sensory activity, EEG, and coordinated, adaptive behavior (or "conscious state"). There is, in the first place, Adrian and Matthews' observation that sensory processes, instead of supporting synchronous, rhythmic firing and large potentials in the EEG, have the opposite effect. They introduce irregularity and flattening of the electrical record. In the second place, large potentials, or "hypersynchrony," negate or may negate normal function (Jasper, 1941). That is, sensory activity breaks up hypersynchrony and makes for normal, coordinated, adaptive activity. Bartley and Bishop (1933) and Adrian and Matthews have even proposed that anesthetics produce "unconsciousness" by suppressing sensory activity rather than acting directly on the cerebrum itself. It does seem clear from the facts discussed, from the large potentials observed in sleep, and from the hypnotic effect of minimizing the normal variation of sensory activity, that the sensory input to the brain has a constantly necessary function, for adaptive behavior. We shall return to this point later (p. 145). For the present, it has been advisable to point out that recognizing the existence of spontaneous neural activity is neither indeterminacy nor a denial of the importance of sensory processes in normal behavior.

2. The nature of synaptic transmission in the central nervous system is also of fundamental importance for the theory of behavior. There are two radical modifications of earlier ideas: transmission is not simply linear but apparently always involves some closed or recurrent circuits; and a single impulse cannot ordinarily cross a synapse—two or more must act simultaneously, and two or more afferent fibers must therefore be active in order to excite a third to which they lead.

The concepts of neural action chiefly developed by Lorente de Nó (1938*a*, 1938*b*, 1939, 1943) are well enough known by now to need no elaborate review. It is necessary, however, to point out that they have revolutionary implications for psychological theory.

In particular, the psychological criticism advanced by Koffka (1924), Lashley (1929*b*, 1930), and Köhler (1929), against the theory of neural connections as the basis of learning, applies only to the older theory of *linear*, sensori-motor connections, in which a single cell was supposed to be always capable of exciting a second cell with which it synapsed. The criticism is effective against the idea that synaptic resistances are all that determines the direction of transmission at the synapse. A radical change in the whole problem, however, has been made by considerations of timing in transmission (Gasser, 1937) and by the conception of "optional transmission" (Lorente de Nó, 1939).

In a single system, and with a constant set of connections between neurons in the system, the direction in which an entering excitation will be conducted may be completely dependent on the timing of other excitations. Connections are necessary but may not be decisive in themselves; in a complex system, especially, time factors must always influence the direction of conduction. The older ideas of neural transmission gave synaptic connections too much rigidity, as a determinant of behavior. The rigidity has now disappeared; the idea of connections can again be useful in psychological theory, and the question of "synaptic resistances" is completely reopened.

Let me now summarize what has been said, in this and the preceding section, about attention, set, attitude, and so on. (1) All psychologists have recognized some such factor in behavior. It undoubtedly exists. (2) Recognizing it is really a denial that behavior is only a series of responses to environmental stimulation. One important meaning of "attention" or the like is the reference to a partly autonomous, or nonsensory, cerebral activity: the "autonomous central process." (3) The problem for psychology then is to find conceptions for dealing with such complexities of central neural action: conceptions that will be valid physiologically and at the same time "molar" enough to be useful in the analysis of behavior. (4) Psychology is still profoundly influenced by the very "molecular" conception of linear transmission through a sequence of single cells. The conception is no longer valid physiologically, just as it has long been without psychological usefulness. The attack on neural connections as an explanation of behavior was really an attack on this particular conception of the way connections operate; modern neuroanatomy and electrophysiology have changed the question completely, and the significance of synaptic connections must be examined all over again.

Our problem, then, is to find valid "molar" conceptions of neural action (conceptions, *i.e.*, that can be applied to large-scale cortical organizations). Bishop (1946, p. 370) has made the point, in another context, that this is an essential problem for neurophysiology also. But psychologists can hardly sit around with hands folded, waiting for the physiologist to solve it. In its essence the problem is psychological and requires a knowledge of the psychological as well as the physiological evidence for its solution.

PERCEPTUAL GENERALIZATION AND THE ASSUMP-
TION OF A STRUCTURAL MEMORY TRACE

Now for a second fundamental assumption of psychological theory: this time, one that must, it seems, be accepted; but in accepting it we must also recognize the difficulties it entails and provide for them. These difficulties in fact determine the main features of the theory presented in this monograph.

The assumption we must accept is that the memory trace, the basis of learning, is in some way structural and static; and the difficulties in the way of making the assumption are mainly in the facts of perceptual generalization that have been emphasized by *Gestalt* psychologists (Koffka, 1935; Köhler, 1929, 1940) and Lashley (1938*b*, 1942*a*). The problem raised by these writers is crucial and must be disposed of before we touch anything else.

Lashley has concluded that a learned discrimination is not based on the excitation of any particular neural cells. It is supposed to be determined solely by the pattern, or shape, of the sensory excitation. Köhler, also stressing the apparent fact that the pattern and not the locus of stimulation is the important thing, has developed a theory of electrical fields in the brain which control cerebral action. Like Lashley, he explicitly denies that the same cells need be excited to arouse the same perception.

This suggests that the mnemonic trace, the neural change that is induced by experience and constitutes "memory," is not a change of structure. Other facts, at the same time, are an even stronger argument that it *must* be structural. A structural trace, as we shall see in a moment, must be assumed; but when we do so we have to find some way of fitting in the facts of perception.

If it is really unimportant in what tissues a sensory excitation takes place, one finds it hard to understand how repeated sensations can reinforce one another, with the lasting effect we call learning or memory. It might be supposed that the mnemonic trace is a lasting pattern of reverberatory activity without fixed locus, like some cloud formations or an eddy in a millpond. But if so it seems that the multitudinous traces in the small confines of the cerebral cortex would interfere with one another, producing a much greater distortion of early memories by later ones than actually occurs.

Moreover, violent cortical storms can occur (as in *grand mal* epilepsy or cerebral concussion) without a detectable effect on earlier memories. That the trace should be purely "dynamic"—a pattern of activity not dependent on structural changes for its permanence—thus seems in the highest degree unlikely. No one has explicitly made such an assumption; yet how otherwise are the known properties of a learned discrimination to be accounted for, with its inevitable tendency to be generalized beyond what has already been experienced by the animal—its apparent independence of excitation in specific cells?

In addition to the facts of perceptual generalization, two other forms of evidence might make it difficult to postulate a structural trace as the basis of memory. One is from Lashley's (1929a) extirpation experiments, showing that the removal of blocks of the rat's cerebral cortex does not affect habits selectively. If one habit is affected, others are also. From this, Lashley has concluded that memory traces are not localized in the cerebral cortex, but himself has pointed out (Lashley, 1929b) another possible interpretation. His evidence is consistent with the idea that the trace is structural but diffuse, involving, that is, a large number of cells widely spaced in the cortex, physiologically but not anatomically unified. This is not, consequently, crucial evidence for or against the notion of structural traces in the cortex.

The other evidence that seemed once to prevent postulating a structural trace is found in the work of Wulf (cited by Koffka, 1935) and later investigators who have interpreted their studies of human memory for patterns to mean that the trace is spontaneously active, and does not lie dormant or merely deteriorate with the passage of time. Hanawalt (1937), however, effectively criticized the earlier evidence for this idea; and Hebb and Foord (1945), having obtained data inconsistent with Wulf's hypothesis, re-examined the later work that managed to avoid Hanawalt's criticism. They have shown that there is no evidence to even faintly support the idea of slow, spontaneous changes in the trace. This conception must be abandoned.

Thus the only barrier to assuming that a structural change in specific neural cells is the basis of memory lies in the generalization of the perception of patterns. Man sees a square as a square, whatever its size, and in almost any setting. A rat trained to look for food behind a horizontal rectangle will there-

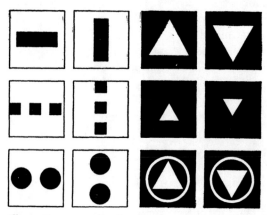

FIGURE 1. Illustrating generalization in perception. A rat is first *trained* with the two diagrams at the top, in the left half of the figure, until he always avoids the vertical bar and chooses the horizontal. He is then *tested* with the next pair of diagrams, the horizontally and vertically arranged squares; and with the next pair, circles side by side versus circles one above the other. Transfer of response occurs, the rat in each case preferring the horizontal diagram, showing that perception of horizontal and vertical is generalized beyond any particular pattern. Similarly, after training with the large plain triangles, top right, the animal is tested with smaller triangles and with circumscribed triangles. If the erect triangle, the one to the left, is positive in training, the rat will choose the left-hand diagram when presented with either of the two lower pairs, again demonstrating perceptual generalization.

after choose almost *any* horizontal figure, such as an interrupted line or a pair of circles side by side (figure 1). Trained to choose a solid upright triangle and to avoid an inverted triangle, he will discriminate consistently between outlines of triangles; triangles with confusing figures added (such as circumscribing circles); and triangles of different size, which cannot thus excite the same retinal cells simultaneously (Lashley, 1938*b*). Rats reared in darkness, then trained in the same way, show the same perceptual generalizations (Hebb, 1937*a*).

These are concrete, undisputed facts of behavior. They have been interpreted as meaning that perception is independent of the locus of excitation; and this interpretation has been tacitly accepted as inescapable. The result is an awkward dilemma for theory, since, as we have seen, it is hard to reconcile an unlocalized afferent process with a structural (and hence localized) mnemonic trace.

Lashley's (1942*a*) hypothesis of interference patterns is the one explicit attempt to solve this difficulty and to deal adequately with both perception and learning. As such it deserves special mention here, although we shall see that in other respects it faces great difficulties.

Other writers have had to choose one horn of the dilemma. Köhler (1940), for example, starts out with the facts of perceptual generalization, in his theory of cerebral fields of force, and then cannot deal with learning. He has no apparent way of avoiding a fatal difficulty about the nature of the trace, its locus and structure. This is another aspect of the difficulty for *Gestalt* theory raised by Boring (1933), who pointed out that at *some* point the perceptual process must act on specific cells in order to determine a specific response.

The theory elaborated by Hull (1943), on the other hand, is to be regarded as providing first of all for the stability of learning. It then has persistent difficulty with perception. The principle of "afferent neural interaction" appears to be a concession extorted by the facts of perceptual generalization. With this, there is some danger that the entire system may lose its meaning. The great value of Hull's theory is in showing how one may conceive of variable behavior as determined by constant causal relationships between stimulus, intervening variables, and response. This is brilliantly achieved, for an important segment of behavior. But then the postulate of afferent neural interaction adds that anything may happen when two sensory events occur at the same time—which of course they are always doing. Evidently no prediction is possible until the limits, and the determinants, of afferent neural interaction can be given in detail. This it seems demands that the neurological reference, already present in the theory, be made explicit, and detailed. For our present purposes, at any rate, Hull must be regarded as not yet having solved the problem of dealing with the perceptual process in a theory of learning, although it remains possible that his program (Hull, 1945) will do so in the future.

THE MODE OF ATTACK

How are we to provide for perceptual generalization *and* the stability of memory, in terms of what the neuron does and what happens at the synapse? We must suppose that the mnemonic trace is a structural change; the difficulty, in supposing it, is a conflict with the idea that only the pattern, and not the locus of sensory stimulation, is important in perception; so let us begin by asking whether that idea is, after all, securely established.

That paragraph puts the theoretical approach of this monograph. I propose to go over the evidence on perception again and show that it is not what it seems. We do *not* know that pattern is everything, locus nothing. Next, an alternative set of ideas about perception will be developed. According to these ideas, perception does depend on exciting specific parts of the receptor surface; mnemonic trace and perceptual generalization need no longer be at odds with one another; and a physiological meaning of attention (or set, or expectancy) shows up.

Now let us see, in the following two chapters, what revisions can be made in current ideas about perception so that they can be extended into a more general theory. The reader will observe that the discussion deals almost entirely with *visual* perception. This is not because vision has any unique significance, but because it is in visual perception, with few exceptions, that the problem of patterning and form has been studied experimentally. It can be assumed that perception in other sense modes does not depend on fundamentally different principles.

2. *Summation and Learning in Perception*

This chapter begins a revision of perceptual theory.* The immediate objective is to show that "simple" perceptions are in fact complex: that they are additive, that they depend partly on motor activity, and that their apparent simplicity is only the end result of a long learning process.

The preceding pages have tried to show that the crucial problem of perception must be dealt with explicitly at the very beginning of a psychological theory; and that one has the choice of two approaches to this problem. One must decide whether perception is to depend (1) on the excitation of *specific cells* or (2) on a *pattern of excitation* whose locus is unimportant. Current opinion seems tacitly to have accepted the *Gestalt* argument (and Lashley's argument) that the only tenable assumption is the second of these possibilities.

The theory to be presented here is diametrically opposed to this aspect of *Gestalt* theory, and is based on assumption 1, that a particular perception depends on the excitation of particular cells at *some* point in the central nervous system. Now the *Gestalt* argument depends, I believe, on another assumption: that when one perceives a simple figure (such as square or circle) one perceives it directly as a distinctive whole, without need of any learning process and not through a prior recogni-

---

* This and the following chapter may be disregarded by the reader who is not particularly interested in the theory of perception. These two chapters are in a sense preventive. The theory of behavior presented later would appear impossible to the reader who is familiar with the current literature on perception if he had not been shown that the alternative (and at first sight preferable) approach of "field theory" or "equipotentiality" has very serious difficulties indeed—more serious than has been recognized.

tion of the several parts of the figure. If one makes this assumption—if the perception of a square is as simple and immediate as it seems to us as adults—I believe that the *Gestalt* argument is unanswerable. But if on the other hand the perception is additive, a serial reconstruction (though very rapid and "unconscious" for the normal adult), the theoretical problem would be very much changed.

In this chapter, accordingly, an attempt is made to show that quite simple diagrams are not perceived directly as *distinctive* wholes—that, though the stimulus has a unitary action in the figure-ground relationship, the perception of identity depends on a series of excitations from the parts of the stimulating diagram. If this can be established, it will remove the *necessity* of accepting field theory; and the following chapter will then attempt to show that field theory actually is not consistent with some of the facts of perception.

The work of Senden (1932) and of Riesen (1947) is fundamental to my argument here. Senden's monograph is a compilation of all published reports on the vision of the congenitally blind given sight by a surgical operation after the patient was old enough to talk to the examiner and describe what he saw. In some respects the data are incomplete, but the report is repeatedly referred to here because it contains the only existent evidence concerning the course taken by the early development of human perception. At first sight, some of the reported facts are literally almost incredible, since they differ so much from what would be predicted by current theory (either of perception or of learning). There is, however, a considerable unanimity among the writers reviewed by Senden, some of whom evidently were not aware of the reports made by others; and the work of Riesen (1947), who reared chimpanzees in darkness to an age when the normal chimpanzee makes an effective use of vision, fully confirms Senden's clinical evidence.

The two reports, by Senden and Riesen, are complementary; and, though many details are not clear, the human and chimpanzee data taken together seem to require radical changes in the theory of perception and of learning.

DISTINCTION OF "PRIMITIVE UNITY" FROM OTHER PROPERTIES OF THE PERCEIVED FIGURE

As a preliminary, certain terms must be defined. I want to show that simple figures do not always act as wholes, innately. But it is undoubtedly true that they sometimes do so in one respect—in the figure-ground relationship: so this property of a perceived figure is to be distinguished from others, in which summation and learning are important. Accordingly, the following are distinguished: the conceptions of (1) a primitive, sensorily determined unity, (2) a nonsensory unity, affected by experience, and (3) the identity (also affected by experience), of a perceived figure.

The primitive unity of a figure is defined here as referring to that unity and segregation from the background which seems to be a direct product of the pattern of sensory excitation and the inherited characteristics of the nervous system on which it acts.

Rubin (1921) elaborated the conception of the figure-ground relationship, in a study of visual perception of patterns with clearly marked boundaries. In order to elucidate the relation of figure to ground (the relation of the perceived object or surface to other objects and surfaces which make up the background) he put particular stress on "ambiguous" figures (figure 2). This is the special case in which either of two parts of a diagram may be seen as figure, each alternating as part of the ground when the other is figure. The principles he established, however, are most fully operative in the unambiguous figure, made up of a homogeneous zone of color surrounded by another color and having a sharply defined boundary—an abrupt transition in brightness from one zone to the other at all points. Such a figure may or may not be regular. It is as well illustrated by a splash of ink or by a silhouette of an animal as by a white circle on a black stimulus card.

An area thus sensorily delimited is seen as *one*, unified and distinct from its surroundings, by any normal person, by the congenitally blind on the first occurrence of vision following operation for cataract (Senden, 1932), by the normal rat (Lashley, 1938*b*), and apparently also at first vision by the rat that has been reared in darkness (Hebb, 1937*a*). The unity and distinctiveness of such figures from their background, then, is independent of experience, or "primitive."

It is not possible to specify exactly the stimulating conditions which determine the primitive figure-ground organization. I do

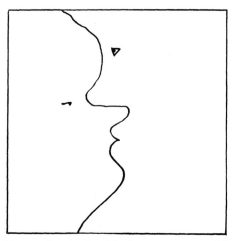

FIGURE 2. Ambiguous figure. In this diagram it is possible to see either of two profiles, but only rarely can the two be seen simultaneously; they alternate instead. When a figure appears on the left, the profile of a rather chubby man, the white area on the left appears as a more solid surface and one that is nearer to the observer. This relationship is reversed when a figure appears on the right—the profile of one suffering from gigantic tumors of the neck and of the frontal bone. The theoretical importance of such reversals of figure-ground relationships has been stressed by *Gestalt* psychologists, though there is considerable difficulty in subsuming the instability under perceptual theory.

not exclude as nonprimitive the perception of groupings; nor the segregation of a patch of color which has ill-defined boundaries. There are suggestions in Senden's (1932) monograph and in rat behavior that the perception of such units in the visual field may also be independent of experience. Senden's monograph is of the first importance for understanding the perceptual process, but in several respects the evidence is far from clear. The earlier writers whose reports are summarized did not recognize some of the psychological problems to which their observations are relevant. What Senden does show, in the fact that patients always responded to certain objects as wholes and could on occasion detect differences between objects even in spite of nystagmus, is that there is a primitive or innate figure-ground mechanism. He does not make it possible to state its limiting conditions.

THE "NONSENSORY" FIGURE

The nonsensory figure-ground organization is defined as one in which the boundaries of the figure are not fixed by gradients of luminosity in the visual field. It is affected by experience and other nonsensory factors, and is not inevitable in any perception. In contrasting the primitive and the nonsensory figure, however, one need not imply that a perceived figure must be either of one or the other kind. They are rather two extremes, and in most perceptions both sensory and nonsensory factors affect figure-ground organization.

The one of these extremes, in which exactly the same figural boundaries are recognized by anyone, has already been illustrated. The other is quite common in ordinary experience, although I have not found any discussion that makes its meaning explicit. It is implied, for example, by Gibson and Crooks (1938) in their discussion of the perceptual field of the automobile driver, and the shrinking or expanding of a perceived zone of safety from *potential* collision. In general terms, the nonsensory figure occurs in perception whenever the subject responds selectively to a limited part of a homogeneous area in the visual field. One may look at the "middle part" of a rope as distinct from the rest, in knot-tying, or perceive the "foreground" of an unbroken landscape. It is a commonplace that in human perception many entities exist, like the place in a continuous expanse of lawn where a flowerbed is to be put in, such that no sensory delimitation of figure from ground can even be suggested. The "corner" of a room certainly does not always refer to a geometrical point; it is extended, and yet does not comprise all of the two (or three) rectangular surfaces which determine it. Its locus is sensorily fixed, but not its boundaries, and language is full of terms with a similar implication for the theory of perception.

Even commoner in everyday perception is the perceived entity in which both sensory and nonsensory factors cooperate. Here the figural boundary may follow one of a number of possible luminosity gradients in the field, the particular one that is effective being usually determined by experience in one form or another. This is illustrated by Leeper's (1935) experiment, which demonstrated a lasting control, *by earlier experience,* of the particular perception that is made with Boring's ambiguous figure, "My wife and my mother-in-law" (Boring, 1930). Another illustration is the process of slow learning to see a configuration in a particular way, as in the gradual decrease of the difficulty a novice has in following the boundaries of a thalamic nucleus that are obvious to the expert.

There is reason to believe that the rat, as well as man, finds some figure-ground relations obvious and inescapable, and detects others only after prolonged experience. That is, the distinction of primitive and nonsensory figures applies also to the rodent's perception. Lashley (1938*b*, pp. 156, 185) points out that success in discrimination and generalization evidently depends on the rat's finding a differentiating characteristic between two figures, or one that is common to a pattern already known and the new one which is presented in the testing situation. It is equally clear that the distinctive part of the test pattern is not obvious to the rat at once; this part, whatever it is, is what determines the response and becomes the true figure (as contrasted with what the experimenter meant to be the figure), the rest merging into ground.

In general, *Gestalt* writers on the organization of the figure have been concerned to show that it cannot be reduced to experience and learning, and have thus selected cases for discussion in which sensory dynamics alone is enough to produce an effective figure-ground organization. They have, that is, concentrated attention on the primitive figure, and they give the impression that the spontaneity of its organization is a property of any figure. True, one can find many passages in the literature on *Gestalten* that refer to figures not sensorily delimited, but no stress on the fact that this implies some role of learning in the delimitation.

Köhler (1929), for example, has written: "Since 'real form' presupposes a segregated whole, the existence of 'form' depends upon factors *of stimulation* similar to those upon which the segregation and organization of wholes depend. Again, definite relations in the total constellation *of retinal stimuli* are found to be decisive for the existence of real form" (p. 202; my italics draw attention to the stress put on sensory factors). Again, after referring to Gottschaldt's experiments, Köhler says: "After these results, whoever defends the automatic influence of past experience upon our seeing definite forms, will have incumbent upon him the task of supporting his theory by other experiments. *If such an influence exists, it must be restricted to rather special cases*" (p. 208; italics mine).

Attention is drawn to this aspect of *Gestalt* theory because it helps one to define the point at which one can diverge from the theory without failing to recognize the great contribution it has made to modern psychology, which has been shaped to a great extent by the impact of *Gestalt* ideas on behaviorism. There are few psychologists who would not own a debt of this kind to *Gestalttheorie,* and few who do not also feel the need of qualifying the theory in some way, though it is not easy to see just how this is to be done without losing the values that have been obtained with its help.

In the pages from which the passage above is taken, Professor Köhler, I believe, provides the necessary clue. His argument appears to depend on a complete antithesis of experience and innate sensory dynamics, and it is this antithesis that we may avoid. The question that is asked by Köhler is whether sensory organization is wholly innate, or wholly experiential.* If these are the only two alternatives, the argument is unanswerable. Köhler and Koffka and Lashley have unquestionably slain the

---

* In the monograph of Köhler and Wallach (1944, pp. 316, 323) there are also passages that seem not intelligible unless one is thinking in terms of such an extreme dichotomy between completely organized sensory processes (innately) and completely unorganized ones. This does not do justice, either to current learning theory, or to the effectiveness of the earlier *Gestalt* arguments in favor of an innate sensory organization.

dragon of pure learning theory, in the field of perception, and no one today would argue that perceptual organization is wholly acquired; there is some innate organization. But this of course does not show that the organization is entirely innate. There is always a possibility that perception has a partly innate, partly learned organization; and that besides the figure that has a "primitive unity" there are "nonsensory figures" in which experience has an important role.

I propose, then, that *Gestalt* theory made an essential contribution when it showed that there are innate factors in perception, but that it has tended to carry the argument too far in denying that learning and experience have any important role in the perception of simple configurations (apart, of course, from learning the *meaning* of the configurations). This, as we have seen, has led to emphasis on a dominant role of sensory dynamics; important as sensory processes are, however, they do not completely dominate either behavior or perception.

It is also important to see that the argument against an effect of experience on perception often requires the assumption that *any* perceived figure is perceived as a whole, in all respects. Thus the upper diagram of figure 3 has been regarded as quite unfamiliar to the observer (Köhler, 1929). Subjects shown this diagram for the first time failed to find another which is concealed in it, and which they had been shown before. The conclusion was drawn that an unfamiliar configuration obscured a familiar, smaller one—that sensory dynamics dominates experience and the effects of learning. But the experimental diagram, actually, was unfamiliar only as a whole: its parts, two parallelograms and a set of parallel lines forming a Z, were certainly not unfamiliar to the experimental subjects. Consequently, the conclusion is valid only if the total figure is an unanalyzable whole, which it surely is not.

In the lower diagram of figure 3, a "4" is concealed. That it may not be recognized is evidence that sensory dynamics on occasion may override experience, in the delimitation of a figure. This is a valid point. But when one looks for it, the 4 can be seen, and this is not explained by *Gestalt* theory. A "special vector" (Köhler, 1929) is operating, but this special vector seems to be the factor of attention and experience that is involved in the nonsensory figure. Our problem is to find out how to modify *Gestalt* theory so that it can comprise this factor of attention and not have to deny the importance of learning in perception.

Furthermore, *Gestalt* emphasis on the primitive figure, which has a marked stability, obscures the fact that in ordinary per-

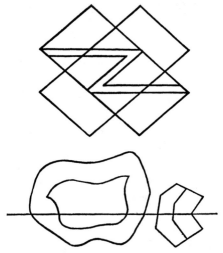

FIGURE 3.   Diagrams from Köhler, *Gestalt psychology*, 1929 (figures 10 and 12). Courtesy of Liveright Publishing Corporation and of the author.

ception any figure-ground relationship is a highly unstable one, with a practically constant fluctuation from one organization to another. Even when one perceives the compact, clearly delimited figure which is such that any observer at once sees it, one finds that the stability of the figure-ground relation is not great; or, better, that its stability consists of a continual *recurrence*, instead of a constancy, of the figure. It is notorious that attention wanders, and this is another way of saying that in perception any figure is unstable; one looks at this part of the configuration and that, and notices its corners or smooth contour, in the intervals between seeing the figure as a whole. In ordinary perception, moreover, the instability is far greater (Boring, 1933; Pillsbury, 1913).

An adequate account of perception cannot be given in terms of a figure-ground organization that has any great duration in time, even when gaze is fixated at a single point in a configuration. The fluctuations of attention which occur point directly to a fundamental importance, in any perception, of nonsensory factors. This of course has already been demonstrated for complex indeterminate figures by Carmichael, Hogan, and Walter (1932) and by Zangwill (1937); I propose that the same factors must be taken into account in the perception of square or circle as well.

"IDENTITY" IN PERCEPTION

Identity is defined here as referring to the properties of association inherent in a perception. The reference has two aspects: first, a figure is perceived as having identity when it is seen immediately as similar to some figures and dissimilar to others—that is, when it falls at once into certain categories and not into others. This similarity can be summed up as spontaneous association, since it may occur on the first exposure to the stimulus object. Secondly, the object that is perceived as having identity is capable of being associated readily with other objects or with some action, whereas the one that does not have identity is recalled with great difficulty or not at all, and is not recognized or named easily. Identity of course is a matter of degree and, as I shall try to show, depends on a considerable degree of experience; it is not innately given.

Thorndike (1931, p. 87) has presented an approach to this conception, using the term "identifiability," and has proposed that identifiability promotes the formation of associations. If one carries the analysis a little further, it appears that the proposition is circular. Identifiability is not merely a perceptible difference of one figure from another when the two are side by side, but implies a rememberable difference—identifiability is clearly, in the instances Thorndike gives, recognizability; and recognition is one form of association. Thus Thorndike's proposition is that associability affects the occurrence of associations.

The real point at which he is driving seems to be that there are genuine differences of associability in different patterns. Also, more is involved in these differences than the number of trials necessary to establish recognition; there are also the spontaneous associations referred to in speaking of similarity. Recognizability goes with selective similarity, or generalization: the figure that is readily remembered is also perceived as belonging to a particular class of figures, and remembered so.

An irregular mass of color or a pattern of intersecting lines drawn at random has some coherence and unity, but one such figure is not readily recognized and distinguished from others when it is seen a second time, and generalization (or similarity) is not selective among a number of such stimuli. There is not a total lack of distinctiveness and of generalization, however. Two of Thorndike's figures which lack identity are not indistinguishable when seen together; and mistaking one figure for another can be called generalization. Lashley and Wade (1946) distinguish between the "so-called generalization" which means only a failure to observe differences and the generalization which involves perception of both similarities and differences. The amorphous figure, lacking in identity, is generalized in the first sense only.

A further illustration of these points is found in the development of identity in the perception of chimpanzee faces by one who has seen no chimpanzees before. Two animals seen side by side are obviously different in details, but the inexperienced observer is not able easily to remember one selectively. Also, all chimpanzees at this stage look alike; the "so-called generalization" occurs. With experience the perception of identity increases. Similarity is still perceived between animals, and confusion between some animals is still possible; but there is a marked change in the perception, as shown in a much more selective similarity of one animal to others, and in the radical increase of the observer's capacity to associate even a new chimpanzee with a specific name. Thus identity is a matter of degree: readiness of recognition, and the extent to which generalization is selective.

This discussion has been meant to establish the conception of "identity" as an important property of perception which should be kept carefully distinct from the "unity" of the perceived figure (as well as from its "meaning"). Unity may be innately determined, an immediate property of sensory dynamics, whereas identity is dependent on a prolonged experience. Because these two things have not been separated in the past, it has appeared that perceptual organization is innate. Some aspects of the organization *are* present, apparently, at the first experience; but others are not.

INDEPENDENCE OF UNITY AND IDENTITY IN SIMPLE FIGURES

The examples of the preceding section dealt with complex perceptions. I wish next to review the evidence that shows that unity and identity have separate determinants even in quite simple perceptions. Seeing a circle as a single coherent object is not the same as seeing it as a distinctive object, selectively recognizable.

First, the evidence for man. It has already been said that the figure-ground segregation is good at the initial occurrence of human vision, as shown by Senden's (1932) reports, at the very time when perception of identity appears to be practically nil. Unity then can be perceived without identity. Investigators (of vision following operation for congenital cataract) are unanimous in reporting that the perception of a square, circle, or triangle, or of sphere or cube, is very poor. To see one of these as a whole object, with distinctive characteristics immediately evident, is not possible for a long period. The most intelligent and best-motivated patient has to seek corners painstakingly even to distinguish a triangle from a circle. The newly seeing patient can frequently find a difference between two such figures shown together, just as the normal adult can readily detect differences between two of Thorndike's figures lacking "identifiability," but the differences are not remembered. There is for weeks a practically zero capacity to learn names for such figures, even when tactual recognition is prompt and complete.

Another facet of the same lack of capacity is the failure to generalize as normal persons do. When the patient first gets to the point of being able to name a simple object promptly, recognition is completely destroyed if the object is slightly changed or put into a new setting. The patient who had learned to name a ring showed no recognition of a slightly different ring;

having learned to name a square, made of white cardboard, could not name it when its color was changed to yellow by turning the cardboard over; and so on. These reports consistently indicate that the perceived whole at first vision is *simultaneously unified and amorphous.* There is not a single instance given in which the congenitally blind after operation had trouble in learning color names; but a great number in which the perception of identity in a simple figure was poor indeed (Senden, 1932, pp. 135–141).

A second evidence comes from species differences in the perception of identity. For coherent patterns and simple groupings the figure-ground relationship appears to be the same from rat to man, so the significant differences of perceptual generalization (one aspect of identity) argue strongly that figural unity and identity have separate bases. (*a*) The discrimination of simple geometrical figures by man and chimpanzee is unaffected by reversal of brightness relations between figure and ground (Gellerman, 1933); a white triangle on a black ground is generalized by these anthropoids to include a black triangle on a white ground. For the rat, such a reversal completely disrupts discrimination, and no amount of training with the white triangle alone will produce "recognition" of a black one. There is some uncertainty about the phylogenetic level at which the capacity for this generalization appears; see Lashley (1938*b*, p. 144), Smith (1936), and Neet (1933); but between the rat, and chimpanzee or man, the difference in this respect seems complete (although for simple figures only; human perception of more complex figures in reversed brightness is definitely defective, as in recognition of photographic negatives). (*b*) The perception of a triangle or square by the rat is not generalized, without specific training, to include a similar rotated figure (Fields, 1932) but is generalized so by chimpanzee and by two-year-old children, although a corresponding head rotation also occurs (Gellerman, 1933). (*c*) Perception of a triangle is not generalized either by rat or chimpanzee to include a triangle made up of small circles, but the generalization is made by two-year-old children (Gellerman, 1933; Lashley, 1938*b*).

Thus the perception of identity is different in different mammals; the perception of primitive unity is practically the same.

Further evidence of the independence of unity and identity is found in the peculiar "equivalences" or generalizations often observed in rat behavior, and in the anomalies to be found in the relative difficulty with which the rat learns to discriminate between certain patterns. Two discriminations that are equally easy, from the human point of view, present very unequal difficulty for the rat. For normal man a square and a circle are no less obviously distinct than erect and inverted triangles; yet the rat readily learns to discriminate between the triangles and consistently has trouble with circle versus square (Lashley, 1938*b*, pp. 155, 156). Some animals that have learned other patterns (thus showing that their acuity is sufficient for the task) show no sign of discriminating circle and square at all. A five-pointed star and an *H* are for man clearly, inevitably distinct, while the rat distinguishes them with difficulty and no faster learning occurs than with quite irregular figures (Lashley, 1938*b*, p. 157). Such facts mean a great difference of rat from man in perceiving the identity of simple, regular figures.

The same is evident in the patterns which may be "equivalent" for individual rats, and in some failures of equivalence. One animal may transfer his response from an erect triangle (versus an inverted one) to a single horizontal line low on the stimulus card (versus another higher on the card), while another animal fails to discriminate the complete triangles with which he was trained, when a slight change is made of their positions on the respective stimulus cards. It is very doubtful in such cases that the rat has perceived the pattern as a distinctive whole, and it seems that a response is frequently determined by only a part of a figure as simple as a triangle.

Lashley (1938*b*, p. 182) has recognized this, but interpreted it by comparing the rat to a ski-jumper who does not pay attention in his jump to nonessentials such as the shape of a spectator's hat. The general interpretation was made that there is little significant difference in the perception of simple figures by rat and man, but this conclusion is not supported by the evidence.

When identity is distinguished from unity, we find great species differences in the perception of identity and not in what is seen as a primitive unity. The analogy between the rat's perceiving all the detail of a triangle in the jumping apparatus, and the ski-jumper's perception of a hat, is valid—except that it sets the human subject a much more difficult task. It is inconceivable that a ski-jumper would not perceive a large triangle as such, fully structured, if it lay close to and marked the point of safe landing in an otherwise plain field, as it does for the rat in the jumping apparatus. The rat, however, may respond selectively to only the part of the figure which lies nearest the point to which he jumps, although his field of vision is wide and although (as Lashley has demonstrated) he perceives much more than he has to in making a discrimination.

These considerations are the more convincing because the evidence of the rat's frequent failure to see the triangle as a distinctive whole figure coincides with Senden's description of the congenitally blind after acquiring vision—the normally reared rat, and a man seeing for the first time, both have precisely the same kind of difficulty.

It is reasonable to conclude that the perception of identity (as defined) follows the same principles in rat and man but is much more highly developed in normal man. Since there is no evidence of any clear difference of the primitive figure-ground organization perceived by these two species, but strong suggestions that it is the same for both, the evidence is consistent with the idea that identity and figural unity have separate physiological bases. They are, that is, psychologically independent. This makes it possible to suppose that additive processes may occur in the development of identity without denying that the figure has a primitive unity.

LEARNING TO PERCEIVE SIMPLE FIGURES

The facts already adduced in the last section have indicated a role of learning in the perception of triangle or square as distinctive wholes. The idea that one has to learn to see a triangle must sound extremely improbable, and so I shall now present the evidence to this effect more systematically.

We have seen that the perceptions of the congenitally blind after operation are almost completely lacking in identity. Senden (1932, pp. 155–157) reports cases in which there was an immediate perception of differences in two figures seen together, but also a number of instances in which even this was not possible. Thus a patient sometimes saw differences between a sphere and cube, sometimes not (p. 91). Color has been found to dominate form persistently in the first vision of these patients. Eleven months after operation the color names learned by a patient in hospital were retained, but the little that had been learned of form was forgotten (p. 135). An egg, potato, and cube of sugar were seen by a patient repeatedly, until naming was prompt, but then were not recognized when put into colored light; the cube of sugar was well named when it was seen on the table or in the investigator's hand but not recognized when suspended by a thread with a change of background (p. 138).

Such patients, when learning has proceeded far enough, manifest the characteristic generalizations of the normal person, so the initial difficulties are not to be put down to structural defects of the sensory apparatus (Senden, pp. 173–175).

Riesen (1947) has fully confirmed the conclusion that ordinary visual perception in higher mammals presupposes a long learning period. His observations concerning the almost complete visual incapacity of chimpanzees reared in darkness, and the slowness of learning, are of the greatest importance. They show that Senden's similar results with man are not due to some inadequacy of the clinical tests, nor peculiarly human.

The course of perceptual learning in man is gradual, proceeding from a dominance of color, through a period of separate attention to each part of a figure, to a gradually arrived at identification of the whole as a whole: an apparently simultaneous instead of a serial apprehension. A patient was trained to discriminate square from triangle over a period of 13 days, and had learned so little in this time "that he could not report their form without counting corners one after another.··· And yet it seems that the recognition process was beginning already to be automatic, so that some day the judgment 'square' would be given with simple vision, which would then easily lead to the belief that form was always simultaneously given" (Senden, 1932, p. 160). The shortest time in which a patient approximated to normal perception, even when learning was confined to a small number of objects, seems to have been about a month.

It is possible then that the normal human infant goes through the same process, and that we are able to see a square as such in a single glance only as the result of complex learning. The notion seems unlikely, because of the utter simplicity of such a perception to the normal adult. But no such argument can be valid, since Lashley (1937) has shown that subjective simplicity and immediacy may be very deceptive as an index of physiological simplicity. There are moreover residual traces of learning in normal perception, and hints of its complexity.

Gellerman (1933) reports that chimpanzees and two-year-old children recognized a triangle that had been rotated through 120° from the training position, but (in the one protocol that is given) responded selectively only *after* a head rotation; and persistent head rotation continued in the later discriminations. Older human subjects do not need to make the same receptor adjustment to recognize the figure in two positions, and so this generalization may be a learned capacity, simple as it seems to us.

Consider also the following evidence, which is suggestive though perhaps not conclusive. When a simple figure such as square, circle, or triangle, subtending a retinal angle of from 2° to 10°, is fixated at one point, it tends in a second or so to become almost amorphous except near the point of fixation. The effect is not due to fatigue alone, nor to poor acuity outside the macular zone: since (1) a single straight line does not suffer nearly as much, (2) shifting fixation back and forth between two corners of a triangle does not restore the clarity with which the third is seen, and (3) an 8° circle drawn with a line 2 mm. wide, and a 4° circle drawn with a line 1 mm. wide, seem to give approximately the same effect.

The factors involved are evidently complicated; it will be found, for example, that with a large figure merely *imagining* eyemovements (of following the contours) will restore definition of the figure. Also, these "imaginary" eyemovements, or subliminal activations of the motor system, occur more frequently and are less easy to control in looking at a smaller than at a larger figure, and it is hard to be sure that the size of the figure is unimportant. But this at least seems definite, that a stable, clear, and effective perception of circle or square is more possible with eyemovement than without. Once the question is asked, anyone can verify for himself the falsity of the implicit assumption (usually made in the study of perception) that the figure acts always as one, without a reinforcing perception of its parts as distinct from the whole.

My point is not that eyemovements are essential to perception by a sophisticated observer (nor, in the following paragraph, that they are completely necessary for an image); but that the perception is definitely clearer, more effective, with them than without. This is really an evident fact. It is to be interpreted in the light of all evidence, cited above, showing that the perception of square or circle is slowly learned *and depends originally on multiple visual fixations.*

Directly in line with such phenomenological observations are the following introspections. I find it very difficult to have a clear image of a triangle, square, or circle without imagining or actually making a series of eyemovements. Several others, asked to make observation on this point, have reported the same thing. It is hard or impossible, that is, to have a clear image of a triangle as fixated at one point. Eyemovements definitely improve the "image." They do not take the form, necessarily, of following the figure's contours, but are apt to jump from point to point, perhaps three to four points in all. Thus the distinctiveness of the image is not merely in the eyemovement pattern, for approximately the same series of eyemovements may contribute to a good image either of circle or square. Activation of the motor system, overt or implicit (even possibly within the cerebrum alone, with no activity of the final common paths), *contributes essentially to the development of visual integration without being sufficient to it.* As I have said, such evidence is hard to evaluate, but it points to the same conclusion as Senden's evidence, already cited, and is supported by it.

Clark and Lashley (1947) have confirmed the observations of Kennard and Ectors (1938) and Kennard (1939), and have provided what appears to be an independent confirmation of the argument above. Kennard found a one-sided loss of vision by monkeys on extirpation of the opposite frontal eyefield, a cortical motor area for head-and-eye movement. Clark and Lashley have demonstrated this phenomenon convincingly, with an adequate method of testing. The most significant and striking observation was startle by the monkey when an object was passed from the blind side into the seeing side, at the moment of passing the midline. One might have argued that the animal could "see" an object in his apparently hemianopic field but was not able to move his eyes toward it. The observation referred to rules that interpretation out, and other observations showed that the hemianopia is a genuine failure to see (though it is transient, disappearing in a week or two).

Now the question is what the motor cortex can have to do with visual perception—unless perception intimately involves a motor activity, liminal or subliminal. There is no reason to think that the frontal cortex has anything to do with the reception of visual sensation, and the alternative seems to be that it must have something to do with the elaboration of sensation into visual perceptions. In Chapter 5 will be found a treatment of perception which supposes that perception of even a simple object involves a "phase sequence." This is a chain of central cortical events with motor links. Although the motor activations may be subliminal and do not always produce overt response, their role is essential in any perception. This would account for the observations of Kennard and Ectors, and Clark and Lashley, which therefore can be considered to be a confirmation of the argument of Chapter 5 as well as the argument of the preceding paragraphs.

CONCLUSIONS

Animal experiments and the human clinical data alike indicate that the perception of simple diagrams as distinctive wholes is not immediately given but slowly acquired through learning. Introspective observations which would not carry much weight in themselves appear to agree fully with other evidence, showing vestiges of a summative process involved in perceiving the identity of circle or triangle; although such a figure is seen by the adult clearly and is effectively discriminated at a single glance, there are still traces left of complexities such as the learning process described by Senden would produce, which for normal persons must have occurred in early infancy and which makes the unified perception possible.

The subjective experience of an irreducible simplicity in the perception of square or circle may then be fully analogous to the illusion of the image of the letter-square (Woodworth, 1938, p. 42), where the subject thinks he has an actual image of the square but can be shown not to have.* Although the perception of identity is good at a glance, it is improved by several glances at different parts of the figure. This process of "successive part reinforcement," as an *aid* to perception, exists at the same time as an essential unity of the whole; and theory must provide for the additive process, with its motor elements, as well as for the primitive unity.

This argument is not in any way a return to the old idea that sensory integration occurs solely through motor activity, or that the distinctiveness of a perception is solely or mainly due to distinctive eyemovement. We know that this is not true. But there are three theoretical possibilities, not two: (1) perceptual integration is wholly the result of motor activity; (2) it is wholly independent of motor activity; and (3) the motor activity is important but not all-important—the position that is taken here.

Grant fully that visual integration cannot be reduced to a synthesis of unrelated elements through effector activity, and the question remains, how much significance the motor factor

---

* The experiment is as follows. The subject is shown a diagram such as

$$x \quad e \quad a \quad q$$
$$r \quad l \quad i \quad s$$
$$o \quad f \quad z \quad g$$
$$d \quad y \quad u \quad p$$

and studies it until he has, apparently, an image of the whole square and can "look at" it and read the letters off, one by one. If he really has such an image, it will not matter in what direction he is asked to "read." Actually, it is found that the subject cannot reproduce the letters as fast from right to left as from left to right, or promptly give the four letters, *p, z, l, x,* that make up the diagonal from lower right to upper left. So what seems a simple, immediately given image of the whole is actually a serial reconstruction of parts of the figure. An "image" of triangle or square is simpler, longer practiced, but may be fundamentally the same. The perception of such figures, also, may involve a temporal sequence.

may still have. Receptor adjustment (head-and-eye movement) is the most prominent feature of visual perception whether in rat, chimpanzee, or man—*except* in long-practiced habits. The assumption has been tacitly made that the adjustments are unimportant for theory (once it was shown that they were not the whole answer). The fact of eyemovement has been treated only as a further (negative) evidence that the locus of excitation in the retina is unimportant, since the changing retinal projection does not disturb perception. But obviously another point of view is possible. The thesis of this chapter is that eyemovements in perception are not adventitious. They contribute, constantly and essentially, to perceptual integration, even though they are not the whole origin of it.

3. *Field Theory and Equipotentiality*

The last chapter examined the proposition that perception is a unitary process, in all its aspects. We can turn now to an investigation of the two theories, Köhler's and Lashley's, that have resulted from that idea. In effect, this will be a critique of the theory of perception, since Köhler and Lashley are the only writers who both recognize the real problem of the neural mechanisms of perceptual integration and attempt an adequate solution. Others have avoided the crucial difficulty of specifying the way in which perceptual generalization occurs. Either like Pavlov (1928, 1932) they have not seen the difficulty at all, or like Hull (1943) have put it to one side for solution later. Hull has discussed the problem, but only to show that it is not necessarily insoluble for his theory of learning (Hull, 1945). For the present, Köhler and Lashley are the only ones who have attempted to say *where* and *how* perceptual generalization takes place.

For reasons already mentioned, however, the line of thought that they have chosen may be a blind alley, and it must be shown that there are other possible solutions. Until someone challenges the theory of innate stimulus equivalence and equipotentiality, and of neural fields and gradients as the only mechanism of integration, any theory with neural connections in its ancestry is damned before it is born. Being gravid, and so disapproving of infant damnation, let me look for another gospel.

CLARIFICATION OF TERMS AND ISSUES

As elsewhere, the issues here have sometimes been lost sight of in the dust of a prolonged battle. There is one main question: whether recognition, or a selective discriminatory response, requires the excitation of specific neural cells or not. The doctrine that it does not, we can refer to as *equipotentiality:* Köhler does not use the term, but his position is the same as Lashley's on this point, and a single term will do.

Explanations of the supposed equipotentiality differ greatly in some respects but agree in their stress on patterning in the central nervous system as against locus of excitation: so we can again use a single term, *configuration theory,* to designate Köhler's (1940; Köhler and Wallach, 1944) explanation by electrical fields in the cortex and Lashley's (1942*a*) alternative idea of irradiating waves of excitation and their interference patterns.

Next, *sensory equipotentiality* can be coined for Lashley's "equivalence of stimuli," which is ambiguous. One may want to refer to a limited degree of equipotentiality, in afferent structures, without accepting the whole theory of equipotentiality in central action, and this term can be used for the purpose.

"Equivalence of stimuli" has a double reference. It may mean only (1) that different stimuli can arouse the same response. This is an observed fact of behavior, whatever one's interpretation of the fact. But Lashley has also used the term to mean (2) that it does not matter what sensory cells are excited in order to get a certain response, and this is interpretation. The fact that two different patterns have the same effect may be due to eyemovement, or to multiple learning processes (the position adopted here); or it may be because similar patterns of excitation have the same ultimate motor effect, innately and necessarily, whether the receptors excited are the same or not. Let us then separate fact from interpretation; and let us refer (1) to the behavioral evidence in speaking of the *equivalence of stimuli,* and (2) to a particular interpretation in speaking of *sensory equipotentiality.*

Finally, the idea of equipotentiality itself should be made more explicit. "Potentiality" literally implies only that different cells are able to acquire the same function in behavior. Anyone must agree that this can happen, with separate learning processes. It is the basic idea of conditioning. But Lashley has given the word another meaning, that all cells in a system necessarily *do* acquire the same function, when excited in a given pattern, so that separate learning processes are not necessary for habits involving different stimuli or different parts of a cortical field.

Suppose for example that a habit is set up in this way: the stimulus is a circle, let us say, that falls always on the same retinal cells in the lower right quadrant; the response is a movement of the left hand. The stimulation then is confined to one half of the visual area in the right hemisphere, and the response is determined by motor systems that are also in the right hemisphere. Equipotentiality implies (1) that any other retinal cells, excited in a circular pattern, will elicit the same response—with either left or right hand; (2) that the right hemisphere may be extirpated, and the left will be found then to have "learned" whatever the right did; and (3) that this transfer of learning from one set of cells, primarily excited, to other sets *does not depend on an earlier experience that set up connections between them.* The idea is that the transfer is an innate property of the central nervous system, so that it is not possible for a particular habit to depend on any particular neural cell within an anatomical system, in any circumstances. If a whole system is extirpated, habits will be lost (as when both visual areas are removed); but it is not possible for a habit to be dependent on one half of an anatomical system only (for the habit to depend on one visual area alone, or on any part of it).

This is obviously a rather extreme position. An alternative hypothesis to be proposed later recognizes a limited field action in the sensory projection areas, and something like a limited equipotentiality between cells that are in functional parallel in physiological systems (this will be clear later on); but in the main it derives transfer of response from earlier-established habits and specific connections.

The issue is thus defined. We must recognize that Köhler and Lashley have been completely successful in their original attack on stimulus-response theory such as Watson's. No one now believes that retinal cells acquire direct connections with muscle cells, as in a child's learning to say "cat" when he sees a cat. The elimination of such oversimplified forms of switchboard theory was a fundamental contribution. One need only glance at the *Journal of Neurophysiology* to see that there *are* gradients of neural activity; there *is* some mutual influence of neighboring parts as an excitation is conducted from the retina to area 17. Electrophysiology has fully confirmed the value of such ideas, and they must enter into psychological theory.

But in fact, they have been generally accepted already, so this is no longer an issue. Pavlov's irradiation and concentration is a field action. Hull and Spence both make use of the notion of gradients. The question now is whether gradients and fields are the only mechanism of a selective neural action or whether they are combined with an equally important mechanism of connections and specialized conduction paths.

In short, configuration theory represents two things. It has been, first, a necessary corrective to earlier ideas, such as Titchener's and Watson's. This positive contribution must be recognized as an important step forward. But there is also an over-reaction from punctate sensory elements and sensori-motor connections that is about as extreme as these older ideas. As a theory, therefore, configurationism is just as vulnerable as structuralism and the early behaviorism were.

Now let us see what the evidence is by which we can accept or reject field theory and equipotentiality. Some of the evidence that has been used to support these ideas actually is not relevant to the question, and such evidence can be discussed first, leaving the more relevant evidence for later consideration.

THE PERCEPTION OF BRIGHTNESS, SIZE, PITCH

In the literature, the perception of relative intensity has been used almost entirely by writers on configuration theory for the embarrassment of learning theory. Actually, it is no easier for configuration theory to explain, and so is not really relevant to the debate between the two. It has been thought to be crucial, however, and so must be considered here. Man or animal tends to perceive relative rather than absolute intensity, extent, or frequency. One can readily train an animal to choose the larger of two surfaces; it is extraordinarily hard to get him to choose a particular size, except when differences are very great. These facts are psychologically important, and they provided a decisive answer to learning theory in its older forms; but we know too little of the physiology of the relative perception to use it as evidence for or against any currently maintained psychological theory.

The actual experimental evidence is as follows, taking the discrimination of brightness as an example.

A rat is trained to go toward a light of intensity 1 and to keep away from intensity 2 (*i.e.*, twice as strong as intensity 1). He is then presented with intensities 2 and 4, and chooses (if he chooses at all) intensity 2—which he was taught to avoid. (In the test, discrimination may break down, choices being made at random. This happens perhaps less than half the time; but a consistent choice of an absolute stimulus value never occurs in the rat in these circumstances, and the relative value is what the animal discriminates, when he does discriminate.)

Or, if the rat is taught in the first place to avoid an intensity 1 and to choose intensity 2, in the test with 2 and 4 he will reject the stimulus he was trained to respond to in favor of a new one, intensity 4. This happens even when the animal has been reared in total darkness and has never in his life seen that stimulus before. This is, so far as one can see, still a conclusive answer to any theory of behavior that deals in connections from specific rods and cones to specific muscle fibers (Hebb, 1937*b*).*

But the perception of brightness is commonly cited in a broader context, as supporting configuration theory in general against "learning" theory in general. By implication, it is treated as support for the idea that discrimination is not dependent on the excitation of any particular cells, at any neural level. This does not follow. The truth is that no one has produced any good explanation of the relative perception, so it does not support one camp against the other; and the truth is, also, that

* This author, however, seems to have supposed that such experiments rule out all possibility that connections are the basis of learning. The hypothesis presented in the following section is enough to show that the conclusion was unwarranted.

we know little or nothing about the locus of the cells whose activity mediates the perception "brighter," or "smaller," or "higher" (in pitch), so the facts neither deny nor support the hypothesis of equipotentiality.

We know, with reasonable certainty, that the training process does not form a connection all the way from receptors to effectors, but it is still possible to suppose that connections may be formed at some intermediate levels. I shall outline here a possible hypothesis, mainly to show that we must know more of the physiology of sensation before brightness perception (for example) can be made an argument for or against any existent theory.

AN HYPOTHESIS OF BRIGHTNESS PERCEPTION

Marshall and Talbot's (1942) treatment of visual acuity makes it possible to assume that the perception "brighter" depends on the activity of particular cortical cells, but not of particular receptor cells. We take for granted that intensity 2 excites a larger population of first-order (retinal) neurons than intensity 1 and with a higher rate of firing. Intensity 4 excites a still larger population. The fact that 2 and 4 may elicit the same selective response is an argument for a *sensory* equipotentiality, but the equipotentiality may disappear farther on in the system.

Marshall and Talbot point out that the whole visual system, from receptors to the several layers of the cerebral cortex, must act to damp strong stimulations, amplify weak ones. See what this means for the behavioral problem. At each synaptic stage in transmission the damping, or amplification, increases. A level X may be reached in the system where the degree of activity is constant for an adapted retinal area, with a brightness in the middle range. The amount of activity at X, then, will be the same whether the eye is adapted to intensity of 1, 2, or 4.

This of course is true only in adaptation. The system must remain very sensitive to changes of stimulus intensity. Therefore, when the eye after being adapted to 1 is focused on 2, the level of activity at X goes up, say, from n impulses per second to $1.5n$. The same would happen when the eye adapted to 2 is focused on 4. In one part of the system, the same central neurons might thus be active in the perception "brighter," regardless of absolute stimulus values. (In other parts, the cells that are aroused would still correspond partly to the absolute intensity, and this helps to account for the fact that absolute values *can* be detected, though the tendency is toward the relative discrimination.)

My point is not that this has explained the relative perception. I do not suppose that the problem is as simple as this has made it sound. The point is that the known facts are not inconsistent with the idea that the perception "brighter" involves an activity in specific neural cells at *some* point in the system, and thus that a perception of relative values is not incompatible with some specific neural connections. Something else, a "sensory equipotentiality" akin to neural gradients and field action, is certainly involved; but the establishment of new synaptic connections is not ruled out as the basis of an animal's learning to respond to the brighter of two surfaces.

In the next two chapters some neurophysiological ideas are proposed about visual perception. They could be elaborated speculatively to deal with the perception of brightness and size, though I have not done so. The perception of size, brightness, and pitch should be written down for the present as not yet accounted for, by any theory. Before they are, we shall have to know much more about the physiology of sensation.

THE PERCEPTION OF PATTERNS

In the perception of patterns we reach surer ground, having more of the relevant physiological information available and being better able to see what bearing the facts have on the theory of equipotentiality.

An animal that has learned to look for food behind a small square and not behind a small circle will, without further training, choose a large square and reject a large circle. Small and large squares are "equivalent stimuli." If each is perceived with a single fixation, it is impossible for the total pattern in each case to excite the same set of retinal cells. The current treatment of perception disregards eyemovement; the inference has been drawn, therefore, that the locus of the cells stimulated by the square is unimportant. Only the pattern of stimulation matters.

But we have seen, in the last chapter, that eyemovement cannot be disregarded. A rat trained to jump toward a square does not respond only to the total figure, but at times clearly responds to parts of it, as separate entities. Eyemovement has never been controlled in animal studies of perception. If the rat fixates parts of the figure in succession the result is to superimpose its parts, one after another, on the same retinal cells that were involved in the original training. The locus of excitation may then be essential. Evidently the equivalence of similar patterns different in size does not in itself provide support for the theory of equipotentiality.

For the evidence to become crucial, two conditions must be fulfilled. The equivalent stimuli must be shown to be conducted to different parts of the central nervous system; and there must have been no previous experience that could have set up connections between those parts before the experiment began.

One of these conditions has been met by Levine's (1945*a*, 1945*b*) experiment with pigeons. The optic chiasm in birds is completely crossed, so one eye conducts to one optic lobe, the other to the other. Levine achieved the truly surprising result of finding transfer for patterns in the lower half of the visual field and not in the upper half. For configuration theory, the best that can be said with these results is that there is a limited equipotentiality, between parts of the optic lobes (from the opposite point of view, these results definitely refute the theory of a general equipotentiality in vision).

Levine's experiment did not, however, control earlier experience in his birds, and it remains possible that even the limited equipotentiality suggested by his results is illusory. It is possible that patterns in the lower half of the bird's visual field— as when the bird is foraging on the ground, or alighting on a perch that extends into the field of vision of both eyes—had established, by perceptual learning before the experiment began, interconnections between the two optic lobes which might later be a basis of transfer. This would not require that the bird have learned beforehand the actual patterns used in the experiment; only that the *parts* of those patterns (or "perceptual elements": see Chapter 5) have been learned.* That this possibility is not far-fetched will be seen as we consider next the instantaneous recognition of patterns by man, where it is evident that the perception of one or two parts of a figure may be the clue to recognizing the whole.

Human beings readily recognize certain patterns in the tachistoscope. The time of exposure of the pattern is of the order of one-fifth of a second. The subject cannot fixate the separate parts of the pattern one after another, and cannot adjust his eyes in advance so as to make it fall on any particular retinal cells. This might be interpreted as equipotentiality, but there are facts that make that interpretation practically impossible.

I propose that the human capacity for recognizing patterns without eyemovement is possible only as the result of an intensive and prolonged visual training that goes on from the moment of birth, during every moment that the eyes are open, with an increase in skill evident over a period of 12 to 16 years at least. The evidence supporting this proposition is found (1) in the errors made in tachistoscopic recognition, (2) in the way in which reading skill develops, and (3) in the rate and course of learning by the congenitally blind after operation.

1. The recognition of patterns momentarily perceived, as in the tachistoscope, is extremely defective except with simple and conventional patterns, or very simple combinations of them. The process is exactly that named by Woodworth (1938) "schema with correction." This means that the pattern is perceived, first, as a familiar one, and then with something missing or something added. The *something*, also, is familiar; so the total perception is a mélange of the habitual.

* In particular, the slope of lines as they extend into the fields of both eyes simultaneously. This explanation by a learning process is not, however, the only alternative to equipotentiality. Another possibility is that part of each optic lobe, receiving impulses from the upper hemiretina only, has a point-to-point projection to the other lobe. Transfer would thus be innately provided for. The explanation by learning, however, should be examined first, by repeating Levine's experiment with pigeons reared in darkness and kept in darkness except when they are actually being trained or tested.

The subject's reports are such as "a triangle with the top cut off" or "a square with a crooked bottom." It is thus clear that the subject is not only responding to the diagram as a whole; he perceives its parts as separate entities, even though presentation is so brief. Errors are prominent, and such as to show that all the subject really perceives—and then only with rough accuracy—is the slope of a few lines and their direction and distance from one another. A drawing or a report of what is seen tachistoscopically is not unlike a paleontologist's reconstruction of early man from a tooth and a rib. There is a clear effect of earlier experience, filling in gaps in the actual perception, so that the end result is either something familiar or a combination of familiar things—a reconstruction on the basis of experience.

All that is needed to account for the recognition of pattern without special adjustment of the eyes, to the extent that such recognition really occurs, is ability to recognize roughly (1) the slope of line, (2) degree of separation of points, in any retinal projection. These in combination cover intersection of lines, sharp inflections of line (or corners), and curvature of line (by the variation of slope at different points, and the absence of sharp inflection). • What I am proposing, then, is that, during the continuous, intensive, and prolonged visual training of infancy and childhood, we learn to recognize the direction of line and the distance between points, separately for each grossly separate part of the visual field.*

* Here, as elsewhere, I have chosen to be more definite than is actually required by the theory to be developed; this is done with the conviction (1) that vagueness is not desirable as such, in psychological theory, and (2) that the more definite assumption may turn out to be correct, and at any rate should be explored.

If it is not correct, however, the later theorizing is unaffected. An alternative possibility to be considered is that some form of Lashley's interference-pattern theory may hold in modified form. Lashley has used the theory to explain perception of a square or triangle as a single unified process, and it will be seen in the later part of this chapter that the theory in this form cannot be maintained; but it might be feasible to apply it to single lines instead. Then the stimulation from a line of a certain slope in one part of the visual field would be innately equivalent to the stimulation of a similar line in another part of the field. I know of no evidence that opposes this, but no evidence for it either.

Psychologically, such an explanation might be more plausible; what it

I have already admitted that such ideas sound unlikely. The perception of simple objects seems so simple and direct, so obviously immediate, that it cannot be complex and the result of a long-drawn-out learning process. But it was shown in Chapter 2 that the learning process *is* necessary, that the end result *is* complex, whatever it may seem.

It should be noted that these ideas do not mean that each separate row of single cells in the retina must be separately conditioned for the perception of horizontal line (*e.g.*) in different retinal projections. Marshall and Talbot's discussion of visual acuity implies a significant overlap of excitation, at the level of the primary visual cortex, from lines that have distinct retinal projections. It is not clear how great this spread is, in terms of retinal angle, but it may be of the order of 2° in central vision and considerably greater at the periphery. Accordingly, the number of separate visual habits necessary to ensure the recognition of horizontal line in any retinal projection might be, perhaps, not greater than 10 or 15. Lines of slightly different slope, likewise, would not have to be learned separately (remember that accuracy in discriminating slope tachistoscopically is not great). The number of separate perceptual habits needed to account for tachistoscopic vision, consequently, is by no means infinite.

Now consider how intensive and prolonged the human visual training is. As we shall see later, every single movement of the eyes, when exposed (as they always are) to an unevenly lighted field, produces a number of excitations corresponding exactly to the excitation from a number of lines all parallel to the direction of eyemovement. The eyes are constantly moving when the subject is awake. Every waking moment then provides the necessary conditions for reinforcing the perception of lines, in every part of the retina.

would postulate is that parallel "ridges" of activity in area 17 would tend to excite the same, diffusely arranged, cells in 18. My neural schematizing, in the following two chapters, would then go on as before, but without the necessity of supposing that different parts of the retina must be separately conditioned to produce recognition of the slope of line in any part of the field.

The question is, I believe, open to experimental test, and will be investigated.

We have already seen that it takes months for the first direct apprehension of a figure such as a plain, well-marked triangle to be established. The normal human infant, apparently, reaches this stage quite early in life; but his further training continues every moment that his eyes are open, and must extend his capacity for prompt recognition of patterns falling outside the macula.

2. Speed of reading increases up to the age of 12 to 16 years, or perhaps even later. This speed, depending on the instantaneous recognition of larger and larger blocks of letters, may be regarded as a function of the training of peripheral vision; it implies that learning to recognize a word immediately (as a single *Gestalt*) in direct central vision does not mean recognizing it immediately at any angle of regard, though this is what the theory of equipotentiality requires.

It might be argued that the theory does *not* require this, because of differences of acuity between central and peripheral vision. Peripheral recognition of a word may depend, for example, more on its general outline and less on particular letters. It might be argued, that is, that an increased speed of reading depends on learning to use different cues from those used in central vision. This may well be true, but such an argument abandons the fundamental thesis of equipotentiality, namely, that the same properties of form are perceived whatever the retinal projection, provided acuity is sufficient. Above all, such an argument would imply that peripheral recognition and central recognition depend on separate visual habits, which is the argument of this chapter.

More direct evidence on the point is available, however, than when the above considerations were first formulated. These considerations suggested the need of a re-examination of some features of tachistoscopic perception, and this has been begun by M. Mishkin and D. Forgays. Their experiments show directly that reading does not train all parts of the retina in the same way, even when acuity does not enter the picture. The work will be reported in detail elsewhere; in summary, the following results have been obtained. Fluent readers of English, used to reading from left to right, are able to recognize words to the right of the fixation point between two and three times as well as words to the left of fixation. Readers of Jewish (in which the words run from right to left) recognize more words to the left of fixation. These results can be obtained when the subject does not know whether an English or a Jewish word is coming next, or whether it will fall to the right or the left of fixation—that is, with a random order of left-right, English-Jewish presentations. The subjects that have been studied were not very fluent in Jewish, apparently, and the left-right difference, with Jewish words, was not statistically significant ($P = 0.15$); but it is certain that whatever factors make the English word better recognized to the right of fixation does not affect recognition of Jewish words. Either there is no difference, or the Jewish word is recognized better to the left.

This shows directly that there is not an equipotentiality between the left and the right hemiretina, or left and right occipital cortex, in man. A learned response can be more readily elicited from one part of the retina than another, which provides a good deal of support for the assumption, made in these chapters, that a separate learning process is necessary for the elicitation of the same response by stimulation of a separate region in a receptor surface.

3. Finally, there are Senden's explicit reports of the way pattern vision develops after the congenitally blind are operated on (see Chapter 2). The patient, despite weeks of practice, must still count corners to distinguish a square from a triangle: here there is no unimportance of the locus of stimulation, no evidence of equipotentiality. When the patient first gets to the point of naming an object promptly, the recognition is destroyed by putting the object into a new setting or by changing its color. The significant fact is that the characteristic normal generalization shows up later, *after* a prolonged and arduous training process. The evidence is clearly that the apparent equipotentiality is the sequel and product of learning; the perception of pattern is specific and limited at first, generalized only with further practice; and in these cases there is no support whatever for the idea that when a pattern is recognized at one angle of regard it will be at once recognized in any other.

CLINICAL AND ANATOMICAL EVIDENCE

We can turn next to the clinical and anatomical evidence that is related to the question of equipotentiality in perception.

The conclusions reached already are supported by the perceptual completions in hemianopia, described by Fuchs (1920) and Lashley (1941). When one occipital pole of the brain has been destroyed by injury, or temporarily loses its function in a migraine attack, the patient becomes blind in half the visual field. If a simple symmetrical object such as a solid white square or a billiard ball is fixated in the midline, the patient nevertheless reports that he sees all of it. That he does not, but instead completes in his perception what he really sees only half of, is shown by another fact. If half the object is presented instead, in such a way that the missing half would have fallen in the blind side, the patient still "sees" the whole object.

What is the basis of this completion? Koffka (1935) treats it as a further evidence of *Gestalt* principles—an instance of the operation of field forces. This, however, is precisely what it cannot be.

In two of Fuchs' cases at least (Fuchs, 1920, pp. 424, 436) the gunshot wound that produced hemianopia must have destroyed one area 17. The bullet entered the skull in the midline at the occipital pole, and could hardly have destroyed the optic radiations on one side without also destroying the visual cortex on that side. But area 17 is the cortical tissue in which a dynamic completion, due to field forces, would have to occur; there is no isomorphism in the excitation conducted beyond 17—conduction is diffuse, and the topological relationship to the visual stimulus that is retained from the retina to area 17 is lost beyond it, so the field-force idea is applicable only at this level. The completion, then, is not the result of a field process.

In the case of migraine scotoma described by Lashley, the symptoms indicate that one visual area was nonfunctional during an attack. But this again is the tissue in which interference patterns would have to originate, to produce the perception of a complete object fixated in the center. According to the theory of interference patterns (Lashley, 1942a) the perception of a semicircle lying immediately to the right of the fixation point depends on the particular interference pattern that is set up by that diagram in the left visual cortex. A whole circle, fixated in the middle, sets up two such interference patterns, one from each visual area. In the hemianopic, only one can occur; why, then, should the patient see a whole circle? The conclusion is

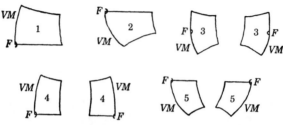

FIGURE 4. Diagramming roughly the changes in cortical projection of a square when the fixation point only is changed: based on the data of Polyak, 1941, and his figure 100, for a square subtending a visual angle of 18° 20′ (the size of the "central area" of the retina). 1, fixation on the upper right corner of the square, which thus falls in the lower left visual field and produces an excitation in the upper right cortex only; 2, fixation on the lower right corner; 3, bilateral projection with fixation on the center of the square; 4, bilateral, fixation on the midpoint of the top line of the square; 5, fixation on midpoint of bottom line. *F*, projection of fixation point; *VM*, vertical meridian.

inevitable that the "completion" occurs in some other, undamaged, area of the cortex—and that it cannot, consequently, be a field process.

Next, consider some of the anatomical properties of the visual cortex in which the field process must occur.

There is a point-to-point correspondence between the retina and the visual cortex, or area 17 (Lashley, 1934; Polyak, 1941). Thus there is an isomorphism of the visually stimulating surface with the resulting excitation in area 17, and both the theories that we are examining assume that this fact accounts for the perception of a square, for example, as a distinctive whole. But there are definite limits to what isomorphism can account for in perception.

Figure 4 represents roughly the patterns of cortical excitation that are aroused by looking at different parts of the same pattern, a square. These show how hard it is to suppose that the perception of a square, as distinct from other quadrilaterals, is determined by the shape of the isomorphic excitation in area 17, since that shape varies so much.

(There are undoubtedly major errors in the figure, which is based on a diagram by Polyak [1941, figure 100]. Polyak made no attempt to represent corresponding retinal and cortical points in detail; the necessary evidence for doing so is actually not in existence. Polyak's diagram also deviates in some respects from his text, which is presumably the more accurate; his figure 100, for example, shows the "central fovea" half as wide as the "central area," whereas his text, pp. 230–231, suggests that the difference in size is greater. Figure 4 follows his diagram, not the text. Finally, the human visual area cannot be represented accurately as a flat sheet.)

Figure 4 is only roughly accurate; it seems certain, however, that the distortion, in the pattern of cortical excitation, that occurs when fixation is changed from one to another part of the figure is at least as great as that diagrammed. If the data of Marshall and Talbot (1942, p. 134) had been used instead, the discrepancies would have been greater. Furthermore, *a difference in size* (in terms of retinal angle) between two squares *would produce even greater changes in the shape of the cortical excitation,* although squares of different size are also supposed to derive their common identity from the distribution of excitation in area 17.

The reproduction of retinal patterns in area 17 is topological, not topographical; and if identity were completely determined by the shape of the cortical excitation, regardless of what the fixation point may be, the perceived properties of a square with shifting gaze or at different distances should change markedly— remaining, it is true, a quadrilateral (topological reproduction provides for this), but not retaining the same proportions. That is, errors should occur, in the perception of quadrilaterals, which do not occur; or in the perception of triangles; and so on. A circle in one angle of regard should be confused with an oval in another angle. One might postulate a differential cell density to correct the distortion of topographical relations which I have diagrammed, but there is no support from histological study of area 17 to support this *ad hoc* assumption, and I can find no way of doing it for one pattern which would not mean an even greater distortion for another.

However, another way of dealing with this obstacle for field theory has been proposed by Köhler and Wallach (1944), who suggest that a differential "satiation" or fatigue would correct the anatomical distortion of the cortical retina. This proposal will be considered with other aspects of their theory of figural after-effects.

THE THEORY OF FIGURAL AFTER-EFFECTS

Köhler and Wallach (1944) have proposed a new treatment of perception which is in some respects very attractive and deals with a certain set of facts very efficiently. On the other hand, I believe that the theory is inconsistent with some of the facts reported by Köhler and Wallach themselves, and that it cannot be considered to have disposed of the anatomical difficulty that has just been discussed.

Following some original experiments by Gibson, Köhler and Wallach have studied certain peculiar fatigue effects resulting from prolonged inspection of visual objects. The method of experiment is this: The subject keeps his eyes fixed, for some two to three minutes, on a single "fixation point" in a large surface on which a diagram is also presented. The fixation point is determined by the experimenter so that the "inspection figure" stimulates a particular part of the retina. Then, after the inspection period, the subject looks at a second surface, again with a fixation point determined by the experimenter, which is placed so that a "test figure" on this second surface also stimulates a particular part of the retina. Thus in figure 5 are represented both an inspection and a test figure, superimposed so that one can see the relationship between the retinal projection of each. The fixation point is shown by a small *x;* the inspection figure (at which the subject stared first) is the large rectangle marked *I*, and the test figure is the set of four small squares each marked *T*. These four squares are so placed that two fall in a region of greater fatigue or "satiation," near the boundary of the rectangle, and two fall farther away, allowing one to discover the changes that occur in the neighborhood of the inspection figure, where satiation has occurred.

When a test figure is projected on the retina near the place at which the inspection figure was projected, several effects can be observed in the test figure. These effects include a color effect (fading), a depth effect (apparent increase of distance from the observer), and displacement effects (apparent change in direction of line, in position, or in size). It is the displacement effects with which we are concerned here. Köhler and Wallach propose, first, that the basis of perception is the occurrence of electric currents aroused by the visual excitation in the cortex of area 17; secondly, that the flow of these currents, in the neighborhood of the excitation, increases the resistance of the tissue through which they flow. This increase of resistance is satiation, and the changes it causes in current flow account for displacement effects. This is on the assumption that perceived distance between two objects "varies with the degree to which corresponding cortical objects [*i.e.*,

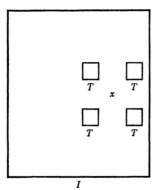

FIGURE 5. Diagram from Köhler and Wallach, *Proc. Amer. Phil. Soc.*, 1944, 88, p. 280. Courtesy of American Philosophical Society and of the authors. The large square, *I*, is the "inspection figure" to which the subject is first exposed; the large square is then removed, and the subject looks at the four smaller "test" squares, each marked *T*.

the excitations in area 17] are interrelated by their figure currents" (Köhler and Wallach, 1944, p. 334). Just what this interrelation is and how it operates is not specified, but its degree decreases when the tissue between two areas of excitation has an increased resistance. The two corresponding objects in the visual field then look farther apart. It is also important to observe that Köhler and Wallach state explicitly (p. 337) that apparent displacements are not dependent on actual changes in the locus of the excitations in area 17: only on an increased resistance to current flow in the tissue between them.

These assumptions account economically for some of the phenomena described by Köhler and Wallach. Other phenomena, however, seem inconsistent with the theory. Consider first the perceived size of a figure within an area of satiation, including the special case where the test figure coincides with the inspection figure. According to the theory, the perceived size of a square or circle should increase with increased satiation, since the greater resistance to current flow between opposite sides should produce an overestimation of the distance between them. In fact, the opposite is frequently reported by Köhler and Wallach: when a test figure, such as square or circle, coincides exactly with the locus of the previously seen inspection figure, its apparent size diminishes. Again, in figure 5, the excitations produced by the two small test squares on the right, near the boundary of the inspection rectangle, are separated by tissue that is more satiated than that separating excitations from the two small squares on the left—yet the two on the right appear closer together than those on the left. This difficulty for the theory is found in the data obtained by Köhler and Wallach with their figures 1, 2, 3, 4, 5, 7, 10, and so on.

The problem has been recognized by the authors and is briefly discussed at the end of their monograph (pp. 351, 356). They suggest two possible solutions: one is that apparent size may be affected by the presence of a large area of satiation surrounding the figure, as well as by the degree of satiation within it (p. 351); another is the possibility that an immediate self-satiation, by the test figure itself, may have a greater effect than immediate self-satiation plus a pre-existent satiation (p. 356). If I understand these explanations, they may undermine all the preceding argument, much as "afferent neural interaction" undermines Hull's theory by removing the definiteness of inference from his other postulates (p. 15). Certainly these two influences, of immediate self-satiation and of a surrounding area of satiation, would have to be reckoned with in the production of other phenomena, else their existence would become an *ad hoc* postulate to be used only where difficulty appears. This of course may mean only that the theory needs to be worked out in more detail, as Köhler and Wallach themselves have pointed out.

Next, a difficulty of a somewhat different kind, related to the anatomical distortions of the cortical retina (the difficulty for configuration theory that was discussed in the preceding section).

To deal with the anatomical fact that objects equally spaced in the visual field are not equally spaced for the cortical retina, the key assumption is made by Köhler and Wallach that a permanent satiation in the peripheral cortical retina would be greater than in the cortical fovea; and, accordingly, that anatomical distortion such as has been diagrammed in figure 4 would be corrected functionally. The greater peripheral satiation is thought to occur as follows. Contours equally spaced on the retina would not be equally spaced in area 17, because the peripheral retina has a smaller cortical representation. So an equal distribution of contours in the visual field, and consequently on the retina, would result in a bunching of contours in the peripheral part of the cortical retina, and a wide spacing of contours in the cortical macula. On this argument, the closer spacing of contours would produce a higher level of satiation in peripheral vision, which would compensate for the fact that a given retinal angle here is represented by a much shorter cortical distance than the same angle in central vision (Köhler and Wallach, 1944, p. 345). Although the cortical distance is shorter, resistance is higher too: so perceived distance remains the same.

But all this has overlooked an essential fact. Acuity in central vision is very much higher than in peripheral vision, and so there is no basis for assuming that the central cortical retina would be the site of a smaller number of excitations per centimeter. Köhler and Wallach's argument assumes, essentially, that all contours in the visual field are supraliminal for the periphery; given this assumption, their argument stands; but we know actually that the assumption cannot be made, that many contours are supraliminal for central vision and subliminal for peripheral vision. These contours, subliminal at the periphery, would fill in the gaps between the more widely spaced excitations in central vision that originate from contours which are supraliminal for the whole visual system, peripheral as well as central. There is no evidence permitting one to be certain that the frequency of contours that are subliminal for the peripheral field is such as to compensate exactly for the greater spacing of other contours in the macular area of the visual cortex; but what evidence we have implies this, since differences of acuity appear to be closely related to the ratio of centimeters of cortex per degree of visual angle (Marshall and Talbot, 1942).

The theory of figural after-effects, therefore, has not avoided the difficulties for configuration theory that are to be found in the anatomy of the visual cortex.

CONCLUSIONS

The conclusions that have been arrived at concerning field theory and equipotentiality, in this and the preceding chapter, may be summarized as follows. The examination of these theories of perception was undertaken in the first place because no way could be found of dealing with attention and attitude, in terms of the configurational hypothesis. This still stands as an essential weakness, which by itself would justify a search for some other approach to perception. On closer inspection, however, one also finds that configuration theory has flaws even in the treatment of perception itself; and some of the flaws are serious. It is not possible to reject the theory finally, for an answer may be found for each of the objections that have been raised, and the alternative treatment that is proposed in the two following chapters has its own difficulties and shortcomings—it is in fact because my theorizing about perception is in some respects implausible that I am obliged to emphasize weaknesses in other theories, just as later (in Chapter 8) a rather vague treatment of motivation is bolstered up by trying to show that Hull's alternative is not as precise as it seems.

The fundamental difficulty with configuration theory, broadly speaking, is that it leaves too little room for the factor of experience. It makes difficulty in seeing how learning can occur (particularly, perceptual learning), and in seeing how autonomous central processes can exist and influence behavior. Association (as distinct from conditioned reflex) theory, on the other hand, may make it possible to adopt a halfway position in which one can take advantage of some of the obvious values both of configurationist and of connectionist theories.

It is important as psychology comes of age to avoid, if possible, the extreme positions that have often been adopted in the discussions of the past. It is consequently relevant here to point out that a large part of the original thesis of the configurationists (the *Gestalt* group, Lashley, Tolman, *et al.*) has already been accepted and is fully made use of in current theorizing; and also that the theory to be presented in the following chapters is explicitly designed to deal from the first with the problems of form perception and attention or set—problems whose existence has been most insisted on in recent years by the configurationists—as well as those problems of learning and memory emphasized by learning theorists. Thus the present argument is based at least as much on *Gestalt* as on learning theory.

The current debate between these two theories cannot be understood on the assumption that they are utterly opposed to each other. It is rather to be seen as like the running battle between the Left and the Right in governmental policy: the Left continually insisting on the inadequacy of present theory, working to broaden and elaborate the conceptual armament of the experimenter; the Right insisting always on the dangers of being too free with changes that may open the doors to animism, on the importance of demonstrable evidence and intelligible definitions, and on the necessity of fully exploring the ideas we have now before rejecting them as insufficient. But in this conflict, as in the political one, it will be found over any great period of time that the Right (in current psychology, learning theory) has adopted again and again the ideas originally advocated by the Left (currently configurationism), once they are properly aged and found not to have spoiled. Thus modern learning theory is "sophisticated"; it deals freely in ideas that were once anathema to it—ideas of gradients, generalizations, interaction among afferent processes as well as the classical afferent-efferent action, and so on. Obviously both Left and Right are needed for the development of psychology, though it may be easy for the configurationist to forget the value of the systematizing and search for rigor made by his opponent, or for the learning theorist to forget where some of his ideas originally came from.

4. The First Stage of Perception: Growth of the Assembly

This chapter and the next develop a schema of neural action to show how a rapprochement can be made between (1) perceptual generalization, (2) the permanence of learning, and (3) attention, determining tendency, or the like. It is proposed first that a repeated stimulation of specific receptors will lead slowly to the formation of an "assembly" of association-area cells which can act briefly as a closed system after stimulation has ceased; this prolongs the time during which the structural changes of learning can occur and constitutes the simplest instance of a representative process (image or idea). The way in which this cell-assembly might be established, and its characteristics, are the subject matter of the present chapter. In the following chapter the interrelationships between cell-assemblies are dealt with; these are the basis of temporal organization in central processes (attention, attitude, thought, and so on). The two chapters (4 and 5) construct the conceptual tools with which, in the following chapters, the problems of behavior are to be attacked.

The first step in this neural schematizing is a bald assumption about the structural changes that make lasting memory possible. The assumption has repeatedly been made before, in one way or another, and repeatedly found unsatisfactory by the critics of learning theory. I believe it is still necessary. As a result, I must show that in another context, of added anatomical and physiological knowledge, it becomes more defensible and more fertile than in the past.

The assumption, in brief, is that a growth process accompanying synaptic activity makes the synapse more readily traversed.

This hypothesis of synaptic resistances, however, is different from earlier ones in the following respects: (1) structural connections are postulated between single cells, but single cells are not effective units of transmission and such connections would be only one factor determining the direction of transmission; (2) no direct sensori-motor connections are supposed to be established in this way, in the adult animal; and (3) an intimate relationship is postulated between reverberatory action and structural changes at the synapse, implying a dual trace mechanism.

THE POSSIBILITY OF A DUAL TRACE MECHANISM

Hilgard and Marquis (1940) have shown how a reverberatory, transient trace mechanism might be proposed on the basis of Lorente de Nó's conclusions, that a cell is fired only by the simultaneous activity of two or more afferent fibers, and that internuncial fibers are arranged in closed (potentially self-exciting) circuits. Their diagram is arranged to show how a reverberatory circuit might establish a sensori-motor connection between receptor cells and the effectors which carry out a conditioned response. There is of course a good deal of psychological evidence which is opposed to such an oversimplified hypothesis, and Hilgard and Marquis do not put weight on it. At the same time, it is important to see that something of the kind is not merely a possible but a necessary inference from certain neurological ideas. To the extent that anatomical and physiological observations establish the possibility of reverberatory after-effects of a sensory event, it is established that such a process would be the physiological basis of a transient "memory" of the stimulus. There may, then, be a memory trace that is wholly a function of a pattern of neural activity, independent of any structural change.

Hilgard and Marquis go on to point out that such a trace would be quite unstable. A reverberatory activity would be subject to the development of refractory states in the cells of the circuit in which it occurs, and external events could readily interrupt it. We have already seen (in Chapter 1) that an "activity" trace can hardly account for the permanence of early learning, but at the same time one may regard reverberatory activity as the explanation of other phenomena.

There are memories which are instantaneously established, and as evanescent as they are immediate. In the repetition of digits, for example, an interval of a few seconds is enough to prevent any interference from one series on the next. Also, some memories are both instantaneously established and permanent. To account for the permanence, some structural change seems necessary, but a structural growth presumably would require an appreciable time. If some way can be found of supposing that a reverberatory trace might cooperate with the structural change, and *carry the memory until the growth change is made,* we should be able to recognize the theoretical value of the trace which is an activity only, without having to ascribe all memory to it. The conception of a transient, unstable reverberatory trace is therefore useful, if it is possible to suppose also that some more permanent structural change reinforces it. There is no reason to think that a choice must be made between the two conceptions; there may be traces of both kinds, and memories which are dependent on both.

A NEUROPHYSIOLOGICAL POSTULATE

Let us assume then that the persistence or repetition of a reverberatory activity (or "trace") tends to induce lasting cellular changes that add to its stability. The assumption * can be precisely stated as follows: *When an axon of cell* A *is near enough to excite a cell* B *and repeatedly or persistently takes part in firing it, some growth process or metabolic change takes place in one or both cells such that* A's *efficiency, as one of the cells firing* B, *is increased.*

The most obvious and I believe much the most probable suggestion concerning the way in which one cell could become more capable of firing another is that synaptic knobs develop and increase the area of contact between the afferent axon and efferent soma. ("Soma" refers to dendrites and body, or all of

---

* See p. 229 for a further discussion of this point and an elaboration of the assumption made concerning the nature of memory.

the cell except its axon.) There is certainly no direct evidence that this is so, and the postulated change if it exists may be metabolic, affecting cellular rhythmicity and limen; or there might be both metabolic and structural changes, including a limited neurobiotaxis. There are several considerations, however, that make the growth of synaptic knobs a plausible conception. The assumption stated above can be put more definitely, as follows:

When one cell repeatedly assists in firing another, the axon of the first cell develops synaptic knobs (or enlarges them if they already exist) in contact with the soma of the second cell. This seems to me the most likely mechanism of a lasting effect of reverberatory action, but I wish to make it clear that the subsequent discussion depends only on the more generally stated proposition italicized above.

It is wise to be explicit on another point also. The proposition does not require action at any great distance, and certainly is not the same as Kappers' (Kappers, Huber, and Crosby, 1936) conception of the way in which neurobiotaxis controls axonal and dendritic outgrowth. But my assumption is evidently related to Kappers' ideas, and not inconsistent with them. The theory of neurobiotaxis has been severely criticized, and clearly it does not do all it was once thought to do. On the other hand, neurobiotaxis may still be one factor determining the connections made by neural cells. If so, it would cooperate very neatly with the knob formation postulated above. Criticism has been directed at the idea that neurobiotaxis directs axonal growth throughout its whole course, and that the process sufficiently accounts for all neural connections. The idea is not tenable, particularly in view of such work as that of Weiss (1941*b*) and Sperry (1943).

But none of this has shown that neurobiotaxis has *no* influence in neural growth; its operation, within ranges of a centimeter or so, is still plausible. Thus, in figure 6 (Lorente de Nó, 1938*a*), the multiple synaptic knobs of fiber 2 on cell *C* might be outgrowths from a fiber passing the cell at a distance, and determined by the fact of repeated simultaneous excitations in the two. Again, the course followed by fiber 7 in the

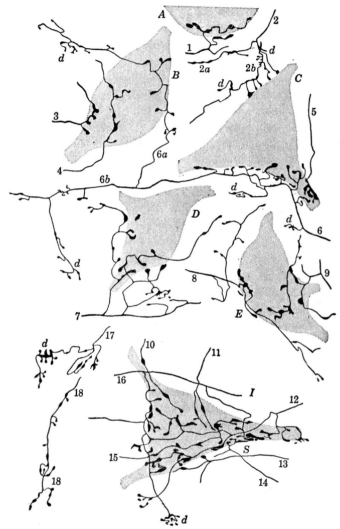

FIGURE 6. Relationships between synaptic knobs and the cell body. From Lorente de Nó, 1938a. Courtesy of Charles C. Thomas and of the author.

neighborhood of cell *D* may include deflections from the original course of the fiber, determined in the same way.

The details of these histological speculations are not important except to show what some of the possibilities of change at the synapse might be and to show that the mechanism of learning discussed in this chapter is not wholly out of touch with what is known about the neural cell. The changed facilitation that constitutes learning might occur in other ways without affecting the rest of the theory. To make it more specific, I have chosen to assume that the growth of synaptic knobs, with or without neurobiotaxis, is the basis of the change of facilitation from one cell on another, and this is not altogether implausible. It has been demonstrated by Arvanitaki (1942) that a contiguity alone will permit the excitation aroused in one cell to be transmitted to another. There are also earlier experiments, reviewed by Arvanitaki, with the same implication. Even more important, perhaps, is Erlanger's (1939) demonstration of impulse transmission across an artificial "synapse," a blocked segment of nerve more than a millimeter in extent. Consequently, in the intact nervous system, an axon that passes close to the dendrites or body of a second cell would be capable of *helping* to fire it, when the second cell is also exposed to other stimulation at the same point. The probability that such closely timed coincidental excitations would occur is not considered for the moment but will be returned to. When the coincidence does occur, and the active fiber, which is merely close to the soma of another cell, adds to a local excitation in it, I assume that the joint action tends to produce a thickening of the fiber—forming a synaptic knob—or adds to a thickening already present.

Lorente de Nó (1938*a*) has shown that the synaptic knob is usually not a terminal structure (thus the term "end foot" or "end button" is misleading), nor always separated by a stalk from the axon or axon collateral. If it were, of course, some action at a distance would be inevitably suggested, if such connections are formed in learning. The knob instead is often a rather irregular thickening in the unmyelinated part of an axon near its ending, where it is threading its way through a thicket of dendrites and cell bodies. The point in the axon where the thickening occurs does not appear to be determined by the structure of the cell of which it is a part but by something external to the cell and related to the presence of a second cell. The number and size of the knobs formed by one cell in contact with a second cell vary also. In the light of these facts it is not implausible to suppose that the extent of the contact established is a function of joint cellular activity, given propinquity of the two cells.

Also, if a synapse is crossed only by the action of two or more afferent cells, the implication is that the greater the area of contact the greater the likelihood that action in one cell will be *decisive* in firing another.* Thus three afferent fibers with extensive knob contact could fire a cell that otherwise might be fired only by four or more fibers; or fired sooner with knobs than without.

In short, it is feasible to assume that synaptic knobs develop with neural activity and represent a lowered synaptic resistance. It is implied that the knobs appear in the course of learning, but this does not give us a means of testing the assumption. There is apparently no good evidence concerning the relative frequency of knobs in infant and adult brains, and the assumption does *not* imply that there should be none in the newborn infant. The learning referred to is learning in a very general sense, which must certainly have begun long before birth (see *e.g.*, the footnote on pp. 121–2).

* One point should perhaps be made explicit. Following Lorente de Nó, two afferent cells are considered to be effective at the synapse, when one is not, only because their contacts with the efferent cell are close together so their action summates. When both are active, they create a larger region of *local* disturbance in the efferent soma. The larger the knobs in a given cluster, therefore, the smaller the number that might activate the cell on which they are located. On occasion, a single afferent cell must be effective in transmission. It is worth pointing this out, also, because it might appear to the reader otherwise that there is something mysterious about emphasis on the necessity of activity in two or more cells to activate the synapse. All that has really been shown is that in some circumstances two or more afferent cells are necessary. However, this inevitably implies that an increase in the number of afferent cells simultaneously active must increase the reliability with which the synapse is traversed.

CONDUCTION FROM AREA 17

In order to apply this idea (of a structural reinforcement of synaptic transmission) to visual perception, it is necessary first to examine the known properties of conduction from the visual cortex, area 17, to areas 18, 19, and 20. (In view of the criticisms of architectonic theory by Lashley and Clark [1946], it may be said that Brodmann's areas are referred to here as a convenient designation of relative cortical position, without supposing that the areas are necessarily functional entities or always histologically distinctive.)

It has already been seen that there is a topological reproduction of retinal activities in area 17, but that conduction from 17 to 18 is diffuse. Von Bonin, Garol, and McCulloch (1942) have found that a localized excitation in 17 is conducted to a large part of 18, a band lying along the margins of 17. There is no point-to-point correspondence of 17 and 18. Excitation from 18 is conducted back to the nearest border region of 17; to all parts of area 18 itself; and to all parts of the contralateral 18, of area 19 (lying anterior to 18), and of area 20 (in the lower part of the temporal lobe).

The diffusity of conduction from area 17 is illustrated by the diagram of figure 7. Cells lying in the same part of 17 may conduct to different points in 18. The cells in 18, thus stimulated, also lead to points in 18 itself which are widely separated; to any part of the ipsilateral areas 19 and 20; and, through one synapse, to any part of the contralateral 19 and 20. Conversely, *cells lying in different parts of 17 or 18 may have connections with the same point in 18 or 20.*

Thus there is convergence as well as spread of excitation. The second point illustrated by figure 7 is a selective action in 18, depending on the convergence of fibers from 17. In the figure, F and G are two cells in area 18 connecting the same macroscopic areas. F, however, is one that happens to be exposed to excitations from both A and B (two different regions in area 17). When an area-17 excitation includes both A and B, F is much more likely to be fired than G. The figure does not show the short, closed, multiple chains which are found in all parts of the cortex and whose facilitating activity would often make it possible for a single fiber from B to fire G. But the same sort of local bombardment would also aid in firing F; and the cell which receives excitations from two area-17 fibers simultaneously would be more likely to fire than that which receives excitation from only one.

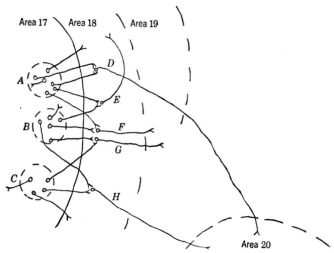

FIGURE 7. Illustrating convergence of cells in Brodmann's area 17 upon cells in area 18, these cells in turn leading to other areas. A, B, C, three grossly distinct regions in area 17; D, E, F, G, H, cells in area 18. See text.

On the other hand, when B and C (instead of A and B) are excited simultaneously, G would be more likely to fire than F. Any specific region of activity in area 17 would tend to excite specific cells in area 18 which would tend not to be fired by the excitation of another region in 17. These specific cells in 18 would be diffusely arranged, as far as we know at random. They would be usually at some distance from one another and would always be intermingled with others which are not fired by the same afferent stimulation, but because of their lasting structural connections would tend always to be selectively ex-.cited, in the same combination, whenever the same excitation recurs in area 17. This of course would apply also in areas 19 and 20. Since a single point in 18 fires to many points throughout 19 and 20, excitation of any large number of area-18 cells means that convergence in 19 and 20 must be expected. How often it would happen is a statistical question, which will be deferred to a later section. The tissues made active beyond area 17, by two different visual stimuli, would thus be (1) grossly the same, (2) histologically distinct. A difference of stimulating pattern would not mean any gross difference in the part of the brain which mediates perception (except in the afferent structures up to and including area 17, the visual cortex). Even a completely unilateral activity, it should be noted, would have diffuse effects throughout areas 18, 19, and 20 not only on one side of the brain but on both. At the same time, a difference of locus or pattern of stimulation would mean a difference in the particular cells in these areas that are consistently or maximally fired.

MODE OF PERCEPTUAL INTEGRATION: THE CELL-ASSEMBLY

In the last chapter it was shown that there are important properties of perception which cannot be ascribed to events in area 17, and that these are properties which seem particularly dependent on learning. That "identity" is not due to what happens in 17 is strongly implied by the distortions that occur in the projection of a retinal excitation to the cortex. When the facts of hemianopic completion are also considered, the conclusion appears inescapable. Perception must depend on other structures besides area 17.

But we now find, at the level of area 18 and beyond, that all topographical organization in the visual process seems to have disappeared. All that is left is activity in an irregular arrangement of cells, which are intertangled with others that have nothing to do with the perception of the moment. We know of course that perception of simple objects is unified and determinate, a well-organized process. What basis can be found for an integration of action, in cells that are anatomically so disorganized?

An answer to this question is provided by the structural change at the synapse which has been assumed to take place in learning. The answer is not simple; perceptual integration would not be accomplished directly, but only as a slow development, and, for the purposes of exposition, at least, would involve several distinct stages, with the first of which we shall now be concerned.

The general idea is an old one, that any two cells or systems of cells that are repeatedly active at the same time will tend to become "associated," so that activity in one facilitates activity in the other. The details of speculation that follow are intended to show how this old idea might be put to work again, with the equally old idea of a lowered synaptic "resistance," under the eye of a different neurophysiology from that which engendered them. (It is perhaps worth while to note that the two ideas have most often been combined only in the special case in which one cell is associated with another, of a higher level or order in transmission, which it fires; what I am proposing is a possible basis of association of two afferent fibers of the same order—in principle, a sensori-sensory association,* in addition to the linear association of conditioning theory.)

The proposal is most simply illustrated by cells *A*, *B*, and *C* in figure 8. *A* and *B*, visual-area cells, are simultaneously active. The cell *A* synapses, of course, with a large number of cells in 18, and *C* is supposed to be one that happens to lead back into 17. Cells such as *C* would be those that produce the local wedge-shaped area of firing in 17 when a point in 18 is strychninized (von Bonin, Garol, and McCulloch, 1942). The cells in the region of 17 to which *C* leads are being fired by the same massive sensory excitation that fires *A*, and *C* would almost necessarily make contact with some cell *B* that also fires into 18, or communicate with *B* at one step removed, through a short-axon circuit. With repetition of the same massive excitation in 17 the same firing relations would recur and, according to the assumption made, growth changes would take place at synapses *AC* and *CB*. This means that *A* and *B*, both afferent neurons

---

* It should be observed, however, that some theorists have continued to maintain that "S-S" (sensori-sensory) associations are formed in the learning process, and have provided experimental evidence that seems to establish the fact. See, *e.g.*, Brogden, *J. Exp. Psychol.*, 1947, 37, 527–539, and earlier papers cited therein.

of the same order, would no longer act independently of each other.

At the same time, in the conditions of stimulation that are diagrammed in figure 8, *A* would also be likely to synapse (directly, or *via* a short closed link) with a cell *D* which leads back into an unexcited part of 17, and there synapses with still

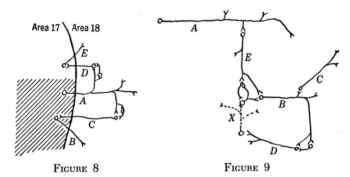

FIGURE 8   FIGURE 9

FIGURE 8. Cells *A* and *B* lie in a region of area 17 (shown by hatching) which is massively excited by an afferent stimulation. *C* is a cell in area 18 which leads back into 17. *E* is in area 17 but lies outside the region of activity. See text.

FIGURE 9. *A*, *B*, and *C* are cells in area 18 which are excited by converging fibers (not shown) leading from a specific pattern of activity in area 17. *D*, *E*, and *X* are, *among the many cells with which* A, B, *and* C *have connections,* ones which would contribute to an integration of their activity. See text.

another cell *E* of the same order as *A* and *B*. The synapse *DE*, however, would be unlikely to be traversed, since it is not like *CB* exposed to concentrated afferent bombardment. Upon frequent repetition of the particular excitation in area 17, a functional relationship of activity in *A* and *B* would increase much more than a relationship of *A* to *E*.

The same considerations can be applied to the activity of the enormous number of individual cells in 18, 19, and 20 that are simultaneously aroused by an extensive activity in 17. Here, it should be observed, the evidence of neuronography implies that there are anatomical connections of every point with every other point, within a few millimeters, and that there is no orderly arrangement of the cells concerned.

Figure 9 diagrams three cells, A, B, and C, that are effectively fired in 18 by a particular visual stimulation, frequently repeated (by fixation, for example, on some point in a constant distant environment). D, E, and X represent possible connections which might be found between such cells, directly or with intervening links. Supposing that time relations in the firing of these cells make it possible, activity in A would contribute to the firing of E, and that in B to firing C and D. Growth changes at the synapses AE, BC, BD, and so on, would be a beginning of integration and would increase the probability of coordinated activity in each pair of neurons.

The fundamental meaning of the assumption of growth at the synapse is in the effect this would have on the timing of action by the efferent cell. The increased area of contact means that firing by the efferent cell is more likely to follow the lead of the afferent cell. A fiber of order n thus gains increased control over a fiber $n + 1$, making the firing of $n + 1$ more predictable or determinate. The control cannot be absolute, but "optional" (Lorente de Nó, 1939), and depends also on other events in the system. In the present case, however, the massive excitation in 17 would tend to establish constant conditions throughout the system during the brief period of a single visual fixation; and the postulated synaptic changes would also increase the degree of this constancy. A would acquire an increasing control of E, and E, with each repetition of the visual stimulus, would fire more consistently at the same time that B is firing (B, it will be recalled, is directly controlled by the area-17 action). Synaptic changes EB would therefore result. Similarly, B acquires an increasing control of D; and whenever a cell such as D happens to be one that connects again with B, through X, a closed cycle (BDXB) is set up.

It is, however, misleading to put emphasis on the coincidences necessary for the occurrence of such a simple closed circuit. Instead of a ring or hoop, the best analogy to the sort of structure which would be set up or "assembled" is a closed solid cage-work, or three-dimensional lattice, with no regular structure, and with connections possible from any one intersection to any other. Let me say explicitly, again, that the specificity of such an assembly of cells in 18 or 20, to a particular excitation *in* 17, *depends on convergences.* Whenever two cells, directly or indirectly controlled by that excitation, converge on another cell (as *E* and *X* converge on *B* in figure 9) the essential condition of the present schematizing is fulfilled; the two converging cells need not have any simple anatomical or physiological relation to one another, and physiological integration would not be supposed to consist of independent closed chains.

This has an important consequence. Lorente de Nó (1938*b*) has put stress on the fact that activity in a short closed circuit must be rapidly extinguished, and could hardly persist as long as a hundredth of a second. It is hard, on the other hand, to see how a long, many-linked chain, capable of longer reverberation, would get established as a functional unit. But look now at figure 10, which diagrams a different sort of possibility. Arrows represent not neurons, but multiple pathways, of whatever complexity is necessary so that each arrow stands for a functional unit. These units fire in

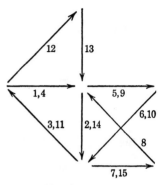

FIGURE 10. Arrows represent a simple "assembly" of neural pathways or open multiple chains firing according to the numbers on each (the pathway "1, 4" fires first and fourth, and so on), illustrating the possibility of an "alternating" reverberation which would not extinguish as readily as that in a simple closed circuit.

the order 1, 2, 3, ⋯ 15. The pathway labeled (1, 4) is the first to fire, and also the fourth; (2, 14) fires second and fourteenth; and so on. The activity 1–2–3–4 is in a relatively simple closed circuit. At this point the next unit (2, 14) may be refractory, which would effectively extinguish reverberation in that simple circuit. But at this point, also, another pathway (5, 9) may be excitable and permit activity in the larger system to continue in some way as that suggested by the numbers in the figure. The sort of irregular three-dimensional net which might be the anatomical basis of perceptual integration in the association areas would be infinitely more complex than anything one could show with a diagram and would provide a large number of the multiple parallel (or alternate) units which are suggested by figure 10. If so, an indefinite reverberation in the structure might be possible, so long as the background activity in other cells in the same gross region remained the same. It would not of course remain the same for long, especially with changes of visual fixation; but such considerations make it possible to conceive of "alternating" reverberation which might frequently last for periods of time as great as half a second or a second.

(What I have in mind, in emphasizing half a second or so as the duration of a reverberatory activity, is the observed duration of a single content in perception [Pillsbury, 1913; Boring, 1933]. Attention wanders, and the best estimate one can make of the duration of a single "conscious content" is of this time-order.)

This then is the cell-assembly. Some of its characteristics have been defined only by implication, and these are to be developed elsewhere, particularly in the remainder of this chapter, in the following chapter, and in Chapter 8 (see pp. 195–7). The assembly is thought of as a system inherently involving some equipotentiality, in the presence of alternate pathways each having the same function, so that brain damage might remove some pathways without preventing the system from functioning, particularly if the system has been long established, with well-developed synaptic knobs which decrease the number of fibers that must be active at once to traverse a synapse.

STATISTICAL CONSIDERATIONS

It must have appeared to the reader who examined figures 8 and 9 carefully that there was something unlikely about its being arranged at the Creation to have such neat connections exactly where they were most needed for my hypothesis of perceptual integration. The answer of course is statistical: the neurons diagrammed were those which happen to have such connections, and, given a large enough population of connecting fibers distributed at random, the improbable connection must become quite frequent, in absolute numbers. The next task is to assess the statistical element in these calculations, and show that probability is not stretched too far.

The diagrams and discussion of the preceding section require the frequent existence of two kinds of coincidence: (1) synchronization of firing in two or more converging axons, and (2) the anatomical fact of convergence in fibers which are, so far as we know, arranged at random. The necessity of these coincidences sets a limit to postulating functional connections *ad lib.* as the basis of integration. But this is not really a difficulty, since the psychological evidence (as we shall see) also implies that there are limits to perceptual integration.

Consider first the enormous frequency and complexity of the actual neural connections that have been demonstrated histologically and physiologically. One is apt to think of the neural cell as having perhaps two or three or half a dozen connections with other cells, and as leading from one minute point in the central nervous system to one other minute point. This impression is far from the truth and no doubt is due to the difficulty of representing the true state of affairs in a printed drawing.

Forbes (1939) mentions for example an estimate of 1300 synaptic knobs on a single anterior horn cell. Lorente de Nó's drawings (1943, figures 71–73, 75) show a complexity, in the ramification of axon and dendrite, that simply has no relation whatever to diagrams (such as mine) showing a cell with one or two connections. The gross extent of the volume of cortex infiltrated by the collaterals of the axon of a single neuron is measured in millimeters, not in microns; it certainly is not a single point, microscopic in size. In area 18, the strychnine method demonstrates that each tiny area of cortex has connections with the whole region. (These areas are about as small as 1 sq. mm., according to McCulloch, 1944*b*.) It puts no great strain on probabilities to suppose that there would be, in area 18, some anatomical connection of any one cell, excited by a particular visual stimulation, with a number of others excited in the same way.

There is, therefore, the *anatomical* basis of a great number of convergences among the multitude of cortical cells directly or indirectly excited by any massive retinal activity. This is to be kept in mind as one approaches the physiological question of synchronization in the converging fibers. In the tridimensional, lattice-like assembly of cells that I have supposed to be the basis of perceptual integration, those interconnecting neurons which synapse with the same cell would be functionally in parallel. Figure 10 illustrates this. The pathways labeled (1, 4), (8), and (13), converging on one synapse, must have the same function in the system; or the two-link pathway (5, 9)–(6, 10) the same function as the single link (2, 14). When impulses in one such path are not effective, those in another, arriving at a different time, could be.

Once more, the oversimplification of such diagrams is highly misleading. At each synapse there must be a considerable dispersion in the time of arrival of impulses, and in each individual fiber a constant variation of responsiveness; and one could never predicate a determinate pattern of action in any small segment of the system. In the larger system, however, a statistical constancy might be quite predictable.

It is not necessary, and not possible, to define the cell-assembly underlying a perception as being made up of neurons all of which are active when the proper visual stimulation occurs. One can suppose that there would always be activity in some of the group of elements which are in functional parallel (they are not of course geometrically parallel). When for example excitation can be conducted to a particular point in the system from five different directions, the activity characteristic of the system as a whole might be maintained by excitation in any three of the five pathways, and no one fiber would have to be synchronized with any other one fiber.

There would still be some necessity of synchronization, and this has another aspect. In the integration which has been hypothesized, depending on the development of synaptic knobs and an increasing probability of control by afferent over efferent fibers, there would necessarily be a gradual change of the frequency characteristics of the system. The consequence would be a sort of fractionation and recruitment, and some change in the neurons making up the system. That is, some units, capable at first of synchronizing with others in the system, would no longer be able to do so and would drop out: "fractionation." Others, at first incompatible, would be recruited. *With perceptual development there would thus be a slow growth in the assembly,* understanding by "growth" not necessarily an increase in the number of constituent cells, but a change. How great the change would be there is no way of telling, but it is a change that may have importance for psychological problems when some of the phenomena of association are considered. This then is the statistical approach to the problem. It is directly implied that an "association" of two cells in the same region, or of two systems of cells, would vary, in the probability of its occurrence, over a wide range. If one chose such pairs at random one would find some between which no association was possible, some in which association was promptly and easily established when the two were simultaneously active, and a large proportion making up a gradation from one of these extremes to the other. The larger the system with a determinate general pattern of action, the more readily an association could be formed with another system. On a statistical basis, the more points at which a chance anatomical convergence could occur, the greater the frequency of effective interfacilitation between the two assemblies.

Psychologically, these ideas mean (1) that there is a prolonged period of integration of the individual perception, apart from associating the perception with anything else; (2) that an association between two perceptions is likely to be possible only after each one has independently been organized, or integrated; (3) that, even between two integrated perceptions, there may be a considerable variation in the ease with which association can occur. Finally, (4) the apparent necessity of supposing that there would be a "growth," or fractionation and recruitment, in the cell-assembly underlying perception means that there might be significant differences in the properties of perception at different stages of integration. One cannot guess how great the changes of growth would be; but it is conceivable, even probable, that if one knew where to look for the evidence one would find marked differences of identity in the perceptions of child and adult.

The psychological implications of my schematizing, as far as it has gone, have been made explicit in order to show briefly that they are not contrary to fact. We are not used to thinking of a simple perception as slowly and painfully learned, as the present chapter would suggest; but it has already been seen, in

the discussion of the vision of the congenitally blind after operation, that it actually is. The slowness of learning, and the frequent instances of total failure to learn at all in periods as
great as a year following operation (Senden, 1932), are extraordinary and incredible (if it were not for the full confirmation by
Riesen, 1947). The principles of learning to be found in psychological textbooks are derived from the behavior of the half-
grown or adult animal. Our ideas as to the readiness with
which association is set up apply to the behavior of the developed organism, as Boring (1946) has noted; there is no evidence
whatever to show that a similarly prompt association of separate
perceptions can occur at birth—that it is independent of a slow
process in which the perceptions to be associated must first be
integrated.

As to the wide range in difficulty of associating two ideas or
perceptions, even for the adult, this is psychologically a matter
of common experience. Who has not had trouble remembering,
in spite of repeated efforts, the spelling or pronunciation of some
word, or the name of some acquaintance? The fact of the unequal difficulty of associations is not stressed in the literature,
probably because it does not fit into conditioned-reflex theory;
but it is a fact. My speculations concerning the nature of the
trace and the aboriginal development of perception thus are
not obviously opposed to the psychological evidence. Further
evaluation can be postponed until the speculations have been
fully developed.

5. *Perception of a Complex: The Phase Sequence*

The reader will remember that what we are aiming at here is the solution of a psychological problem. To get psychological theory out of a difficult impasse, one must find a way of reconciling three things without recourse to animism: perceptual generalization, the stability of memory, and the instabilities of attention. As neurophysiology, this and the preceding chapter go beyond the bounds of useful speculation. They make too many steps of inference without experimental check. As psychology, they are part of a preparation for experiment, a search for order in a body of phenomena about which our ideas are confused and contradictory; and the psychological evidence does provide some check on the inferences made here.

Although this discussion is not anchored with sufficient neurophysiological evidence, it still has a compass. It is guided throughout by the necessity of conforming to the concrete evidence of behavior, and any virtue it may have derives from coordinating the two sources of information. The details of these two chapters, speculative as they are, have to be given for two reasons.

First, competent psychologists have asserted that field or configuration theory is the only conceivable solution of the problems of behavior. The argument is stronger when a physiologist such as Sherrington (1941), without benefit of field theory, can find no possible way of reducing "mind"—which must be the control of behavior—to neural action. The argument is even strengthened by the vagueness of Hull's treatment of perception: "afferent neural interaction" and generalization gradients have the smell of brimstone about them and, when they are made specific, in neurological terms, may turn out to be only a new form of field theory (just as Pavlov's waves of inhibition and excitation are field theory). Improbable as Köhler's theory of electrical fields may be, hard as it may be to reconcile Lashley's theory of interference patterns with the anatomical and clinical evidence, these writers still have a powerful argument for holding psychology to what I believe is a blind alley, so long as it remains true that an alternative explanation cannot be elaborated in enough detail to be conceivably an account of real processes.

So one must speculate. But there is a second reason for the form of the discussion in these two chapters. In speculating, one can at least be specific enough so that, when further anatomical and physiological information is made available to the psychologist, the errors of earlier speculation such as this will be apparent at once, and the necessary changes clearly indicated.

In this chapter, accordingly, the new foundation for association theory is to be completed. The preceding chapter dealt only with the effects of a single visual stimulus, with a constant retinal projection. We can next ask how the several effects of a variable stimulation may be combined, or associated.

LINES AND ANGLES IN PERCEPTION

It has already appeared that the corners of a rectilinear figure are of special importance in first vision. The first crude perception of an object in the visual field as distinctive, as having identity, seems to be related to the sharp inflection of contours and the direction of line. Senden describes the congenitally blind patient, after operation, as frequently not being able to distinguish (for example) square from circle; but when the distinction is made, it is through a search for corners, apparently as foci in an otherwise amorphous mass of light. There is also evidence of an immediate distinction between narrow strips of light, when one is vertical and one horizontal in the visual field. Here again the perception of identity in such objects is defective, since the patient is extremely slow to learn names for the two visual patterns, although he can name horizontal and vertical at once by touch. From Lashley's experiments, it is also evident that line and angle dominate the rat's perception of patterns. We may therefore consider that these things are among the elements from which more complex perceptions develop. "Perceptual element" is meant to contrast sharply with the punctate sensory elements of classical association theory, on the one hand; and, on the other, the term does not imply that the perception of line and angle is fully innate. There is a prolonged learning period before these "elements" are promptly and clearly perceived, either by rat or man.

The evidence on this point concerning man is to be found in Senden's (1932) compilation and has been cited earlier; some evidence follows which indicates that the rat also has to learn to see lines distinctively.

Eighteen rats reared in complete darkness (Hebb, 1937a) were trained, following Lashley's procedure exactly, to discriminate horizontal from vertical lines. The only comparable data for normal animals are from Lashley (1938b), who gives a mean of 21 trials for normal learning of this discrimination. The mean number of trials for the rats reared in darkness was 129, six times as great, with a range from 40 to 190. These animals had been trained first to jump to an open window, and then to discriminate black and white cards (as were Lashley's animals) before being trained with the horizontal and vertical striations. In subsequent tests they behaved like normal animals, showing that the slow original learning with striations was not due to structural defects.

It is to be observed, in this experiment, that the range of learning scores overlapped the normal range. Some animals reared in darkness learned as quickly as some normally reared. Also, in preliminary experiments, two animals showed a prompt but not completely consistent discrimination of horizontal and vertical line. These facts fit with Senden's, for human subjects, very closely; they indicate that both rat and man have a crude immediate perception of a difference between the horizontal and vertical, but that the identity of these perceptions is radically improved with experience.

It may not be necessary to seek far for a physiological understanding of the primitive significance of line and the sharp inflection of line. In their stimulating statistical approach to the
problem of visual acuity, Marshall and Talbot (1942) have discussed a mechanism of summation at the borders of the projection of a visual excitation in area 17. In the absence of other
influence, the heightened activity corresponding to the margin
of a figure might dominate the total process. Walker and
Weaver (1940) have shown a direct control of eyemovement by
peripheral stimulation of the visual cortex. The movement is in
such a direction that the light source which produced such a
peripheral activity would be fixated. In view of Walker and
Weaver's work, Marshall and Talbot's discussion suggests that
there would be a tendency to fixate, successively, various parts
of the contour of an object. Also, with the intersection of lines
there may be a further summation of the border effects, so that
the foci of greatest activity aroused by a pattern in the visual
field would correspond to its corners.

It is important to observe that the figure made up of straight
lines, instead of irregular curves, has special physiological properties. When one point of a straight line is fixated, every point
to one side of the fixation tends to arouse exactly the same direction of eyemovement, and every point in the line on the other
side exactly the opposite direction. At times the two vectors
may balance, but often they will not. It follows that there is
a strong tendency for the eye to make a sweep along the line,
in one direction or the other; and, as the sweep is made, at the
moment when a corner is reached the stimulation of the intersecting line is at the maximum, since at this moment every point
in the second line has the same vector, for a new direction of
eyemovement. It appears from these considerations that the eye
would tend to seek out the contours of a figure and follow them—
irregularly, and with reversals, it is true, and subject to disturbance by other events, but it seems that such a tendency must
exist.

It is also important to note that every movement of the eye
in a single direction, for whatever reason, stimulates a "ridge"
of activity in area 17 corresponding to the projection of a straight
line, wherever the visual field contains a point of light. Except

in the special case of a field consisting of uniform parallel striations, every change of fixation from one point to another means
that rows of cells in area 17 are excited together or left unexcited
together. From the assumptions of the preceding chapter, the
first visual learning would to a great extent be the integration
of the effects, in the peristriate region, of the action of such rows
of cells in the striate region. This is a further emphasis on the
importance of straight lines in perception, and, as I have argued
(in Chapter 3), makes it possible to assume, from such a constant and extended training, that the characteristics of adult
tachistoscopic vision may be accounted for by a learning process.

Lines and angles, then, can be treated as perceptual elements,
not fully innate in perception, but partly so, and likely to be
learned before more complex patterns are. A very incomplete
analogy will serve here as a mnemonic device, to help keep in
mind the different processes that enter into perceptual learning.
If line and angle are the bricks from which form perceptions
are built, the primitive unity of the figure might be regarded as
mortar, and eyemovement as the hand of the builder. The
analogy is poor because the bricks contain mortar, they grow
while they are being used, and the house may change beyond
recognition as it is being built. Nevertheless, two things must
be kept in mind. First, the primitive figure-ground relationship
stressed by the *Gestalt* psychologists remains of fundamental
importance even though one recognizes that it is not the be-all
and end-all of perception. Secondly, one may agree with Lashley and the *Gestalt* psychologists that motor activity in itself
cannot possibly explain the organization of perception and nevertheless recognize that it has an essential role. Bricks alone are
not enough for building, nor yet is mortar.

A triangle then is a complex entity in perception, not primitive. As a whole, it becomes distinctive and recognizable only
after a prolonged learning period in which there is a good deal
of receptor adjustment—head-and-eye movement—as the psychological evidence of Chapter 2 showed. From the point of view
we have now arrived at, the difficulty of explaining the experimental facts of pattern equivalence has been greatly reduced.
Similar triangles of unequal size, a solid and an outline triangle,
even a solid plain triangle and one circumscribed with a circle

(Lashley, 1938*b*) contain a number of identical elements—lines and angles with the same orientation. (For some readers, "identical elements" will be an invitation to battle: let me say again that these are not the sensory elements of the classical dispute.)

It is of course still necessary to show how these elements, the parts of the figure, are integrated in perception. This I shall try to do next, taking an example that is as simple as possible. The present schema of perception and perceptual learning deals only with the case in which changes of visual fixation and some locomotion occur freely. The problem is to show how the variable stimulation which results from such movements can have a single effect, the perception of a single, determinate pattern.

MOVEMENTS DURING PERCEPTUAL INTEGRATION

In the perception of a triangle, there are three nodal points in the pattern on which fixation would be made repeatedly. A single fixation point was assumed in discussing perceptual integration in the last chapter. Let us next try to elaborate the schema to provide explicitly for movement of the eyes, and for those movements of the whole animal that produce variations in the size of the retinal projection of the stimulating pattern.

The account of neural integration now needs to be elaborated in three respects: (1) The activity in the peristriate, temporal, and other association areas of the cortex, that is aroused by fixation on any one of the three corners of the triangle *ABC* (figure 11), is always accompanied by motor processes which control the changes of fixation to the other corners. (2) Because of these changes, the integration of activity in area 18 and beyond occurs without constant conditions of excitation in area 17: when for example *B* is fixated, which cells will be excited in 18 is determined in part by the preceding activity in 18, and this varies according to whether the preceding fixation was on *A* or on *C*. (3) Finally, each of the three retinal patterns produced by fixation on the corners of the triangle is itself variable, with different distances of the animal from the stimulus object.

To show as simply as possible what these three points involve, suppose now that an animal sees a triangle repeatedly, having had no previous visual experience and having no other stimulation at the same time. Disregard any changes of background activity in the brain, apart from those induced by the changes of fixation mentioned; and, as a final simplification, treat the three angles *A, B,* and *C* of figure 11 as the only perceptual elements involved: that is, disregard fixation on the sides of the triangle, and the perception of the lines as distinctive entities.

The three changes to be made in the schema now can be dealt with one by one.

1. First, the concomitant motor excitation: with fixation on *A,* as represented in figure 11, *B* and *C* falling outside the macular field, the peripheral stimulation of *B* and *C* excites two motor responses simultaneously. The excitation may of course be subliminal, particularly at the first moment of fixation on *A,* since a fixation often endures for an appreciable time. The relative strengths of the motor components of the excitation aroused by *B* and *C* can be supposed to be the same, statistically, as

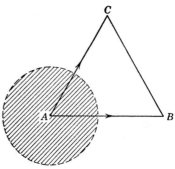

FIGURE 11. The triangle *ABC* is seen with fixation on the point *A.* The macular field is represented by the hatched circle, so that the points *B* and *C* fall in peripheral vision. Arrows represent the direction and strength of eyemovement tendencies aroused by the stimulation from *B* and *C.*

shown by the vectors (the length of the arrows) in the figure. At any one moment, variations of excitability would make one dominant over the other, but one can suppose that on the average they are equal. Looking at *A* would be followed by looking at *B* about as often as *C.*

In the normal adult animal, at least, the control of the direction and extent of eyemovement is accurate within quite narrow limits and does not work through a series of gross approximations. This means that the neural activity leading to the motor centers, *before* an eyemovement begins, is determinate, and specific to the locus of the peripheral stimulus. Fixation on *A,* then, has two effects: one "central" (*i.e.,* the arousal of specific cells in the peristriate and temporal regions, without a direct motor significance); and one primarily motor (*i.e.*, the arousal of specific fibers in a pathway that is not known but which originates in the visual cortex and which presumably involves the frontal eyefields [Clark and Lashley, 1947]).

These two effects, central and motor, correspond roughly to a dichotomy of the total excitation in area 17. The central effects are mainly determined by the part of the excitation falling in the macular zone, where acuity is greatest and the motor components least; the motor effects, by the peripheral part of the excitation, where acuity is poor, the ratio of cortical cells to degrees of visual angle least, and the motor limen lowest (Walker and Weaver, 1940).

If the cells in area 18 and beyond which are aroused by fixation on *A* are designated by the letter *a*, the composition of *a* is determined by the whole triangle, but the angle *A* has a disproportionately great influence because it falls in the field of central vision. Millimeter for millimeter, the part of the triangle which falls on the macula excites more cortical cells. Thus the main determinant of the central effect of fixating *A* is the angle *A* itself, rather than *B* or *C*. We shall also find that this influence of *A* in organizing the neural structure *a* must be further increased if the triangle is seen at a variable distance; but it is important to remember that *a* is defined originally as made up of the cells in the association areas of the cortex that are activated, not by *A* alone, but by the whole triangle when fixation is on *A*.

In the same notation, *b* and *c* are aroused by fixation on *B* and *C*. The distinction of *a* from *b* is a distinction of the excitations aroused with two retinal projections of the same figure. In brief, the angle *A* is the main determinant of the structure *a*, but not the only one; while *B* and *C*, when *A* is fixated, are the main determinants of the subsequent motor response.

As the integration of *a*, *b*, and *c* proceeds, repeated fixation on the three corners of the triangle slowly establishes three diffuse, irregular cell-assemblies (Chapter 4), each of which is capable of acting momentarily as a closed system. As this goes on, the activity of each structure would at all stages of its development be accompanied by two specific motor excitations. Activity in *a* occurs in the constant presence of a liminal or subliminal excitation tending to move the eyes to the right (fixating *B*, figure 11) or upwards and to the right (fixating *C*). From the assumptions of the preceding chapter, this means some mutual facilitation between *a* and the motor activity in question. Psychologically, in the particular limited conditions of the schema, perception of the triangle with fixation at one corner would involve a set to look at one of the other two corners (facilitation by *a* of the motor responses, strengthening the motor facilitation from *B* and *C*); and a sensorily aroused change of fixation from *A* to *B* would produce an expectancy of seeing the triangle with fixation at *B* (facilitation from the motor activity, arousing or reinforcing activity in *b*).*

2. The second point (on which the schema as it appeared in

* That is, when the animal looks at *B* after looking at *A*, the assembly *b* is excited in two ways: centrally, by the facilitation from *a* and from the motor activity; and sensorily, by *B* itself. In these circumstances, the two facilitations would just about coincide in time. "Expectancy" implies that the central facilitation definitely precedes the sensory, so it would be better to speak here of *attention* (central reinforcement of a sensory process). But the same process is called expectancy when the sensory reinforcement is delayed.

The later chapters will consider the interaction of sensory and central facilitations, and the disturbing effect on behavior when they conflict or when an expectancy fails to get sensory reinforcement. In a thoroughly familiar environment, the two facilitations would be synchronized, mainly because of the motor links in the central "phase sequence" discussed in the following pages. The facilitation of *a* is equally on *b* and on *c*; so *a* might arouse either one. But the cortical motor activity that results in looking from *A* to *B* is specific to *b*; and the animal will not "expect" to see the point *C*.

None of these relationships can be so precise outside of this schema, but the principles can hold. Central and sensory processes will stay more or less in synchrony in a familiar environment, both because of the motor links in the central sequence, and because the facilitation of a perception *X* will not be specific to another particular perception *Y* unless *X* was invariably followed by *Y* in past experience—the sight of an unsupported object, and the sound of a crash. But a sequence of visual sensations which is *not* organized by one's own eyemovements can be very disturbing to behavior, as the occasional case of seasickness at the movies shows. Again, the sight of a large body of calm water is not disturbing in a strange landscape, where one's expectancies are not specific, but would be very much so if it followed a movement of the head and eyes toward a place where one had always seen dry land. These points are developed further in Chapter 7.

the last chapter must be modified) has to do with an interference between the suprasensory effects of fixation on different points in the stimulating pattern.

It was proposed that the cells which are excited in area 18, by the first visual stimulation, are determined by chance anatomical convergences. Those which are active when the angle A is looked at must, on a statistical basis, include some which are active when B or C is looked at. The number of convergences in common would also be increased by any overlap in the retinal projections of a figure. Consequently, when A and B, or B and C, are looked at in close succession, there must be an influence of the one activity, in the peristriate region, on the next. When B is looked at, some cells in 18 will be active if A was looked at just before, but not if C was; others inhibited, or refractory, following a look at A. In the early stages of the visual development, there must be an interaction between a, b, and c, which in this schema amounts to an interference. In the ordinary course of perceptual learning, evidently, where the eyes are first opened on the complications of an ordinary room without the artificial limits of the schema, the amount of interference between the first perceptual activities must be much greater.* The interference has to be fully recognized here if the schema is to have any theoretical value later.

Such an interference, it seems, can occur only in the first stages of perceptual development and would disappear later. It is important to recognize it, however, since it affects the course that integration takes. In terms of the notation used above, the organization of the structure a (excited by fixation on A) must proceed mainly in cell groups (effective units of transmission) which are reliably excited whenever fixation is on A, whether B or C, or neither, had been fixated just before. I have

---

* And the resultant generalization of perception will be greater also. In this schematizing, the conditions of visual learning have been simplified to an absurd degree, but the ideas that emerge from it can be applied to behavior in more natural circumstances. The initial interference between the three primary visual habits epitomizes a relationship between a much larger number of habits in real perceptual development. The larger number of habits means that each one will be more an abstraction, less a perception of a particular angle (or line) in a particular setting.

emphasized that there must be fractionation and recruitment, or growth, as the individual closed cell-assembly becomes physiologically organized. When the growth occurs in a variable background of visual stimulation, those cells which are affected by the variability would not be consistently active at each repetition of the specific stimulus which excites the assembly, and therefore would not be part of it. In other words, as growth proceeds in *a*, *b*, and *c*, fractionation would eliminate elements that are active only when a certain fixation has preceded, and those which are inactive following any particular fixation. Activity in *a* can therefore occur independently of *b* or *c*, once the integration of these assemblies is complete.

In general terms, what has just been discussed is the case in which sensory events recur in random order in a short time interval, as one must suppose visual fixations to do. The alternative is a fixed sequence of sensory events, which of course also happens in normal perceptual development. The difference between the two cases is instructive.

Using the same notation, let us consider for a moment what would be the result of looking at *A*, *B*, and *C* always in the same order. (*A* is now a "signal" for *B*, and *B* for *C*, but this is not an analogue of the conditioned reflex: in the hypothetical conditions of the schema, *B* occurs *only* following *A*; in the classical conditioning procedure, *B* is an event such as feeding which follows *A*, the conditioned stimulus, but which also occurs at other times.) With a fixed order of stimulation, activity in the assembly *b* occurs always in the same setting, the after-effects of activity in *a*. The structure *b* therefore would include transmission units whose activity is especially facilitated by *a*, whereas, when stimulation occurs at random, *b* must be made up of units that are independent of the preceding activity. Also, when activity in *a*, *b*, and *c* occurs always in that order, no reverberation in *a* can be expected to coexist and be independent of activity in *b*, but must fuse with it. Any reverberatory after-effects which are not extinguished by the changed sensory influx are constantly present during the physiological integration of *b* and could not be distinct from it.

When fixation is at random among *A*, *B*, and *C*, however, we have seen that fractionation would tend from the first to keep the structures *a*, *b*, and *c* distinct, and make activity in *b* possible without preceding facilitation from *a*. This leaves the possibility that the three assemblies, once integrated, could still develop the interfacilitation that is discussed below, while the three are independent in the sense that one can be active apart from another, or that two may be active at the same time.

3. The third point, on which the schema as it was developed in the last chapter is to be elaborated, concerns the effect of a variable distance of the animal from the stimulus object. The result must be an increased importance of the part of the pattern which falls in the field of central vision.

When an animal looks at any part of a rectilinear pattern while moving toward it, the excitation aroused by the part looked at, falling in central vision, remains constant. The rest of the excitation, in the peripheral field, varies steadily. If the point of fixation is, say, the midpoint of one of the sides of the figure, the locus of the retinal projection of that line does not change, except to be extended at each end. If an angle of a triangle is fixated, as in figure 11, the projection of two lines and their intersection in the macula is unchanged as the animal moves closer to the figure; the third line, and the two remaining intersections, move farther and farther toward the periphery of the visual field.

The rat in the Lashley jumping stand, learning to discriminate a square from a triangle, does not see the figures at a constant distance. The retinal angular extent might vary by 50 per cent. The variability is very much greater in a Yerkes box, where the animal runs toward, or may back away from, a door on which the stimulus figure is placed. Now, using the same notation, in the composition of the assembly *a* (the organized structure in the association areas of the brain which is aroused by looking at the point *A* in figure 11), the influence of the angle *A*, relative to *B* and *C*, becomes even greater. The two lines and their intersection, fixated at a variable distance, have a constant effect; the other two intersections have a variable effect and do not repeatedly excite the same cells in area 18. In the growth of *a*, *b*, and *c*, fractionation would eliminate most of the cells whose excitation is due to the extramacular part of the figure. This excitation would of course always coexist with the activity of the organized assemblies, but it would remain unorganized. The organized activity would have to be determined by the macular excitation, *which, with appropriate fixation, is constant despite a variable angular size of the stimulus object.* This conclusion is clearly significant in understanding stimulus equivalence, as demonstrated by a rat's choice of a large triangle after learning to choose a small one.

THE SPATIAL HYPOTHESIS AND PERCEPTION OF THE REMOTE ENVIRONMENT

My discussion is already getting pretty far from the actual known facts of neural function. If it is not to become fantasy, it must at least stick close, at every point, to the facts of behavior. Here I digress for a moment to consider a group of facts that are well known but have not been explained. They serve as a check on the present theorizing.

The preceding discussion implies that a variable stimulation from the same stimulus object would retard the rate at which the subject could learn to perceive it *de novo.* Some of the discussion has suggested that differences of size, in terms of retinal angle, might not greatly affect learning; but differences of pattern, as an irregular object is seen from different directions, would be more important. Each grossly different pattern of stimulation, as the object is seen from one side or another, requires the establishment of a separate set of cell-assemblies. I can anticipate the discussion of the following section, and add that when this happens the various sets of assemblies would gradually acquire an interfacilitation—if sight of the object from one angle is often followed by sight of it from another. Arousing one set would then mean arousing the others, and essentially the same total activity would be aroused in each case.

Each perception would thus involve a conceptual activity (an activity, *i.e.,* not *directly* controlled by sensory processes). There is plenty of evidence in children's drawings, and in adult errors in perspective drawing, to show that a person looking at an object thinks he sees more of it than he does. What he knows about the object appears in his drawing, as well as what is visible at the moment; and the significant fact is that neither child nor adult can usually say where his drawing departs from what is actually presented to the sense organ.

An object seen from various aspects, then, requires a more complex learning process for its recognition than one seen always from the same direction and the same distance. Such learning should take longer; and, if we assume that a smaller number of cortical cells means a greater limitation to the number of assemblies that can be set up as separately functioning systems, learning to recognize a variably stimulating object should be harder for lower animals than recognizing a constant object.

Now it happens that the visual activity of lower species is dominated by the perception of place. This turns out experimentally to mean a dominance of cues from remote objects instead of near ones; and remote objects provide the most stable and constant stimulation of the animal's environment.

In discrimination training, the "position habit," which Krechevsky (1932) has called a "spatial hypothesis," is a constant nuisance in animal experiments. The method of training is to offer a choice of two alleys, or doors or windows, one of which leads the animal to food. He is also given a sign as to which one contains the food: the correct door has a black card on it, or a circle, say; the wrong one has a white card or a square. Food, and the sign of food, are sometimes on the right, sometimes on the left. But what the rat, dog, or chimpanzee persistently tries to find out is something different. He wants to know whether food is always on the right, or always on the left; or perhaps, in desperation, whether it alternates, once right, once left, and so on. He wants nothing of the rarefied intellectual problem of the signs the experimenter has put on the doors; it is only after repeated discouragement of the position habit—the attempt to find the food in some one *place*—that one can get him to learn anything else.

It has sometimes been supposed that this is a visual lack, or that the vision of lower animals is dominated by other senses. But this interpretation is not right, for two reasons. First, the position habit is just as annoying when one is trying to get blind animals to discriminate tactual cues (Smith, 1939) or auditory ones (Pennington, 1938). Secondly, the perception of place itself is visual, as much as kinesthetic or tactual. When visual cues from the distant environment are available, they dominate behavior. So the difference between lower and higher species is that the lower species is more dominated by the least variable of the environmental stimulation, not that vision in general has less influence.

This can be demonstrated strikingly in the rat. The rat is first accustomed to feeding on a bare table. He is then taught to run across the table, from a fixed starting point, to a food dish that is always in the same place on the opposite side of the table. The table is then rotated through 90°, but nothing else is changed: the rat is dropped at the same place on the table, with the food still opposite him. He runs at least once to the side of the table where the food used to be, with respect to the room, although neither food nor food dish is there now.

If one changes the method slightly, the dominance of room cues as against table cues becomes clearer. Put four small shields on the table, one in the middle of each edge. Mark the one that contains food by painting it white and making it larger than the others. Train the rat first to run to that one only, by putting no food in the others. Then rotate the table through 90°, and put food in all four shields. The rat will choose, not the plainly marked shield he was taught to go to, but the unmarked shield which, after rotation, now occupies the place *in the room* that the food used to occupy (Hebb, 1938*a*, 1938*b*).

A still more striking demonstration has been mentioned by Lashley (1938*b*) and further investigated by several students of Queen's University (Hebb and Williams, 1941, and further unpublished experiments). Teach a rat to jump from a small platform to another one near by. The second platform is just large enough for him to land on safely, and holds food. After he has made ten jumps, move the second platform through 90°. The rat hesitates, shows disturbance, but finally jumps—into space, in the former direction of food.

A final demonstration that visual cues are controlling the response can be made in a small cabinet, 6 by 6 feet square and 6 feet high, in a building quiet enough to provide no auditory cues to direction. Each wall is identical with the others, and each contains a door. The ceiling is homogeneous. One door is opened only, and a thin curtain is hung over it to admit light without allowing the animal to see outside. Now the rat is again taught to jump from one platform to another, in this cabinet. When he has learned to jump, the door that was opened is closed, and one in the next wall, at a 90° angle, is opened, and screened as before. Nothing is changed but the more distant visual cues of the door; the nearby platform remains as it was; but the rat now jumps out into space, at a 90° angle from his goal.

Why? And why is the position habit so persistent? The answer seems to be that the animal mainly perceives, and responds to, the least-variable objects in his environment, which are the ones at the greatest distance.

The stimulation received from any object varies with the animal's movements, but there are important differences that depend on the distance of that object. When the animal turns round, excitation is changed equally from near and far objects; but not when he moves from one place to another. Changes of position affect retinal locus, extent, and intensity only slightly when the stimulus is remote, very greatly when it is near. Even with body rotation, the order in which nearby objects are seen has no constancy, unless the animal always turns at precisely the same point. But the order in which distant objects are seen is the same, no matter where the animal is in the experimental apparatus.

It seems therefore to be true that, *the more constant the stimulation from an object is, the more readily it will be identified and responded to,* as the schema of these chapters requires. This is relevant also to the fact that as one goes up the phylogenetic scale one finds an increasing tendency toward visual discrimination of objects, without special training. The rat shows no sign of distinguishing between persons, or between inert objects visually presented; the dog often distinguishes a number of objects by vision, and probably a few persons; the chimpanzee is very selective in his behavior toward a great many objects, and is clearly able to distinguish a large number of persons (whom he sees often) from strangers.

The fact therefore is that perception of the intrinsic visual properties of a near or movable object is a less primitive and more difficult feat than perception of its place. This too is relevant to the fact that spatial delayed response is obtained easily in monkey and chimpanzee, nonspatial only with the greatest difficulty (Riesen and Nissen, 1942).

My account in these pages evidently has a long way to go before the generalized human concept of a triangle, or any other figure or object, is provided for; but it is essential to remember that the rat's perception is also a long way removed from man's. He does not recognize the triangle he was trained to recognize if it is rotated by 60°, nor a black triangle on a white ground after learning a white one on a black ground. He has, in fact, some considerable difficulty in seeing the difference between a triangle and a square when their base-lines are identical. Normal man can recognize simple regular figures at a single glance, but it is very unlikely that a rat does. When some change in the training figure is made, such as making it larger, the rat's behavior is clearly disturbed, while man might be quite unaware of the change; and the rat often discriminates only part of as simple a figure as a triangle.

None of these differences between rat and man is accounted for in current theories of perception. The critic of the account of perception that is offered here is likely to find it distasteful because it implies that with limited visual experience perception would be little generalized. Clinical and experimental evidence, however, does not support the objection but shows that the characteristic human perception of a triangle is the product of a long experience. Thus the schema agrees with fact on this point and in addition has the advantage of suggesting, at least, why the perception of place and direction is so prominent in animal behavior.

THE DEVELOPMENT OF SUPERORDINATE
PERCEPTIONS

We can now turn to the question of an integration of the several parts of a figure into a distinctive whole, as contrasted with the amorphous whole that is perceived in first vision.

The most direct way of accounting for the superordinate integration is as follows, as long as this is still recognized as frankly schematic. Activity in the assembly *a*, aroused by fixation on an angle *A* of a triangle, can occur independently of *b* or *c*. When *A, B,* and *C* are looked at successively, in any order, but in a short period of time, activity may continue by reverberation in two of the structures while the third is sensorily aroused. Just such a series of fixations would be the result of the behavior described by Senden, as the congenitally blind patient after operation learns to count the corners of a square or triangle and becomes quicker and quicker at doing so before he learns to recognize the figure at one glance. In these circumstances, conceivably, there is a frequent occurrence of activity in the three assemblies *a, b,* and *c* at the same time. These lie interlaced with each other in what is grossly the same tissue of the cerebrum, and according to the assumptions of the last chapter the simultaneous activity would result in an integration of the three systems.

It is perhaps necessary to remind the reader that the three systems do lie in the same tissue, although two of the sensory excitations concerned are unilateral, one in one striate area exclusively, one in the other. All such suprasensory systems must develop in parallel, in both hemispheres. The purely sensory activity, up to and including area 17, is unilateral when the stimulating diagram falls wholly to one side of the fixation point. But when area 18 is strychninized, it fires into the contralateral 18 as well as into the ipsilateral 19 and 20 (von Bonin, Garol, and McCulloch, 1942). The suprasensory integration initiated by a unilateral sensory event must be bilateral and consist of two halves, in the two hemispheres. Each half has the same functional significance—that is, it mediates the same perception and facilitates the same responses—even àpart from a coordinating action of the corpus callosum and other cerebral commissures (though the *development* of the contralateral half depends on the commissures). This is evidently relevant to the clinical and experimental reports of slight effects from damage to the callosum (Bridgman and Smith, 1945), or failure to find an effect of unilateral extirpation of association areas; but it is important for the present as showing that the assemblies *a* (excited by a figure which falls wholly in the right homonymous visual field) and *b* (arising from the left visual field) are structures which must develop in the same gross tissues of the brain.

According to the assumptions made earlier, simultaneous activity in *a, b,* and *c* would establish facilitation between them, through their chance anatomical interconnections and the enlargement of synaptic knobs. An effective facilitation from one system on another means a change of frequency characteristics in the system receiving the facilitation. It therefore means some fractionation and recruitment in the constituent units (p. 76). With three extensive systems involved, each facilitating action in the other two, these growth changes must be considerable. The resulting superordinate system must be essentially a new one, by no means a sum or hooking together of *a, b,* and *c.* Instead of *abc,* which might suggest such an idea, a better notation for the new structure is *t:* the assembly of cells whose activity, in the schema, is perception of the triangle as a distinctive whole. As *Gestalt* writers would say, this is something other than the sum of its parts; but, unlike *Gestalt* theory, the schema derives the distinctiveness of the whole from perception of the parts.

Now for the defects in such a formulation. Supposing that the general idea is right, it is still unlikely that the synthesis of *t* from *a, b,* and *c* would be made as a single step, however gradual. A single step would depend on simultaneous activity in three systems and so requires a frequent fixation of the three corners of the triangle in quick succession. Looking at two of the corners only would not contribute to the integration.

A much more plausible idea is that one or more intermediate stages would occur, such as an integration of *a* with *b* before that of "*ab*" with *c* (*ab* is used for brevity, though it is misleading in the same way as *abc* in the preceding paragraph). This would call for simultaneous activity in only two systems at a time. I mention *ab* as the first stage, rather than *ac,* because the horizontal line (*AB,* in figure 11) seems of fundamental importance in human perception, and certainly is so for the rat in the usual conditions of testing. The perception of lines as distinctive entities has been disregarded in this schema, in order to avoid a cumbrous and unwieldy discussion; but as we have seen the perception of lines is primitive, as the perception of angles or corners is, and a triangle has six instead of the three perceptual elements dealt with by the schema. This would make probable the occurrence of several intermediate stages between the perception of "elements" only, and perception of a distinctive total figure.

The argument up to this point can be summarized in general terms. Reasons have been given for believing (1) that fixation on each of the several parts of a figure would have an increasingly determinate effect, as arousing one specific structure; (2) that these structures, each corresponding to a frequently made fixation, are anatomically diffuse and interlaced with one another in the same gross cerebral tissue; and (3) that the several activities may coexist, and be aroused in any order. It is a reasonable inference (4) that two of these determinate actions simultaneously would have a determinate effect, tending to excite specific transmission units, and that the action of these units would tend to organize in the same way that the earlier established systems were organized. *Activity in a superordinate structure* (in this case, *t*) *is then best defined as being whatever determinate, organized activity results from repeated activity in the earlier-developed or subordinate structures giving rise to it* (in this case, *a*, *b*, and *c*; or "*ab*" and *c*, assuming two steps in development, and that *a* and *b* are first integrated).

THE PHASE SEQUENCE IN PERCEPTION

Next, let us consider the temporal relationship of activity in these various structures. During the development of the assemblies *a*, *b*, and *c*, arousal of *a* as we have seen is accompanied by two motor activities. Of these, one always becomes liminal (producing a change of fixation) before *b* or *c* is sensorily aroused. The sequence of events can be schematized as

$$a\text{--}b\text{--}c\text{--}b\text{--}a\text{--}c\text{--}a\text{--}b\text{--}a\text{--}$$

and so on. Each of these events is associated with two specific motor excitations. One of them at least is subliminal, and one becomes liminal as an event intervening between *a* and *b*, for example, or between *c* and *a*.

This "ideational" series with its motor elements I propose to call a "phase sequence."

When the assembly *t* has become organized, the psychological evidence indicates that its activity intervenes between the activities of the subordinate assemblies *a, b,* and *c* and does not supersede them. The sequence now becomes something like this:

$$a–b–t–a–c–t–c–t–b–$$

Such complication of a simple perception has important consequences for theorizing. The reader is briefly reminded of the reasons for thinking that perception of a simple pattern is not a single lasting state, terminated by an external event, but a sequence of states or processes. The congenitally blind patient after operation at first sees any figure as an amorphous mass, but may be able with effort to count its corners; the perception is then alternately of the whole and of its parts. As the figure becomes a distinctive whole, there is still the same fluctuation of the figure-ground relationship—attention directed now to the whole, now to its parts. This is a phenomenon which as a matter of common observation is always present in perception (and in a "concept," as one thinks about an object), as Chapter 2 showed, although the fact is not recognized in current discussions of the figure-ground relationship. Exactly the same sort of thing is implied by Lashley's inference that the rat successively isolates (*i.e.,* sees as figure) various parts of a unified pattern before making a response.

In terms of the schema, the alternate perception of whole and parts is an alternation of activity among *a, b, c,* and *t,* with corresponding directions of fixation (except for the entity *t,* which is accompanied by no determinate eyemovement; since the *average* values of the six eyemovement vectors associated with the three part perceptions of the triangle add up to zero, but also fluctuate from moment to moment, their resultant would fluctuate in direction and amount, and would produce neither a fixation of gaze nor any predictable change of fixation).

It follows that the integration of *t,* the basis of perceiving a distinctive total figure, essentially involves a sequence of cortical events with motor components. Activity in *a* facilitates the arousal of both *b* and *c,* with the appropriate intervening eyemovement, and activity in *b* or *c* facilitates the arousal of *a* in the same way. Whether *b* or *c* is aroused following *a* would depend on the momentary conditions of excitability. Activity in *a* would also facilitate that in *t*. In the early stages of perceptual development, *t* might be excited only after repeated activations of *a*, *b*, and *c*, but later (with the extensive development of synaptic knobs in the system and the consequent increase in the strength of facilitation) might be aroused following sensory activation of *a* alone, so that the triangle would be recognized with a single glance at *A* (figure 11). But the activity so aroused must be transient, as we have seen; perception of the whole as such is momentary, and alternates with perception of the various parts. Instead of an indefinitely prolonged reverberation, interrupted only by some event outside the system, excitation in one of the assemblies *a*, *b*, *c*, and *t* is an unstable equilibrium which moves readily into another phase.

The schema that has been developed requires only that reverberation continue in one of these structures long enough so that temporal overlap can occur. The psychological evidence reinforces the idea, based on the physiological evidence, that reverberation is short-lived: if the duration of an idea, or a perception, is the duration of reverberatory activity in a closed system, one can say that the pattern of activity rarely lasts without change for as long as a second. The stability of a perception is not in a single persistent pattern of cerebral activity but in the tendency of the phases of an irregular cycle to recur at short intervals.

It will be proposed in the following chapter that the train of thought is also a "phase sequence" of the same kind, but more extended, consisting of a series of phase cycles. The present discussion, besides dealing with perception, is also meant to lay a groundwork for dealing with the temporally organized processes of thinking.

THEORETICAL PROPERTIES OF THE SCHEMA

With this we are done schematizing. It remains to ask what theoretical significance the schema has, and how its ideas are to be applied to the development of behavior in normal circumstances.

Actually, all the rest of this monograph is devoted to answering the questions, but it will be worth while first to strike a trial balance and see what has been accomplished already. The main conceptions used in the following chapters have now been developed. The relationship of the schema to the following chapters will be more easily kept in mind by making its psychological reference more explicit.

Within limits imposed by the needs of exposition, a conceptual system has been elaborated which relates the individual nerve cell to psychological phenomena. A bridge has been thrown across the great gap between the details of neurophysiology and the molar conceptions of psychology. The bridge is definitely shaky in the middle, but it is well buttressed at each end; and we have a psychological bridgehead which can be widened and which already includes some strategic points. In other words, the schema has some theoretical value already. It shows, more or less explicitly, how it is possible: (1) to conceive of a conjoined action of the primitive figure-ground mechanism, eyemovement, and learning (specifically defined synaptic changes), in the development of simple perceptions; (2) to provide for an action of set, attention, or expectancy, also defined physiologically, in the perceptual process; and (3) to provide at the same time for *Gestalt* completion; similarity; generalization; and abstraction—these, with attention also, being essentially different aspects of the same process and closely related to association itself.

1. The interrelationships of eyemovement, figure-ground segregation, and learning are explicit in the schema. Perception depends on learning first to see the parts of an object clearly, a process involving a series of visual fixations, and proceeds from seeing, at first, an amorphous mass containing several foci (the corners), to seeing a distinctive figure at a glance. Even at this final stage we know that perception of the whole is dependent on eyemovements for maximal clarity (Chapter 2). According to the schema, the perception is constituted by a temporal sequence of activity in suprasensory (or association-area) structures, which owe their organization to changes at the synapse: it is an irregular cycle of recurring events which *can* continue momentarily without the corresponding sensory stimulations, but

which is reinforced by them and by the appropriate eye-movements.

2. References to set, attention, and expectancy were made in developing the schema, which can be more precise here. The term "attention" is ambiguous in the literature, and has several meanings: it may refer (*a*) to the state or end result of attending—the subjective clarity of what is attended to, or the necessary receptor adjustment; (*b*) to the selectivity of the process; (*c*) to the hypothetical agency or process which produces the selectivity; and (*d*) to various properties of "mind" which apparently cannot be defined or understood. It is in the third sense (*c*) that the term is used here, and in the schema attention may be defined as a central facilitation of a perceptual activity. So used, "attention" has exactly the same meaning as a "perceptual set," a process which makes one thing seen more readily than another. When this facilitation is effective in advance of the corresponding sensory process, expectancy is said to occur.

In the notation of this chapter, activity in the cell-assembly *a* facilitates an arousal of the assemblies *b* and *c*, as well as facilitating two motor responses, to fixate *B* or *C* (points of the triangle *ABC*, figure 11). In one way or another, this facilitation has inherent in it the notions of association (the whole schema makes this explicit), attention, and expectancy. Activity in *b* may be aroused in two ways: sensorily, by looking at *B*, or centrally, by the "association of ideas." When *B* is looked at just after *A*, activity in *b* is aroused in *both* ways, and the central facilitation, from *a*, is an instance of attention: a central reinforcement of a particular sensory event.

This illustration of the physiological meaning of attention is complete logically but is not particularly effective, since it does not make the selectivity of the process explicit. Our hypothetical animal has not been allowed to see a variety of patterns as yet, among which selectivity could operate; but this will be clearer in a moment, in discussing abstraction. Similarly, an eyemovement from *A* to *B* may be aroused in two ways: by the sensory stimulation from *B*, or by the facilitation from *a* on the motor system. Here the selectivity of the central facilitation is more evident. Eyemovements may be made from *A* to *B* or from *A* to *C*, and which of these is made evidently depends often on central events. We have seen that the relative strength of the two motor facilitations from *a* fluctuates from moment to moment; when one becomes liminal—that is, becomes decisive in determining which eyemovement is made—the selectivity of the "motor set" is illustrated.

3. Suppose now that our hypothetical animal, after thorough habituation to his limited environment ("limited" puts it mildly,

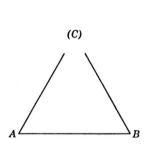

FIGURE 12. The triangle of figure 11, lacking its apex.

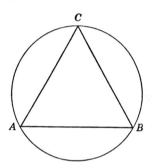

FIGURE 13. The triangle of figure 11, circumscribed by a circle.

since he was permitted no experience except to see a single triangle, at varying distances but always with the same angle of regard)—suppose that the animal is now tested with the two patterns represented in figures 12 and 13. Let him first see figure 12, a triangle such as he is used to, but with apex missing. What neural processes will result, according to the schema?

Fixation near the top of the figure will have no organized effect (remember that the schema disregarded perception of lines as distinctive entities, discussing the intersection of lines only). If the animal looks at *A* and *B*, however, the assemblies *a* and *b* are excited, with facilitation on each other, on *c*, and on *t*. A momentary excitation in *t*, a perception of the whole triangle, is then possible. Here is an instance of *Gestalt* completion, but derived as an associative process, with no field forces operating. According to the schema, it could happen only with a simple and thoroughly familiar figure (or thoroughly familiar part of a complex and unfamiliar figure), which agrees with the experimental facts. It is evident that such a completion becomes a simple corollary of association, once we can provide for a perception of parts without denying the unity of the whole. So too are similarity, abstraction, and generalization. Given perception of the various parts or properties of a pattern, separately; and the possibility of an association of these perceptions with a perception of the whole: we have given at once the possibility of a single response to two patterns which differ in their total properties but which have a property or properties in common. This of course is not new. What is new in the schema is showing how, conceivably, perception of part and of whole can be related to each other and to the nerve cell, and to changes at the synapse. An immediate dividend is the possibility of clearly stating, in physiological terms, the meaning of words like abstraction or similarity which are necessary to describe behavior but which have had, to say the least, a touch of mystery about them.

When the animal whose perceptual processes have been schematized looks at the point C in figure 13, at the apex of the familiar triangle, the intersection of the two straight lines produces an organized neural activity, plus an unorganized one due to the unfamiliar presence of the circumscribing circle. In the notation of the schema, c is aroused, but also a new and random activity of cells in area 18 and beyond. To interpret the effect of the random firing in 18 we must fall back on the statistical ideas of the last chapter. The number of convergences of this new activity on the organized cell-structure c would vary from animal to animal, since it is a chance matter; and in any one animal, from moment to moment, with variations of excitability in the individual unit of transmission. Accordingly, the organized activity in the assembly c would sometimes be disrupted, sometimes not. So with activities of a and b, when the other corners of the triangle are fixated.

When the organized activity does occur, the triangle is "recognized"—the *similarity* of the figure to the familiar plain triangle (figure 11) is perceived, the animal has *abstracted* from the total complex, and *generalization* of perception has occurred. Here too the selectivity of *attention* is more evident: once c is aroused, a fixation immediately afterward on A will be more likely to arouse the organized activity of *a*—the sensory effect of the triangle is selectively reinforced by the facilitation from *c*, that of the circle is not.

The purpose of this schema has been to arrive at conceptions that will be as near physiological fact as possible and that will enable us to deal with the cerebral control of behavior and its temporal integration. From this point onward, it is assumed that some such structure as the cell-assembly is established as the result of repeating any particular firing combination in an afferent system, and that assemblies interact in some such way as that proposed in the schema.

What follows is an attempt to generalize the ideas that have been developed in these two chapters (4 and 5), rather than an attempt at rigorous explanation by means of the assumptions that have already been made. Two implications of those assumptions, however, may be made explicit, since they broaden the applicability of the schematizing to real problems:

1. The different properties of a single sensory event may have separate central effects. This can be conceived of as follows: The infant's hand making contact with two or three objects in succession may receive from them stimulations which differ except in one respect, such as the degree of pressure on the skin as the hand closes. In the schematizing, there was only one stimulating object in the environment; in the environment of an actual infant, stimulation involves a number of objects and a *cumulative* effect of stimulation would be established most promptly by *the property that several of these objects have in common*. Such a consideration makes abstraction fundamental in the first learning; thus, in the context of one group of stimulating objects, a metal bar on the crib might contribute only to the development of the perception of *hardness;* but, while contact is being made intermittently with another set of objects, the same bar might contribute to the perception of (tactual) *roundness*.

2. Another aspect of sensory processes can be taken account of, in the temporal sequence of stimulating conditions. The problem of the perception of *black* in the visual field, for example, comes from the fact that this is not a static perception determined only by an absence of light in part of the visual

field, but is transient and requires temporal as well as spatial contrast for the full effect. A frequently repeated condition in the optic system is a decline of activity up to and including the lateral geniculate. During such a decline, and determined by it, there may be a predictable and selective activity in areas 17 and 18, by cells which are not active in the same combination during equilibration or during an increase of intensity. The repeated activity of such a particular group of cells would develop an assembly whose activity would be the perception of black.

In general, then, whenever a change of stimulation produces a transient but selective activity (that is, in certain cells only), in the sensory projection areas or in the neighboring association area, the necessary conditions are provided for the formation of a cell-assembly. Such assemblies would be the basis for perceiving contrasts, and the relative properties of stimulation: of colder, larger, higher in pitch, and so on. By the very conditions determining their occurrence, such perceptions must be transient and brief but may nonetheless be definite and distinctive for the period of their duration.

6. Development
of the Learning Capacity

In the schema of perception, motor learning got a foot inside the door through the emphasis on eyemovements. These movements were treated as having a variable relationship to sensation. They may be elicited (1) directly, by stimulation of the peripheral retina; (2) less directly, by a foveal stimulus that arouses an assembly action, this in turn facilitating eyemovement; or (3) still less directly, through a phase sequence, or succession of assembly actions. The stimulus may arouse assembly a, a then arousing c, at which point the motor limen may be low enough so that the activity of c results in overt eyemovement.

This epitomizes the treatment to be made of motor learning. The behavioral evidence shows a considerable variation in the directness of sensori-motor control. Some responses have, at maturity, all the properties of a reflex and yet are known to be learned. Others remain quite unpredictable from a knowledge of the stimulus alone; they are, that is, determined by an interplay of sensory stimulation and the autonomous activity of the cerebrum (set).

We must remember both kinds of learning: the set-influenced and the non-set-influenced. The reaction against early switchboard theory and connections, and the current dogma that learning occurs only with special conditions of motivation, have both tended to draw attention away from a kind of learning that, once established, is little affected by set and does not seem to need reinforcement.

In the adult animal the eyeblink to a rapidly approaching object, for example, is practically in the class of a spinal reflex.

Unlike the learned response studied in the usual experimental approach, it is extremely resistant to extinction, and to distraction ("external inhibition"); and, in human subjects, very hard to change by verbal preparation. Yet Riesen (1947) has shown that it is in fact a learned response. It is absent at the twentieth month in the chimpanzee reared in darkness, but then appears slowly with visual experience; and it is found at about three months in the normally reared animal. Such learning must be thought of as depending essentially on sensori-motor connections. The connections are presumably not from specific receptors to specific effectors; but they must be rather direct between afferent and efferent systems, since the response is without important influence from the autonomous central process (set, attention, or the like).*

The responses that have this property, however, appear to be acquired early. They are by no means a paradigm of learning in general.

At another extreme are those learned acts of the half-grown or full-grown animal that we call both learned and "voluntary" (a term that will be defined later). They are completely subject to extinction, and no matter how thoroughly learned they remain completely a function of set and drive. There is no possibility of direct sensori-motor connections here; to understand such behavior, and such learning, we shall first have to understand the organization of the controlling cortical activity.

It is implied that the nature of the learning process changes significantly with development; and the application of the ideas of the schema of perception to the real behavior observed in an experiment will best be seen in considering first the changes of the learning capacity with growth.

---

* Which means that the learned eyeblink may be about as close as mammalian learning ever gets to setting up S-R (stimulus-response) connections. The experimental criterion of such a response is dual: its independence from set and attention, and its resistance to extinction in Pavlov's sense. This comes down essentially to a single theoretical criterion: the predictability of the response to a particular stimulation, in any circumstances, as long as no other physically incompatible response is aroused at the same time. This is what sensori-motor connections imply. But when a response is predictable only in the experimental apparatus, or following verbal preparation, we are dealing with another class of behavior.

It was possible to be specific about a hypothetical perceptual learning as it is not possible about the motor learning of the mature animal. Perception is firmly tacked down to known stimulating conditions; its antecedents can be discovered. Motor learning at maturity, however, is conditioned by all the unknowns of cortical action. But with the schema as a starting point, and considering some properties of behavior that are often overlooked, it will be possible to set up a tentative account of learning at maturity.

THE RELATION OF EARLY TO LATER LEARNING

In this section I shall bring together the behavioral evidence on the relationship between learning in infancy and that of the normal adult animal, before returning in the next section to the question of neural mechanisms.

It is proposed that the characteristics of learning undergo an important change as the animal grows, particularly in the higher mammals; that all learning tends to utilize and build on any earlier learning, instead of replacing it (Mowrer, 1941), so that much early learning tends to be permanent (Tinbergen, 1942; Hunt, 1941); and, finally, that the learning of the mature animal owes its efficiency to the slow and inefficient learning that has gone before, but may also be limited and canalized by it.

THE GENERAL PROPOSITION. It is of course a truism that learning is often influenced by earlier learning. Innumerable experiments have shown such a "transfer of training." Learning *A* may be speeded up, hindered, or qualitatively changed by having learned *B* before. The question for debate is how great the effect may be in general behavioral development (as distinct from the effect of some one specific habit on some other) and what theoretical use is to be made of it.

McGeoch,* for example, has said:

After small amounts of learning early in the life of the individual, every instance of learning is a function of the already learned organization of the subject; that is, all learning is influenced by transfer.····

* *The psychology of human learning,* copyright Longmans, Green & Co., Inc., 1942, pp. 445–446. By permission of the publishers.

The learning of complex, abstract, meaningful materials and the solution of problems by means of ideas (reasoning) are to a great extent functions of transfer. Where the subject "sees into" the fundamental relations of a problem or has insight, transfer seems to be a major contributing condition. It is, likewise, a basic factor in originality, the original and creative person having, among other things, unusual sensitivity to the applicability of the already known to new problem situations. Perceiving, at whatever level, is probably never free of its influence; and there is no complex psychological event which is not a function of it.

Those are strong words, and I propose that they must be taken literally—as presumably they were meant to be taken. Unless we are to regard them as just a lip service to logic and the known facts of behavior, they must influence general psychological theory profoundly. If the learning we know and can study, in the mature animal, is heavily loaded with transfer effects, what are the properties of the original learning from which those effects came? How can it be possible even to consider making a theory of learning in general from the data of maturity only? There must be a serious risk that what seems to be learning is really half transfer. We cannot assume that we know what learning transfers and what does not: for our knowledge of the extent of transfer is also derived from behavior at maturity, and the transfer from infant experiences may be much greater and more generalized.

An example, in itself important for the theory of learning, will also show the dangers of generalizing from adult to infant behavior with regard to transfer. A student once pointed out to me that James' famous experiment on memorization begged the question. James wanted to see if practice in memorization would increase the ability to memorize. He found it did not; and later writers have found the same thing. As a result, it has been concluded that practice *per se* has little or no transfer value, without instruction as to better methods of learning. But all this is done with adults who have had long practice already, and the student pointed out that the transfer effects *must have been complete before the experiments began,* and could not be demonstrated by the method used. James (1910) used highly educated adult subjects, Woodrow (1927) college sophomores.

What would have been the result with subjects who had done no memorization before? We do not know, but it is certainly quite illogical to conclude that undirected practice has no transfer value because we find no evidence of it where there is no reason for expecting it. Above all, it would be illogical to conclude from this sort of evidence that the incidental learning of infancy has a negligible effect on later learning.

It has already been emphasized that perception is affected by past experience (Gibson, 1929; Carmichael, Hogan, and Walter, 1932; Leeper, 1935; Zangwill, 1937; Krechevsky, 1938). What is learned is in terms of what is perceived: what is not perceived can hardly be remembered. Koffka (1935) has emphasized that patterns may be seen and remembered by the arousal of "older trace systems"; Woodworth (1938) says that all perceiving is "schema with correction," that is, in terms of earlier perceptual habits. How do these habits get established in the first place? What are the properties of the learning that sets up the "older trace systems," of learning in its first stages, before there are any earlier habits to help it along? These questions cannot be completely answered at present, but even the skimpy evidence we have is enough to reorient the whole problem of learning.

THE FIRST LEARNING OF PRIMATES IS EXTREMELY SLOW, AND VERY DIFFERENT FROM THAT AT MATURITY. There are two kinds of learning. One is that of the newborn infant, or the visual learning of the adult reared in darkness or with congenital cataract; the other that of the normal adult. I have repeatedly cited the behavior of the patient born blind and given his sight after motor (and speech) development was well along, to show that the first learning is extremely inefficient as far as detectable effects on behavior are concerned, despite the completion of physical maturation (Senden, 1932). Here it is referred to once more, partly to show that the early inefficiency is not due to poor motivation and partly to make a comparison of man with other species.

Senden reports a serious disturbance of motivation, apparently in all cases, at one stage of learning. But this cannot be the main cause of the slowness of learning, for two reasons.

1. Motivation is not disturbed in the first stage, immediately upon beginning to use the eyes. At first there is a period of

delight, particularly in colors, and apparently a complete pre-occupation with the new experience.

Before long, the patient finds out how hard it is to get an effective use of pattern vision. The "crisis" of motivation then ensues. Until that point there is interest and application; things that are easy to learn are learned and not forgotten; color names are readily remembered, but it takes a long apprenticeship before any useful or demonstrable learning occurs in pattern vision.

Learning is evidently going on in this period, as long as the patient continues to keep his eyes open and makes any effort, but it can hardly be demonstrated except in the later increase of efficiency.

2. The second reason for denying that poor motivation explains the poor learning of man, in his first visual experience, comes from the observations of Riesen (1947). His chimpanzees, reared in darkness, were certainly motivated: both by hunger, and by their strong drive to find and cling tightly to an attendant, when they were out of their living cages. Yet there was no sign that either hunger or the desire to cling had taught them, in 40 to 50 hours' visual experience, how to discriminate the white-clad attendant from any other part of the environment. Astonishing as it was, the chimpanzees appeared to be completely avisual at this stage of the experiment.

Moreover, in further tests, a strong electric shock failed in a dozen trials to set up any avoidance whatever of a large, distinctive stimulus object. After a single trial, normal animals of the same age and in similar circumstances showed violent avoidance of the object with such painful properties. In the slowness of their first visual learning, man and chimpanzee are in the same class. The human slowness is not due to defects of motivation, but points to some fundamental property of the learning process in primates.

RELATIONSHIP OF LEARNING TO PHYLOGENESIS. The conclusion that the first learning differs radically from the later needs one most important qualification: the difference depends on phylogenetic level.

The evidence so far has been for the higher primates only. It was shown in an earlier chapter that training in pattern vision is slower for the rat reared in darkness than for normal rats, but the difference is not nearly as great as for chimpanzee or man. The rat reared in darkness is capable of a selective visual discrimination, definitely learned, after a total visual experience of less than 15 minutes (Hebb, 1937a, pp. 113–115). He requires six times as many trials as the normal to learn a discrimination of horizontal from vertical stripes, and twice as many for erect versus inverted triangles, but within an hour or so his behavior cannot be distinguished from that of normal animals. As we have seen, the corresponding time for primates is a matter of weeks or months.

There are no comparable data for other species, but some insect behavior suggests strongly that the first learning of the invertebrate is still quicker, and much prompter in reaching full efficiency than the rat's. What learning ability there is seems to appear full-blown, with little or no apprenticeship needed. The bee for example on first emerging from a completely dark hive flies off and is able to find the entrance to the hive again. We know also that finding the hive depends on vision. The behavior indicates that the insect's learning starts out, from the very first, at the mature level of efficiency. (Much that we attribute to instinct, because no *prolonged* learning is evident, might thus be due to learning that needs only a few seconds for its completion. The associations that are formed may be only certain ones to which the nervous system is especially adapted [Tinbergen, 1942, p. 82]: heredity would still have an overmastering importance, but learning may nevertheless be essential to some apparently instinctive acts.)

As we go up the phylogenetic scale, then, we find in mature animals an increasing ability to learn complex relationships, but also, surprisingly, a slower and slower rate of learning in infancy.

This does not refer merely to the fact that higher animals have a longer period of physical maturation. We have always known that a rat grows up, and develops whatever capacities the adult rat has, in three months—or a dog in six months, whereas a chimpanzee takes ten years, and a man twenty years. We have thought, I suppose (if the question ever came up at all), that this longer period of behavioral development meant only that maturation takes longer in the primate, and that with less instinct he has more to learn. But the clinical and experimental evidence points to an additional factor. Given a really new and unfamiliar set of sensations to be associated with motor responses, selectively, the first definite and clearcut association appears sooner in rat than in man, and apparently sooner in the insect than in the rat.

We commonly regard quick learning as the main distinction of higher species, and in certain conditions this is true. Normal man can glance once at a face and remember it for years. The chimpanzee Bimba was pricked once with a lancet and never again would permit it to be brought near her—but with no avoidance of other objects of the same size or roughly the same proportions.* This is something completely outside the rat's scope. We think of it as intelligent learning, and are prone to regard it as an innate property of the primate brain. It cannot be innate, however, as Riesen's evidence shows. So also with the ability to remember faces: Miner's (1905) patient, described as exceptionally intelligent despite her congenital cataract, two years after operation had learned to recognize only four or five faces and in daily conferences with two persons for a month did not learn to recognize them by vision. The human baby takes six months, the chimpanzee four months, before making a clear distinction visually between friend and enemy. Evidently, this is a period of learning as well as of maturation: not just a matter of waiting until certain neural structures are fully grown, with learning then at a typical adult rate.

There have been, in general, two schools of thought concerning the rate of learning. The configurationists, stressing the importance of insight, have been inclined to hold that learning occurs as a single jump, an all-or-none affair proceeding by discrete steps ("noncontinuity theory"); their opponents, that

* Dr. Glen Finch: diary of Bimba, Yerkes Laboratories of Primate Biology, 1940. It is relevant here, in discussing the nature of learning in higher species, to add a reference also to the remarkable learning capacity of rhesus monkeys that Harlow (*Psychol. Rev.*, 1949, *56*, 51–65) has demonstrated in a long series of experiments. Harlow's whole argument, showing how the learning capacity may be changed out of all recognition by prolonged experience, is a powerful reinforcement of the position adopted in these pages.

learning is graded in amount, built up steadily by small increments, and typically independent of any special factor of insight ("continuity theory").

But it is impossible to avoid the conclusion that both types of learning occur, and that one is characteristic of the mature animal, the other mainly of the infant. There *is* insightful, single-trial, all-or-none learning—in the mature animal, but never in the infant of a higher species. There *is* a slow-increment learning in the infant, in which no trace of insight whatever can be found, and in the mature animal also when he has been reared in darkness and is learning to use vision. It is reasonable to suppose in general that, the less familiar the situation or the task to be performed, the more important slow-increment learning becomes. But it seems also that few situations can be set up in which there is nothing familiar, so that it would be very hard to find an instance of learning in the mature animal in which there is not some effect of insight.

We are now in a position to define the relationship of the learning capacity to phylogenetic level. There is no evidence to support the idea that learning *in general* is faster in higher species—even at maturity. In the infant, the evidence is conclusive that the rate of the first learning is slowest in the highest species, quite apart from slowness of maturation. The distinctive characteristic of learning in higher species is the ability to handle complex relationships, and handle them as quickly as lower species can handle simpler ones. Man can learn to unfasten a latch quicker than the chimpanzee, the chimpanzee quicker than a rat; but, if we take the learning at which each species is most efficient, there is no good evidence that one is faster than another.

Lashley (1929*b*) has made this point effectively. After discussing an experiment by Pechstein in which rats and human subjects learned mazes of identical pattern, and in which the rats showed to rather good advantage—in one respect their scores were better than those of the human subjects—Lashley goes on to point out that with simple enough habits lower species and the feebleminded learn about as fast as normal man. Such habits are not retarded, in rate of formation, by extensive brain damage. There is also reason to think that immediate incidental memory occurs in lower species, and Lashley concludes: "The comparative study of learning in different animals gives little evidence that evolution has brought any change in the rate of formation of the simpler habits. On the other hand, there is a fairly consistent rise in the limits of training and in the formation of complex habits with ascent in the phylogenetic scale."

In summary, then, the phylogenetic changes in the learning capacity are as follows: (1) more complex relationships can be learned by higher species at maturity; (2) simple relationships are learned about as promptly by lower as by higher species; and (3) the first learning is *slower* in higher than in lower species.

CONCEPTUAL DEVELOPMENT AS THE BASIS OF LEARNING. Finally, before turning to the question of neural mechanisms, I want to bring together some of the behavioral evidence that throws light on *how* the learning capacity changes with growth. In general, it is a conceptual development, rather than the elaboration of a number of specific motor responses. Perceptual organization is also involved, but percept and concept are intimately related, and the term "conceptual development" will do to cover both.

The best single illustration of how one set of experiences can facilitate the formation of a new habit, involving a new stimulus and a new response, is one that has already been given: in learning to distinguish chimpanzee faces and remember them (or of course the old example of the westerner's difficulty in recognizing a particular Chinese face, before he has seen many Chinese). Learning to name *Pan, Jack, Frank, Don,* and so on, makes one later able to name a new chimpanzee, *Balt,* much more quickly. The exposure to a number of individuals sets up some sort of conceptual type, from which individual deviations become very noticeable.

This sort of facilitation in learning seems quite general, particularly in what can be called intelligent (as distinct from rote) learning, with meaningful material. That such a facilitation affects intelligence-test scores was the only interpretation that seemed possible of certain aspects of behavior following brain injury, or in old age (Hebb, 1942a). In a later chapter I shall present evidence showing that the behavior of the blind rat is permanently changed by earlier visual experiences. Jackson (1942) and Birch (1945) have independently shown an influence of experience on the insight of young chimpanzees. Birch has made it clear that this does not reduce insight to rote learning (thus Köhler's classification of behavior retains its value), and yet insight depends on the earlier experience.

How then does the earlier experience work? In the very first stages, to judge from Riesen's experiment and the material brought together by Senden, it operates to establish the perceptual elements discussed in Chapter 5. These are the entities that make up more complex perceptions. Organizing such elements in the various sense modes would lay the foundation of all later responses to the environment. Secondly, there is a period of establishing simple associations, and with them conceptual sequences—the period in which meaning first begins to appear. Finally, the learning characteristic of the mature animal makes its appearance.

This later learning is essentially conceptual. Even in the rat, maze learning requires the notion of the stimulus as acting to arouse conceptual activities, which in turn control motor activity (Lashley, 1944; Tryon, 1939). In man the conceptual activity has an even greater and more obvious role. There have been a number of attempts in psychology to treat language theoretically as a collection of conditioned reflexes, specific stimulations directly controlling specific responses. But consider such peculiarities of human learning as the following.

Certain features of the development of language in small children are very instructive. With opposites such as *up-down, back-front* (of a house), *in-out,* or *left-right,* a very interesting confusion can be observed in some children at about the age of two to four years. (Some doubt about *left* and *right,* of course, is often seen in adults; while other opposites, such as *hot-cold,* or *black-white,* never seem to give any particular trouble.) The confusion of *up* is only with its opposite and never with "in" or "back." This means that the word has first acquired an association with a definite, limited set of conceptual coordinates. The confusion, when it is observed, may last for months. In this period the word *up* has its prompt, clearcut association with the vertical dimension, but no association with a particular motor act such as raising the hands or looking upward at sky or ceiling. With such facts, it becomes nonsense to explain man's conceptual development as exclusively consisting of verbal associations.

The relationship of (*a*) stimulus, (*b*) central activity or concept, and (*c*) motor response is clearest in the notorious difficulty of choosing between *left* and *right*, to be observed by anyone who tries to teach twelve-year-old children to "right turn" promptly on command. Here we have a definite auditory stimulus, the word *right*, and a definite motor act to be associated with it. One might expect the association to be immediate, or at the very least to be set up as a conditioned reflex in a few trials—the more so since the child has had some such training since infancy. But we know that this does not happen; the discrimination is certainly much harder to make than that of *up* and *down*, and this in turn harder than *black* and *white*. The child can very readily learn at the age of three that "right" and "left" each refers to a side of the body—but ah me, which one?

Here, in the discrimination of right and left, is the real paradigm of adult learning. What is set up first is a conceptual organization. By the age of six the word "right" clearly and immediately means sidedness to the child. A considerable conceptual elaboration has already occurred, and the stimulus effectively arouses that structure; but it arouses no prompt, specific response. The response may come later, but for long it remains vacillating and unpredictable.

Consider again the role of analogy in human thought, and the figures of speech that betray it even in scientific work. The *pons* and *island* and *aqueduct* of cerebral anatomy; the *wave* of sound and *cycle* of sunspots in physics and meteorology; the *rise* of the blood-sugar *level*, and the *limen* of stimulation in physiology—all these are as enlightening, concerning the nature of learning and intelligence, as the child's confusion of left and right. Such figures of speech are at the very least an aid to memory; even when it has a totally new reference, the familiar term is more easily recalled than a neologism. Using it is therefore more than an economy of language. The underlying analogy with something known already is an economy of thought as well, an economy of effort in learning and understanding.

This fact is at the least surprising, since exactness of meaning is essential to scientific thought, and since the laws of learning as we know them would suggest that there must be a considerable interference between the old meaning and the new one given to a familiar term. That is, there should be interference *unless terminology corresponds to thought and the new concept is only a modification of the old.*

The worker in the laboratory does not merely report and expound by the aid of analogy; that is how he thinks, also. The atom was once a hard little round particle, or later one with hooks on it. Recently it was a solar system. The classical dispute of physics about the nature of light was really asking, Is light like a shower of pebbles, or like ripples in a bathtub? The ultimate answer, Both, was one that was hard to accept. Why? Because it fitted into no pre-existing conceptions; waves are waves, and pebbles are pebbles—there is nothing in common experience that has the properties of both. We know well that scientific thought travels by short steps; the individual thinker never gets much in advance of his fellows, and his ideas are born of existing ideas. A new conception, like Woodworth's "schema with correction," must be mainly composed of earlier ones. New learning is facilitated by old.

But, as the history of the theory of light suggests, it may be limited or canalized as well. I have used the analogy of an apprenticeship, in visual learning. Now an apprenticeship in one trade may help in another, but not as much as the one directly studied. It is not just *any* learning that facilitates any other learning at maturity.

Nissen, Machover, and Kinder (1935), for example, have shown how the visual learning of childhood may be selective in its later effects. West African natives made low scores on form boards, in an intelligence test. In this sort of test the subject is asked to fit a series of wooden blocks with simple geometrical shapes into holes with the same shapes, as fast as he can. In conversation, Dr. Nissen has made the point that the low scores were not due to slowness of movement, but to a slowness in identifying shapes—a slowness of perception.

At the same time, he found himself just as inferior in seeing things in the bush that seemed completely obvious to the native. Suppose now that a native and a city-dwelling scientist were shown the trail of a *new* animal in the same habitat: though it is strange to both, which would remember it better, and be able to recognize it on a second occasion? What a native could learn from a text on geometry, or what one of us could learn about following a trail, must be far more a function of pre-existent learning than of the inherited properties of our respective brains.

It is of course a commonplace that the experiences of childhood have a permanent effect on one's attitudes, interests, and even abilities. Lorenz (cited by Tinbergen, 1942) has demonstrated the effect experimentally in birds. With mammals, everyone knows that taming is easiest in infancy, with a lasting effect. The gun-shy dog, conversely, is an example of a lasting failure of emotional adaptation: though the disturbance need not be set up in infancy, it does demonstrate an intractable effect of a first experience. Hunt (1941) has shown an effect of early hunger on later hoarding by the rat. As to abilities or intelligence, it is now generally accepted that races and peoples cannot be compared in hereditary endowment, since low scores may be due to cultural background. That the level of problem-solving at maturity, then, may be permanently influenced by childhood experience is an accepted psychological principle, despite a certain inconsistency of the theorists who think that the Negro's low IQ is to be explained so, but seem to have forgotten that the poor white's may be in the same class.

To this point we shall return, in discussing the nature of intelligence. Here I have attempted to define the general relationship of first learning to later learning, in terms of the behavioral evidence. Let us now turn to the physiological processes that must explain the relationship as well as the peculiarities of primary or aboriginal learning.

THE STAGE OF PRIMARY LEARNING

Among others, the preceding discussion has raised the problem of explaining the greater inefficiency of early learning in higher species. To deal with it, we can return to the schema of perception and repair a deliberate omission. The schema made almost no mention of the spontaneous firing of the association areas of the cerebral cortex. Taking this into account, a question is raised that has really wide significance. For the moment, it can be put in this form: In what circumstances can one suppose that a stimulus will have the same central effects on two different occasions, so that cumulative learning is possible?

It has already been said that an afferent excitation does not arouse inactive tissue but feeds into an activity that is already going on. A constant net result, when a stimulus is repeated, requires some constancy in the spontaneous activity in the association areas upon which the afferent activity impinges. The perceptual learning that has been schematized in the preceding chapters depends on *some* consistent central action of a repeated stimulus. We need not assume a constant pattern of the background activity, at all times, to satisfy the schema; but it does demand at least a frequent recurrence of the same pattern. This is necessary if the stimulus is to have a cumulative action and build up the "assembly" of cells that constitutes the first learning.

In the answer to this problem lies an explanation of the slower first learning in higher species and, indirectly, as we shall see in later chapters, an understanding of some of the problems of motivation and emotion in the half-grown or full-grown animal.

There seem to be two main factors that would make for some consistency in the activity of the association areas at different times. One can be referred to as an intrinsic organization, in that activity; the other is the steadily increasing influence of the infant's environment.

The *intrinsic organization* of cortical activity is so called because it is opposed to the organization imposed on the cortex by sensory events. It appears at birth * in the large slow waves

---

* *I.e.*, it is "innate"; but it may or may not be unlearned. There are two possibilities: (1) that there are pacemakers which are inherently such as to dominate other neural cells and produce the synchronous firing; and (2) that the synchrony is "learned"—established *in utero* as a result of the neural activity itself. The comparatively slow change of the infant's EEG toward the adult pattern, and the lack of any sharp discontinuity between the two extremes, suggest the second interpretation. Supposing that the

of the infant's electroencephalogram, and in the sleep or coma of older subjects. At birth, that is, the intrinsic organization is completely dominant; in psychological development its dominance decreases, but it continues to recur periodically, generally in a diurnal rhythm. Its behavioral correlate is a heightened limen for sensory stimulation and a marked absence of the persistently directed activity that we call voluntary and purposeful.

This does not mean that there is any sharp line that divides infant behavior, or sleep, from the behavior of the wakeful adult; it does not mean, either, a hard-and-fast distinction between the corresponding EEG's. But there appear to be two extremes in the organization of cortical activity that correspond exactly with the two extremes of learning ability discussed in the last section. One is established early; interrupted rather than supported by a varied sensory activity, once the alternate organization begins to appear; manifested by large potentials in the EEG; and correlated with an inactivity of the musculature or an aimless, undirected activity and a slow and inefficient learning.

firing of central cells is originally at random, the synaptic changes discussed earlier would lead to an increased coordination of firing and the establishment of massive self-exciting systems. These might be comparatively simple closed circuits at first but would tend to steadily recruit other cells and later other circuits. This is the "growth" referred to in the discussion of perceptual development (p. 76). Without the constant sensory disturbances resulting from the motor activity of the waking animal, the growth would make for *local* integration, and hypersynchrony; with them, the integration is in anatomically diffuse systems and reduces local synchronization.

This discussion makes a good deal of the electroencephalographic evidence as the most direct index of physiological organization in the normal living brain. It is wise to recognize explicitly, however, that the index is a very rough one. I have treated the slow waves of the infant's EEG, and those of adult sleep and coma, as having the same meaning. Apparently they may have, in one respect: as indicating a local synchrony of firing in cortical neurons (see the assumption made earlier, p. 8). But in other respects there may be significant differences. Indeed, there must be; and future developments in electrical recording may reveal them. For the present, the important thing is to see that there is in one respect an identity of cortical activity in infancy, sleep, and pathological conditions which is at the opposite extreme from that of the normal waking adult, as seen both in the electrical record and in the presence or absence of sustained purposeful behavior.

The other is slowly acquired; dependent on a constant change of the sensory influx for its maintenance for any period of time; produces a flattened, irregular EEG; and is the precondition of the normal adult waking behavior and the adult level of learning. Note that what is discussed here is a variation of *organized* activity in the cortex. In the later discussion of fear and neurosis the notion of a disorganization will appear, producing neither quietude nor purposeful activity but incoordination and autonomic activity. Intrinsic or primitive organization, and disorganization, are to be distinguished.

Against the background of the intrinsic organization, the infant's first visual learning could proceed steadily, although slowly, with no disruption. If the first sensory excitation feeds into an organized activity, where cells are firing rhythmically in large populations (which I assume is what the large waves of the infant's EEG mean), the argument of the schema can still stand, although visual learning must be slower than if the cells of area 18 were always ready to be fired, and never refractory, when an impulse arrives from 17. The only change in the schema is to show still another reason for the slowness of first learning in the higher primates.

At the same time, an explanation of the difference from lower species appears. The process of perceptual learning must be thought of as establishing a control of association-area activity by sensory events. The larger the association areas, both absolutely and relative to the size of the sensory projection areas, the slower the establishment of such a control must be and the less rigid and more complex its final form.

Let us suppose, as we safely may, that the principles of central organization in other sense modes do not differ from those of vision. Anatomical differences in the various sensory systems may affect the complexity of discrimination, fineness or acuity of discrimination, and so on. They may lead to a greater relative importance of temporal integration in one sense and of spatial in another, as in hearing and sight. But these anatomical differences do not imply different principles of central neural integration in sight and hearing, or in touch and smell.

Our problem essentially is to see how a particular sensory event can have the same central effects on different occasions despite spontaneous central activity. If we conclude with Adrian (1934) and Weiss (1941a) that the unstimulated neural cell must eventually fire spontaneously, we must also accept Adrian's conclusion that this cannot happen in the cell that is exposed to persistent bombardment. As long as the receptor surfaces are being stimulated, therefore, the sensory projection areas of the cortex must remain completely and constantly under environmental control.

Also under control are the fibers that lead from the sensory areas into the association areas. According to the schema of perception, this control is extended gradually, synapse by synapse. Considering the association areas as made up of a population of transmission units, two factors must affect the length of time needed to bring all these units under control. One is the number of controlling fibers leading from sensory areas into association areas. The second is the number of transmission units in the association areas themselves.

With cortex of a given size, these two factors may be considered to be roughly proportional to the size of the total sensory cortex, and the total association cortex. It then follows that the length of the primary learning period will be roughly proportional to the ratio

$$\frac{\text{total association cortex}}{\text{total sensory cortex}}$$

which can be called the A/S ratio. The sensory projection areas are directly under environmental control; and if they are large, with respect to the association areas, and so project a large number of fibers into the association cortex, their control should be quickly established. If the sensory projection is small, association cortex large, the control will take longer; the period of "primary learning," that is, will be long.

But we may have to consider a further factor. With the same A/S ratio, but with different absolute size of brain and a larger absolute number of transmission units in the association areas, it seems that the larger brain might also make for slower first learning. A larger number of transmission units means a greater variability in the spontaneous activity of the association areas, as well as a larger number of synaptic junctions over which sensory control must be extended. It will be recalled that the synapses in question are not the minimum number through which an afferent excitation might conceivably reach the motor cortex. We are dealing with recurrent circuits and complex closed systems. An absolutely greater number of transmission units in the association areas would probably make for greater variability in early spontaneous activity and a greater ultimate complexity of organization. Both imply that a sensory control might be established more slowly in a larger brain, even with the A/S ratio constant.

The sensory projection areas are widely separated in the brain, almost as if to maximize their influence. Only in the frontal pole in primates (and to a less extent in the temporal pole) is there cortical tissue that is far removed from a sensory projection area. *We can then regard the stage of primary learning as the period of establishing a first environmental control over the association areas*, and so, indirectly, over behavior. With this proposition we have at once an explanation of the slowness of the first learning in primates, in which brain and A/S ratio are larger, and of the ultimate level of the primate learning capacity.

The numerical aspect of this fraction cannot be stressed, since presumably there are other factors of finer neural anatomy, of metabolism, and so on, to be taken into account. It may be suggested, however, that the size of association cortex, and the A/S ratio, when these can be expressed in terms of cell counts, may provide the basis of a better morphological index of the level of behavior than the brain-weight/body-weight ratio. This of course is not testable at present. No cell counts are available, and psychology has so far found few satisfactory comparisons of intelligence as between different species. We have not even any exact data on the gross size of the sensory cortex in different species.

But, for widely differing phylogenetic levels, a hierarchy of "intelligence" (or psychological complexity: McBride and Hebb, 1948) can be assumed, which corresponds to gross differences (1) in size of the cerebrum, or (2) in the proportion of afferent to internuncial neural tissues. In the lower vertebrates, the cerebrum is small, and the afferent systems are massive in comparison with the internuncial. Within the mammalian series, there are differences both of absolute and relative size of association cortex which may be assumed (in the total absence of any exact data) to have a relevance to the greater speed with which the "lower" species can learn to respond selectively to the environment, and to the comparative simplicity of the behavior when it is fully developed.

These anatomical considerations draw attention to another point. The learning ability of higher species at maturity is not merely the capacity for a greater number of associations or for associations that involve finer sensory discriminations. The behavior also shows a less direct control by the stimulus of the moment, from the immediate environment. In larger association areas the central phase sequence can be more complex: it must still be organized and ultimately controlled by the relatively smaller sensory projection areas, but the phase sequence can escape the direct control more frequently and for longer periods. The possession of large association areas is an explanation both of the astonishing inefficiency of man's first learning, as far as immediate results are concerned, and his equally astonishing efficiency at maturity.

MECHANISM OF ADULT LEARNING

The question has been raised as to how, if the association areas of the brain have a continuous and variable activity, a repeated stimulus can have the same central effect on separate occasions, to make cumulative learning possible. The question was answered for the infant, and the answer helped to account for the slow first learning of higher species. It can now be answered for the adult.

Fortunately, it is no longer necessary to account for a cumulative effect of stimulation that is superimposed on an *independent* activity of the association areas (fortunately, because this activity must be extremely variable in the waking adult). The learning occurs when the events to be associated can already command organized trains of cortical activity; in other words, when the environment has a control of the association areas that can be repeated, so that the central activity is *not* at random and the stimulation *can* impinge on the same central pattern when the training situation is repeated.

I have made it an essential condition of learning that two central events occur together. The reader is reminded, however, that this is not always a sufficient condition. In discussing the question earlier (p. 77), I considered the probability that two systems would acquire an interfacilitation by being active at the same time. The systems referred to, at that point in the development of the theory, were newly organized ones, and the question was of the *first* association of one system with another during primary learning. The conclusion was that the ease of association must vary greatly, even when the two systems lie intertangled in the same gross region of the brain. They might promptly coalesce, at one extreme; or might, at the other, fail to do so despite often being active at the same time, over a long period. It was concluded also that the larger the system the greater the probability of its establishing an effective inter-facilitation with another—provided that the two are well organized, so that arousing part of one will arouse the whole.

But we are now interested in the associations formed at maturity, between much more complex processes. Learning at maturity concerns patterns and events whose parts at least are familiar and which already have a number of other associations. This changes the problem considerably. It means that the learning is not an association between totally unrelated processes. It must concern a complex of cell-assemblies, and elaborate phase cycles (in the jargon of my schema); and amounts to a strengthening of facilitations, not a setting up of new connections between wholly unrelated activities.

The characteristic adult learning (outside of psychological laboratories) is learning that takes place in a few trials, or in one only. It seems always to involve a recombination of familiar perceptions and familiar patterns of movement. Thus one can typically remember a new name when given name and surname are already familiar, or a new face when it is one of a racial group to which one has long been exposed. Vary these conditions, and repeated effort may not do the trick. Complicate the problem even by requiring that the new name and new face be learned simultaneously, and the difficulty is increased; it is usually overcome only by repeating the name and looking at the face a number of times in a short interval. So adult learning is typically an interaction of two or perhaps three organized activities; being organized, they are capable of a continued existence after cessation of the stimulation that set them off, which gives time for the structural changes of permanent learning to take place. *For the theory being developed, a prompt learning is possible when the stimulation sets off well-organized phase sequences, but not otherwise.* This organized activity of the association areas is subject to environmental control. To the extent that the control is effective, and re-establishes the same central pattern of activity on successive trials, cumulative learning is possible.

Adult learning is thus a changed relationship between the central effects of separate stimulations, and does not directly concern the precipitating stimulus or, primarily, the motor response whose control is imbedded in the central activity.

The same conclusion is reached from another approach. Experiments on learning have shown again and again that the nonsense syllables *tob, del, rec, til,* and so on, are harder to memorize than the more complicated items *tob*acco, *del*ights, *rec*ommend, and hear*til*y; and still harder than the sentence "I recommend the delights of tobacco heartily." The event with meaning is best remembered; moreover, it is the meaning that is remembered rather than the specific stimulation that aroused meaning (McGeoch, 1942). That is, the central effects of sensation are what enter into an association, rather than the comparatively simple sensory event itself. This seems especially true of the most efficient learning—the kind that is established most easily and persists longest.

Such learning may be diagrammed as in figure 14, where each circle represents a conceptual activity. The concept of an object or place is an irregular cycle, each phase of which is the activity of a cerebral cell-assembly. If a large enough part of this phase cycle is aroused, the whole becomes active. Thus in figure 14 the concept *A* was originally organized by an interaction of hearing, touch, and vision. Once organized, it may be aroused by hearing alone, or perhaps by hearing and touch; but the essential association between *A* and *B*, resulting from simultaneous activity, would be the same whether each was aroused by vision, or whether one was aroused by hearing and the other by touch.

In this way learning may be "free" of any particular sensory cues (Tryon, 1939). The rat may learn a maze by the aid of cues from vision, smell, touch, and kinesthesis; the maze once

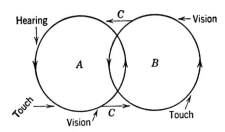

FIGURE 14. *A* and *B* represent two conceptual activities. *C, C,* possible connections between *A* and *B*. These are not simple closed neural circuits, nor even the more complex "assemblies," but "phase cycles": systems of assemblies whose several activities are temporally integrated and tend to recur in an irregular cycle. *A* was originally organized by auditory, tactual, and visual stimulation (that is, it involves assemblies in each of these modes); *B*, by visual and tactual stimulation. When these cycles are well organized, their activity may be initiated by part of the original stimulation—*A* for example by hearing, touch, *or* vision. When *A* and *B* are simultaneously active, they may acquire an interfacilitation which is diagrammatically represented by *C* and *C*. The learning is independent of any particular stimulation; the association might be set up by two visual stimulations, but be manifest later when *A* is aroused by hearing, or *B* by touch.

having been learned, any of these cues may be disturbed or removed, but the learning persists and utilizes those that remain. We shall see in a later chapter that the behavior of the blind rat is permanently affected by his having had vision during the period of development. The rat blinded at maturity solves certain problems that rats blinded at birth do not. The properties of the concept *A* (figure 14) depend originally on vision; but a rat might be blinded, after *A* had been developed, and still retain the concept as one that can be aroused by hearing and touch alone.

Now as to the mode of association between two such concepts. The two neural structures may have enough chance anatomical convergences (Chapter 4) that a direct interfacilitation is established. This is represented (still quite diagrammatically) by C, C in figure 14. Then, even though the stimulation arousing A and B is brief, they may continue active long enough for synaptic knobs to develop. The result would be one-trial learning, involving two separate neural systems.

But this, it seems, is unlikely. When new connections are to

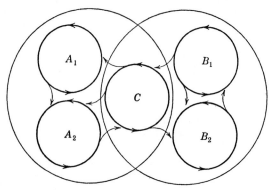

FIGURE 15. To illustrate the possibility that a subsystem, C, may act as a link between two systems (conceptual complexes). One concept is represented by A_1, A_2, and C; the second by B_1, B_2, and C. The two systems have a subsystem, C, in common, to provide a basis of prompt association.

be set up, as in figure 14, it is probable that a number of trials would be necessary, and the diagram is best considered as representing rote learning. The facts already discussed have indicated that one-trial learning occurs only as the association of concepts with "meaning"—having, that is, a large number of associations with other concepts. Figure 15 diagrams another possibility, which can be given more weight. A perceived object consists of a number of perceptual elements (p. 83). The same elements recur in different perceptions, so that two concepts to be associated may have phases (assembly actions) in common. These would be ready-made links, needing only to be strengthened to establish the association.

But more: the perception of an actual object (that can be seen from more than one aspect, and touched, heard, smelled, and tasted) involves more than one phase cycle. It must be a hierarchy: of phases, phase cycles, and a cycle or series of cycles. ("Cycle" is of course temporal: referring not to a closed anatomical pathway but to the tendency of a series of activities to recur, irregularly.) The two ideas or concepts to be associated

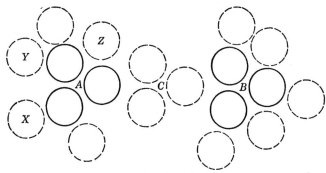

Figure 16. Diagramming in another form the same principle as in figure 15. The complexes A and B are sensorily aroused at the same time. Solid circles represent systems that are reliably aroused; broken circles, ones that are facilitated by the activity of adjacent systems, but not reliably aroused by them. That is, the "fringe" systems X, Y, Z, C, and so on, receive a facilitation from A which is often not sufficient to arouse them; which ones are active will depend on preceding activity in the tissue and accidents of concomitant stimulation. The complex C might or might not be aroused as a sequel to A, or to B; but when both are active simultaneously, C is more likely to be aroused. Thus the subject associates an object B with the object A, because both are associated with something else, C: a familiar trick in memorizing lists of words or nonsense syllables in learning experiments. But the processes A, B, and C all occur within what is grossly the same tissue, not spaced as in the diagram; and when by virtue of C's activity A and B are persistently active together, they may slowly build up a direct interfacilitation—so that C can drop out eventually, leaving A linked to B directly, by a short-circuiting. (Woodworth, 1938, p. 34; McGeoch, 1942, p. 166.)

might have, not only phases, but one or more subsystems in common. This is suggested by the diagram of figure 15. It should provide an even more effective link. Such a mode of association is possible only between complex systems, and it may be recalled again that a complexity of meaning is more readily remembered than a simpler perception without meaning.

The same general principle is involved in figure 16. This

represents the familiar fact that a subject required to learn pairs of words with no obvious relationship will invent relationships, and will himself supply extra terms in doing so. The subject trying to associate *conceal* with *above* may do so by thinking *above* = CEILING–*conceal;* or with *marble–punish,* may think of being *punished* FOR PLAYING *marbles* FOR KEEPS (Woodworth, 1938). The subject is making his task more complex when he chooses to remember three or four terms instead of two, but he also makes it easier. Thus figure 16 shows how two concepts *A* and *B* may be associated if a third one (*C*) is aroused to which *A* and *B* are already related.

The prompt learning of maturity is not an establishing of new connections but a selective reinforcement of connections already capable of functioning. Observe, however, that this account differs from traditional association theory in at least one respect, which is of the greatest importance for applying the theory to the results of experiment. *Two concepts may acquire a latent "association" without ever having occurred together in the subject's past experience.* Although the "association by similarity" of older theory recognized this fact, the explanation seemed to depend on the idea of identical sensory elements. The present theory suggests that the identical elements may be conceptual rather than sensory; that is, two things may seem similar without exciting the same receptors.

The concept *A* in figure 16 is capable of arousing, or facilitates, *C;* but the facilitation may be from one of the subsystems of *A* on a subsystem of *C,* so that *A* and *C* need never have been active together at any earlier time. Or, as in figure 15, two systems may coalesce promptly because of having a subsystem in common. It seems likely that something of this sort is the explanation of the happy figure of speech, which links two sets of ideas not previously associated: the more unlike they are, superficially, the more effective the figure; and yet it is effective only because something about the structure of the two ideas is the same. (For examples of such pairs of ideas, the reader may consult the discussion of scientific analogies earlier in this chapter.)

My treatment of learning here is tailored carefully to the experimental facts, but it also follows naturally from the original neural schema. At this point, in the emphasis on pre-existent associations in learning, we have come to a classical problem that we can examine a little more closely: the meaning of "meaning."

The implication of the preceding paragraphs is that a concept is not unitary. Its content may vary from one time to another, except for a central core whose activity may dominate in arousing the system as a whole. To this dominant core, in man, a verbal tag can be attached; but the tag is not essential.* The concept can function without it, and when there is a tag it may be only part of the "fringe": sometimes aroused with the dominant subsystem, sometimes not. The conceptual activity that can be aroused with a limited stimulation must have its organized core, but it may also have a fringe content, or meaning, that varies with the circumstances of arousal.

Thus in figure 16 the activity of A may be accompanied by the activity of X on one occasion, or of Y and Z on another. Which will happen is not indeterminate, but depends on the excitability of each subsystem at the moment, and on the facilitation from other concurrent sensory and central activities.

Now consider the subject learning a list of words again. Following one train of thought, in which an activity occurred which facilitates activity in C (figure 16), the occurrence of A and B (also facilitating C) leads at once to the sequence A–C–B. On another occasion, A and B at first might have excited no common system. In such circumstances, the subject would look at the words, "think" about them (that is, A and B are persistently active, with a varying fringe activity), until the facilitation on C

---

* It seems likely that there is a great deal of conceptual activity that is unreportable (and so "unconscious") in human thought: above all, in what can be called intuitive judgments (Hebb, 1946a). Despite reliable and predictable verbal responses in the recognition of emotion, for example, a subject may be quite incapable of saying what considerations determined his choice of terms. There may, consequently, be concepts in man that do not have a verbal element, just as there are in animals. On the other hand, it seems quite clear that many concepts are fundamentally and essentially verbal—the "core" is a word or other symbol, without which the concept could no longer be an element in thought (function as a neural system). If we recognize, first, that there are nonverbal concepts, we must recognize secondly that some concepts are verbal only.

from some one of the fringe activities suddenly becomes liminal, and the relationship A–C–B is "perceived."

Evidently such changes are what has been called, in the psychological literature, a "restructuring" of thought; and the sudden activation of an effective link between two concepts or percepts, at first unrelated, is a simple case of "insight" (p. 158). This is a topic that will be discussed more fully in the following chapter. The mechanism of the sudden perception of new relationships is, I propose, the one that has just been discussed, in its simplest form.

This account does not, however, sufficiently recognize the orderly, directed, persistent feature of the phase sequence that leads to insight: a problem that presents major difficulty (Humphrey, 1940), and is considered in the following chapters in the treatment of attitude, motivation, and pleasure. For the present theory, insight is a "chance" combination of facilitations from different phase sequences; but this is chance only in a limited sense, and given phase sequences that persistently return to a certain conceptual activity (motivation to solve a problem) the ultimate occurrence of insight may be quite predictable. What may not be predictable is just when the occurrence will take place, and this of course agrees with the facts of behavior.

MAZE LEARNING

Having considered how a certain kind of human learning might occur, in which the subject given one word must reproduce a second, let us next see how the theory of phase sequences and "concepts" can be applied to the learning of a rat in a maze.

Suppose that we have a simple maze with a starting point A, three choice points B, C, and D, and a goal E. As the rat runs the maze correctly, the environmental or sensory sequence would be A, B, C, D, E. The phase sequence determining such a run cannot be so simple, because of the central facilitation that may arouse a conceptual activity in advance of its sensory arousal ("expectancy"), and equally may arouse the concept of a point that has already been passed ("recollection"). This can be diagrammed as

$$A\text{–}e\text{–}b\text{–}B\text{–}a\text{–}c\text{–}C\text{–}\cdots E$$

where the small letters represent centrally aroused complexes
(each corresponding to the recognition of a point in the maze),
and capital letters represent sensorily aroused ones, or actual
perceptions.

The existence of the procurrent items in the sequence above
is both an inference from the neural schema and a reasonable
inference from the literature on expectancy. The recurrent
item (*a* following *B*) is mainly an inference from the schema;
but it is suggested also by the backtracking done by sophisticated rats in a simple maze.

In a long and complex maze, with unsophisticated rats, re-
tracing is usually thought to be simply an error, part of the rat's
effort to reach food as quickly as possible. But in the method
of testing intelligence described by Hebb and Williams (1946),
the rat often acts in a way that suggests something different.
After reaching the food box the animal may turn and explore a
blind alley, or retrace the entire maze (sometimes without a
single error). His return to the food box is usually at a higher
speed than the first part of the run, and he eats enthusiastically—
on the *second* time of reaching food. Behavior is determined
by the central phase sequence, and this means that the sequence
is recurrent as well as anticipatory. Similarly, "mental backtracking" is reported by the blindfold human subject learning a
stylus maze (Woodworth, 1938, p. 143).

Also, when one is finding one's way through an unknown city,
or by compass through the deep woods or at sea, one has a continual awareness of the supposed direction (1) of the goal and
(2) of the earlier route, though the apparent direction of either
may be quite wrong. There are indications in both animal and
human behavior that learning depends on setting up a unifica-
tion of the total situation even when it cannot be surveyed as
a whole. It is not necessary for the learning that an accurate
picture of the situation be achieved (Brown, 1932), only that
the goal-concept dominate the phase sequence, and that each
particular complex in the sequence corresponding to a correct
run reliably evoke the next complex, with the resultant recognition of the direction of the next choice point.

As an illustration: when driving to the neighboring city, 18
miles away by a winding route (on a modern highway, that is,

on which all the turns are very gradual), I persistently feel that the part of the highway on which I am at the moment leads nearly straight toward my objective. When a bend in the road approaches, the apparent direction of the city changes; each turn is remembered, inconsistently, as a turn toward the goal, except when two turns are close together. I am unable to list all the different segments of the route from memory, in the right order; all I can do reliably is make the right turns at the right time.

This proves nothing, perhaps, except that I am easily confused; but it illustrates the point that a series of correct responses can be organized into a smooth sequence under the influence of a goal anticipation without requiring that the subject (whether rat or man) have any accurate or detailed image of the total situation. The phase sequence determining such behavior need not be so well organized that it can run off complete without sensory support. As I start driving, it consists of little more than an awareness of the starting point, the goal in a certain direction, and the next distinctive point in the route.

How is the sequence established? It will be clear, from the facts reviewed in the early part of this chapter, that the half-grown or adult animal comes to his task with an elaborate conceptual organization ready made, and that the learning is a modification of this to fit the particular properties of the new situation. Before one can attempt anything like an explanation of adult learning, therefore, it will be necessary to find out much more about the ontogenetics of behavior. The experiments reported in the following chapters hardly amount to a beginning at this task; until they are carried much further a discussion of the details of maze learning must be speculation only. The experiments referred to suggest, for example, that much of a rat's learning to run a maze is done in his home cage, before he ever enters the maze at all. What I propose to do here and in the following chapters is outline the *approach* that is implied by the theory and define the problems that it raises for research.

One of these problems is the development and control of hunger. Experimental evidence presented later (p. 193) indicates that there is an important element of learning in hunger.

It is not always enough to have an animal lack food in order to get him to eat. At the same time, the analysis of the control of eating made by Morgan (1943) shows that no simple learning formula will provide for the known facts. This problem, then, must be left to one side for the present. Assume here that the foundations are laid: the rat put into the apparatus will eat food when he finds it, will move about until he does find it, and has

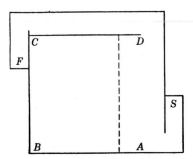

FIGURE 17. A simple maze problem, the simplest of those used in the method of testing rat intelligence, that is briefly described in Chapter 11. S, starting box; F, food; A, B, C, D, points in the maze. The line C–D represents the single barrier used in this test problem; in the preceding problem, four barriers, differently placed, presented the rat with a more difficult problem. Crossing the broken line constitutes an "error."

become used in preliminary training to the general situation and has organized his perception of room cues, the remote objects that determine perceived position (p. 92).

With a simple problem such as that of figure 17, one of those used in a rat "intelligence test" (Hebb and Williams, 1946), learning takes from 1 to 5 trials. In this method the food box is always in the same place, but there are movable barriers that are changed for each test, so the rat is used to finding food by a different route each day. With the problem shown, a bright rat is likely to enter the error zone *BC* once or twice, and then make no more mistakes, following the route *A–D–F* consistently.

At the point *A*, the rat's behavior on the first trial is determined by his experience with preceding problems. He has sometimes found food by going toward *B* followed by a right turn, sometimes toward *D* followed by a left turn, and always in the general region of *C* and *F*. At *A*, accordingly, the phase sequence is variable (unique at any one moment, but changing from one moment to another as "meaning" varies—p. 133). With each phase sequence, there is a selective influence on the motor system, determining head-and-eye movement toward *B, C,* or *D*. Further, the phase sequence is dominated by two things: an anticipatory concept or expectancy of reaching food, and perception of the rat's present place in the maze. Each two conceptual complexes are linked by activity of the cortical motor system facilitating not only movements of the head but also locomotion. The latter facilitation is not always liminal, but when it is liminal the rat runs, in the direction determined by the earlier movement of head and eyes.

The sequence of events, as the rat reaches *A*, might then be as follows: perception of *A*—expectancy of food, with orientation toward *C*—running—perception of *C*—expectancy of an alley leading to *F*. No alley appears, and either of two things may result.

1. The first possibility is that the controlling phase sequence is not strongly established and readily gives way to another which determines a different direction of movement. Expectancy was not confirmed; the original phase sequence has not been reinforced by a corresponding sensory sequence, and the probability of its occurrence when the rat next arrives at *A* is—at most—not increased. On a second trial, the run may be toward *D*. Now the expectancy of an alley beyond *D* is reinforced sensorily. The individual phase in the phase sequence is aroused both by a sensory and a central facilitation, strengthening interphase facilitations and so increasing the probability that on a third trial the rat will go from *A* direct to *D*.

2. As the rat approaches *C* on his first run, the second possibility is that the phase sequence determining this behavior is strongly established, with a strong motor facilitation. The end of the cul-de-sac not only fails to provide sensory reinforcement for the phase sequence but disrupts it. There is a conflict between the original phase sequence and a new one aroused by contact with the end of the cul-de-sac, which has been associated in earlier experience with a right-about turn. This conflict may appear as an emotional disturbance (anticipating the

discussion of emotion in the following chapter), and amounts to breaking up a link in the chain of the recurrent organization of the phase sequence. In succeeding trials when the rat reaches the point A in the maze, the phase sequence may be, as before, perception of A—expectancy of food, with orientation toward C—anticipation of C. But the anticipatory concept of C is now linked with a disruption of cortical organization. The cyclical series A–C–F–A–C–F, and so on, is broken up, permitting another cycle A–D–F (originally less strongly established) to occur instead.

This, in outline, is the approach to adult learning that is suggested by the phase-sequence hypothesis. As I have said, there are large gaps in the evidence, and when these are filled in the hypothesis may be found to need serious modifications. It has not made use of motivation or insight as special processes independent of the phase sequence, because these with emotion seem already subsumed by the hypothesis. I shall try in the following chapters to show how such processes may be dealt with in more detail.

7. *Higher and Lower Processes Related to Learning*

The course of learning is rarely a smooth accession of motor skill, or a closer and closer relationship of response to some particular environmental event, as the learning process goes on. Learning curves, for the individual animal, show great fluctuations from day to day—now backsliding, now sudden improvement. It is only by averaging the results from a number of animals, trial by trial, that one can manage to get a simple curve showing steady improvement with practice.

It is usually considered that these fluctuations are caused by a number of factors that are independent of learning and of each other. Just what factors are invoked depends on the individual writer and his theoretical point of view. In general, they include (1) processes that guide and strengthen learning: physiological needs and motivations (in one kind of theory), or such things as attention, expectancy, and insight (in another); (2) processes that weaken or disrupt learning, such as emotional disturbances; and even (3) the innate processes of instinct that are thought to take the place of learning.

The question of differences in the learning of different species has already been broached. Amplifying this topic will also serve to fill in some of the more important details in the account of learning that has been outlined in preceding chapters. In the present chapter, accordingly, the "higher" processes of consciousness and insightful behavior will be discussed together with the "lower" factor of instinct, and, more briefly, the relation of these to emotion and motivation, leaving a fuller account of the latter processes to following chapters.

ENDURING SELECTIVITY IN CENTRAL ACTION: ATTITUDE

An important aspect of an animal's behavior is the occurrence of periods of directed behavior, in which one kind of action appears only, or in which responsiveness is to one kind of stimulation. This selectivity appears to be like the selectivity of attention but lasts longer and is less specific. It might be referred to as attitude, interest, or intention (though these terms may be objectionable), to distinguish it (1) from the more briefly lasting attention, and at the same time (2) from the stable selectivity that may be either inborn (and referred to as instinct) or established by slow learning, and remains unchanged from one day to the next. The behavior discussed here is behavior in which responses are now to one class of stimulus, now to another, in the same environment.

At a purely descriptive level, this aspect of behavior must be considered when one attempts to deal with species differences. It seems first that the duration of the selectivity—the amount of time likely to be spent continuously in one kind of activity—may vary for higher and lower species. Periods of spontaneous play are shorter in the rat than in the dog, and still shorter than in man; the period of emotional disturbance following momentary stimulation seems progressively shorter as one goes down the phylogenetic scale; and so on. Secondly, the number and variety of the distinctive forms of behavior involved is greater in higher species—the number of recognizably different attitudes or interests, that is, is greater. And, finally, the variability of action that still remains selective is also greater in higher species: an aggressive attitude, for example, has a much more variable expression in the chimpanzee than in the dog.

At a theoretical level, it seems further that there can be no explanation of learning and problem-solving in any mammal without reference to the persisting central neural influence that sustains activity in one particular direction. Even in the rat, learning continually shows this selective responsiveness to one aspect or part of the environment. In higher forms, where expectancy has been most clearly demonstrated, it seems often to be organized by an expectancy of a particular reward or goal. This is clearly not sensory but a conceptual process (to which, however, sensation must continually contribute).

To account for a series of responses to the environment in which a lasting central influence is evident, it would be convenient to be able to think of reverberation in some thalamo-cortical system, acting without interruption to influence other cerebral systems in a particular way for extended periods of time. But this is at the least unlikely. Even if such a system were unexposed to external disturbance, simple reverberation without afferent support cannot be expected to last more than a fraction of a second (Lorente de Nó, 1939). The schema of neural action on which the present theory depends has made it appear that there is no constant, uninterrupted activity determining behavior, no one enduring pattern of neural firing, but a continual fluctuation. If the theory up to this point is to be accepted, a selectivity of behavior that may last for minutes or longer must be ascribed to some other limitation on the variability of firing pattern in the cortex. How might this occur?

First, there may be classes of associated cortical activities. Because of having occurred together frequently, each activity in a class *A, B, C, D,* and so on, would facilitate other activities in the same class more than those in another class *L, M, N, O.* Arousal of any one activity *A* would then arouse others *B–C–D–A* · · ·, but none of *L, M, N, O.* Each letter here stands for a conceptual activity, or phase cycle, not a cell-assembly action. The duration of each phase cycle might be a matter of seconds; of the series of cycles (or conceptual series), correspondingly longer. This would be one mechanism of a persisting attitude, with a mainly intracerebral origin. Its maintenance might also be contributed to by sensation; the behavior would amount to a seeking out of certain stimulations rather than others, and these might be such as to reinforce the selectivity of further response.

But secondly, if the initiation of one of these protracted and selective conceptual series involves some lasting bodily condition such as lack of food, which in the presence of a particular environment sets up an expectancy of eating, the expectancy might dominate the series and have a further organizing influence. (The assumption is that hunger pangs, or a low level of blood nutrients, would have a selective effect on the limen for the conceptual activities determining eating. This assumption will be discussed later, in relation to the problem of hunger.) If A then stands for the expectancy of eating, and B, C, D for conceptual activities associated with eating, the series might be A–B–A–C–A–B–D–A, and so on, with A in a dominating role. Thus a lasting bodily state might repeatedly induce a conceptual activity whose frequent recurrence would act to organize a conceptual series and restrict its content. This second mechanism presumably would make possible a longer duration of attitude than the first alone.

The duration of a self-maintained activity, as contrasted with an activity that is frequently reinstated sensorily, depends on the complexity of the system in which it occurs. A simple closed circuit may reverberate for perhaps 0.001 to 0.05 second; the cell-assembly, in which an alternating reverberation is possible (by-passing refractory transmission units), has been assumed to be capable of activity for periods as great as half a second (p. 74); a phase cycle, or sequence of recurring assembly actions, might then endure for perhaps 1 to 5 or 10 seconds (the apparent duration of conceptual processes in man). I have assumed in the preceding paragraphs that a series of such cycles or concepts might last for minutes or longer and constitute a transient attitude. A greater complexity does not ensure a longer persistence of self-maintained activity in the system, but may permit it; and at the same time it permits or depends on a greater variability of specific content from moment to moment. In the conceptual class A, B, C, and so on, A facilitates B, C, and D. A temporarily high limen in B at the time of A's activity would not prevent continuance of selective behavior, since C or D may be aroused by A if B is not. The idea in essence is that a conceptual series A–B–C–D–A–B–C–D, and so on, might have a greater duration, at its maximum, than A–B–C–A–B–C, and so on.

In a higher brain, accordingly, in which more assemblies are organized by learning and may occur in more varied combinations, the upper time limit of a selective central influence is greater and the selectivity at any one moment is less specific.

The anatomical factor here is both absolute size of the association areas and the A/S ratio (p. 124). This provides some rationale for the observed relation between (1) phylogenetic level and (2) the complexity and duration of attitude and interest. The problem dealt with here has not of course been solved. It will be returned to in Chapter 9.

Now the behavior that shows this sort of control is the behavior that is called conscious or voluntary. These two terms are not in good standing in modern psychology, and yet they refer to an important psychological distinction: not only for the clinic, where it is fundamental, but even in the experimental laboratory, where for example the differences in conditioning voluntary and involuntary responses are well known. It is not important whether one is to continue using the words conscious and voluntary in psychological discussion; it *is* important to have the distinction to which they refer made explicit, and to be able to deal with it theoretically.

Let us start by recognizing that the distinction is not between discrete, unrelated states but between the extremes of a continuum. The important thing is to define the continuum, not to decide just where a line should be drawn to divide one end from the other, or even to divide it at all.

The preceding discussion of attitude makes a theoretical definition of "voluntary" and "conscious" possible, and, just as important, draws attention to what seems to be the empirical meaning of these terms, quite apart from theory. For the present theory, a voluntary act is one that is determined by a phase sequence or conceptual series with some duration in time, to which both sensory and central facilitations contribute constantly. These sequences are recurrent as well as anticipatory, so the voluntary act is influenced by immediate memory and set as well as by an expectancy of the future—particularly, an expectancy of the immediate consequences of the act. This theoretical definition is considered also to cover the adjective "purposeful"—from the point of view of *mechanism,* there is no apparent basis for distinguishing "voluntary" and "purposeful" (the distinction in usage may actually be a distinction between the circumstances in which a single kind of process occurs).

Empirically, a voluntary act appears during periods of selective responsiveness, conditioned both by earlier stimulations (the influence known as set) and by present stimulation. The influence of present stimulation is not always obvious, since the act is not necessarily initiated by an environmental event. It becomes evident, however, whenever an environmental change occurs during the act that would change its effect. There is at once a variation of muscular pattern that is such as to tend toward a constant end effect. This muscular variability with a single result has been called "motor equivalence" by Lashley (1942a). It is an essential mark of the voluntary act (and is essentially the only meaning of the adjective "purposeful").

The form of an involuntary act is characteristically not a function of set, or any preparation of the subject by instruction or the like (Hilgard and Marquis, 1940). It is determined by the stimulation of the moment plus the general physiological condition of the animal, and does not show motor equivalence. The *occurrence* or *strength* of an involuntary response may be subject to the influence of set, as when ghost stories facilitate a startle reaction, but the startle is involuntary as long as it maintains the characteristic rigidity of pattern. The distinction is of course between two ends of a continuum, not attempting a sharp separation of two totally different kinds of behavior. Some involuntary acts may show "purposeful" motor variability, or vary in pattern as a function of set, but the more they do so the less certain the classification must be.

Consciousness then is to be identified theoretically with a certain degree of complexity of phase sequence in which both central and sensory facilitations merge, the central acting to reinforce now one class of sensory stimulations, now another. The cortical organization consists of a diffuse firing in a succession of assembly actions or phases that are organized first in phase cycles (conceptual activities) and then in series of such cycles that maintain a selective influence on behavior for appreciable periods of time, but always with the possibility that the current organization may be changed or disrupted by an unusual sensory event. The limen for the unusual, that is, remains low. The unresponsiveness to some stimuli that is characteristic of the conscious animal is always for familiar features of the environment. Finally, this organization is opposed to the intrinsic organization of infancy and sleep (p. 121), and appears to be maintained by the constant sensory flux to which motor activity contributes. It is rarely possible for any prolonged period of unchanging sensory pattern (when sleep or catalepsy is likely to ensue).

Empirically, in behavior, the most important mark of consciousness is the continually changing selective responsiveness to different aspects of a familiar environment, the *unchanging* responsiveness to unusual or unexpected events, together with the continual presence of "purpose," "means-end-readiness" (Tolman, 1932), or motor equivalence. Another mark might be the occurrence of "operants" (Skinner, 1938), or actions not initiated by an environmental change. However, these occur also in earliest infancy, in very primitive organisms, and in sleep, and so do not very clearly distinguish a conscious from an unconscious animal.

MODES OF SENSORY-CENTRAL INTERACTION

The chief need left by this discussion of attitude, or enduring selectivity of central action, is a more detailed treatment of the interplay of sensory and central facilitations. I have said that the phase sequence persistently escapes from a direct sensory control. But this by no means implies a total lack of sensory influence, at any time. By "direct" control is meant that association-area activity is determined by the pattern of immediately preceding sensory stimulation; since this activity determines behavior, a direct control would mean that with any given sensory stimulation an animal would respond in only one way. This, as we know, does not occur in higher animals in a familiar environment. At the same time, it is quite evident that there is a continual influence, of some kind, from sensation.

Defining this influence in its various forms raises a number of problems. The schema of neural action made the mode of sensory-central interaction explicit as far as momentary excitations are concerned, but new difficulties appear when one is dealing with lasting central activities and a series of sensory events. Some of these are handled reasonably well in the phase-sequence hypothesis. Others remain as problems for experimental investigation. They can be defined here and at least related in a general way to the hypothesis.

At each point in a conceptual series, the ensuing activity is determined by the total pattern of sensation at that moment and by the residue of facilitation and negativity from the preceding central activity. In general terms, this means that there are three possible ways in which sensory and central facilitations may interact. (1) They may conflict, producing phase sequences that are mutually incompatible; (2) they may have unrelated effects, tending to set up independent phase sequences in parallel; and (3) they may reinforce one another's action, both facilitating the same subsequent pattern of cortical action.

The second and third of these possibilities are the subject matter of later sections, dealing respectively with the relation of attention to learning, and the role of expectancy in a skilled motor performance. The first possibility, a conflict of facilitations, is related to the problem of emotional disturbance.

THE RELATION OF EMOTIONAL DISTURBANCE TO LEARNING

The original idea of emotion was probably a reference to the demons that now and then disturb ordinary behavior. Demons or no, let it be observed that this was an inference from *behavior,* demons (including the soul itself) not being easily seen by most people.

Very much later a quite different idea appeared, and is still current. Emotion is now generally thought of as an awareness, a distinctive conscious process that is quite separate from intellectual processes. This notion has led to a good deal of confusion, for it has gradually become clear that no such distinct kind of awareness exists (a surprising unanimity of psychological opinion has been reviewed elsewhere—Hebb, 1946a). In this sense, the term emotion has lost much of its meaning. Further, it is meaningless as referring to any momentary muscular or visceral response, for here also no distinctive pattern can be found (Dashiell, 1928).

But it is still true that emotional disturbance exists, and can be recognized as a long-term deviation from an animal's ordinary behavior (Hebb, 1946a). Something causes it. I propose that we return to an earlier, behavioral, interpretation (but substituting neural events for the demon), and define emotion as the neural process that is inferred from and causes emotional behavior, with no reference to consciousness. However, for reasons to be considered later (Chapter 10), we shall be concerned in the present chapter with *emotional disturbance* rather than emotion.

Now as to mechanism. The causes of rage (Hebb, 1945a) and fear (Hebb, 1946b) are extremely diverse. Unless we are to suppose not only that there are a number of separate emotions, with independent neural mechanisms, but also a number of angers and fears, each equally independent, we must ask what these various causes can have in common.

One answer to this question has already been suggested. Emotion may be a disruption of cortical organization, which could occur in several ways: the occurrence of incompatible phase sequences; the absence of a sensory facilitation that has always contributed to the phase sequence; "pain" stimulation that can be supposed to be innately disruptive of cortical activity (see Pain, Chapter 8); and chemical change of the blood content, altering the rate of firing of individual neurons and so disrupting a cortical organization that is fundamentally a matter of timing (see the discussion of hunger and addiction, Chapter 8).

Some of the points involved must be left for later chapters. For the present we are concerned with the possibility of a sensory disturbance of the phase sequence, as an influence on learning. In the schema of neural action, it was concluded that a neuron, or group of neurons acting as a transmission unit, must be expected to enter into more than one assembly if the assemblies are organized at separate times. In two assemblies involving some of the same transmission units, a simultaneous activity would not be possible. The activity of one would prevent activity in the other.

In assemblies of cells that are frequently active at the same time, fractionation eliminates from each the transmission units whose action is interfered with or controlled by others (pp. 88–9). In a familiar environment, therefore, such conflict would not usually occur. The same process would also gradually eliminate conflict occurring at the first presentation of a new stimulus combination; as the combination is repeated, the make-up of one or both conflicting assemblies would be changed by fractionation, and the disorganization would decrease. The strange combination would now be familiar and no longer disturb behavior.

In the phase sequence, the central facilitation from one phase on the next is usually not specific, since sensory events occur in a variable order; and, because of this, the facilitation from one phase cycle or conceptual activity is not completely specific but tends to arouse one of a *number* of subsequent activities (pp. 133–4). This flexibility of the phase sequence permits a considerable variation of the sequence of sensory events without a disturbing effect. Such considerations do not permit one to say how great an environmental change must be to produce an overt disruption of learned behavior; but the assumption that disruption of cortical organization may vary in extent *and* in duration, and the assumption that the disruption when it has more than a momentary duration means some incoordination of effectors, make sense of the emotional disturbance that appears when environmental change is great enough. What I postulate is that, up to a certain point, lack of correspondence between expectancy and perception may simply have a stimulating (or "pleasurable") effect (Chapter 9); beyond this point, a disruptive (or unpleasant) effect.

The changes that disturb behavior must also include the absence of a customary stimulation. The phase sequence is a continual interaction of central and sensory events, and the background facilitation from a constant sensory facilitation must affect the composition of the cell-assembly, during its organization, and be a factor in its later arousal. The absence of a customary stimulation will be "strange," and exciting. But again, if this condition is repeated, a reorganization of assemblies and change of interassembly facilitations can re-establish the stability of the phase sequences concerned. With a varied experience, the animal will become less and less dependent on any particular stimulation that is not a constant feature of his environment.

This is an effect of learning on emotion, a mechanism of

adaptation to the strange. The converse is a directing influence of emotional disturbance on learning, a problem raised in the preceding chapter. It has been concluded that the prompt learning of maturity depends on a phase sequence with a recurrent organization. Disruption of any link in this disrupts the whole. Hypothetically, the disturbance varies in extent: when it is widespread, it may cause deterioration of other, alternate, phase sequences—an extreme instance, presumably, being the paralysis of terror. With less marked disturbance, the effect may be to prevent activity in the current phase sequence only, and so allow another integrated sequence to take its place. In this case, there would be little sign of emotion in the behavior, although the disturbance would have its effect in a changed direction of response.

This is supposed to be the way in which emotional disturbance guides learning. An example will make the proposed idea more definite. Let us suppose that a rat is being trained to avoid a darkened door, by being given an electric shock, and being allowed to find food when he goes through a lighted door. As the rat makes his choice, suppose also that his perception is of the relation of the right-hand door to the distant environment, the relative brightness of the door not arousing a conceptual activity. He approaches the right-hand door, and receives a shock. The disruptive effect here is on the conceptual series: *perception of present place—door A—expectancy of food—door A*, and so on. Back at the choice point, an alternate series involving perception of *door B* can displace the first, the rat goes through *B*, and finds food. The effect of this one trial is to teach the rat to go through the left-hand door. Unless there was a conceptual activity aroused by the different lighting of the two doors (p. 106), this trial would not set up a tendency to avoid a *darkened* door as such.

Subsequent trials, with the dark door sometimes right and sometimes left, would accumulate a disruptive effect on *both* "spatial hypotheses." But on any trial when the conceptual content includes phases determined by the brightness or darkness of a door, an association of darkness with shock can begin to be established. With this, the phase sequence will alternate between: *perceiving present position at the choice point—per-*

ceiving a brighter door—expectancy of food; and *perceiving present position—perceiving darker door—expectancy of food.* The first is reinforced by a corresponding series of sensory events, as the rat runs under its influence; the second is unreinforced, and, further, disrupted. When this stage has been reached, the final learning of the task should be prompt.

This, and the discussion of frustration in the preceding chapter (pp. 138–9), represent in principle the role of emotional disturbance as it might affect learning in an experimental study. A special relationship between emotional disturbance and learning will be dealt with in Chapter 10, which tries to show how learning might develop typical rage and fear, with their distinctive patterns of organized response, out of what (in its origins) is simply disorganization.

INTENTION AND ATTENTION AS FACTORS IN LEARNING

We can now turn to the second way in which sensory events may be related to the current central process. The first possibility, just discussed, is that the two may conflict. The second is that they may neither conflict nor reinforce one another, but determine independent phase sequences. This possibility bears directly on the commonly held opinion that no learning is possible without intention to learn, no memory of a sensory event unless it was "attended to" at the time of its occurrence.

It is often supposed also that there is an extraordinary unity about attention—that one can attend to one thing, or to another, but not to both at the same time unless the two are a single unit, responded to as a whole. These conclusions need qualification.

There is actually no evidence to justify the general statement that learning never occurs without the help of attention (though my treatment in the following paragraphs assumes that this is in a sense true). It has been shown repeatedly that a subject may not remember what he did not attend to, or that he remembers more with attention than without. But other things are apt to be remembered to some degree. It is common experience to remember details of a situation to which one did not, appar-

ently, attend—when the details later have become relevant to
one's thought. Similarly, the remark made by someone else,
when one is reading, may not be noticed or responded to in any
way, as far as anyone can tell; and yet 30 seconds or a minute
later one becomes aware of the remark and answers it. The
event was remembered. Are we to postulate an "unconscious"
attention to explain the fact? If so, attention is no longer unitary—even if there were no other objection to such a treatment
of the problem.

This is a point, it seems, at which such theoretical conceptions as attention and intention are no longer precise enough.
I have already defined attention as the immediate facilitation
from one phase, or assembly action, on the ensuing one, with
no implication that two such processes might not occur at the
same time. In so far as the term is to be useful, it should be
restricted to this very brief central facilitation. "Intention"
seems a still more slippery term, related to "attitude" but with
the implication that motor components are prominent. If the
term has any intelligible reference to neural function, it must be
to the *enduring* selectivity of central action that was discussed
earlier.

There is a certain unity about this action, but not at all the
absolute unity with which attention, at least, has been endowed
in the older literature. There may be more than one phase sequence in the association areas at one time. The discussion of
meaning in the preceding chapter implied also that the phase
sequence may continually tend to branch out in more than one
direction, ameba-like—some, or all but one, of the branches eventually becoming abortive for lack of the general background
facilitation of "attitude" that determines the general trend of the
phase sequence. I have emphasized the idea that the motor
facilitation of phase or phase sequence may be subliminal; and,
to the extent that attention has the unity it is supposed to have,
the unity may consist of a control of the motor system by one
phase sequence only, when two or more run in parallel. Even
then it should be remembered that we very often carry on two
familiar activities at the same time. Arguing and driving a car
will do as an instance; neither seems possible without "attention."
It certainly seems that the unity of attention has been exag-

gerated, and the phase-sequence hypothesis, at least, suggests that it may often be multiple.

Memory for an incidental stimulation then may occur because the stimulus has aroused a second phase sequence without interrupting the prior dominant one. This can happen only with familiar activities and perceptions, and only if a phase sequence *is* aroused by the stimulus in question; and, in agreement with the importance of meaning for learning, only if the incidental phase sequence has a certain degree of complexity and persistence. There will consequently be plenty of occasions on which "unnoticed" events are not remembered, as the experimental literature has shown.

So also with the effect of set on perception (perceptual set is another aspect of the phase sequence, closely related to attention). It has been shown that in certain circumstances one sees what one expects, or is set, to see. But this is no general rule, else one would be incapable of seeing the unexpected. When a stimulation is sufficiently strong or distinctive from its background, and familiar or composed of familiar parts, it will be capable of initiating its own phase sequence, regardless of what other phase sequence may be going on at the moment. (If the new phase sequence is incompatible with the pre-existing one, startle or emotion may result.) The sensory event is capable of taking control of central action, just as in other circumstances the central action is capable of reinforcing one sensory event at the expense of a second.

MOTOR EQUIVALENCE

Two modes of sensory-central interaction have been discussed. The first, a conflict of sensory and central processes, was regarded as a source of emotion; the second, in which a sensory event has central effects that neither support nor conflict with a prior central process, was treated as accounting for certain kinds of incidental or unintentional learning.

The third mode, an active support and direction of the phase sequence by sensory processes, is at least as important. It is best exemplified in the phenomenon of motor equivalence: a variability of specific muscular responses, with circumstance, in such a way as to produce a single result. The phenomenon and its importance for the theory of learning have been emphasized by Tolman (1932), Hull (1934), and Lashley (1942a). At the same time, theory has not handled the problem very successfully. It is usual, and in practice necessary, to define an animal's response in terms of its end effect: the rat reaches and enters the food box, the chimpanzee's hand makes contact with a stimulus plaque and moves it. It would be impractical to record the actual series of muscular contractions that brings such an event about. But one must not then assume that a common end result means a single pattern of contractions.

It is necessary to use very special conditions of training indeed to establish a "learned response" as a constant *effector* response. A rat trained to depress a lever to get food may do so from any of several positions, in each of which the muscular pattern is different. He may climb on the lever; press it down with the left forefoot, or the right; or use his teeth instead. Very often, all that can be predicted after the response is learned is that the lever will be moved downward. It is not necessary here to multiply examples of such behavior; it will be evident to anyone who cares to watch animal or man carry out a learned response. With long overpractice it may seem at times that the subject has settled down to the use of a specific muscular pattern, an exact duplication of his movements from one trial to the next. When this happens, however, it will rarely be difficult for an experimenter to change that pattern and still observe approximately the same end effect. (Timing, however, may be disturbed.)

In general, the variability of motor pattern in a hungry animal's reaching food becomes comprehensible if it is supposed that the behavior is determined both by an expectancy of the immediate result of each movement and by a continual perception by the animal of his own locus and posture at each stage of his response. The problem has sometimes been discussed as though the motor variability occurred despite a constant set of stimulating conditions. Sometimes, indeed, it may, when there are two or more equally efficient modes of solution available to the animal. But the variability characteristically appears when there is a variation of the animal's initial posture, of his locus with respect to the goal, or of intervening barriers.

The animal must perceive his own posture and his place in relation to the goal; and his behavior must be affected by this perception as much as by his anticipation, expectancy, or foresight of the state of affairs in which food has been found in the past (remember that we are discussing the variability that occurs after learning is established). The monkey that must lift the lid of a box to get food has an expectancy of the lid's rising in contact with his hand; and he knows where his hand is at the moment. The question then is, what neural mechanism will account for a movement of the hand direct to the edge of the lid?

Here we have an example of motor variability in a learned response that is about as simple as can be. The muscular pattern of response, when the hand moves direct to the lid, is obviously different for each initial position of the hand. We cannot, I believe, accept the solution of this problem proposed by Hull (1934), in his concept of the habit-family hierarchy, for he assumes that the final muscular event in the sequence is constant, though earlier ones can vary. Here even the final pattern of contractions is variable, depending on the monkey's position with respect to the box; and we know that the monkey will open the box despite changes of distance from the retaining cage or changes of the box's orientation.

But we can follow the general line of Hull's argument and assume (I believe, necessarily) that an earlier generalized learning of infancy provides the basis of response, together with an expectancy by the animal of his own later movements. The only thing that seems common to the various responses is a perception of the hand in final contact with the lid of the box. In the normal primate, this perception certainly involves vision. I assume thus that the movement of the hand primarily follows an eyemovement that fixates the point of contact. Part of the learning of infancy must establish an ability to move either hand or foot directly from any point to the line of vision. Given this, the behavior is explained, my earlier schema of neural action having provided for eyemovement in perception.

The schema has also shown how the cortical process controlling eyemovement might be subliminal for actual movement and yet have a facilitating action on other cortical processes. The first learning involving manipulation, in the normal primate, would be accompanied by eyemovements; but later, in man at least, there is a capacity to move the hand to the point one only "thinks" of looking at. In this case it is assumed that the motor process is subliminal for eyemovement, but still with an integrating function for other cortical processes. My account is explicitly in terms of visual processes, but I will add that the arguments applied (in the earlier schema) to eyemovement might as easily have been applied to movement of the hands; so this does not mean that the variable motor behavior of the congenitally blind is unaccounted for, or different in principle from that of the seeing. Further, there is plenty of evidence to show that the space perception of the congenitally blind is radically defective (Senden, 1932)—which justifies an emphasis on the role of vision in the manipulative activity of normal subjects.

In the specific example discussed above, the hungry monkey might equally raise the lid of the box with either hand, with a foot, or even with a stick: all that is necessary to account for the behavior is that the foot, or the end of the stick, be seen in its present position, that its end position in contact with the lid be conceived of in advance, and that the monkey have learned to move it from one position to another presently being looked at.

More complex patterns of manipulation require only a number of such steps: a continual awareness of the present position of the hand (or foot), and at each point in its movement an anticipation of the next point in space to which it must be moved. At all times the behavior is under the control of these two things; the muscular pattern of the half-grown or adult animal is so variable simply because the subject is not learning now to make specific movements (as he is earlier, perhaps, when he is learning to bring the hand to the line of vision), but learning a relationship, an association, between perceived environmental events. This makes adult learning primarily perceptual; but, in accordance with the developmental changes of learning discussed in the preceding chapter, it still leaves a great emphasis on the motor learning of infancy, which frequently can be regarded as purely sensori-motor.

In this section I have tried to present my solution of a ubiquitous, fundamental psychological problem. It would be wrong to leave the impression that the solution can be regarded as complete. The solution says in short that motor learning at maturity is perceptual learning in the first place. It also says that a true motor learning of infancy is an essential element in the equivalence of adult responses. The adult who learns to operate a slot machine learns, that is, that a quarter's moving into and falling down a slot will be followed by the appearance of a package of cigarettes. He learns that the depression of a certain lever starts the motor on his car. He does *not* learn to make a certain series of muscular contractions; but, once the perceptual relationship between depression of the lever and starting the motor is learned, an earlier infant learning is enough to provide for the adult's being able to put a hand or foot—or a stick—in contact with the lever and depress it. But all this is in very general terms.

I believe that such conceptions will be a good basis for the study of motor learning, but it should be emphasized that the study is still needed—that nothing more has been provided than a rational approach which may or may not be found adequate in the long run. The discussion has said nothing about the changes of skill with practice. What is their nature? Are they to be comprised in the conception of changes in the cell-assembly due to an increased frequency of activity? Does the subject revert to his first clumsiness of performance when he is required to use a new muscular pattern? Does his *perception* of the situation change with practice, or his muscular timing—or both? Above all, *is he still responding to the same cues?*

We still have a great deal to learn about the modification of motor performance with practice. It should be said explicitly that this discussion has not attempted to cover the development of motor skills involving a precisely timed series of movements, nor such learning as that demonstrated by Sperry (1947), which monkeys are capable of and rats are not.

INSIGHT AND HYPOTHESIS

A somewhat different aspect of the problem of learning, and its phylogenetic correlations, brings us to the question of intelligence or insight in learning, and the related question of "hypotheses" in animals. These ideas have occasioned a good deal of dispute, and some confusion, in the psychological literature.

The analysis of animal intelligence, by controlled experiment, has been a slow process. Mainly, the trouble has been to make the transition from an earlier subjective psychology (resorting freely to the notion of "mind" or conscious awareness as an *agent* in behavior) to an objective theory of neural action, without oversimplifying the facts.

If an animal shows "intelligence" in his learning and problem-solving (Hobhouse, 1915), "ideation" (Yerkes, 1916), or "insight" (Köhler, 1925), can the fact be dealt with in a strictly monistic theory with no hidden thread of animism? It was hard to find a way of doing so. What psychologists really needed, of course, was a physiological mechanism of thought to supplement their frankly physiological treatment of afferent and efferent mechanisms. The failure to suggest any intelligible mechanism of insight, or ideation, led to two sharply opposed points of view. One group—in general, those I have called learning theorists—began by denying that the facts were what they seemed, and argued that insight must be reducible to simple learning.

The other group—in general, the configurationists—proceeded by urging the need for a better theory of learning, whether it could be found at once or not, and continued a search for evidence to show that the need existed; that animals do have ideas, or insight, or intelligence.

As a result of this undertaking, psychological knowledge made a considerable advance. I am going to argue that such notions as insight have a limited value, and that something with more precision will be needed for the further development of theory; but it should be recognized that these ideas have led to an improved analysis of animal behavior and its qualitative variations at different phylogenetic levels.

Besides Hobhouse, Yerkes, and Köhler, already mentioned, Lashley (1929a, 1938b) and Krechevsky (1932) should be listed as making major contributions to the difficult problem of analyzing animal intelligence; and Tinklepaugh (1928), Tolman (1932), and Cowles and Nissen (1937), as well, for demonstrating expectancy (a form of ideation) in animals and establishing the value of this notion in the theory of behavior.

It is generally conceded by now that learning involves more than the gradual reinforcement of responses originally made at random. "Sophisticated" learning theory recognizes the fact as much as configuration theory (Spence, 1938, 1940). Learning is often discontinuous; error curves show sharp drops without warning, and the kind of error that is made on one day may be quite changed on the next. The great disagreement that still continues in psychology does not concern the existence of some factor producing these effects, but its nature: how it operates, and how it is related to learning as such.

Let me make this a little clearer. In the first efforts to be rid of anthropomorphism in animal psychology, "learning" theory said something like this: When an animal is faced with a new problem, we can avoid any reference to intelligence or comprehension and describe the cat's attempts to open the door of a problem box (for example) as at first a series of random movements. Some one of these movements will eventually open the door, by chance. The tendency to make that movement is then increased because it was rewarded (the "law of effect").

On each trial, the tendency is further increased. Eventually, the cat opens the door immediately—not because of any separate process of intelligence or understanding, but because a specific association has been built up. This is the "naïve" theory of learning by trial and error; it is no longer maintained, largely because of the work of Hobhouse, Yerkes, Köhler, Lashley, and Krechevsky, together with an important analysis by Adams (1929) and the later work of Thorndike (1931). But it had its value. It was a necessary corrective to the vagueness of other theories, and though in development it has become rather vague itself it still represents a line of thought that insists, rightly, that theory must aim at definable conceptions and a clear statement of its original assumptions.

The configurationist attack on the earlier, "naïve" learning theory proceeded as follows. A search was made for tasks to set an animal, of just the right degree of difficulty for each species to demonstrate the operation of intelligence. The task must neither be so easy that the animal solves the problem at once, thus not allowing one to analyze the solution; nor so hard that the animal fails to solve it except by rote learning in a long series of trials.

With a problem of such borderline difficulty, the solution may appear out of a blue sky. There is a period first of fruitless effort in one direction, or perhaps a series of attempted solutions. Then suddenly there is a complete change in the direction of effort, and a cleancut solution of the task. This then is the first criterion of the occurrence of *insight*. The behavior cannot be described as a gradual accretion of learning; it is evident that something has happened in the animal at the moment of solution. (*What* happens is another matter.)

The second, and essentially more important criterion, involves a comparison of species. To the human observer, a monkey's efforts to get at food may at times appear utterly stupid. It is one of the great achievements of modern psychology to show that the stupidity is always a matter of degree, and to make a beginning at saying what intelligent behavior is, in its various manifestations. The description of intelligence is a more difficult task than it sounds; this is one matter in which appearances are really deceptive. The box-stacking of the chimpanzee, for example, is a very clumsy performance indeed. The chimpanzee has no notion of statics and must pile his boxes by trial and error until finally they will stay piled and bear his weight (Köhler, 1925). But comparison with other species reveals a considerable intelligence in this performance, nonetheless. The dog is not low in the intellectual hierarchy, and yet he is unable to see the possibility of moving even one box to a place where he wants to climb. Physically, this is possible for him, though piling one box on another may not be. The failure is thus intellectual.

The dog, again, shows his great superiority to rat or hen in his skill at passing obstacles, and reaching a goal by the shortest route (psychologically a more brilliant achievement, more insightful, than it may sound).

It is often said that most human beings never think, and go by habit instead of intelligence. The dullest person who can earn a living in this culture, however, continually functions at a level well above the chimpanzee's—complex as the chimpanzee intelligence is—and it becomes nonsense in view of this fact to suppose that a man could ever get along solely by routine without the continuous operation of whatever it is that we call intelligence. This becomes even clearer when one looks at cases of aphasia. As we shall see later, aphasia is by no means a mere loss of speech; the patient has lost something else as well, an intellectual capacity that no chimpanzee will ever have and one that every normal person has and uses continuously (even if he never sits down, puts his chin in his hand, and announces in so many words that he is about to "think"). Without the study of insight in animals, we should not have been able to see how much is involved in ordinary, everyday behavior that seems elemental in its simplicity but is not.

There is an unsuspected degree of intelligence in even the simplest behavior of normal man. Krechevsky (1932) established a similar point for the rat, showing that apparently simple learning is more than an uncomplicated acquisition of stimulus-response connections; it involves "hypotheses" as well.

Briefly, what Krechevsky found is this. A hungry rat is given a repeated choice of two doors, one left and one right, one white and one black (for example). The white door is sometimes on the left, sometimes on the right; and food is to be found by going through one of the doors (the other being locked). With such a problem, the rat does not choose at random. At first he is almost certain to persistently try the door on one particular side, trial after trial; and later, to try the other side in the same way. Still later, he may alternate, one left, one right, and so on; or choose always the white door, whichever side it may be on, until finally one of these systematic attempts at solution is consistently rewarded. The rat is then said to have had a series of hypotheses, and it is clear that his learning is not a gradual strengthening of responses that were at first made at random. The behavior is stupid enough, by primate standards, but it involves intelligence of a kind and it throws a good deal of light on the behavior of higher species.

DIFFICULTIES OF THE CONCEPTION OF INSIGHT

So much for the value that psychology has drawn from the conceptions of insight and hypothesis (the latter evidently a form of insight itself). We can next ask in what respect such conceptions are unsatisfactory, and the inquiry will lead us to recognize a complementary value in the "learning" theory that has been consistently opposed to the theory of insight.

From the first the meaning of insight and hypothesis, as exact scientific terms, has been left confused. Their connotations obviously are anthropomorphic and unfortunate. This might have been less important if the terms had been well defined, but they were not.

"Hypothesis" has been defined as a form of behavior: a set of responses that deviates systematically from a chance performance. This will not do at all, as Prentice (1946) has pointed out; it confuses cause and effect. An hypothesis, it becomes evident, is something postulated, hypothetical, *inferred* from behavior.

Psychology has sometimes in the past been too free in postulating special processes to explain behavior. Now it is doing penance by going to another extreme, scientifically just as sinful. This current misconception of the scientific method makes any hypothetical entity somehow disreputable. Psychologists now seem to feel that it is risky indeed to depart from statements of fact; nothing should be mentioned that is not "operationally" demonstrable. Thus in another field we find emotion defined as a bodily reaction, which it is not; or neurosis as a set of neurotic symptoms. At the same time, the context in which such definitions appear makes it obvious that the writer has in mind something inferred from behavior, not the behavior itself, just as the rat's hypothesis is inferred. It is completely necessary to keep out of such confusion (in the first place; and in the second place, to realize that neither operationalism nor logical positivism really discourages inference or postulate but only seeks the rules by which inference is to be made).

Insight, again, has on occasion been defined as a sudden change in behavior, or as a conscious experience that one may have in solving a problem. Neither definition gets at the real meaning, which is that of a causal factor in behavior.

When this is clear, it becomes clear also that there is no need to say that a rat has an hypothesis only when he makes a series of systematic choices. The hypothesis might endure only for one trial, or part of a trial; though it could not then be directly detected, it would still exist. In the same way, it is not necessary to limit insight to those occasions such as when a chimpanzee, at first failing to reach a banana outside his cage, suddenly turns away, looks for a stick, and rakes in the food. These are the occasions on which it is evident that something has changed in the animal and has led to a solution. But if it is insight that solves a problem following error, it is no less insight when an animal makes no errors and sees the solution at once. When the solution is seen at once, there must be at least as much insight as when the solution is delayed.

In this sense "insight" is fully equivalent to "intelligence"— the term that Hobhouse used. The term insight therefore seems to have two references, one to an enduring factor in behavior, the other to a variable one. Both "insight" and "intelligence" are probably unsatisfactory terms—it will be seen in the following chapter that they may be hard to distinguish from some uses of "motivation" except as different aspects of the same thing—but it may be suggested that, if they are to be used, "intelligence" should refer to the enduring aptitude, the existence of a causal factor in problem-solving that may or may not lead to the solution of a particular problem; "insight" to refer to its operation in the particular instance.

There is still a difference of opinion as to what this causal factor in behavior is, and how it operates: is insight or hypothesis— or, in the broadest terms, intelligence—something distinct from the mechanism of association? And here, I think, we must take a long step toward the position of those theorists who originally denied the existence of insight but who now, like Hunter (1934) or Spence (1940), are concerned to show that it can be derived from a theory of learning.

Whatever insight is, we now know that it continually affects the learning of the adult mammal. This has been maintained by those who have emphasized the value of insight as a theoretical conception; if we grant it, the conception does not become more valuable for theory, but less.

We find at once the need for more precise conceptions. The original value of the notion of insight lay in the distinction between intelligent and rote learning. Now all behavior involves intelligence, and the distinction is a matter of degree: *how much* insight (or intelligence) is present? Further, if all learning is insightful we can no longer speak of insight as if it were a separate process and distinct from learning.

The conception of insight was a valuable first approximation, but a first approximation only. Insight is not distinct from attention or expectancy (which are also first approximations), just as it is not wholly separate from rote learning. Postulate insight to account for the discontinuity of a sudden improvement in learning, and sooner or later we shall have to add other postulates (temporary forgetfulness, frustration, loss of interest, and so on) to account for the regressions and disruptions that also occur in learning.

It has already been seen how insight, as a sudden perception of new relationships, can result from the simultaneous activity of two conceptual cycles in adult learning (pp. 133–4). This need not be elaborated further; the new relationship is a change of the phase sequence, and each phase sequence has its distinctive motor facilitation, so the change would be evident in a discontinuity of behavior—the actual evidence from which the insight is inferred.

Apart from the special case of a sudden solution following failure, insight is essentially the phase sequence itself, the autonomous central factor in behavior. It is that which makes behavior directed, instead of random; the mechanism that is both anticipatory, adjusting behavior to an obstacle *before* the obstacle is reached, and recurrent, so that the chimpanzee, trying to reach a banana, *remembers* the stick he saw a moment before, goes and gets it, and rakes in the fruit.

Phylogenetic differences of insight are thus the differences in the complexity of phase sequence that is possible in the brain of a higher or lower species. The lack of insight in the earliest learning of primates becomes comprehensible, since the phase sequence must first be organized.

Also comprehensible is the slowness with which insightful learning develops in these species, by the very mechanism that makes their ultimate level of behavior more insightful than any other. The larger association cortex of primates, both in absolute terms and in A/S ratio (p. 124), means a slower establishment of sensory control, and so a longer time to set up the phase sequence and insight. At the same time, in a larger association cortex the number of assemblies of cells that can function as separate closed systems will be larger. This means that the higher animal at maturity will see any particular situation in a larger number of ways. The comparatively small sensory projection means also that the phase sequence can escape from complete sensory control more frequently, and for longer periods, so that the insightful behavior of higher species is less a response to the immediate environment and more an integration of serial stimulation from situations that cannot be surveyed as a whole.

Finally, all this explains how insight depends on experience and yet is not a simple, direct result of learning, or the operation of specific habits (Birch, 1945). The perception of new relationships discussed above is usually not delayed, but immediate; the animal put into a new situation will perceive its parts as familiar, and as related in a meaningful way (that is, by the mechanisms discussed on pp. 130–4). The behavior is then insightful, as an organized set of responses to a new total situation. An organization that consists of a *new* temporal combination of elements which themselves were organized by experience obviously depends on learning, but is not learned. Heredity sets a limit to the amount of development of the phase sequence and determines the principles of development, but experience is necessary as well.

THE RELATION OF INSTINCT TO LEARNING

The problem of instinct is the correlative of that of intelligence, or insight, and of learning. It has just been seen that intelligence is not an entity that is quite distinct from learning; and we may now see that instinct, also, is not to be cut off sharply from either.

The term "instinctive" will be used here to refer to behavior, other than reflex, in which innate factors play a *predominant* part. Empirically, this is behavior in which the motor pattern is variable but with an end result that is predictable from a knowledge of the species, without knowing the history of the individual animal. This class of behavior must be recognized, and we are no farther forward by coining a new name for it. "Instinct," however, is less useful. It suggests a special agent in behavior, just as "intelligence," "insight," or "drive" may. Essentially, we are involved here in the difficulties of the constitutional-experiential dichotomy that are discussed later (Chapter 10). We must distinguish, conceptually, the constitutional factor in behavior from the experiential, but there is presumably no mammalian behavior that is uninfluenced either by learning, or by the constitution that makes some learning easy or inevitable. We need not consider (1) that instinctive behavior is sharply distinct from other behavior, or (2) that it involves some special process that is radically different from those involved in other behavior. Ultimately, our aim must be to find out how the same fundamental neural principles determine all behavior.

There is a means at hand for attempting this. Consider first Lashley's (1938*a*) useful distinction between reflex and instinct. A reflex may be defined as innately determined behavior that is controlled by stimulation of a specific group of receptors and takes the form of a predictable set of muscular contractions. Instinctive behavior, on the other hand, is more than a complication of reflexes, although of course it involves reflex elements. It is not always controlled by a specific stimulation, and may in fact be aroused by a perceptual lack ("reaction to deficit," Lashley, 1938*a*; "vacuum activity," Lorenz, cited by Tinbergen, 1942). Instinctive behavior does not consist of a predetermined sequence of muscular contractions, and yet it has a constant and predictable end result. The spider of a given species will spin a web highly specific in design, though the movements necessary to produce it vary with the distance of the objects to which it is attached; the kind of movements and number of trips made by a bird in building a nest (in those cases where the design can be foretold from the bird's species) depends on the kind of material used and the shape and size of the crotch or ledge that supports it; and so on.

All this means that the behavior, though it cannot be called reflex, is still continually under sensory influence, more or less direct. At each stage in the construction the muscular activity varies with circumstances and is such as to produce a certain perceptual effect. This indirect sensory control is demonstrated whenever accident destroys part of the structure. The muscular activity then does not continue in a predetermined sequence, but reverts to an earlier stage, in such a way as to restore the missing part. Since the behavior is continually responsive to such events, it must be under afferent influence throughout.

Now we have already seen that the A/S ratio, or proportion of association-area cortex to sensory cortex, affects the directness of sensory control over behavior and the promptness with which it can be established. In order to make this relationship meaningful for lower forms in which the cerebral cortex is absent or insignificant, let me speak here of the proportion of internuncial to afferent cells (association/sensory *cortex* being only a particular case of this more general relation). A massive afferent system and a negligibly small internuncial one implies an immediate and direct sensory control of behavior, and one in which any particular sensory constellation would tend to have a single effect on behavior. The larger the internuncial system, the more slowly can a sensory control be set up. A sensory control that is established only with experience, however, means that there is an element of learning in the subsequent behavior—and so an increased variability. Thus, with phylogenesis, the predictability of instinctive behavior would steadily decrease as the ratio of afferent to internuncial tissues becomes smaller.

This does not of course explain why the instinctive behavior of any one species takes the particular form it does; but at this point we do have an explanation for the fact that instinct is most evident in lower species, in which internuncial structures are small, both absolutely and relative to afferent ones. Before specific instincts can be explained, much more must be known about the behavior in question and the finer nervous structures that determine it. It is a reasonable expectation that the knowledge will be obtained, and that the explanations when they are found may be much simpler than one would suppose.

To show that the expectation is not chimerical, that this does not simply dodge a crucial difficulty for the present theory of behavior, let me cite the earlier discussion of the "spatial hypothesis" or position habit. The position habit of course is not called instinctive by psychologists, presumably because it only shows up during the course of learning; and learning and instinct are supposed to be incompatible. But it is so completely predictable in the rat that it might well be called instinctive. Before a means was found for analyzing the behavior (Hebb, 1938*a*, 1938*b;* Hebb and Williams, 1941) it almost appeared that the rat had a thoroughly mysterious capacity for perceiving compass direction. It turns out, however, that his behavior is simply response to the most constant stimulation of his environment (pp. 91–5).

Eventually, explanation at a similar level can be expected for other species-predictable—or instinctive—behavior. It is almost certain that the mysteriousness of the processes determining instinct is generally overrated; when analysis has finally succeeded, the process turns out to be quite different from what it appeared at first (Schneirla, 1948). The nest-building of the pregnant rat may be the simple result of a disturbed temperature control (Kinder, 1927). The visual preference of the honeybee for complex flower forms appears to come from the fact that these forms produce a greater flicker frequency in the bee's eye (Wolf and Zerrahn-Wolf, 1937) and thus have a maximal stimulating value. The preference is not at all an innately determined perception of a particular pattern as distinct from other patterns. There is still an innate factor, but a much simpler one than it seemed at first to be, and the evidence does not require the assumption that some special and complex process is involved in the behavior. Another example is the apparently purposeful behavior of the newly hatched loggerhead turtle in going directly to the sea (Daniel and Smith, 1947), which, however, is phototropically determined.

I have already suggested that "instinct" may fundamentally involve some learning even at lower phylogenetic levels, if the kind of learning is strictly limited and if it may occur in a matter of seconds (pp. 113, 115). This is quite speculative at present; but one thing is clear, at least, that there is no evidence to justify the *a priori* assumption that the control of learned and the control of instinctive behavior are quite separate processes (Beach, 1937, 1939). In mammalian behavior, certainly, we cannot separate out one group of responses that are innate, others that are learned. Constitution (the factor of heredity) may dominate in determining some properties of behavior, experience (the factor of learning) in others; but there must be a gradation from the one type to the other.

In the same way, instinct is not a separate process from intelligence or insight. It is intelligence, or insight, that is innately limited in variety. An animal low in the scale must see a particular situation in a particular way because of the overwhelming mastery of afferent over internuncial activity, whereas a higher animal with a more variable association-area activity, under imperfect sensory control, may see it in a number of ways and respond accordingly: now to one property of the stimulation, now to another. But the mechanism of response is not different in the two cases, except in complexity.

This should be more explicit in one respect. It has been argued that *expectancy* is an essential explanation of motor variability in mammalian behavior. At the same time, it must be clear that instinctive behavior does not involve an expectancy of its remote biological results (this would be the worst sort of teleology).

I have said that instinct and intelligence differ in complexity of mechanism; and one of these differences is in the degree of anticipatory central action that is called expectancy, and in the temporal extent that expectancy can span. At the lowest levels of instinctive behavior there can be no expectancy whatever, where the internuncial activity is completely under sensory control, without intermission. At intermediate levels, there may be an expectancy of the immediate consequences of the single act in an instinctive sequence (the bird may have an anticipatory concept of a twig placed in a certain part of the nest, before it is actually laid there; the rat whose pups have been scattered may possibly retrieve them under the influence of an expectancy of perceiving them in the nest again). Even this degree of expectancy, however, involves learning; expectancy must be an association between a present state of affairs and one that has followed that state of affairs (or similar ones) *in the past*. The temporal span of expectancy in instinctive behavior must vary, from zero to the human expectancy of pregnancy and birth nine months after copulation (and the difficulties of rearing a child for twenty years after that). To the extent that expectancy occurs it must represent an influence of learning, not an inborn knowledge of the future.

8. *Problems of Motivation: Pain and Hunger*

This chapter and the next aim at a broader picture of the problem of motivation than is usually drawn when neural mechanisms are to be discussed. The biologically primitive hunger, pain, and sex drives are important in behavior, but these are not all of motivation. In particular, there is an essential problem in play, and in the changes of motivation that occur when bodily condition (including humoral factors), and the environment in all important respects, seem unchanged.

In the present chapter, motivation is dealt with first as a theoretical conception, particularly in relation to the theory of learning; we can then try to see how the more general ideas that result from this examination are to be applied to the specific problems of pain and hunger. The following chapter will be an attempt to round out the picture by treating the spontaneous variations of motivation that appear in such different aspects of behavior as play and sleep.

THE CONCEPT OF MOTIVATION

The term motivation concerns two distinct questions: (1) why is an animal active at all, and (2) why does the activity take a particular form? Ostensibly, (1) is the fundamental question. Actually, it is (2) that modern psychology is usually concerned with—though the writer who uses the term often seems to be talking about (1).

We have seen (Chapter 1) that early experiments with nerve-muscle preparations made it easy to think of the nervous system as inert, unless stirred up by some outside irritant. It then seemed necessary to look to sensory stimulation for the cause of any muscular contraction.   Now, however, it is known that the central nervous system is continuously active, and the necessity has disappeared, as long as we do not ask about the patterning, the timing, of muscular contractions.

In fact, most of the musculature itself is continuously active (for whatever reason), and the chief problem the psychologist is concerned with, when he speaks of motivation, is not an arousal of activity but its patterning and direction.   Little time is spent discussing the source of an animal's tonic contractions and random movements, in the first stage of a learning experiment.   What we have usually wanted to know is why the random movements change and become directed.   The main question for psychology concerns the *timing* of muscular contractions, not their arousal.

There seems still to be some confusion on this point.   Psychological theory sometimes seems to be still looking for some extraneural irritant to account for maternal behavior, for example.   In an earlier day, it was thought that maternal behavior must be aroused by the sensory stimulation of distended breasts, male sexual behavior by distention of the seminal vesicles; the search for food or water by stomach contractions or dryness of the throat; and so on.   Without exception, these ideas have broken down.   Desire to drink can occur when the throat is moist or anesthetized, eating continues after the stomach has been surgically removed.   This point has been adequately discussed by Morgan (1943).   The older manner of thinking persisted, however.   As contradictions accumulated, a tendency appeared instead to postulate "central receptors" instead of peripheral ones as motivating agents.   By this device, it is still possible to discuss motivation as a *stimulation* that arouses activity of a particular kind.*

---

* The implied distinction between theories of motivation does not merely concern use of the word "stimulation."   It is more than a question of definition.   The sex hormones, for example, are known to have a primary action on the central nervous system.   This action might be either (1) by exciting specific cells—in which case it would be meaningful to speak of a "central stimulus"—or (2) by changing the excitability or frequency prop-

It has frequently been proposed that all behavior, and all learning as well, must be motivated. The proposition may be taken in either of two ways. First, we can treat it as a fundamental assumption. We then infer the existence of a motivation, known in no other way, when an apparently unmotivated act is seen. (When the rat reaches food and, before eating, goes off to some other part of the maze, he must have an exploratory drive or motivation. He has a hoarding motivation when he gathers pellets of food without eating them.) Such a use of assumption is often legitimate; what it really does is define motivation or drive, and such definitions have been an essential part of the scientific method. But here the term motivation becomes so broad, when all the deviations of behavior are considered, as to have little usefulness, except as a convenient reference to the fact that behavior in general is directed and organized. The fate of the term becomes that of insight when all learning is said to be insightful.

Or, secondly, one can define motivation independently, as an extraneural bodily condition or an irritant that acts on specific neural cells. The proposition that all behavior and learning are motivated then becomes untrue, on the existing evidence, and with it the proposition that learning is directed only by motivation.

And yet there is an important problem here. In its simplest terms, the question that has bothered psychologists is this: An animal learning to solve a problem makes some right movements, some wrong. What is it that reinforces the right ones and discourages the wrong? Why are the right ones remembered in later trials, the rest forgotten? This has been a persistently baffling problem; and its solution is essential to the theory of behavior.

The difficulty may seem trivial. If so, however, the reader may be begging the question by saying to himself, in a common-sense (and animistic) way, that the animal of course can *see* that one of his movements has had the right effect, others not. But if the question is asked, What neural processes constitute the

erties of a system of cells, without being able to induce activity in the system directly. If the term "stimulus" is to have a determinate meaning, it should not perhaps be overextended to include the second reference (2).

"seeing"? the solution is evidently as far off as ever. The simplicity of the question of reinforcement, or selective retention of some responses and not others, is like the simplicity of the fundamental postulates of mathematics that are taking centuries to ravel out. A simple common-sense answer has no value whatever; the first thing one has to do is get away from the animism that saturates common sense. Having done that, there remains an uncommonly difficult scientific problem.

What it involves will perhaps be seen best in showing its relationship to Pavlov's theory of conditioned reflexes. Pavlov's failure to solve the problem is one of the decisive reasons why psychologists have had to abandon or change the theory.

THE THEORY OF CONDITIONED REFLEXES

Pavlov (1927, 1928) formulated a simple rule for the occurrence of learning. Any stimulus that acts repeatedly at the same time as a response will form a connection between the cortical cells involved. Subsequently, the stimulus will be sufficient to arouse the response. (The classic example is a bell rung at feeding time: after a number of trials, ringing the bell alone makes the animal's mouth water.) The original or unconditioned stimulus (food in the mouth) has an innate relationship to the response. The substitute or conditioned stimulus (the sound of the bell) has an acquired relationship. The relationship is supposed to be set up in connections from sensory to motor area in the cortex.

This assumption is the keystone of the theory. The theory as a whole is of course much more elaborate, with a number of other assumptions, but I have not oversimplified the point under discussion. An afferent activity at one point in the cortex, and an efferent activity at another point, at the same time or immediately after the afferent one, is all that is needed (with enough repetitions) to establish a sensori-motor connection; and all behavior is determined by such connections, innate or conditioned.

This means that all acts at the time of a particular stimulation would be associated with it; and the act that has most frequently occurred would be most strongly associated. Now in problem-solving, or any learning situation in which a number of acts are possible but only one rewarded with food, "mistakes" occur frequently. Often, in the first trials of maze learning, the same mistake is repeated much more frequently than the "correct" behavior. Yet the net effect is that mistakes vanish, and leave only the correct responses. Instead of being associated, the act that occurred frequently is forgotten. Its elimination, also, can hardly be ascribed to an inhibition. Pavlov defined inhibition as producing a cessation of activity and leading directly to sleep. But repeated mistakes do not tend to make the animal drowsy or motionless. They are often followed by an increased activity.

Maze learning, however, is not a very clearcut instance. For the theorist, a more crucial argument has been found with Pavlov's own procedure, and minor variations of it. This argument is in the fact that the conditioned stimulus does *not* evoke the unconditioned response, as Pavlov implied (Zener, 1937; Hilgard and Marquis, 1940).

The conditioned response is not a duplicate of the unconditioned, but something new. All the elements of the unconditioned response may be there, but if so some of them are minimal, and the total pattern is significantly changed. When the dog hears the bell, he does not usually make eating movements, with his nose in the food dish, until the food itself appears. Conditioned and unconditioned stimuli, then, are not just two ways of arousing the same combination of effectors.

If the objection is made that no one would expect the dog to chew and swallow until food shows up, the answer is that Pavlov's theory says he will. The conditioned stimulus is supposed to set up connections *with any following effector activity;* and eating movements follow the conditioned stimulus as much as the secretion of saliva does. If the critic of this argument points out that a dog is too intelligent to respond to a bell in such a way, he is really criticizing the original theory. A separate intelligence, to tell the dog when his conditioned reflexes may operate, would be a *deus ex machina.* One may suppose that the dog is intelligent, but not that his intelligence is separate from his neural activity; and we are examining the theory that all higher neural activity consists only of conditioned reflexes.*

---

* The physiological and clinical literature suggests that a number of workers still feel that Pavlov's conclusions are a factual statement of what

MOTIVATION IN CONDITIONED-REFLEX THEORY

Now let us see whether some principle of motivation can be added to the theory and thus make it able to account for the facts. Hull (1943) has made this addition explicitly to show why "right" responses become conditioned, others not. Hull proposes that those acts that are immediately followed by a "need reduction" are retained; and he believes that with this change Pavlov's main structure can stand, successfully reducing behavior to a set of conditioned reflexes. That is, Hull has introduced motivation as a supplementary principle. The idea was used earlier by Thorndike, who called it the law of effect.

The law of effect is roughly this. An act that is closely followed by satisfaction, pleasure, or comfort will be learned; one that is followed by discomfort, forgotten or eliminated. Partly because of the result of subsequent experiments, Thorndike's (1931) later treatment is not in terms of pleasure and pain but refers to a very vaguely defined condition of "belonging" as the factor that makes for learning. The response that will be re-

is known to go on in the cerebrum. It is important to see the difference between the facts he demonstrated and the theory based on the facts. Pavlov has deservedly had a great influence on psychology, and his theory has not been rejected because it is too physiological but because it does not agree with experiment. Apparently, Pavlov isolated himself from the contemporary literature, and his theory took no account of psychological discussions after 1900. Criticism at present is based on later experiments, physiological as well as psychological.

The main points can be listed briefly: (1) Simultaneous sensory and motor activity is not enough to establish a conditioned reflex when the motor activity is directly aroused by stimulation of motor cortex (Loucks, 1935, 1938). (2) The data published by Pavlov do not agree with his theory of a slow irradiation of excitation across the cortex (Loucks); and the strychninization method reveals a kind of cortical organization quite unlike what Pavlov assumed (Hilgard and Marquis, 1940). (3) Irradiation, by which Pavlov accounted for stimulus generalization, does not provide for generalization of stimulus intensity (Hovland, 1937; Hilgard and Marquis), and the theory also has considerable trouble with the kind of pattern generalization illustrated in figure 1. (4) Finally, it does not seem possible to translate Pavlov's system into terms of problem-solving or serial learning without serious modification. This is the point discussed in the text.

membered and repeated is one that "belongs" in the total situation. Unfortunately for the older and simpler law, punishment by electric shock for the *right* response may help the subject to learn as much as punishing wrong ones. Mild punishment for either may be better than no punishment, whether with animal or human subjects (Muenzinger, 1934; Drew, 1938; McGeoch, 1942). It is therefore not possible to say that discomfort always acts to eliminate a response. The vast literature on this issue, and the facts that led Thorndike along with many others to abandon the original law of effect, have been surveyed by Postman (1947).

To substitute belongingness for comfort and discomfort makes the law of effect extremely vague and says nothing about physiological processes. The theory presented here can be regarded as an attempt to fill in the gap left by Thorndike's treatment of this point. In psychological approach his ideas are in many ways identical with those that were outlined earlier (Chapter 6). They constitute, that is, a theory of association, as distinct from a theory of conditioned responses, in which an association may be between autonomous central processes instead of between afferent and efferent processes.

Hull (1943) has attempted to deal with the problem in another way, essentially by going back to the earlier law of effect without the vagueness of Thorndike's later formulation. Unfortunately, he has done this by retaining the idea of motivation as stimulation, and of all learning as consisting fundamentally of sensori-motor connections.

"Effect" becomes a reduction of need, and a need is defined as follows: "When any of the commodities or conditions necessary for individual or species survival are lacking, or when they deviate materially from the optimum, a state of *primary need* is said to exist" (Hull, 1943, p. 17). Further, the need affects behavior by stimulating special receptors, either peripheral or in the brain itself. (Hull actually starts out by saying that they "probably" do [p. 18] but thereafter takes the point for granted; his argument and diagrams deal with stimulations of particular hypothetical cells.)

What the theory says in short is this. All behavior is determined by sensory stimulations. All learning consists of forming or strengthening S-R connections. An S-R connection is strengthened whenever the stimulus, S, and the response, R, occur together and *some need stimulation, N, decreases at the same time.* The S-R connections amount to conditioned reflexes. What Hull has done, in this modification of Pavlov's ideas, is to postulate a special class of stimulus that (1) must be present before learning can occur, and (2) must then decline. The decline, and the decline only, determines the occurrence of new connections. No way is suggested as to how the decrease of stimulation promotes the formation of connections.

To Hull's system as a whole vigorous objections have been made by other psychologists. Its weakest point, and clearest departure from the facts, is in the treatment of motivation as biological need.

In the first place, the apparently clear and precise definition of a need will not hold water. A need occurs "when any of the commodities or conditions for individual or species survival are missing." One of these needs is "the occasional presence and specialized reciprocal behavior of a mate." But the absence of a mate cannot excite sensory receptors. By this definition, evidently, another need is for testes in the male animal and simultaneously ovaries and uterus in the female. Species survival is not possible otherwise. But lack of testes is not usually a motivating condition, nor can it excite receptors. The injection of male hormone would not affect the needs of the animal, as defined, since he is still incapable of fertilizing a female and contributing to survival of the species. Yet his behavior sexually is that of a normal animal once the injection has been made.

The preciseness with which "need" has been defined is illusory. It is a biological statement that does not coincide with the psychological conception Hull had in mind when he wrote. First, then, it must appear that Hull's reformulation of the law of effect is not the precise postulate that it was meant to be. A system of deductions that makes repeated use of it may have a fundamental flaw.

Secondly, the law of reinforcement, as it is now called, is open to the same criticism that made Thorndike abandon the law of effect in its earlier form. As we have seen, pain does not always act to eliminate a response. Incidental learning, unaccompanied by reward or the avoidance of punishment, does occur. According to the theory, the rat in the maze should learn nothing about it until one of his responses is accompanied by a decrease of hunger or thirst, or escape from electric shock, or some similar reward. In actual fact, when he is allowed to run in the maze without reward or punishment the rat learns a good deal about it. This is shown by the small number of errors he makes later, when he is put into the maze hungry and allowed to find food there (Blodgett, 1929, cited by Hilgard and Marquis, 1940).

The third point is the extreme narrowness of the range within which needs as Hull has defined them must operate. This is a return to the old idea that the only sources of action are such things as hunger, thirst, pain and concupiscence, with mother-love thrown in for good measure. Stimulation that is frequently associated with one of these is supposed to acquire the same kind of influence. It is not denied, therefore, that man or animal may act without prospect of primary reward. But according to the theory these secondary motivations can be set up only by repeated coincidence with a primary one, and the connection between the two must be frequently reinforced thereafter.

Emphasis on biological needs seems to limit animal motivation much too narrowly. It excludes conditions that clearly influence behavior and learning (Allport, 1946, p. 342), and it may have the unfortunate effect of preventing the student who takes the hypothesis seriously from seeing many of the facts of behavior. For example, children spontaneously avoid dark places even though no unpleasant event has been associated with darkness (Chapter 10). They can *learn* what to do to make their parents come into the bedroom and turn on the light. But the "need" here is for more stimulation, not less. It is the theoretical preoccupation with hunger, thirst, sex, and avoidance of pain, as sources of motivation, that has led many child psychologists to deny that there is any emotional response aroused primarily by perceptual lack, such as darkness. Nevertheless, the evidence is strong that such responses occur.

The point has been labored enough. As far as one can see at present, it is unsatisfactory to equate motivation with biological need. Theory built on this base has a definiteness that is very attractive; but it may have been obtained at too great cost. To follow this line seems to require either a persistent disregard of facts such as those referred to above or the continual addition of new assumptions as soon as one gets beyond the subject matter of the classical experiments on rote learning in animals.

It is clear of course that the primitive drives of pain, hunger, and sex are often of overwhelming importance. We need an approach to motivation that neither minimizes these things nor fails to provide for the unrewarded learning that also occurs when the animal's belly is full and his sex drive satiated.

AN ALTERNATIVE TREATMENT OF MOTIVATION

The alternative treatment of motivation that is required by the present theory is here introduced in general terms and is made more precise in the following discussion of pain and hunger. This will still have some of the essential points of conditioning theory as developed originally by Pavlov and later by Hull. The differentiation of two stages or levels of learning (first, the assembly of cerebral cells, and second the establishment of connections between assemblies) makes it possible, perhaps, to treat motivation in a Pavlovian way without inserting a special postulate in the theoretical structure. Pavlov necessarily thought in terms of a sensori-motor conditioning; but, with the data available from electrophysiology of the central nervous system, one can conceive of conditioning as the establishment of relations between cerebral neurons (in the first place) and between systems of neurons (in the second). The result, as I have suggested, is a theory of associations; from another point of view, it is a way of incorporating some of the advantages of association theory into a theory of conditioning—a common ground perhaps for Thorndike (1931) or Woodworth (1938), with Hull (1943) or Guthrie (1946).

Learning according to the present ideas consists of a lasting change of facilitations between the activities of specific neural structures. The change results when two structures (single pathways *or* assemblies) that have sufficient anatomical connections are active at the same time. The first learning establishes an organization of individual transmission units into an assembly. But later learning, the kind that is usually studied experimentally, is a change of facilitation between organized systems, a changed interaction between one complex of assembly actions and another. In the terminology of Chapters 5 and 6, learning is a change of relationship between cortical phase sequences—or conceptual activities—because of their having occurred together.

It then follows that the experimenter who wants an animal to learn some particular thing must achieve some control of the phase sequence. In a single environment, the phase sequence may be extremely variable. Putting an animal into a particular situation does not determine what particular conceptual activity will result. Therefore, it cannot determine that a facilitation will be established between the conceptual activities the experimenter is interested in. When the experimenter takes further steps to limit the variety of conceptual activity that will occur in an animal, he sets up a *motivation*. The term motivation then refers (1) to the existence of an organized phase sequence, (2) to its direction or content, and (3) to its persistence in a given direction, or stability of content.

This definition means that "motivation" is not a distinctive process, but a reference in another context to the same processes to which "insight" refers; it also means that the waking, normal adult animal always has some motivation (because of items 1 and 2 in the definition) though its persistence in any one direction (3) may not be great.

If a bodily need is found to limit the variability of central neural action, it can be used experimentally to control learning; but this of course is quite different from saying that the animal will learn nothing unless he has first been deprived of food or injured by electric shock. Without such means of control one is less able to predict what will be learned in a given situation, but one would still expect *some* learning to occur.

Now we have to ask how such bodily conditions can control conceptual activities. First, pain.

PAIN

The relationship of pain to learning has already been taken for granted, in the assumption that certain afferent processes act primarily to disrupt central neural activities (p. 150). Disruptive processes are a general classification that includes more than pain. In most sensory modes there is an intensity limen at which avoidance appears. Below this point, the stimulation may be sought out—that is, it is "pleasant"; above it, the same kind of stimulation produces avoidance and, if the avoidance is unsuccessful, behavioral disturbance. With different kinds of stimulation, the avoidance limen falls in a different part of the intensity range. Pain is not unique, but may seem so partly because there is a great range of intensity above the limen of initial avoidance. Pain, therefore, as a particular class of event, is regarded here as a disturbance originating in the somesthetic afferent system, though its mechanism may be like that of disturbance originating from certain sounds, smells, or tastes.

It should be understood that we are not mainly concerned here with the conscious experience of pain, and consequently that the class of event discussed is not quite coterminous with pain as discussed in the introspective literature. There is, for example, what has been called "pleasant pain," which will not be discussed apart from pointing out that the phenomenon may be exactly parallel to "thrill" or pleasant fear (p. 233).

I class pain then as a disruptive somesthetic event. The disruptive action is usually limited, and is mainly at higher levels in the brain stem or in the cortex. At the spinal level, tissue injury may arouse only integrated reflex responses (Sherrington, 1906). At the thalamo-cortical level, the disturbance must still be focalized, since of course pain is referred to specific parts of the body. Its effects may be widespread, but if the disturbance becomes really general it is emotion, not pain.

With these assumptions, it has been shown how pain might control learning by disrupting one phase sequence, leaving another unmolested. Essentially, this is a limitation of conceptual processes in a given environment. Pain then is a means of channeling motivation, as motivation was defined in the preceding section. It is not a source of learning, from this point of view, but limits and directs it. However, pain does have an energizing effect on behavior, and in some circumstances it appears to facilitate learning directly. To this possibility I shall return.

Now let us see what the assumptions mean concerning pain

itself. There have been in general two theories of pain (Morgan, 1943). In one, pain is not a special sensory mode but an effect of overstimulation of receptors for heat, cold, or pressure. In the other, pain is a sensory mode with its special receptors, peripheral nerve fibers, and conduction paths in the spinal cord. Each of these theories has its difficulties; each has something to recommend it. The two seem to have been thought of as mutually incompatible, and exhaustive: if one is proved wrong, the other must be right. But following up a suggestion made by Nafe (1934),* and making a comparatively small change in each theory, we can find a way of combining them. The combination has the best features of both, and covers certain facts that may be equally destructive of either theory singly.

Against the first, peripheral-intensity theory, is the existence of pain spots in the skin: here a weak stimulation can arouse pain, although a much stronger stimulation elsewhere does not. Pain seems also to depend mainly on the activity of C fibers in the sensory nerve. This in itself denies that intensity is all that matters in pain; but, even more, intensity in neural terms must be a matter of impulses per second, and C fibers are the very ones in which conduction is slowest and which deliver the fewest number of impulses per second to any one point in the nervous system.

However, there are strong arguments against the alternative, sensory-mode theory. If pain is a sensory mode, it is known that its receptors must be free nerve endings, and free nerve endings are also known to mediate pressure. There may of course be two kinds of free nerve ending, histologically indistinguishable. However, very weak or very brief stimulation of pain spots or pain fibers produces no pain; as Nafe has pointed out, this has obliged supporters of the sensory-mode theory to hold that there may be "nonpainful pain."

Also, it is not at all clear that pain can be permanently abolished by clean surgical section of one or two of the tracts only,

* And see Weddel, Sinclair, and Feindel (1948), whose views in some respects are identical with those elaborated here. Wortis, Stein, and Jolliffe (1942) have also anticipated some of this treatment. They suggested that the faster-running impulses in A fibers can prevent C impulses from traversing certain synapses, so preventing pain.

in each side of the spinal cord: there are tracts that are mainly involved in the production of pain, but are they solely involved in it? Finally, there is no specialized cortical area for pain as there is for touch, and apparently no specialized pain nuclei in the diencephalon or lower brain stem: if specialized tracts for the conduction of pain do exist, what do they conduct to, other than the centers of somesthesis?

The suggestion of Nafe, to which I have already referred, is that pain somehow concerns the patterning of central activities aroused by the pain stimulus; and with this it seems that the main contentions of both classical theories can be combined. Let us forget *peripheral* intensity, as the essential determinant of pain, and think instead of a central intensity that could, as we shall see in a moment, be initiated by a weak stimulus in the periphery as well as by a strong one. Let us also suppose that the pain fibers do not inevitably mediate pain; that the slow impulses, and the central connections of these fibers, are such that they are peculiarly effective in producing sudden massive discharges in somesthetic nuclei at thalamic or cortical level, with a widespread effect. This would be pain. Isolated stimulation of a pain spot then would not necessarily produce pain but would usually do so.

It is a highly significant fact that pain is often the result of conditions that must decrease sensory activity, including activity in the pain fibers or their central connections. As Lashley (1938c) has observed, pain is often an accompaniment of injury to the somesthetic system all the way from peripheral nerve to thalamus. In some cases, the pain may be due to irritation; but in many cases there is little basis for the assumption, if the facts can be explained without it. As the work of Adrian (1934) and Weiss (1941a) has shown, an essential function of normal sensation is a regulation of central firing; without control, the firing is spasmodic or with a local hypersynchrony; with it, the cells do not build up to the point of spontaneous discharge but are fired diffusely in a frequently varying pattern. If higher somesthetic nuclei are deafferented, everything we know about neural function indicates that the cells must eventually fire, and fire more or less in synchrony, with massive jolts to other nuclei connected with them. When it is supposed that pain may be a disruptive activity at the cortical level, it must be supposed also that a conceivable source of pain is a decrease or absence of peripheral sensory activity, even in pain fibers. This hypothesis does not specify what kind of disturbance constitutes pain. Evidently there are deviations from normal sensory function, including hypofunctions, that never involve pain; so the hypothesis is certainly not complete. As for pain in healthy persons, the predominantly slow impulses in the sensory nerve may produce pain only (1) because of some peculiarity in the pattern of thalamic activity they arouse, apart from total frequency of impulses in a given part of the afferent tract (*i.e.*, apart from intensity at this level). Alternatively, pain may occur (2) because the slow impulses are peculiarly effective in arousing excessive bursts of firing from the thalamus. Either explanation will suit my more general thesis, though the second is the one I have preferred. But the essential point is this: a theory of pain must provide for the fact that an increase of pain often results from hypofunction in afferent structures.

I have already referred to Lashley's observation, that pain may follow lesions anywhere in the somesthetic system up to the thalamic level. In Head's (1920) classic experiment on the regeneration of cutaneous nerve, hyperalgesia was prominent. According to Boring (1916) the hyperalgesia is not a lowering of the pain threshold. Thresholds, including that for pain, are raised; yet the pain when it does occur may be of extreme severity. Wolff and Hardy (1947, p. 173) make the same point, concerning patients with thalamic lesions. It seems obvious that the rise of threshold means a decrease in the total amount of afferent activity. The pain that is so often felt in the phantom limb (Riddoch, 1941) also seems an obvious accompaniment of a decreased sensory activity. After amputation, regenerating nerves may form neuromas that are a source of sensory irritation. But it is very unlikely that the total of this afferent activity can be as great as would result from the use of the whole limb; and why should pain fibers in the neuroma be more irritable than in the normal limb? Neuralgia, finally, is usually thought of as an irritation, as a hyperfunction that must be reduced by deadening the nerve. But only too often an injection of the nerve fails to work—just as might be expected if the pain, in such cases, is essentially related to a *hypo*function. The original source of the neuralgia must have been a pathological process in the nerve or the nuclei to which it leads. It is highly improbable that a pathological process can increase the efficiency of any fiber, even a pain fiber; is it not more likely that total afferent activity has decreased, and that a disruption of central timing has resulted from an incomplete peripheral control of central activity?

Return for a moment to the older theories of pain. The evidence concerning hypofunction directly denies the theory of *peripheral* intensity. It also makes difficulty for the sensory-mode theory, but a more clearcut argument against the latter is found in the fact that the pattern or combination of stimuli is often the decisive factor for the occurrence of pain. Stimulation of *A* produces pain; of *A* and *B* together, no pain. The clearest example has been provided by Head (1920). Stimulating the tip of the glans penis with water at 45° C. is painful; but the pain totally disappears when the glans is immersed more deeply in the water. Such facts might be accounted for if pain impulses are "inhibited" by other sensory impulses, but this explanation has really grave difficulties.

The difficulties of the inhibition idea are clearest if we consider an organ, such as a sound tooth, that contains pain fibers but has never been the site of pain. We can hardly suppose that there are normal nerve fibers that have never once been active over an individual's lifetime. If we suppose that they are active, but at a low level that is not recognized as pain, then we have conceded that the activity of the pain fiber does not essentially mediate pain; and the alternative is to suppose that an inhibitory action of other fibers has throughout a lifetime prevented the occurrence of pain. It is very doubtful that an inhibitory process can be so uniformly and continuously efficient (p. 212).

It seems in short that the pain receptors in a sound tooth, or in the cornea of an eye that has had no grit in it for months, must have some other function—with weak or brief stimulations, that they are pressure receptors as well. It is still reasonable to think of them as pain receptors if, as it seems, the thalamus innately has a very low tolerance for the activity they initiate; if their action tends innately to result in a disruption of any behavior that is accompanied by tissue damage.

It may be objected that pain is a unique sensory experience, and therefore that it must have its special receptors and central connections which serve no other function. But competent introspective observation has always found more than one kind of pain experience, and Titchener (1920) gives four: prick, clear pain, quick pain, and ache, each no more closely related to

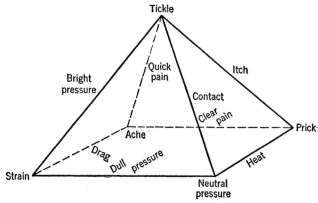

FIGURE 18. Diagram from Titchener, 1920, showing the independence of various kinds of pain, introspectively determined. By permission of the *American Journal of Psychology*, Karl M. Dallenbach, Editor.

another according to his diagram (figure 18) than quick pain is to bright pressure or to itch.* Clearly, the subjective evidence in itself does not establish a separate modality of pain, internally unified, and distinctive from others. How then have we arrived at this impression of uniqueness?

I have already suggested that pain may seem unique because the limen of avoidance in the intensity range of the pain

* Professor Dallenbach, in a personal communication, has pointed out that other evidence may render this account of pain, by Titchener, out of date. I cite it here, however, as showing that competent introspective observation does not inevitably find pain to be a single entity, whatever the conclusion from other experiments may be. Professor Dallenbach has drawn my attention also to his ingenious experiments with Burns, Stone, and Edes (Dallenbach, K. M., "Pain: history and present status," *Amer. J. Psychol.*, 1939, 52, 331–347), which controvert the theory that pain is intensive stimulation of tactual receptors only, but do not appear sufficient to show that it is a separate and coequal sensory mode.

stimulus is so low.   It may also seem unique because the characteristic event causing it, damage to body tissue, is not immediately reversible.   Once the damage is done the stimulation of nerve continues and avoidance does not put an end to it.   It is common knowledge that there are noises that are almost unbearable, although the fact is hard to demonstrate in the laboratory (Miller, 1947).   But one can move away from the noise or cover the ears, at once decreasing the intensity of stimulation.   These conditions must tend to determine a special kind of learning related to pain, with a more strongly marked avoidance and a greater emotional element, even though the mechanism of the disturbance when it does occur is the same in different sensory systems.

Let me say again that this hypothesis of pain is incomplete. Hypofunction often occurs without pain; syringomyelia, a degenerative disease of the cord, provides an outstanding example. The hypothesis is of value in suggesting how pain *may* result from hypofunction, and in reconciling divergent views of normal pain.   Intensity is still a factor, but at the cortical or thalamic level; and the arousal of *C* fibers may still have a special sensory *quale*, not disruptive of behavior at the very lowest level of intensity or duration, but promptly becoming disruptive unless they are part of a much more extensive stimulation that has a thoroughly well-organized central action.   This central organization would be a diffuse firing, and would make impossible whatever pattern of local synchronization it is, in the ventral nucleus of the thalamus, that leads to local disruption in the cortical somesthetic area and so constitutes pain.

It may be proposed that the optimal condition for the arousal of pain without gross bodily injury is a punctate stimulation of the relatively inefficient *C* fibers—being inefficient, they do not readily set up a well-organized central action; and, accordingly, that it is not a complete hypofunction of afferent systems that conduces toward pain, but a decreased efficiency.   Higher somesthetic nuclei then lack their normal degree of sensory control and become hyper-responsive, and yet are still exposed to an intermittent "triggering" from peripheral stimulation.   A complete deafferenting consequently would fully eliminate pain, while pathological changes without complete destruction, up to and perhaps including the nucleus ventralis thalami, would increase it. Specifically, lesions of peripheral nerve would then be considered to have reduced the efficiency of *A* fibers to that of *C* fibers—that is, make them into pain fibers; higher lesions would have a similar effect by reducing the efficiency of *A*-fiber control of thalamic and cortical tissue. It would thus be conceivable also that "quick pain" could be aroused by undamaged *A* fibers, though less readily, since their control is more efficient than that of the *C* fiber.

It is possible now to complete the picture of pain as related to learning, and especially as having a positive value in learning. The psychological entity pain must be a disruptive action at the cortical level, but the pain stimulus has other effects. In the spinal animal, it may arouse only a well-coordinated reflex avoidance (Sherrington, 1906). In the diencephalic animal, it is likely to produce sham rage, with an integrated action of the whole organism (Bard, 1934). It has been seen in the preceding paragraphs that the stimulus that by itself arouses pain may have no such effect when combined with other stimulation. The pain stimulus arouses pain when its central action is unorganized and interferes with other, organized action, but not when it enters into and forms part of an organized neural action.

Pavlov (1928) and Liddell (1944) have shown that the disturbing effects of cutting and burning the dog's skin disappear completely when the pain stimulus is regularly followed by feeding, in the conditioned-reflex procedure. The transformation from typical pain responses to feeding responses was gradual; once it was established, there was immediate relapse when the site of pain stimulation was changed to new parts of the body.

This means that there were synaptic changes in the cortical region in which the focal pain disturbance originally occurred, leading to the disappearance of pain from one region of the body, not from others. In that one region, the pain stimulation now aroused organized cortical activity. This conclusion is meaningful for the observation of Muenzinger (1934) and Drew (1938) that giving a rat electric shock for the correct response (followed of course by food) increases the rate of learning. In Drew's experiments, when the food itself was electrified so that the rat got a shock with every bite, eating was voracious. In such a case, once the central effects of the pain stimulus have become organized, we must regard the stimulus as essentially motivating: just as a blow of the whip may be motivating and energizing to a racehorse that appears already to be exerting himself to the utmost—a further stimulation that adds to the effectiveness of a pre-existent cerebral control of behavior.

HUNGER

The treatment by Morgan (1943) is taken here as a basis for discussing the problem of hunger, with two questions to be kept in mind: how the approach to motivation outlined in this chapter accords with the experimental facts of hunger, and whether it can be of any further value for understanding the behavior involved.

The fundamental problem is to know what controls the initiation and termination of eating (or drinking). Hunger is defined here as the tendency to eat; conscious awareness or verbal report of hunger is important only as a convenient index of that tendency. Eating is not necessarily dependent on the occurrence of stomach contractions, since the surgical removal or denervation of the stomach does not prevent or decrease it. It is not necessarily dependent on blood-sugar level, since hunger is reported when the blood-sugar level has not changed (Scott, Scott, and Luckhardt, 1938). Both stomach contractions and blood sugar are related to hunger, but in no simple way.

The termination of eating also has no simple control. The animal that has been starved eats more than one that is well fed, but the termination of eating comes before the food can have much effect on bodily tissues. A thirsty animal will drink approximately the amount of his water deficit, and stops drinking before the water has been absorbed. The experiment can be done in fact with a dog with a fistula in his throat, so that little if any of the water is absorbed, yet "satiation" occurs (Bellows, 1939).

The problem is complicated but not fundamentally changed by the demonstration that there is not one but a number of hungers (Richter, Holt, and Barelare, 1938; Young, 1941). The rat lacking any one of a dozen or so substances will choose a diet containing that substance, selectively correcting a specific deficiency. We still have the same problem: what is it that initiates the eating of salt or sugar, or drinking water; and what terminates it? Appetite and satiation are selective, but it is desirable if we can to avoid postulating fifteen or twenty mechanisms (allowing for future discovery of other hungers besides those we already know), all in control of normal eating. If possible, we must find a single mechanism to comprehend the facts.

The neural mechanism that determines such motivated behavior as eating or sex activity Morgan has called the "central motive state." This, for the theory presented in this book, evidently is a phase sequence or conceptual activity. It does not require that we postulate a special process to deal with hunger, but only that the process already postulated have some distinctive feature for each of the separate hungers. Conceptual series *A, B,* and *C* might correspond to one hunger; *A, B,* and *D* to another, and so on.

The total process would fit Morgan's specifications for the central motive state, since: (1) the phase sequence is independent of input from any specific sensory mode; (2) it has a central priming action that reinforces some sensory stimulations and not others; and (3) it evokes specific forms of behavior, since each phase in the phase sequence may have its specific motor facilitation. Morgan's final specification (4) is that the central motive state arouses general activity or restlessness: for the present theory, this is qualified by saying that the restlessness must occur only when the environment fails to supply the specific stimulation that the central motive state would reinforce—that is, when the hungry animal is not exposed to food, or the sexually motivated animal does not have a sex partner at hand.

This point is of some importance. We must distinguish between an integrative, motivating effect of a lack of food, and a disintegrative one. The integrative action appears in any purposeful search for food, and in eating. That it occurs, in the experienced animal and in a familiar environment, is an evident fact; it is the real fact with which most discussions of hunger have been concerned. But the picture will not be complete if we recognize only this aspect of the problem, and assume implicitly that the physiological need of food equals hunger (that is, the tendency to eat).

There are two reasons for denying such an assumption. One is that learning is involved in hunger, as we shall see in a moment. The other is that, until this learning has occurred, the lack of food is apt to be disruptive of behavior. The effect of the lack appears in restlessness, which is not directed behavior but implies an instability of direction: restlessness as such is not a purposeful seeking but activity without purpose. With more experience, the restlessness becomes a directed search. Biologically, it has served a purpose, having made a certain kind of learning possible; but this does not make it, from the psychological point of view, purposeful—and the point here is that the *first* effect of a lack of food is not an increased directedness in behavior (unless the mouth happens to be in actual contact with the nipple, when there is directedness at the reflex level).

Even in experienced subjects the need of food has disintegrating effects. The relation of hunger to emotional disturbance is notorious, and Goodenough (1931) has shown it clearly in a study of anger in children. Lack of food, or of some particular element in the diet, such as salt (Saphir, 1945), can produce profound and lasting emotional disturbances.

Furthermore, hunger itself—the tendency to eat—may be disrupted by a lack of food. Hunger practically disappears about the fourth day of starvation in man, and there may even be a "repugnance" to food (Carlson, 1916). In the rat, the rate of eating is markedly lowered by the fourth day, and the amount eaten is also low (Bousfield, 1935). Physical changes in the alimentary canal would account for the smaller total intake, and even perhaps for a 50 per cent decline in the rate, but they would not account for a total loss of human appetite if the *neural* mechanism of hunger were undisturbed.

In chronic starvation, however, the hunger mechanism seems undisturbed even though the degree of malnutrition may be great. Is it possible that the difference here is due to learning, in the same way that learning changes the restlessness of the first need of food into a directed search? Let us look at some evidence concerning the relation of learning to hunger, before returning to the question of how a lack of food might disorganize behavior.

It is common knowledge that a person eating on an irregular schedule when he is used to a regular one, and so without his usual environmental cues for eating, may be "hungry without knowing it." With a deficiency sufficient to produce headache and irritability, he may find out what is wrong only when food tastes unusually good or when his symptoms disappear as a consequence of eating. The fact obviously suggests that eating is partly a learned response to certain environmental events. Hunger, defined as the excitation of a neural mechanism that controls eating, is not a simple direct product of a need for food. There are cognitive factors to be considered when hunger is studied in the mature animal.

It does not affect the value of Richter's study of food preferences (Richter *et al.*, 1938) to recognize that his method clearly permits of a short-term learning as a factor in preference. Young (1944) and Beebe-Center, Coffin, and MacLeod * in fact have shown that the learning has a strong influence.

Also, it is well known that tame laboratory rats deprived of food, taken from their cages and offered food in a strange place, will for some time eat little or nothing. Before he will run in a maze for food reward, the rat must be given the routine "preliminary training," extending over a period of days. Inanition, meanwhile, may become extreme. It has been generally supposed that the failure to eat is due to an independent emotional disturbance, but some preliminary experiments (to be reported in more detail elsewhere) suggest strongly that this is not the whole explanation.

Six rats were thoroughly habituated to an enclosed field, containing a number of movable objects, over an 8-day period. Then they were deprived of food for 24 hours, and put into the field with food and water present. The amount of time each rat spent eating, in a period of 120 seconds, was recorded. The procedure was repeated a number of times as one would carry out a learning experiment, to see whether the amount eaten would be affected by "practice"—whether it would be small at

---

* Personal communication from Dr. J. G. Beebe-Center.

first, and increase on subsequent days; whether "forgetting" would occur when practice was interrupted; and whether changes in the environment might change the response, but without inducing emotional disturbance to account for failure to eat.

The amount that a rat can eat in 120 seconds is not nearly enough to maintain health, but the average time spent eating in the first test was only 79 seconds, one rat eating for as short a time as 35 seconds. On subsequent days, the amount increased; dropped whenever practice was interrupted (*i.e.*, after the rats had been left for a few days in their cages with food and water present, before being tested again) and rose once more when practice was resumed; and dropped with each change in the arrangement of objects in the experimental environment. The changes induced exploration but no evident signs of emotion. It is also important to note that there was no tendency to take a bite of food and then explore, or even to take a quick bite whenever exploration brought the animal near the food (this shows up later, as the rat becomes more sophisticated).

A second experiment was done to check on these results, and also to see what would happen when exploration was eliminated. In this experiment 10 rats (from another colony) were tested individually in a living cage, being allowed food for 300 seconds after a 24-hour deprivation, and again after a 48-hour deprivation. The average time spent eating was again low on the first test—41 seconds: one animal ate for as short a time as 5 seconds. On the second test, the average rose to 140 seconds. But the total amount eaten was still estimated to be not more than one-tenth of what would be necessary to maintain even a depleted body-weight.

It seems therefore that the rat must *learn* to eat the amount he needs; and "satiation"—cessation of eating when no external event has occurred to interrupt it—occurs before the physiological needs of the unsophisticated animal have been met.

These results agree with the indications that human hunger is partly dependent on being aroused by events associated with eating. They also show that a theory of hunger does not necessarily have to account for an automatic regulation of the amount eaten, that will just equal the amount needed. The termination of eating or drinking may be determined by experience, in part at least (but partly as the termination of other pleasurable activities is determined, by a kind of fatigue: Chapter 9). This learning process is prolonged. I have the impression that the rat, offered food for short periods only, at 24-hour intervals, will take from 3 to 5 weeks before he gets to the point of promptly eating the amount of his food deficit as soon as food is made available.

Must there not be something of the same sort of learning in the hunger of the dog and cat? The experiment suggests that when hunger in the dog is to be studied it will be necessary to know the animal's history or, better, to rear the animal in the laboratory with a systematic control of his experience of the need of food. Data obtained when this has not been done may make hunger appear more an innately established process than it actually is.

METABOLIC FACTORS DISTURBING BEHAVIOR

The evidence discussed in the preceding section has indicated, first, that lack of food tends to disrupt behavior, producing restlessness, discomfort, irritability, and, in the extreme degree, emotional apathy. Secondly, a learning process seems to be involved in transforming this primitive disturbance into hunger as we know it in the adult animal or human being.

We may now ask what the source of the original disturbance is before considering (in the next section) the processes that transform it. The present discussion, primarily of the origins of hunger, has a broader implication and will be relevant also to the problem of emotional disturbance due to metabolic disorders.

It is well established that the need for food affects the central nervous system directly, through changes in the blood content (Morgan, 1943). (There may of course be peripheral effects as well.) The effect of chemical changes in the blood content would influence the rate of firing of the nerve cell. A nutritive deficiency may be thought of as usually lowering the rate, though a calcium deficiency might raise it (Lehmann, 1937a; Bronk, 1939), the important thing being the change of rate rather than the direction of change. It must also be assumed that any particular chemical influence would not affect all cells equally. There is a considerable variety in the make-up of central neural cells and their reaction to changes of blood content. This is shown in the selective susceptibility of particular parts of the central nervous system to particular diseases and toxins; it is also shown in the differential effects of anoxia and of various anesthesias. The firing of some cells may be especially changed by a lack of thiamin; others by hypochloremia, and still others by hypoglycemia.

Now it has been seen that neural integration is fundamentally a question of timing, quite apart from the particular theory of integration that has been developed in these pages. Metabolic changes, by altering time relations in neural firing, must tend to disrupt behavior—not merely slow it up, but disorganize it.

In the present theory, timing has its effect in the functioning of the cell-assembly and the interrelation of assemblies: diffuse, anatomically irregular structures that function briefly as closed systems, and do so only by virtue of the time relations in the firing of constituent cells. Synaptic changes are necessary to the setting up of an assembly, but these act by coordinating the action of two or more cells. The firing of one cell immediately after another is not determined by synaptic knobs alone but also by what is going on in some other cell or cells. Synaptic knobs alone cannot determine that a particular system will function as such.

Furthermore, an individual cell or transmission unit may enter into more than one assembly, at different times. Which it will form part of, at any moment, depends on timing in other cells; and to enter into any assembly requires that its frequency accord with the time properties of the active system. If a metabolic change affects one cell much more than other cells in the system, it must drop out; if enough cells drop out, the assembly does not function.

If, instead, all the cells in an assembly are affected to about the same extent, the system would continue to function; but the facilitation delivered to other assemblies might be modified in a way that would disturb, or redirect, the phase sequence (that is, the sequence of assembly actions).

At any one moment, the action of an assembly may be considered to be on an all-or-none basis; the system functions as such, or it does not. But an affected assembly might function at one time and not at another, in agreement with the statistical approach of Chapter 4. Suppose for example that the functioning of an assembly requires the activity of n pathways in parallel at some point in the system, and that $n + 4$ are anatomically available. At any time, some pathways are refractory but there is normally a margin of 4 at this point, maintaining the operation of the system. If now a change of blood content lengthens the recovery cycle of some of these cells, the average number of refractory pathways might rise from 2 to 3, say, and the upper limit of the number from 4 to 6. When 5 or 6 are refractory, the number of available pathways would fall to $n - 1$ or $n - 2$, and the assembly does not function for the moment. A half second later, it might again be responsive.

One might assume that longer-established assemblies would have in general greater safety margins. With the greater development of synaptic knobs, due to more frequent activity, the number n might decrease (p. 66). This would imply that older habits, and longer-established memories, would be most resistant to disruption by metabolic changes of blood content.

In general terms, these ideas provide a rationale for the actually observed disturbance of behavior that may result from changes of blood content, whether in hunger or otherwise. In hunger itself, the blood change might be a lack, as in hypoglycemia, or it might be the addition of the "hunger hormone" of Luckhardt and Carlson (1915) and Morgan (1943). This would be a substance liberated by depleted body tissues, with a selective effect on the firing of neural cells.

THE MECHANISM OF LEARNING IN HUNGER

The facts discussed earlier, showing an element of learning in hunger, leave room at present for a considerable difference of opinion as to how large a part it plays. In order to further define the problem for research, let us assume for the moment that the innate factor consists only of the reflexes of sucking, chewing, and swallowing, of spitting out noxious substances, and of the activities of the gastrointestinal tract—that all else is learned.* The deficiencies of this approach will help us to discover what facts are needed for a better understanding. Stimulation of the lips of the newborn infant elicits sucking, as a reflex activity. The same stimulation stops hunger contractions, and the effect is increased by the stimulation of taste buds and by swallowing (Carlson, 1916). In the adult at least the effect of stomach contractions is related to pain ("hunger is an uncomfortable pain sensation caused by stomach contractions": Carlson, p. 97)—mild, but painful. In the infant, also, the behavior accompanying strong stomach contractions is in general not to be distinguished from the effects of a loose safety-pin in the diaper.

Consequently, hunger contractions should have the same role as pain in their effect on learning. As the contractions begin and get stronger, some time after suckling, there would be an increasing disturbance of the intrinsic organization of activity in the infant's cerebrum (p. 121). This organization it will be recalled makes for inactivity in behavior, other than reflex behavior; as it is broken up, an increasing restlessness should be expected. As a result, the moving mouth is likely to make contact with the nipple. Reflex sucking follows, with a further stimulation of taste buds and swallowing: stomach contractions cease, and the restlessness disappears.

Later, as the infant becomes more mobile and explores more of his environment, other things are investigated and enter the mouth, with similar effects. Some things produce, perhaps, too strong a stimulation of salt, sour, or bitter receptors and are spit

* In correcting proof I realize how misleading this statement may be. Obviously, I assume that the "innate factor" also includes all the mechanism that determines what kind of learning will take place. It includes for example the susceptibility of cortical organization to disturbance by hunger pangs or lowered blood nutrients.

Throughout this book the reader may feel that the emphasis is too much on learning. But this is only verbal. Whenever one could think of several ways in which some particular learning might happen, but recognizes that the facts of anatomy or physiology allow only one of them, one is recognizing the existence of the innate peculiarities of the central nervous system. All mammalian behavior involves learning; but the innate factor is always there, determining what learning occurs and how.

out. Others fall below the avoidance limen, reduce to paste and are swallowed. These edible substances, not only stimulating taste receptors but also being retained in the mouth and eventually swallowed, are evidently the ones that most effectively interrupt stomach contractions: they provide more of the inhibiting stimulation, and more-prolonged stimulation.

The conditions necessary for learning are provided in this sequence of events. As the sequence is repeated, the sensory stimulation—visual, olfactory, gustatory, and kinesthetic—organizes assemblies of cells with a motor facilitation of the various activities of eating. This brings eating farther and farther under cortical control, and so increases the possible influence of learning. The sight, smell, and taste of food, the tactual stimulation of mouth and throat, and kinesthesis from chewing and swallowing are the stimuli that arouse this assembly action. To a certain extent, the sensation from stomach contractions itself would become conditioned to arouse the same activity. Though primarily disruptive, like pain, this sensation should like pain be capable also of being conditioned to eating responses. It has been seen that the potentially painful stimulation is not disruptive (that is, it is not pain) when it forms part of a stimulation that has well-organized central effects. Finally, the development of conceptual processes controlling eating makes possible an association of eating with other conceptual processes.

Schematic and oversimplified, this discussion still shows the way toward avoiding oversimplification. It points out three ways in which hunger—an organized activity in the cortico-diencephalic system—can be aroused: (1) by the sight and smell of food and the sensation of eating itself, (2) by stomach contractions, and (3) conceptually, as the sequel to a train of thought. These agencies may summate. One, on occasion, may not be effective by itself, but becomes effective when another is added to it. Hunger can then be aroused or further increased by an attractive appearance of food, or by its smell and taste.

Such effects are familiar; but since they do not fit into the rubric of hunger as a bodily need, or alternatively as sensations from the stomach, we are apt to forget them. Consider the salted-nut phenomenon. Ordinarily, one can take salted nuts or let them alone—until one has eaten a mouthful, when it becomes much harder to let them alone. Hunger has increased: but how? A lack of food cannot be increased by eating something, and stomach contractions are stopped by chewing and swallowing. If, however, we consider hunger to be neither a particular condition of the body, nor a set of sensations from the stomach, but an organized neural activity that can be aroused (like any other conceptual process) in several ways, the puzzle disappears. The schematizing of the preceding paragraphs, then, has developed some of the further possibilities of Morgan's conception of the central motive state.

The puzzle just referred to has been dealt with in the past by a distinction of hunger from *appetite*. ("A taste of salted nuts does not increase hunger; it only increases appetite.") The solution is not a good one because no one has been very clear as to what appetite is, if it is not hunger. It seems in fact that hunger cannot exist without appetite; and "appetite" seems in practice to be a term that is applied to the tendency to eat when eating is not biologically desirable or valuable, "hunger" when it is desirable. Such a distinction has no place in discussion of the physiological control of eating.

If the explanation proposed in this section is right, cutting the vagus in the newborn infant will retard the normal development of hunger, by preventing the postulated role of hunger pangs in the learning process. Cutting the vagus does not stop eating in the adult, but it may have more effect at an earlier stage. This would provide a direct experimental test of my schematizing. It is not predicted, however, that no learning could then take place, since there is still a mechanism of addiction to food to be discussed, which would also provide a basis for learning. The explanation predicts that cutting the vagus would retard the development of hunger, perhaps seriously, but would not prevent it entirely.

HUNGER AS AN ADDICTION

I have already discussed the metabolic changes due to lack of food as a disturbing influence on behavior. The treatment of hunger can now be completed by considering the relation of these changes to the learning process: a relation that makes eating, in the mature animal, equivalent to an addiction, as Carlson (1916) long ago suggested. It may be objected that hunger cannot be related to metabolic changes, because of the experiment by Scott, Scott, and Luckhardt (1938) in which it was found that hunger can occur in human subjects with no change of blood-sugar level. This experiment is valuable, but in the light of present knowledge, and the discussion of the preceding pages, it needs two things to be complete:

1. In the first place, we need to know about other blood components besides glucose. Glucose is only one of a number of substances involved in hunger: if there are nine specific hungers besides those for oxygen and water (Morgan, 1943), there are nine substances whose concentration in the blood must be examined before it can be concluded that hunger is not determined directly by the blood content.

2. In the second place, since we know also that there is an important element of learning in hunger, the experiment should be repeated with subjects in early infancy. Only then will it be possible to say that stomach contractions are not determined, originally, by changes of blood content, or to conclude that the development of hunger is independent of such changes. The obvious experiment, dealing with both points 1 and 2, is to determine the levels of thiamin, chlorides, and so on, in addition to the level of glucose, at the time when a need of food begins to disturb infant behavior or when the adult actually reports hunger.

Until such an experiment is done we can only speculate, but a little speculation may help to define the problem. Return to the learning process of the last section. In general, the cell-assemblies whose activity is hunger would be organized *in a condition of mild deficiency*. We do not know whether this condition is enough to produce a lowering of blood nutrients, or secretion of the hunger hormone; but, if it is, observe that a *mild* deficiency would be the optimal condition for the functioning of the assemblies in question. It is not a low blood sugar, or low chlorides, that would be disruptive of an assembly, but a change from the level at which the assembly was organized. If hunger is established originally in the presence of a slight deficiency, the return of blood sugar and so on to normal would tend to disrupt it, and equally, a more extreme lowering of the blood-sugar level. This accounts for a loss of appetite in starvation, and is a first step toward accounting for satiation.

Suppose that an experienced, adult animal is exposed for the first time to a severe lack of food. Both the increased hunger pangs and lowered blood nutrients contribute to a disturbance of cortical organization and so of behavior. If the disintegration of the hunger mechanism itself has gone so far that there is indifference to the thought of food, or if the animal put where he can find food makes no effort to seek it out—that is, if the hunger mechanism is not excitable conceptually—the sight and smell of food may be more effective; or food in the mouth may be. This sort of thing of course has been observed in starvation. The animal is apathetic about food until he has eaten a mouthful, and then shows an increased hunger (the "salted-nut phenomenon" again). Once swallowed, the food is absorbed and reverses the slow fall of blood nutrients, increasing the possibility of actual hunger as an organized cerebral action.

Now observe that each occurrence of such a sequence of events in chronic starvation would tend to set up new cell-assemblies (or modify old ones) by the same process that set up assemblies in the normal infant. The new assemblies, however, would be such as to function best in a condition of low blood nutrients. The learning then would establish a hunger that could occur strongly in the presence of starvation, and not as before only with a minimal need of food.

Hunger established in the presence of lowered blood nutrients, and having the effect (through eating) of raising them, would be physiologically the equivalent of an addiction—biologically valuable, but still an addiction. There has occasionally been confusion in distinguishing between addiction and habit. Some writers apparently have seen no difference (except possibly in strength) between a habit of drinking milk at breakfast and a habit of drinking coffee. But an addiction involves more than a relationship of overt response to certain sensory stimulations: otherwise Sanka, with the taste and smell of coffee but without its caffeine, would satisfy every need that coffee does and could be substituted for it without the victim's knowing that anything had happened. Unfortunately, it cannot: the addict may not know what has happened, but he will know that something is wrong. An addiction, therefore, besides involving habit, also acts so as to maintain a blood concentration of some substance that is necessary to stable neural functioning, or whose absence results in emotional disturbance, restlessness, and discomfort or pain. This is a trite statement, but one of its implications should be considered. What has happened to prevent integrated neural function, in the absence of the drug?

We know, first, that there is always a period of "learning" or apprenticeship, in addiction; and we know also that an addiction lasts longer than the overt withdrawal symptoms of physiological disturbance. It may be proposed, therefore, that the learning is a genuine learning; and that it consists in part of the change of assembly action discussed above in relation to starvation. It follows that an addiction must be considered to be more than a metabolic reorganization: it includes a neural reorganization also, and one that tends to persist, since (as any tobacco addict or alcoholic knows) a "cure" is apt to be unreliable and the addiction can be reinstated much more promptly than acquired for the first time.

It is this very learning in addiction that we must know more about, to understand hunger. The learning can be described as an association between a sensory event and the subsequent euphoria: being at peace with the world follows a full belly, or an injection of morphine. The reference to "association," however, is misleading if it suggests that we understand the mechanism involved. We do not.

The problem of a learned preference, either for a drug or a needed food substance, can be seen better in the light of Spragg's (1940) study of morphine addiction in chimpanzees. For example, his experiment has demonstrated the difference between physiological dependence on a substance, and addiction to it. Daily injections established a dependence on morphine, demonstrated by withdrawal symptoms when the drug was withheld. But his chimpanzees still took a considerable time—from three weeks to three months—before they discovered the connection between (1) injection of the drug and (2) feeling better. This exemplifies an *intermediate stage* of addiction. Eventually, the chimpanzee in need of morphine tried hard to get an injection (by struggling to get to the accustomed room, getting the hypodermic needle and giving it to the experimenter, and so on). The learning that leads to this final stage of addiction presents us with our problem, the same one that is involved in hunger.* It has sometimes been said that the rat in need of salt learns to eat it, by "experiencing its beneficial effects." Spragg has shown that an association of this kind can occur, even if its mechanism is not at all clear, and his data should be kept in mind in dealing with the problem of the self-selection of diet.

When a rat is suddenly put on a salt-free diet, he may be considered to be in the intermediate stage of addiction. His behavior shows that he has a physiological dependence on salt, but he may still have to learn to look for salt-containing foods and eat them selectively.

The immediacy and reliability with which an animal will correct a dietary deficiency seems to have been overestimated—at the least, overemphasized. I have already cited Young (1944) and Beebe-Center (personal communication) as showing that the rat's preference for a needed food is not immediate, but learned. With a low concentration of the needed substance, preference is established slowly; it may require as long as 7 days. With stronger concentrations, the preference appears early. But showing that a rat already has a complete preference at the end of 24 hours does not show that no learning has occurred. We badly need a detailed study of what learning may occur in the first 10 minutes, or first hour, of a rat's exposure to a choice of foods.

The Editors of *Nutrition Review* (1944) in a summary of the history of this topic, and a paper by Pilgrim and Patton (1947), have drawn attention again to the unreliability of the self-selection method in many circumstances. The failures must be kept in mind as well as the successes, if selective hungers are

---

* Dr. Austin H. Riesen has pointed out, in a personal communication, that another example is the slowness with which air crews learn what to do about oxygen deficiencies, when oxygen is available.

Obviously the law of effect would be the very thing to invoke to account for such learning, but I can still find no satisfactory way of fitting it into the present set of physiological conceptions.

to be explained. Man is notoriously capable of malnutrition while freely choosing his own diet. This might be put down to bad habits, interfering with an innately sound mechanism of choice; but such an explanation would hardly account for hypochloremia, promptly relieved by taking common salt (Saphir, 1945), in men who had access to salt-shakers. Their symptoms were severe, and their condition once more can be properly likened to that of Spragg's chimpanzees when they had withdrawal symptoms without seeking a morphine injection. Man must often *learn* to take more salt when he moves to a tropical climate, and the learning is not automatic.

Until such learning has occurred, it appears that the only direct effect of a need of some particular food, or of food in general, is restlessness, emotional disturbance, and malaise. The lack of specificity in this disturbance may well be a clue to the nature of pathological eating, arising from emotional disturbance, or of the alcoholic's tendency to eat a less and less adequate diet. Clinically, there is an inescapable relation between drug addictions, food habits, and chronic emotional disturbance. The fact has some meaning on the assumption that the need of food or drug, and emotional disorder, have a common element in a disruption of timing in the firing of central neural cells, and on the further assumption that this disruption is transformed into an organized action by a process of learning.

An hypothesis dealing with part of this learning process has been set forth in the present chapter, but there remains a part about which the hypothesis must be so vague as to have no present value. Once more, Spragg's experiment makes the matter clearest. He found it possible, once a full addiction was established, *to abolish withdrawal symptoms by an injection of saline only*—briefly, but nonetheless effectively (Spragg, 1940, pp. 95–96). Similar effects are known in human addicts, and "explained" by a reference to suggestion. Here we have a sensory and perceptual event substituted effectively for the physiological presence of a substance in the blood stream. The analogue in hunger is the occurrence of satiation long before a meal has been absorbed from the stomach and intestine. It has been argued that withdrawal symptoms, or the restlessness and discomfort of hunger, are the result of a disturbance of central organization. If so, the sensory stimulation of seeing the hypodermic needle and feeling its jab, or the sensations of eating, must have some rather direct action in restoring the normal time relations in the firing of central neural cells. Some such possibility has actually been envisaged in supposing that sensory processes may actively support and direct a given cerebral organization. This of course is in extremely general terms, and no details relevant to the present problem can be proposed. A more specific hypothesis may be possible later, when some of the experimental evidence is available whose need has been shown in this chapter.

9. The Problem of Motivational Drift

The two primitive motivations of pain and hunger can be regarded as mainly determined by specific bodily conditions—tissue damage and lack of nourishment—although, as we saw in the preceding chapter, neither of these relationships is simple and neither is as yet really understood. Hunger, particularly, must be a very complex process.

A third motivation, biologically primitive, is that of sex. The sex drive is also tied to a definite physiological condition, the presence of certain hormones in the blood stream. But it would once more be an oversimplification to make this the only factor: like eating, sex behavior is not reducible to any simple formula (Beach, 1947*a*), and it serves especially to make clear a further complexity of the problem of motivation. This concerns the time relations in the organism's responsiveness to a particular class of stimulation. In sex behavior, the problem appears in the comparatively slow build-up of *interest* (that is, responsiveness to or seeking out of genital stimulation) and its frequently abrupt decline, following orgasm: humoral conditions presumably remaining constant. A roughly parallel course of events is to be seen in other behavior, particularly in the alternation of sleep and waking, but also in almost any behavior that is a source of pleasure. It should therefore have an important place in the theory of motivation.

A constant property of mammalian behavior is a variability of responsiveness to the environment that cannot be ascribed to conditions originating outside the nervous system—it appears, that is, to reflect something intrinsic to the organization of cerebral activity. I have already emphasized in Chapter 7 this variability of attitude (or interest), and I propose now to look closer at its neural basis. The reader will recall, further, that "motivation" has been treated not as a distinct process, separate from learning, insight, or attitude, but as a useful first approximation whose main reference is to the temporal organization of cerebral events (Chapter 8). The present discussion accordingly deals with the slow change or "drift" of motivation, but interprets motivation in a rather broad sense.

THE PROBLEM OF A LASTING EXCITATION, FATIGUE, OR INHIBITION

The problem of this chapter is the relationship between cyclical changes of responsiveness in the whole animal and events in the nervous system. A permanent change of responsiveness, of course, is called learning, and does not concern us here; but one that involves a continuing alternation of responsiveness to some stimulation, each phase lasting perhaps for hours before reverting predictably to the other, is a different matter. In describing the behavior, such transient conditions may be called excitation or fatigue, which is a commonly accepted and useful terminology. It has, however, certain dangers and may conceal certain complications for the theory of behavior. "Excitation," "inhibition," and "fatigue," as prolonged neural conditions * determining the behavior of the whole animal, are conceptions which perhaps are not a primary concern for the neurophysiologist but which certainly need examination in psychological theory.

When an animal is "excited" what happens—simply an increase of total cortical activity? What changes take place when excitability, or responsiveness to a particular kind of stimulation,

---

* It will be evident that a discussion of fatigue on this basis is not very closely related to the undertaking of Bartley and Chute (1947), who define fatigue as a form of experience that is the outcome of mental conflict. They have not been mainly concerned with the neural mechanism of this conflict, or with the nature of the "loss of interest" which contributes to it. Their emphasis on the complexities of fatigue, however, strengthens the present argument that it should not be lightly invoked as an explanatory conception.

increases over a period of hours, days, or weeks? Is there simply a decrease of cortical firing in "mental fatigue"? When the cortex inhibits a certain hypothalamic pattern of response, is one group of cells preventing the firing of another group? Presumably, these questions cannot be definitely answered at present; but it should be seen that the answers are not obvious, and that, when the temporal characteristics of excitation are taken into account, the question of its neural basis becomes a crucial one, for physiological psychology at least. And so with inhibition and fatigue.

Consider excitation first. There are two aspects of the problem: one is simply the duration of the excitation following brief stimulation. It seems generally recognized now that an excitation which endures for minutes or longer at once raises a question of the special mechanism involved. The all-or-none excitation in the nerve cell is almost infinitesimal in duration, bearing little relation to behavioral excitations that take an appreciable time to develop. The widespread theoretical interest in reverberatory or re-entrant pathways as the basis of a continuing excitation in the central nervous system shows that this side of the problem has been recognized (unlike the problem of a continuing inhibition, as we shall see in a moment).

But another aspect of the problem of excitation needs more attention. A behavioral excitation, an increase in some bodily activity, is not necessarily a sign of an increased neural activity either in the brain as a whole or in some one part of it. The point is well illustrated by the process of getting drunk. A small amount of alcohol may be an excitant—socially, and in its immediate net effect on behavior—but this of course does not prove that alcohol is a neural excitant; it does not even prove that lower centers are being released from cortical inhibition.

There is a fallacy here which is most likely to be made when one is thinking of different kinds of behavior as controlled by different parts of the brain: "There is an increase in certain behavior, therefore some part of the brain is more active, therefore—supposing that alcohol is not a neural excitant but a depressant—a higher inhibition has been removed."

Perhaps this is what happens. The point, however, is that it is not logically inescapable. A change of behavior does not necessarily mean that some neural units, active before, have become inactive, and that inactive ones have become active (except at the level of the final common path, and very often not even here since the same effectors may enter into different responses). The same neural cells may still be active, but in new combinations, when a different response occurs. This is one of the profoundly important implications of recognizing the role of timing in neural transmission and of such conceptions as that of "optional transmission" (Lorente de Nó, 1939). Stimulate *AB* and *CD* and the excitation follows one set of pathways; stimulate *AC* and *BD* and the excitation may follow different efferent pathways and determine a totally different response—although the same internuncial cells are active.

The behavior of the drunk may be produced because alcohol, depressing *all* neural cells, depresses some more rapidly than others and so changes the pattern of firing throughout the cerebrum. The cortex of course may be more affected than the rest of the brain; but this is different from saying that the activity of the brain stem actually increases with the administration of alcohol. The idea that cortical function can be almost eliminated before lower centers are affected is scarcely tenable; and in fact the drunk, up to the moment of collapse, does not in any way resemble a decorticate preparation but continues to manifest behavior that we know is fully dependent on the cerebral cortex. The behavior changes and may be less adaptive, but is it less "cortical" and more "hypothalamic" or more "mesencephalic"?

The theory that drunken behavior is due to loss of cortical inhibition is open to these objections: first, it implies that the inhibition, during long periods of sobriety, has an astonishing duration and efficacy—a point to which we shall return; and secondly, it seems to imply that all drunks should act much more alike than they do, perhaps approaching the picture of sham rage before passing into stupor. The other possibility, suggested above, is that alcohol from the first knocks out cells in the hypothalamus and striatum as well as in the cortex, and slows up firing rates, thus reducing the complexity of cerebral organization but leaving until the last some cortical as well as subcortical function. Whether this is so or not, it is enough to show that there is no logical necessity of regarding drunken rudeness or hyperactivity as a loss of inhibition that permits an absolute *increase* of neural activity in some part of the brain.

Two points have been made concerning a lasting excitation in behavior: the long duration must be accounted for, and an increase of some kind of behavior does not always or necessarily mean an increased activity in some region of the central nervous system. The same two points apply to inhibition and fatigue.

If a decrease of bodily activity that lasts more than seconds is to be explained by a neural inhibition or neural fatigue, some explanation is needed of the duration; and secondly, the decrease of bodily activity is not *a priori* proof that such an inhibition or fatigue exists. There is risk in assuming that *any* prolonged change in some aspect of behavior means a parallel change in some one part of the brain: that mental fatigue is a neural fatigue, or that a suppression of anger means that some one set of cells (preferably cortical) suppresses the firing of some other set (preferably hypothalamic). A decrease of bodily activity does not always mean a decrease of neural activity: sleep may consist only of a change of the combinations in which cortical cells fire—*i.e.*, may essentially be hypersynchrony, with no decrease of total activity; and the EEG offers evidence that immobility and unresponsiveness can accompany a considerable cortical activity (Jasper, 1941).

It is commonplace to say that an organic whole has properties other than the sum of the properties of its parts in isolation. The necessary corollary is this: do not take for granted that the parts of a neural complex—or that any one part—must act in parallel with the action of the whole. The fatigue that leads to prolonged sleep, or the disappearance of sexual responsiveness after ejaculation—often for hours afterward—is not proof of fatigue in cortical cells, or of an inhibition of sexual centers, for corresponding periods of time.

Fatigue as demonstrated physiologically in the neuron (the refractory period) has a duration measured in milliseconds. "Mental fatigue" may be a phenomenon of behavior, but its duration gives us no warrant for identifying it with a primary neural fatigue. Similarly, the inhibition that is studied in lower neural centers (where a fairly direct inference is possible concerning what happens in the single neuron) is a briefly lasting process that is promptly followed by excitation. In a matter of seconds it becomes possible for any strong excitation to break through. Consequently, to speak of an inhibition that lasts indefinitely is not just making use of the established conception of spinal reflex inhibition but introducing a different one. The conception may be quite valid, but it is not necessarily the *c.i.s.* of Sherrington (1925).

This point applies to the idea that pain fibers in a sound tooth can be continuously prevented from firing (p. 186); that the sham-rage center in a good-natured, normal cat is continuously inhibited by the cortex; or that a conditioned inhibition (Pavlov, 1928) can account for schizophrenic catatonia or for long-standing Freudian repressions. Some of these ideas assume first that each form of behavior is determined by a separate part of the central nervous system, and all of them assume secondly that inhibition may have an extraordinary degree of persistence.

When for example damage to the frontal lobe is followed by an increased appetite, or increased sexuality, or increased responsiveness to carotid-sinus stimulation, some clinical writers are prone to take for granted that this is of necessity evidence that the frontal lobe normally inhibits whatever lower centers are involved. Not at all; the normal action of the frontal lobe (and of the rest of the cortex) may be only to stimulate lower centers, but determining at the same time a particular timing of action in those centers. The behavior that results is a function of this timing; removal of the *stimulation* (not inhibition) from the frontal lobe means a different pattern of firing and so a change in behavior. It must be realized that when a patient says nasty things to his friends after lobotomy he uses the same effectors as when he is polite—but in a different firing combination; and the appearance of rudeness following brain damage does not show that there is a rudeness center in the brain, normally inhibited by the region that has now been damaged.

Decerebrate rigidity, again, may imply *either* (1) that the cerebrum acts primarily to diminish the activity of ventral-horn cells, *or* (2) that its action stimulates only, and in stimulating continually modifies the activity of the intrinsic circuits of the spinal cord which if left to themselves would simply raise the level of tonic contraction. It is legitimate (though possibly confusing) to speak of the cerebrum here as "inhibiting" the action of these circuits; my point is to draw attention to the difference in meaning between such usage, and the usage when one speaks of inhibition as the suppression, by one cell, of activity in another. I have argued that the physiological evidence does not justify the idea that pain fibers, for example, may be indefinitely inhibited. It is a long step of inference from the prolonged inhibitory action of one complex set of neurons upon another to an inhibition of the individual cell.

As a last example of this problem, consider the "suppressor areas" of the cerebral cortex (von Bonin, Garol, and McCulloch, 1944; McCulloch, 1944a, 1944b).

These areas, in or near areas 2, 4, 8, 19, and 24 of Brodmann, are widely spaced in the cerebral cortex and appear superficially to have a primary inhibiting action. Stimulation of one of them in the anesthetized animal may have two effects: relaxation of the musculature on the opposite side of the body, and disappearance of electrical potentials throughout the rest of the cortex. This might appear to be a direct suppression of neural activity, as a positive action by one set of cells in the cortex that prevents the activity of other cells. It might appear to justify, once and for all, the conception of a primary inhibitory function of the cerebral cortex.

The experimental evidence, certainly, has made it clear that stimulation of a suppressor area may produce a decrement of activity. But this leaves two questions: is this inhibition, in the sense that the vagus inhibits heart muscle, the same inhibition that presumably must operate in Lloyd's two-neuron spinal reflex arc (Fulton, 1943)? and does it occur as a result of the normal action of suppressor-area cells, or only as a function of massive nonphysiological stimulation by electrical current or strychninization?

Suppose for a moment that the normal action of the suppressor area is a *facilitation* of other cortical activity; that the function of areas 4s, 19, and so on, is like the function of the reticular substance in its facilitation of oculo-motor reflexes (Lorente de Nó, 1939). On the lines of the theory of the preceding chapters, integrated behavior requires a diffuse firing in the cortex. But a massive electrical stimulation would fire all the cells in one region together and prevent their entering into the diffuse patterns of firing necessary to the normal cortical control of behavior. That is, the "inhibition" would be a loss of essential facilitation only.

The evidence presented by McCulloch (1944b) fits into such a picture. Suppressor areas are directly connected with the caudate nucleus, and direct stimulation of the caudate produces "large, long voltages" in thalamic nuclei. McCulloch, accordingly, has suggested that the action of the caudate, in "suppression," is not a positive inhibition but the induction of rhythms of thalamic activity that are incompatible with normal thalamo-cortical reverberation.

Finally, it is important to see that the suppression cannot be a direct inhibitory action from one part of the cortex on another, both because the strychninized suppressor area does not appear to fire directly to other areas in the cortex and because of the observed time relations: The first effect of suppressor-area stimulation is the appearance of spikes in the immediate neighborhood, but with no simultaneous loss of potentials elsewhere. Next, a spreading extinction of potentials moves outward from the point stimulated, affecting the suppressor area before affecting others. If the cells in this area were inhibitory, a high level of firing here should coincide in time with a low level elsewhere; but this is not what happens. The suppressor area suppresses *itself* first, and then, after it has itself become inactive, makes others inactive. Obviously, this does not fit in with the idea that suppressor-area cells are inhibiting other cells but does fit in with the idea of a slowly spreading loss of facilitation—the implication of McCulloch's remarks.

It is still early for final interpretation of much of the work that has been done in this field. The nature of even spinal inhibition is still a disputed question, and there are serious dangers in applying the conception directly to the complexities of cerebral function, especially when the time properties of a decrement of activity are found to be markedly different. If it were safe to assume a true long-term inhibition (or, equally, fatigue) in cerebral action, it would greatly simplify the task of the psychologist. As matters stand, however, this is not justified. It is necessary to recognize the problems for behavioral theory that result from this fact. Now let us see more specifically what some of these problems are.

THE TIME COURSE OF SEXUAL MOTIVATION

What we are interested in here, essentially, is the nature of a behavioral excitation, and this perhaps would present no particular problem if it were not for the way in which excitability and excitation develop and decline. The difficulty is clearest in sexual behavior.

The review of studies of mammalian sex behavior by Beach (1947*a*, 1947*b*, 1948) makes for emphasis on an interaction of sensory and central factors. It has been clearly shown that the arousal of sex behavior does not depend on any particular sensory stimulation—on olfactory, visual, or auditory stimuli, nor on somesthetic stimulation from the genitalia or from other regions of the body. If gonadal hormones are also considered to be stimuli, arousing receptor organs in the brain, even this stimulation is not always essential to sexual arousal (since gonadectomy frequently does not put an end to copulation). Nevertheless, all these factors normally play a part in the arousal. Their effect is additive.

The presence of gonadal hormones in the blood stream does not often produce continuous sexual excitement, and it appears that a normal level of hormone facilitates certain effects of sensory stimulation, selectively, rather than itself producing any specific pattern of coordinated responses. When essential stimulation is lacking, the motor pattern of copulation is apt to deviate from the norm or not to be completed. Also, "There is evidence ··· that the cortex is involved in the arousal and maintenance of the male's sexual excitement; and reduction in susceptibility to sexual arousal subsequent to cortical injury appears to be proportional to the amount of neopallium removed" (Beach, 1942, p. 187). The evidence thus gives us a picture of sexual excitation as being produced by the close collaboration of sensory and central mechanisms.

During courtship and during copulation up to the point of

orgasm, activity in the "central excitatory mechanism" (Beach, 1942) summates, cooperating closely with sensory stimulation and producing forms of behavior which increase that stimulation, until the joint effect of sensation and central facilitation reaches a final limen of response. Then, abruptly, the central excitatory mechanism is somehow discharged; or, alternatively, an inhibition or fatigue not evident before suddenly assumes maximal effectiveness and may last without interruption for hours.

It is, I believe, the first of the alternatives—a slow growth of excitation followed by a condenserlike discharge—that should be explored theoretically. It has already been said that it would be very desirable for psychological theory to be able to postulate an inhibition or fatigue in such cases to explain the transient disappearance of responsiveness. But there are difficulties about doing so, as we have seen, and for the present there is no advantage in postulating a special inhibition in sexual behavior—as if we understood the excitation but not its absence. Really, we do not understand either, and a transient disappearance of excitability may be inherent in the nature of the behavioral excitation itself. Nothing that has been said in this discussion has made it impossible to suppose that the inhibition referred to above does exist; but if this is assumed, the essential problem of the time relations remains. The inhibition must be such as to last for days, on occasion, waning slowly in the older subject who may be capable of copulation only after days of recuperation from an earlier copulation (Kinsey, Pomeroy, and Martin, 1948). This is no easier to explain than an equally slow rise of *excitability*.

Let us turn now to the similar problem of sleep, before asking how this problem might be solved.

THE ALTERNATION OF SLEEP AND WAKING

The comparatively well-defined course of sexual arousal provides a clear example of a generally unsolved problem concerning cyclical changes of excitability. It cannot be asserted that fluctuations in sexual excitability, and the diurnal fluctuation of general excitability called the sleep cycle, must have the same mechanism; but the two have important similarities, and it may be profitable to proceed on the working hypothesis that the problems are in essence the same. The course of sexual motivation suggests that a cyclical change may be inherent in the process of excitation, so that an extended period of arousal must eventually be followed by an extended period of unresponsiveness (though the reason is hard to see); and this of course is exactly what happens in the alternation of sleep and waking.

Physiological study of sleep has centered about two questions: (1) whether sleep may be determined by one of several conditions external to the nervous system, such as muscular fatigue, the accumulation of toxins, and so on; (2) whether it may be due to the action of a sleep center, or inaction of a waking center, within the nervous system itself (Kleitman, 1939; Nauta, 1946). Research has emphasized the importance of a waking center in the caudal hypothalamus; its action evidently has much to do with regulation of the sleep cycle. Further knowledge on these two points must be obtained by physiological methods, and the present discussion will not contribute to it.

But there is also (3) a psychological factor of "interest" or "boredom" in sleep (Kleitman, 1939). With this we are directly concerned. The theory developed in the preceding chapters has definite implications about sleep; sleep has in fact been referred to repeatedly because it seems not to be an isolated phenomenon but an aspect of processes fundamentally involved in learning, for example, or volition or emotional disturbance—and these implications make it possible to deal with the "cortical" or "higher" components in sleep.

Return to the earlier discussions of spontaneous neural activity, and its relation to sensation and consciousness (pp. 9, 121–4, 146). We have, to start with, (1) the suggestion by Bartley and Bishop (1933) and Adrian and Matthews (1934) that unconsciousness may be the result of a lack of afferent activity, and (2) that this excitation normally has the function of breaking up the synchronous spontaneous firing of central nervous tissue. Add to this (3) that the EEG in sleep shows a marked hypersynchrony and (4) the general conclusion of Jasper (1941) that hypersynchrony may be opposed to adaptive behavior. We then have (5) a picture of sleep as a state in which sensation has lost its usual control of central neural firing, and in which a large segment of the cerebrum has drifted, from the diffuse firing necessary to adaptive behavior, into the hypersynchrony of unconsciousness.

From such ideas it is a short step to thinking of sleep as a functional deafferentation of the cerebral cortex (Kleitman, 1939). But this phrase should be used cautiously. It may suggest for example that consciousness is a function of the cortex alone, or that the cortex is an isolable unit physiologically.

Even in the anesthetized animal, cortical action is closely related to activity in cortico-diencephalic circuits (Morison and Dempsey, 1943; McCulloch, 1944*b;* Murphy and Gellhorn, 1945). There is probably a continuous interaction with the striatum as well (McCulloch, 1944*b*). Also, the term deafferentation may overemphasize the role of sensation in the sleep cycle of the normal animal. Important though it is, the level of sensory activity does not alone determine sleep or waking. This of course is the point made by Kleitman's "wakefulness of choice" as well as by his emphasis on boredom as a source of sleep. Wakefulness of choice is mainly a characteristic of higher animals: when a point is reached in the cycle at which sleep may occur, whether it does or does not depends on certain cerebral activities (referred to as conscious in man), as well as on the subject's environment.

With some qualification, however, the idea of a functional deafferentation is valuable. How would it occur? Structural connections with the sense organs are, presumably, unchanged as one goes to sleep. The waking center in the posterior hypothalamus, whose destruction leads to a continuing sleep, is not the portal by which afferent excitation reaches the cortex. It cannot therefore simply act like a valve, periodically cutting off the cortex from stimulation. However, it could be an essential link in a system "priming" the cortex for the reception of afferent impulses (Morgan, 1943). This would imply that the diffuse firing of the cortex cannot be maintained by afferent impulses alone; in terms of the present theory, it implies either that one cell-assembly cannot arouse the next, in a "phase sequence," without supporting facilitation from the waking system, or else that some significantly large fraction of assemblies incorporate cells from the waking system. Damage to this system, or synchrony of firing in it, would then interfere with assembly action and consciousness.

This does not localize consciousness or the waking state but assumes that the kind of activity *throughout the cerebrum* which we call consciousness is dependent on activity within a more limited region: primarily, the waking center in the mammillary bodies, or in the neighboring posterior hypothalamus and anterior mesencephalon (Nauta, 1946); and the intralaminar and midline nuclei of the thalamus (Penfield and Jasper, 1946; Jasper and Fortuyn, 1946). The essential structures in waking may also include the anterior cingular region (Brodmann's area 24, one of the suppressor areas). The cingular area is connected with the waking center *via* the mammillothalamic tract and the anterior nuclei of the thalamus, and Smith (1945) showed that stimulation of the area produces a transient condition apparently equal to sleep, except in duration.

At first glance, this would mean that the cingular area is a sleep center, not a waking center; but the function of a waking center is to maintain a diffuse firing, and a strong electrical stimulation firing a large number of cells in the area all at once would prevent it from having this function—the same point that was made in discussing the action of other suppressor areas.

If thus the activity of the posterior hypothalamus is necessary to the maintenance of diffuse firing, the anterior hypothalamus may have a similar function, a pacemaker for the synchronous cortical firing of sleep. It may, that is, be a sleep center, as Nauta (1946) appears to have demonstrated experimentally. I shall urge in a moment that sleep is not a negative thing, not a mere lack of the organized activity of consciousness but the presence of an alternative organization, and the existence of a sleep center fits into this conception.

From this point of view, we might consider that the cerebrum deafferents itself to produce sleep: by failing to provide the facilitation that is necessary for environmental stimulation to maintain any control of cerebral firing. The cerebrum also deafferents itself indirectly by ceasing to initiate motor activity, which at once means a decrease in sensory stimulation. But we must go farther than this. The conditions that produce sleep

The Problem of Motivational Drift

are not merely negative: the fact is that some stimulations contribute positively to sleep, and sleep is reinforced by learning. Physiologically, also, it is evident that hypersynchrony is not a random affair but organized, so that going to sleep means the positive substitution of one organization for another. This was referred to in an earlier chapter as the intrinsic organization of cerebral action, and it was suggested there how a prenatal learning process might contribute to it, if the organization is not simply due to the action of inherited pacemakers in the cerebrum (footnote, pp. 121–2).

On the same assumptions that justified the conception of the formation of cell-assemblies (Chapter 4), an afferent activity that coincides frequently with a synchronous firing will establish synaptic knobs between the afferent fibers and any members of the synchronously firing pool with which they come into contact. Repetition of that afferent excitation will then tend to support the synchrony, or re-establish it, which means a mechanism of learning to go to sleep. One may have to learn to sleep easily in the daylight or in unusual conditions; an habitual posture often helps one to get to sleep; and even habitual noises may do so, the lack of familiar stimulation delaying the onset of sleep or—if it occurs in the night—waking the sleeper. Kleitman (1939) considers that the sleep cycle of the adult is a function of learning; and in old age, when other learned behavior is deteriorating, we find the cycle also tending to return to a more infantile stage. Thus an accustomed stimulation may actively support hypersynchrony, as a learned relationship that is affected (just as other learning may be) by cortical atrophy. All this involves a further qualification of the "deafferentation" idea; one might suggest perhaps that sleep is more a de-*ef*ferentation.

The rationale of the de-efferentation should perhaps be made explicit here. It is simply that normal waking behavior is a highly selective set of contractions of muscle, in which it is usually quite essential that antagonists are not both at peak activity simultaneously, but in alternation, and in which a particular contraction must have a particular strength and endure only for a particular length of time. It is this that requires a dispersed firing in the cerebral cortex. I have referred to Jasper's conclusion that hypersynchrony *per se* is opposed to adaptive behavior; it is evidently opposed also to the process of thinking, which tends to break up even the moderate synchronization of the alpha rhythm. Similarly, Kleitman has remarked the negative correlation between (1) hypersynchrony in sleep and (2) the responsiveness of the sleeper or the extent to which his dreams are organized and rememberable. Finally, Loucks (1938) found that a conditioned response to *direct stimulation of the visual cortex* could not be elicited in the sleeping animal: here, clearly, deafferentation of the cortex is not an explanation of the failure of stimulation to elicit a response.[*]

These facts appear to mean that the pyramidal-tract control of ventral-horn cells and cells of the motor nuclei of the brain stem depends on a dispersed firing in the efferent fibers from the cortex, except when a very high degree of synchronization produces an outright convulsion. It can be supposed, then, that the degree of synchrony in sleep (and in petit mal) is too great for the temporally integrated control of muscle and too low to produce convulsions.

One consequence of such ideas is the conclusion that sleep produces relaxation as much as relaxation produces sleep. This makes possible a vicious circle, or cumulative reciprocal influence, that partly explains the gradualness of change from waking to sleep and *vice versa*. The drift from a dispersed firing to synchrony might be initiated within the cerebrum; if there is a sleep center in the anterior hypothalamus, cells in this region would start to recruit others and might assume control of local cortical areas, which in turn would mean a decrease in the number of cells available for assembly action and a decrease in muscle tonus. The consequent lowering of afferent excitation would further the same drift into hypersynchrony.

In waking, on the other hand, sensory stimulation would be considered to wean transmission units away from the pools of synchronous firing; each accession to this asynchronous assembly

---

[*] This one experimental fact alone might justify the treatment of sleep that is made in these pages. The cortical transmission that would be involved in a conditioned reflex, according to the phase-sequence hypothesis, depends on the series of assembly actions that is replaced in sleep by a local synchrony of firing, so even when a stimulus is applied directly to the cortex it could not elicit an adaptive response (in *deep* sleep).

action would increase muscle action and increase afferent excitation; and so on.

The experimental evidence has shown that a particular region has a crucial role in such changes; there is a waking center, and Nauta has given reason for thinking that there is a sleep center as well. But such centers may be necessary only in coordinating the action of the relatively large mammalian cerebrum, and the same kind of process might occur in a smaller brain without special pacemaking centers. Also, even in man, waking or sleep may not be necessarily initiated by changes in such centers. Sleep is produced by *cortical* lesions (Davison and Demuth, 1945) and may be interrupted by nightmares—a "conscious" activity. It may be profitable to consider sleep and waking as an alternation of excitability to which any central nervous tissue is prone, but which can be coordinated throughout the whole cerebrum only by the regulating action of special structures in the hypothalamus. When the action of these structures is impaired, disorganization of neural firing is possible: producing emotional disturbance. Interference with the sleep mechanism is accompanied by irritability (Nauta, 1946); and the irritability commonly seen when sleep is *abruptly* cut short, but which nevertheless disappears soon, as the subject becomes fully awake, indicates that between the intrinsic organization of sleep and the conscious organization of waking there may again be an interval of disorganization of cortical firing.

The role of psychological influence in determining the rate of drift from the diffuse organization to the intrinsic organization appears to mean that some phase sequences are more firmly established than others: that is, are more capable of perpetuating themselves. The level of stimulation from sense organs affects the persistence, and a phase sequence may perpetuate itself by raising this level, as when one knits his brow and pinches himself to stay awake.

Other phase sequences doom themselves to a short career by lowering the level of stimulation, except for stimuli that make for hypersynchrony. When such a phase sequence is in command, we say that the subject "tries to sleep," seeking relaxation, darkness, and quiet. But as we have seen there is a further cerebral factor, which becomes our next concern.

This is the factor of *interest* or *motivation,* which is provisionally translated into the stability and persistence of the phase sequence. It appears first in the fact that no amount of muscular relaxation and quiet is likely to put the subject to sleep in the morning just after he has slept through the night; or, in other circumstances, in the fact that a good light, a loud voice, and a hard pew are not enough to keep one's eyes open. Again, if the reader cares to make a little experiment and turns from this book to a detective story, costume thriller, or sentimental family piece—whatever his preference may be—he will find himself wide awake again though he sits in the same chair, with the same light and the same degree of quiet, with the same degree of eyestrain in reading the same 26 letters of the alphabet (but happily contrived in other words). The problem raised here concerns the relationship between sensory input and the phase sequence; what characteristic it is, in this relationship, that tends to prolong the phase sequence and avert sleep.

Another facet of the relationship can be added at once: no matter how exciting a first reading of the detective story may have been, it will have lost this property on rereading unless considerable time has elapsed. To common sense, the reason is obvious. The fun is gone when you know exactly what happens next. But it is not obvious theoretically—if the book kept one awake yesterday, why not today? If a particular sequence of sensory events tones up the waking center, keeps hypersynchrony to a minimum, and maintains pyramidal-tract control of the muscles, why should it not have the same physiological effects a second time?

In this, as I shall try to show, there is a clue to the sources of motivation, and "pleasure." In view of the definition of motivation proposed in the preceding chapter, that it consists of the directedness and persistence of the phase sequence, we must consider sleep to be the extreme case of a loss of motivation. From the discussion in the present chapter, it has appeared that sleep is not an isolated topic—not an isolated phenomenon dependent only on certain nuclei in the hypothalamus and amounting only to an intermittent cessation of cortical function. The frequently slow transition from unresponsiveness to full responsiveness (that is, from sleep to being wide awake) presents the same difficulty for theory that the slow development of sexual responsiveness does; and in his conception of "wakefulness of choice" Kleitman has evidently related waking and sleep to a much wider problem of motivation. Let us see what approach can be found in the commonplace, but theoretically peculiar, fact that an event which is exciting and interesting on its first occurrence is likely to be dull and sleep-provoking on its second.

EFFECTS OF MONOTONY ON LEARNED BEHAVIOR

Certain changes in the form of learned behavior, resulting from repeated or prolonged stimulation, do not seem to agree with the fact that repetition is usually what established that particular form of response in the first place, and is also necessary to maintain it. Dunlap (1932) has shown how the deliberate repetition of a response may eliminate, instead of strengthening, it. Hovland (1936) has described an "inhibition of reinforcement" from too many successive practice trials of a conditioned response. As Hilgard and Marquis have remarked, Pavlov (1928) found it advisable to space trials widely, in setting up a difficult discrimination; and it is well known that in ordinary learning massed practice does not have the same effect as distributed practice. Since a few seconds between trials should be enough to avert fatigue in the neural cell, one might think that longer intervals would only promote forgetting; but this does not seem to be true.

Presumably related to these effects of repetition is the "fading" discussed by Gardner and Nissen.* In prolonged training, there are often periods when practice seems to have a negative effect. The more he tries the worse the subject does. In man this is apt to go with a motivational disturbance, or loss of interest. One thinks little of it when repeated failure reduces motivation; but after all, why should it? Also, even if the reason for this were self-evident, a deterioration in performance can take place when the human subject is still "trying as hard as he can," or in an animal, working for a food reward, that continues to be

* L. Pearl Gardner and Henry W. Nissen, "Simple discrimination behavior of young chimpanzees: comparisons with human aments and domestic animals" (in press, *J. Genet. Psychol.*).

genuinely in need of food and apparently makes every effort to get it. In almost any discrimination training there are periods of deterioration of performance which are usually disregarded as due to chance but which, as Gardner and Nissen point out, seem to require some further explanation.

All these things might suggest that the connections involved in learning are (1) somehow weakened by being activated, and need a period of recovery before they can function well a second time; but (2) are strengthened, instead, when the period of recovery has been permitted. Hull (1943) has shown the explanatory value of such an idea, though he has put the weakening influence as a separate inhibitory process ("reactive inhibition"). How are we to deal with the apparent weakening in the present theory?

Two possibilities may be considered—that the cell-assembly tends to be disrupted by its activation, or that the relationship between assemblies changes and affects the phase sequence. There are indications that both things may occur, and can be distinguished one from the other by behavioral signs; and, also, that the effect we are interested in is primarily an effect on the phase sequence, not the assembly. The argument is as follows:

The assumptions made in Chapter 4 about the formation of assemblies implied, first, that self-maintained activity in the assembly would stop after a very short period (up to half a second). If nonetheless the arousing sensory stimulation persists without intermission, forcing a continued activity, the tendency would be to induce a change of frequency properties in the assembly. Some fractionation and recruitment would thus be expected (p. 76). The facilitation delivered to other cerebral systems would then be changed, which means some change in perception. Theoretically, this appears to be exactly what happens in the notorious effect of prolonged staring at a word or repeating it over and over to oneself: the familiar perception tends to become something strange and unrecognizable. Such effects can be regarded, then, as evidence of deterioration in the assembly due to *continuous* activation.

But the assumptions of Chapter 4 also implied, secondly, that when an assembly has become inactive it might be aroused again in a matter of a second or so, and after the same short interval aroused once more: and so on, indefinitely. The be-havioral evidence seems to support this, indicating that the single assembly or small group of assemblies can be repeatedly aroused when some other activity intervenes: in vision, for example, the perception of vertical line must occur thousands of times an hour; in conversation, the word "the" must be perceived and uttered with very high frequency; and so on.

According to the theory, then, the deteriorative effects of re-peating the same long series of words over again (loss of in-terest on rereading a novel), or of repeating the same group of attempted solutions (loss of motivation in problem-solving), should be in the phase sequence instead of the assemblies that compose it: that is, in the relation between constituent parts, not in the parts themselves. The same conclusion is indicated by the fact that the individual words of the reread story, or the details of the unsolved problem, do not appear different (as the stared-at word does) but have an annoying sameness. Also, a very ingenious experiment briefly reported by Lewin (1938) strengthens the argument:

The subject was required to write a word over and over until the task became intolerable. The experimenter accepted his refusal to write the word again, agreed to stop the experiment, but casually requested the subject to write the word on the back of one of the work sheets, to identify it. The subject did so without difficulty. Thus a change of set, or intention, banished fatigue. The assemblies directly necessary to writing the word may have been somewhat impaired, but not to the point at which they could not function: and the mental fatigue must have mainly concerned the accompanying assembly activities which constitute the subject's attitude or motivation. The re-covery in this experiment seems closely related to the increased output of industrial workers when a change is made in their attitude toward a monotonous task (Roethlisberger and Dickson, 1939). The theoretical significance thus is the same as that of the revitalizing effect of "insight" (a new combination of assem-blies—p. 134) on interest and motivation. This effect is greatest on the first occurrence of the new assembly combination; on repetition, the stimulating value declines, just as when a joke or a story is heard for the second time.

These considerations imply that the phase sequence continually needs new content to maintain its organization and persistence.* It appears that the individual assembly may be rearoused indefinitely at short intervals, but that the phase sequence as a whole cannot be—it must continue to *develop* if motivation is to be maintained. "Develop" here means to lead to new combinations of assemblies, which in turn means new perceptions, new insights, new ideas. As we know, such events are exciting. But why should new combinations be continually necessary to maintain the phase sequence, and with it a normal level of excitability? An answer can now be proposed which, in its wider significance, will also concern the nature of pleasure.

AN HYPOTHESIS OF THE RELATION OF EXCITABILITY TO MEMORY

To the psychologically naïve there is no riddle about the fact that hearing a story for the second time makes poor entertainment—the better you remember the details of the first telling, the less your interest in the second. Common sense thus ascribes the change of excitatory value to a change in *memory;* and I shall try next to show how this idea may be utilized theoretically.

Our question is why it is not possible to repeat a prolonged

---

* This conclusion is not contradicted by the fact that long periods of monotonous work are possible in the factory, where no change of insight or the like is possible. Habituation to monotony is apt to be accompanied by complex daydreaming, which means the development of a parallel phase-sequence activity, so the total pattern of cerebral activity is not at all repetitive. The work of Roethlisberger and Dickson, referred to above, also shows that the behavior is related to the ancillary cerebral activity.

Another possible objection can also be considered here. According to the hypothesis presented in the following section, the infant's capacity for an endless repetition of some action or set of words is possible because the phase sequence is not yet well enough consolidated to lead to short-circuiting. The following section modifies the conclusions of this section in one respect, suggesting that it is only the highly organized phase sequence that cannot be repeated in detail; if the sequence loses in degree of organization with the passage of time, it can occur again. Accordingly, the infant's repetitive action is considered to occur during the period when organization is being established. With completion of that process, the repetition disappears.

phase sequence in its entirety—why it must always lead to new assembly combinations, or else give way to some other cerebral activity. The answer may be that the mere occurrence of a particular phase sequence, once, induces changes at the synapse (memory) that make it impossible for exactly the same sequence to occur again, unless the synaptic changes have disappeared with time. This can be made more specific, and made to comprise an explanation for the slow development of excitability that has been discussed in this chapter. This is done by slightly elaborating the assumptions about the memory trace that were made in Chapter 4. The implication is that an immediate re-arousal of a phase sequence is quite possible, but that the synaptic changes of memory then tend to make the sequence short-circuit * and run off so quickly that it cannot hold the field long; if it is to endure, and remain coordinated with environmental stimulation, new elements not so well integrated with it must enter to delay its course.

Nowhere in the preceding chapters has there been any assumption as to the permanence of the synaptic connections established by learning (though it has been concluded that early learning has, in one way or another, permanent *effects* on later learning). This is because until now, at least, there has been no decisive reason to assume either that synaptic knobs once formed are permanent or that they deteriorate with disuse. If (1) they are permanent, one has accounted directly for the permanent effects of early learning, and may assume that forgetting occurs as an addition of new learning: the establishment of further connections changing the time properties of assembly function and so changing the facilitation delivered to other cere-

---

* The reader will recall that the phase sequence is "recurrent" and "anticipatory," containing cyclical conceptual activities schematized as

$$A–B–A–C–B–D–E–F–D–E–G–F–H, \text{ etc.}$$

"Short-circuiting" might cut such a sequence down to

$$A–B–D–H, \text{ etc.}$$

That is, on repetition the sequence might touch only the high spots; after some synaptic knobs have deteriorated, however, D might be no longer able to arouse H directly—only when E, F, and G are also aroused.

bral systems. The connections originally established would still be there, but the original habit would disappear, replaced by a new one. Alternatively, (2) one might assume that a knob disappears with disuse, which accounts directly for forgetting; and, since we have seen reason (in Chapter 6) to think that new learning incorporates earlier learning as a "transfer" effect, the persistence of early memory can be accounted for because most early connections are maintained by the exercise they receive as they take part in the learning of maturity. Either of these two assumptions might thus be made without disturbing the main structure of the theory.

But for the problem now being considered, a solution may be found if we can adopt assumption 2, that an unused connection decays; or, better yet, if we can assume that a very frequently and long-used connection becomes permanent, but that there is a stage in the development of synaptic knobs before which the development is reversible. The old, long-established memory would then last, not reversible except with pathological processes in the brain; less strongly established memories would *gradually* disappear unless reinforced.

Now: suppose a man picks up the book he read last week. The title and the first paragraphs recall the story—the phase sequence runs off quickly, short-circuited, leaving many of the cell-assemblies briefly refractory before they can be aroused by the rest of the printed matter. No cooperation is then possible between sensation and central facilitation; the latter is too far ahead. Something of this sort would account for the continued need of some degree of novelty to maintain wakefulness of choice. The thoroughly familiar arouses a well-organized phase sequence; the very fact that it is well organized means that it runs its course promptly, leaving the field for less well-established sequences: and so, from this theoretical point of view, one would find behavior dominated always by the thought process that is not *fully* organized—one that is achieving a new organization or one in which synaptic decay makes it necessary that organization be reachieved.

This means that the subject will not linger over the thoroughly familiar event even though this is the one that is most capable of arousing and controlling central processes; the control may be momentary only. The totally unfamiliar does not arouse a phase sequence, so "interest" and "motivation" are likely to be preoccupied by whatever is new in the combination of familiar events, and by events that produce *some* frustration or *some* fear (which tend to break up the phase sequence—Chapter 10). Rereading a half-forgotten novel would thus be possible; immediately after the conclusion of any exciting or interesting series of events a repetition would not be exciting (or not as exciting, depending on the degree to which synaptic changes have produced short-circuiting); in the following minutes, hours, or days the subject's responsiveness to that sequence of events would steadily rise as the synaptic changes regressed. Similarly, the psychological function of a night's sleep may be to permit a certain decay in the particular connections that were established or strengthened by the previous day's behavior, so that the behavior may recur again as a cooperation between sensory and central processes.

If it should be true that such reversible growth processes occur, the problem of the slow changes of excitability might thus be solved. Is the idea at all plausible? One is accustomed to thinking of the nerve cell as a static structure (as it is after being fixed and stained), and of growth as a very slow process. Yet it may be recalled that Cajal (among others) conjectured that the change at the synapse in learning is an ameboid outgrowth of the cell (see, *e.g.*, Freeman, 1934, footnote p. 23), which might need very little time for its occurrence.

Cajal's proposal has been disregarded by psychologists and no longer figures in discussions of learning. Presumably, this is partly because the whole theory of synaptic connections and resistances fell into disrepute some time ago. But it has been seen (Chapter 1) that modern neurophysiology makes it possible to reopen this entire question, and so Cajal's idea cannot be at once dismissed as fantastic.

As to the time needed for an outgrowth of the cell wall, we may note (1) that the actual distance involved may be very short indeed, and (2) that reverberatory activity in the assembly would serve to prolong the time in which a structural change could be completed. An ameboid outgrowth would be reversible; but the mere absence of the electrochemical influence which produces the outgrowth might not act as forcefully and promptly as its presence. So it is possible to assume, in the light of the psychological evidence, that synaptic decay occurs slowly and perhaps is never quite complete. Thus each repetition of the ameboid change at a particular point might leave a higher residual level, and with a frequent occurrence the outgrowth might become permanent. These assumptions then would correlate directly with the fact that memory can be quickly established but declines slowly, and with the fact that there is apt to be little or no forgetting of the long-practiced response.

It is proposed therefore that some such postulate should at the least be considered seriously, for it would help us to deal not only with (1) the facts of learning, but also with the formidable difficulty of understanding (2) the reversals of motivation discussed in this chapter, (3) the length of time over which excitability (rather than excitation) may on occasion increase, and (4) mental fatigue without a fatigue of the neurons and effectors that enter directly into the response. The assumptions discussed above do not help particularly to deal with a behavioral excitation (except to suggest that its time course may depend on the rate of establishment of new—and reversible—connections); but they do appear to account directly for long-term changes in excitability, and in general for the *psychological* component in sleep and waking, in sexual responsiveness and so on, and in the effects of novelty on these conditions. It is of course evident that some degree of novelty, combined with what is predominantly familiar, is stimulating and exciting over a wide range of activities—from sexual responsiveness (Beach, 1947a; Kinsey, Pomeroy, and Martin, 1948) to the appreciation of painting or music, or the pleasures of exploration.

I do not propose to discuss the neurological assumption further, but only point out once more that the decay of memory allows what has been experienced to become relatively novel again and, therefore, exciting; so that the necessity of a lapse of time between repetitions of some activities can now be fitted into a more general statement of the conditions of pleasure.

THE NATURE OF PLEASURE

The theory that has been developed implies that pleasure is not the activity of particular structures in the nervous system, and not even a particular kind or pattern of cerebral organization, but fundamentally a directed *growth* or *development in cerebral organization*. It is thus necessarily a transient state of affairs in which a conflict is being reduced, an incipient disorganization being dissipated, or a new synthesis in assembly action being achieved. The preceding section has tried to explain why such states of affairs should dominate cerebral processes; in other words, to explain why pleasure should have the peculiar place in behavior that it has, without covert recourse to an animistic consciousness; just as the discussion of emotional disturbance and pain, in other chapters, has tried to provide mechanically or deterministically for the avoidance of certain activities and situations.

Those sensory conditions are called pleasant, then, which contribute to the current development in the cerebrum, or which consist of the decline of a sensory process that interferes with development. If going to sleep is, as has been suggested, the establishment of an "intrinsic" organization, the process according to the definition above should be pleasant—as in fact it is; and to the drowsy subject those stimuli are pleasant which actively support the development of hypersynchrony. But some eight hours later, as the subject is waking up, the pleasant sights and sounds are those that "catch his interest" and promote another kind of organization, without hypersynchrony. The *same* stimulus is thus pleasant at one time, not at another; when the event that could be interesting later occurs too soon in the waking-up process, and disrupts hypersynchrony without promptly establishing a phase sequence, it is the very reverse of pleasant.

In view of the discussion in the preceding section of the effect of short-circuiting on motivation, there is a paradoxical implication here. Sensory events should not support the phase sequence too strongly, so that it runs its course immediately and cannot continue to dominate association-area activity. The well-developed phase sequence depends, for a continued existence, on repeated checks from the environment. Hence, as we saw in the preceding section, the preoccupation with what is new but not too new, with the mildly frustrating or the mildly fear-provoking. Many adult sports of course depend for their pleasure on the presence of some danger; and both Woodworth (1921) and Valentine (1930) have remarked on the tendency of children to seek out the frightening situation in which the degree of emotional stimulation remains under control and can be terminated at will. This seems wholly parallel to an adult's reading of "thrillers" and ghost stories.

Similarly, problem-solving involves frustration, and many of the activities that are sources of pleasure actually depend on problem-solving—not only in games like bridge or chess, but also, as Woodworth and others have remarked. in art appreciation and novel reading.

In music, again, the dissonances that are harsh and disruptive at first become pleasant as they become more familiar, but finally are dull and boring (Chandler, 1934). The course of events is: first, a dissonance with too much conflict to elicit an organized cerebral action; secondly, with the establishment of new assemblies, or modification of existing ones (due to repeated stimulation by the new tone combination), an organized activity is aroused, in which, however, some conflict remains; and, finally, organization reaches a point at which the sensory stimulation no longer offers any check to the phase sequence, and pleasure has disappeared. This phenomenon in music might be subsumed quite well under Woodworth's generalization concerning the role of problem-solving in art appreciation, but still more easily by the present formulation. What I have sought here is a generalization that would subsume not only the problem-solving factor, but also the effects of novelty and of a mild degree of fear, in contributing to pleasure.

In its relation to the rest of the theory presented in this book, the discussion of pleasure has had two significances. First, it is important to show that the theory of emotional disturbance in the following chapter does not require that all conflict is unpleasant and grossly disruptive of behavior; on the contrary, some degree of conflict is stimulating and necessary to the maintenance of normal responsiveness to the environment.

Secondly, whether it is eventually found to be adequate or not, this discussion of pleasure together with the hypotheses of the nature of pain and emotional disturbance represents my attempt to be rid once and for all of the little man inside the skull who *approves* of some sensory events relayed to him by the nervous system, *disapproves* of others, and guides behavior accordingly: who encourages stimulation of the afferents from the genitalia in his crafty and teleological aim to perpetuate the species, and who for the same purposes becomes violent when C fibers are stimulated or when he foresees that they are going to be. By some such approach as the one suggested, it may become possible to understand the directedness and order in behavior, and the variability of motivation, as produced by neural functioning alone.

10. *Emotional Disturbances*

The discussion of emotion has been about as confused as that of any topic in psychology, partly because the terminology is often equivocal and partly because tradition carries great weight in this part of the field and it is hard to keep a modern point of view consistently. The present chapter deals with emotional disturbance instead of emotion, for reasons to be made plain; and the discussion is limited in other respects. It is not concerned mainly with sham rage and the hypothalamus, or with emotion as a kind of awareness, or with emotion as it may exist in states of quiet affection and the like. "Emotional disturbance" here is used to refer to the violent and unpleasant emotions, roughly, and to the transient irritabilities and anxieties of ordinary persons as well as to neurotic or psychotic disorder. Let me offer what justification I can for such an arrangement of topics.

EMOTION AS DISTINCT FROM SHAM RAGE

Since the work of Bard (1934), the phenomenon of sham rage and its dependence on the posterior hypothalamus have held the center of the stage in the theory of emotion. But the analyses of Lashley (1938c) and Masserman (1942), particularly where they have dealt with the clinical data that were supposed to establish the diencephalon as the seat of human emotion, have limited the emotional functions of this region to a motor integration. An equally significant modification of his earlier work has been made by Bard (1942) himself: He has reported that rage can be evoked from cats in which the pos-

235

terior hypothalamus *only* has been destroyed—a most important observation.

Thus, "rage" is not localized in the hypothalamus. Also, the rage of the decorticate cat is markedly different from the normal, so the name "sham rage" was properly chosen and should be taken literally. Sham rage is different in its time properties, lacking duration or after-discharge following stimulation; it is different in the rigidity of its pattern, having almost none of the normal variability of motor expression; and it differs radically in the limited range of stimulation that is adequate to elicit it. Also, Spiegel, Miller, and Oppenheimer (1940) have reported the production of rage by lesions of (1) tuberculum olfactorium, (2) hippocampus and fornix, and (3) amygdaloid complex; and slight, transient signs of rage from damage to (4) the pyriform cortex.

Apart from these considerations, there are other emotional processes besides those that produce overt rage behavior. It is true that fear as well as rage has been evoked from the decorticate cat, but apparently only by auditory stimulation and with considerable difficulty. Further, strong emotional disturbance can exist in the intact animal without producing either clearcut attack or cowering and flight. The problem of emotion, in short, is not simply the problem of the motor pattern of sham rage (or "sham fear"). It is of course essential to have discovered the unexpected extent to which rage and fear patterns may appear in the decorticate animal. Bard's work was one of the most important single contributions to understanding emotion. But, given that knowledge, we must go on next to ask how the hypothalamic expression is modified by the presence of a large thalamus and cortex, how learning affects emotional behavior, and the relationship of emotion to perception and thought.

EMOTION NOT A STATE OF CONSCIOUSNESS

Traditionally, emotion is an awareness, an event in consciousness. Here, perhaps more than anywhere else in psychology, a traditional interactionism (which is animism) tends to persist. The afferent excitation is thought to produce a feeling or awareness, *and that feeling then acts on the nervous system*—it must do so, according to such ideas, for it is the *feeling* that makes the subject sweat or tremble or run away, and the sweat glands and the legs are controlled by nerve fibers.

Just such an inconsistency of thought has led to an endless, and pointless, debate on the James-Lange theory of emotion. What James and Lange were accounting for, again, was that emotional feeling or awareness; they postulated that the awareness is a set of sensations, that the awareness follows and does not cause emotional behavior ("I see the bear, I run, I feel afraid"). Their critics proceeded to show that emotional expression is still there in the dog whose sensory processes have been interfered with, and thought this a refutation of the theory. But such an argument is totally irrelevant; James did not say that emotional *behavior* depends on sensations from the limbs and viscera.

It is equally irrelevant to show that emotional expression is centrally organized, in the hypothalamus. If James had raised the question at all, he must have assumed something of the sort; remember that what he denied was that consciousness intervenes between stimulus and response. Therefore, showing that the "higher" centers of the cortex are not needed for the response is clearly support for his position. The extraordinary *non sequitur* of such criticisms, made by some very distinguished critics indeed, would not be possible if there were not the immutable idea that *only* emotional awareness or feeling can produce emotional response. If the response is there, the feeling must be also. Such illogic, assuming James to be wrong first, in order to prove him wrong, is the clearest evidence of the hold traditional ideas have on psychological thought.

But we must get rid of the tradition both for scientific consistency and because psychological observers have been unanimous in denying that there is any special, fundamental category of consciousness that can be called emotion. "Emotional experience ⋯ is a highly variable state [and] often partakes of the complicated nature of a judgment" (Landis and Hunt, 1932). I have reviewed the evidence on this point elsewhere (Hebb, 1946a) and need not go into it again. Since it seems that the term emotion does not refer to a special kind of event in consciousness, and since in any case we must not slip into the inconsistency of treating an immaterial awareness as a causal agency, the term is not very useful in its traditional significance. At the same time, we must postulate that the disturbances of emotional behavior have a neural origin; and the term emotion still can be useful to refer to the neural processes that produce emotional behavior.

It is important to be clear that in this discussion "emotion" is a reference to the hypothetical neural processes that produce emotional behavior; explicitly, it refers neither to an immaterial state of consciousness nor to the observable pattern of emotional behavior.

EMOTION AS A DISORGANIZING INFLUENCE

The third point to be clarified is the distinction between emotional disturbance and those processes (also called emotional) which are inherently organizing and motivating. A paper by Leeper (1948) has urged that all emotion be considered to have such an integrating function. He has expressed a commonly held point of view, and has at the same time I believe clouded the issue with which he dealt. His position demands consideration.

Leeper has shown effectively that regarding emotion as disorganizing has led some of us into an inconsistency, but he has proposed another inconsistency to take its place. He points out that others have first defined emotion as a disorganization of behavior and have then gone on to give mother-love as one example of emotion. This is certainly inconsistent. But how is it different logically from defining emotion as something that makes behavior more efficient and at the same time giving, as examples, the stage fright that ruins a performance, the anger that makes a boxer less skillful, and the mental depression that makes a man unable to earn a living? I must add at once that Leeper anticipated this criticism. He answered it by saying that, though emotion may sometimes disorganize, the disorganization is not characteristic because it occurs only (1) when emotion is extreme, or (2) when the emotion conflicts with some other motivation. As far as one can see, however, the first of these explanations depends on a mistaken use of analogy, the second begs the question.

1. It might be doubted whether emotion is disorganizing only when extreme. A touch of shyness or of self-consciousness, for example, may sometimes ruin one's conversational skills. Leave this to one side, however, and accept the assumption that only strong emotion disrupts behavior.

The idea that such an effect does not indicate the true nature of emotion depends on this analogy: An excess of salt or oxygen has toxic effects, "but we do not use this as a means of determining the normal functions of such products. The same logic, then, should apply to emotional processes" (Leeper, 1948, p. 15). But we must really use the same logic. We must, that is, ask the same question in both cases. The question does not concern the "normal function" of emotion, but what emotion *is*. No one doubts that fear has a useful function, aiding survival; the question is, how? Might fear not be a simple disrupter of behavior and still be useful, if the disruption is mainly of the behavior that gets us in trouble? Emotion could then be disorganization and still have its survival value, because the disorganization is selective, eliminating some actions and allowing others to take their place.

If we accept the analogy between emotion and salt we still can say that emotion is disruptive of behavior, that it generally has a useful function when it occurs in moderate degree and bad effects when there is too much of it—exactly as with salt or oxygen.

2. In discussing the stage fright that keeps a pianist from giving a good performance, Leeper says the emotion is not a disorganizer of behavior because, by itself, it would produce only flight—a well-organized pattern of behavior. This seems to beg the question, since the pianist neither runs away nor stays to play well. Leeper says it is not the emotion that produces his incoordinations, but the conflict. But if there were no conflict at all, would there be any emotion? Are the conflict and the emotion quite independent?

The difficulty here is clearest by Leeper's own criterion of "organization." He points out first that any directed behavior means the suppression of conflicting tendencies; so conflict is not *ipso facto* disorganization. The test is "whether [an] interference is relatively chaotic and haphazard, or whether the suppressions and changes of subordinate activities are harmonious with some main function that is being served." The trembling, palmar sweating, disturbance of breathing, and incoordinations of the pianist's fingers, obviously, are not harmonious with the main function being served—until he actually runs away. Could we regard his emotion as solely organizing even then? See what this implies. If we are really consistent in saying that any disorganization in emotion is accidental, that emotion is essentially an organizer only, then a well-organized avoidance is at least as much an instance of fear as an ill-organized one. Consequently, the pianist who anticipates the possibility of stage fright, and calmly decides to keep away from the stage, provides as good an example of emotion as the one that trembles before an audience. We have deliberately got rid of any criterion of emotion except that it "arouses, sustains, and directs" behavior. We have equated avoidance and fear, aggression and anger. But these surely are not identical.

The upshot of such an argument is to broaden the category of emotion so much that it includes all psychological processes. We should then have to find another name for the distinctive event that—at present—is called emotional.

How are we to find some halfway point between this position and the one that Leeper has criticized so effectively? I think it is evident that Munn, Young, Dockeray, Woodworth, Landis, and so on (authors criticized for treating emotion as disorganization), were after all not as absurd as Leeper thought them; at the same time, he has made untenable the proposition that "emotion" simply means a disruption of behavior.

A way out, I believe, can be found if we do two things: first, stop talking about emotions as a single, fundamental kind of unitary psychological process, and separate (1) those in which the tendency is to maintain or increase the original stimulating conditions (pleasurable or integrative emotions) from (2) those in which the tendency is to abolish or decrease the stimulus (rage, fear, disgust), including, however, depressions in which the organism may discover no way of escape from the condition giving rise to the emotion. Secondly, if it is assumed that stimuli in class 2 above are essentially disintegrative, it must also be recognized that the disintegration in rage or fear is often *incipient* or *potential* and likely to be successfully averted by the aggression or avoidance of the subject.

As to the first of these points, we have no need to bring together pleasure-seeking and melancholia, mother-love and temper tantrums, always in the same single category—"emotion." I have, in the preceding chapter, discussed pleasure as a special problem; and I propose in this one to try to deal with a quite different sort of process. Since "emotion" undoubtedly will often continue to mean affection or pride as well as anxiety or shame, "emotional disturbance" is a better way of designating the subject matter of the present chapter.

RAGE AND FEAR IN CHIMPANZEES

The theory of emotion proposed by Watson (1924) is by now classical. It held that there are three innate emotions, rage, fear, and love: rage aroused by a restriction of physical movement, fear by a loud noise or sudden loss of support (and presumably, pain), love by stimulation of the genitalia. These stimuli may then serve to condition others: if a child fears animals, it is because he has been scratched by a cat or knocked over, perhaps, by a friendly dog while learning to walk. As soon as one tries to apply this theory to the emotional disturbances that are actually observed in children, serious difficulty shows up; it is not really plausible, and it has been subjected to powerful criticism by Dennis (1940) on rage, by Jones and Jones (1928) on fear, and by Valentine (1930), also on fear. But it has been hard to document the criticism with experimental evidence, for two reasons. First, it is not safe or socially permitted to arouse a strong degree of emotion in human subjects for experimental study. Important as the topic is, consequently, we have surprisingly little exact information about the causes and consequences of human emotion—above all, of adult emotion. Secondly, when one studies emotion as it occurs socially, outside the laboratory, it is almost impossible to know the antecedent conditions as they must be known if one is to understand the present responses of the subject.

But neither of these objections need apply to the study of emotion in animals, and the chimpanzee fortunately has an emotional repertoire that is very like man's. The things that annoy us are apt to annoy him, and he shows his annoyance much as we do; his fears in some respects are astonishingly like man's—in what is feared, in complexity of the causes of fear, in the relation of fear to intellectual development, in resistance to extinction or reconditioning, and in the marked individual differences between one subject and the next. Even more, there are data on what were with practical certainty two cases of neurosis or psychosis in mature chimpanzees whose histories were known from birth or very early infancy, one born in the Yerkes Laboratories of Primate Biology and one captured in the first year of life. These animals of the Yerkes colony can be studied as human subjects cannot. Their histories are known in detail, being recorded in individual diaries. With these data, one is in a position to see just what complexity of response must be provided for in a theory of emotion, chronic as well as acute.

The causes of rage may have nothing to do with physical restraint of movement. When the chimpanzee Dita, in heat, would sit where he could watch her from the next cage but one, Don seemed calm (if not content); but he had a temper tantrum repeatedly whenever she left the outer cage for an inner room where he could not see her. When Mona had a noisy temper tantrum because Pan had stolen a peanut from her, Pan was finally enraged to the point of beating her up. A chimpanzee may be angered by a reproof, by being startled, or by being obliged to look at something unpleasant such as a model of a snake. These causes act "spontaneously"; that is, the emotional disturbance does not have to be learned, any more than a human being must learn specially to be angry at disturbance of the peace, at being shown something nasty, or at being momentarily scared by a practical joker (Hebb, 1945a)—although, as we shall see, a certain kind of learning, in infancy, may have to have been established first.

The causes of fear include not only loud noise or sudden fall, but snakes with which an animal has never had contact (this can be known certainly with some chimpanzees reared in the nursery), solitude, and the strange or mysterious. McCulloch and Haslerud (1939) have analyzed such fears in a young chimpanzee reared quite apart from others, and were thus able to show that they are not necessarily acquired by "social conditioning" or imitation. I discovered accidentally that some of the chimpanzees of the Yerkes colony might have a paroxysm of terror at being shown a model of a human or chimpanzee head detached from the body; young infants showed no fear, increasing excitement was evident in the older (half-grown) animals, and those adults that were not frankly terrified were still considerably excited. These individual differences among adults, and the difference of response at different ages, are quite like the human differences in attitude toward snakes, the frequency and strength of fear increasing up to the age of seventeen or so in persons who had never been injured by a snake (Jones and Jones, 1928). The increase fits in with the conception that many fears depend on some degree of intellectual development, and so with the idea that the range of such fears is characteristic of "higher" animals like man and chimpanzee (McBride and Hebb, 1948).

The observations using detached heads were then followed up by others, using various stimuli: an isolated eye and eyebrow, a cast of a chimpanzee's face, a skull, a cured chimpanzee hide, an anesthetized chimpanzee.

Two things appeared: first, that such stimulation may be primarily a source of profound *excitation,* rather than specifically fear-producing; the excitation was usually followed by avoidance, but sometimes by aggression, and sometimes it produced a marked autonomic reaction combined with apparent friendliness. On occasion, a confusing mixture of all these reactions was seen.

Secondly, this primitive excitation appeared to be fully parallel to the human emotional disturbance that may occur at the sight of a badly deformed face, in watching a major operation, dissection, or autopsy for the first time, or as a result of contact with a dead body (Hebb, 1946*b*). This human disturbance, like the chimpanzee's, is not specific—it may take the form of nausea, of vascular disturbance and dizziness, of disgust or fear, or may even facilitate anger (*e.g.,* at "desecration" of the dead). It is important to recognize individual differences of sensitivity to such experiences, and the loss of sensitivity with repeated exposure (which is presumably an effect of learning); but this does not mean that the responses are wholly learned. The evidence is very definitely to the contrary: the degree of excitation is likely to be strongest on the first exposure, provided certain *other* experiences have preceded. On the other hand, the disappearance of response with repetition must be an effect of learning, and I believe we must assume that it is learning also that establishes any integrated response to such stimuli, transforming a nonspecific emotional disturbance into an organized flight (disturbance plus a tendency to flight then constituting fear) or aggression (constituting rage).

The complex origin of emotional disturbance may be clearest in the infant fear of strangers. About the age of four months the chimpanzee reared in the nursery, with daily care from three or four persons only and seeing few others, begins to show an emotional disturbance at the approach of a stranger (Hebb and Riesen, 1943). The disturbance increases in degree in the following months. This is "shyness" but may become much more violent than that term would usually imply. It commonly shows up in the human baby about the sixth or seventh month. (The age difference is in keeping with the fact that chimpanzee development generally takes only about two-thirds of the time for the corresponding human development.) Everyday experience tells us that shyness does not occur in the human child that is continually in contact with strangers; and that it is very strong, as a distrust or fear of "foreigners" (even in adults) in isolated communities. We might then suppose that the excitation out of which the fear develops is aroused innately at the sight of a stranger, but extinguished if enough new faces are seen with no accompanying injury. But this supposition is wrong: there is definite evidence that the response is *not* innately established.

Dennis (1934) pointed out that human patients, congenitally blind and operated on to restore vision, have shown no emotional disturbance at the first sight of a human face. Chimpanzees reared in darkness, and brought into the light at an age when the response normally would be at its strongest, show not the slightest disturbance at the sight of either friend or stranger. *But* some time later, after a certain amount of visual learning has gone on, the disturbance begins to appear exactly as in other animals.

So it appears that the emotional disturbance is neither learned nor innate: a certain learning must have preceded, but given that learning the disturbance is complete on the first appearance of certain stimulus combinations. Dennis (1940) has also made it clear that temper tantrums are not learned, and still require that other things have been learned first. We are accustomed to think of any particular response as either learned or innate, which is apt to be a source of confusion in thinking about such things as far apart as an insightful act or neurotic behavior—is the response inherited, or acquired? The answer is, Neither: either Yes or No would be very misleading. The irrational emotional disturbances of man and chimpanzee are fully dependent on learning, but are not learned in the usual sense of the term.

On the other hand, in order to account for the specific processes of rage and fear, and the integrated, adaptive responses of aggression and flight, we must I believe give learning its role. This point will be returned to after broadening the field of our inquiry by considering two cases of mental illness in chimpanzees.

MENTAL ILLNESS IN CHIMPANZEES

Now, before turning to the mechanism of these responses, let me report two cases of apparent neurosis or psychosis in the chimpanzee. Here again we have the advantage of knowing more of the previous experience of the patients than is possible with most human patients in the clinic. We have no verbal recollections to go by (recollection in clinical cases, after all, is apt to be unreliable); but the animals' experience, in cage life, is much less varied than a man's would be and—once more—the chimpanzees of the Yerkes colony have been under daily observation by trained observers who have faithfully recorded at the time of its occurrence any observed illness, unusual experience, or peculiarity of behavior.

We have further, in the particular cases to be discussed, the invaluable asset of control subjects. It happens that four chimpanzees were reared together for a large part of the developmental period, in the same circumstances: Alpha, Kambi, Bula, and Bimba. Alpha and Bula were born in captivity, Kambi and Bimba were captured wild, at about nine months of age. Nothing was recorded, and nothing could later be recalled, by the trained workers who reared them, that would account for any great differences in the adult personalities of these four chimpanzees. Yet, by the time of adolescence, one of the four (Kambi) was a hypochondriac—as far as behavior could show; and one other (Alpha) in full maturity suddenly developed an extreme phobia. Let me give these histories in more detail.

Alpha was born in 1930, the first chimpanzee to be born in the Yerkes colony. She was taken from her mother immediately and reared apart from other chimpanzees until she was one year old (Jacobsen, Jacobsen, and Yoshioka, 1932). She then was brought into the laboratory, as one of the group of four to which I have already referred. The menarche was at age eight, and her sexual behavior with males has always been entirely normal. The concensus of the staff was that Alpha, as she became mature, had a strong liking for human company, was not particularly bright and was very obstinate but still a good experimental subject. Otherwise she was just a chimpanzee. Chimpanzees, like men, have their individual peculiarities, and no great prognostic significance was attached to some small peculiarities of Alpha's— although, in the light of her later psychiatric problem, some of the peculiarities were peculiarly Freudian. Alpha would definitely not have anything to do with any carrot with a forked root, nor usually with any long cylindrical vegetable such as okra, though when carrot or okra was cut up before her eyes she would accept and eat the pieces immediately. Finally, she had a marked tendency to masturbate, frequently against the water faucet projecting from the wall of her cage, whenever a human being came in sight.

In 1942, when Alpha was twelve (corresponding roughly to full maturity), a serious disturbance of behavior appeared. With no warning signs, she suddenly refused all solid foods, despite being very hungry. It then appeared that she would eat at once if food was cut small for her; and a number of tests showed conclusively that she was violently afraid of contact with any piece of food more than an inch or so in length or thickness. Considerations given elsewhere (Hebb, 1947) lead me to believe that this behavior cannot be sufficiently explained as due to injury, as from a thorn or stinging insect in the food, though such event may well have been the precipitant. The fears fluctuated considerably, but waned gradually until they had completely disappeared two years after the original onset; then, after another year, they reappeared with equal suddenness and severity (this second episode clearing up more promptly, however).

A further phenomenon, of the greatest importance for showing the parallel with clinical cases, was observed during the first of these two neurotic or psychotic episodes. Four months after the first onset, when the fear of food had greatly decreased, Alpha out of a blue sky developed a strong fear of me, later a violent aggression, and then (having been soaked with water from a hose for her persistent attacks) became quite friendly, at the same time reverting to her fear of food.

Two friendly critics, on the occasion of the original report of this case, were able (with serious intent) to diagnose the case and explain the cause of illness. Alpha, in short, was in love with me; the earlier fear of forked carrot and of cylindrical objects, and the masturbation against a projecting water faucet, were not the only Freudian features of the case. The aggression occurred because Alpha had had to repress her unmaidenly desires, with an inevitable result. This is an interesting idea; liking chimpanzees (or some chimpanzees), it would please me to think them capable of such delicacy, such capacity for repressing vulgar desire—in short, to think of chimpanzees as having Superegos.

But if Alpha had a Superego its operation was rather hit-and-miss, and in many of her dealings with other chimpanzees (or with the staff), and in some of her personal habits, there was little sign of self-imposed restrictions. If Alpha was in love, it must have been with someone else; and her emotional disturbance had no relation to fluctuating level of sex drive, which in chimpanzees is directly correlated with the menstrual cycle. It might be amusing to try to psychoanalyze Alpha, but it seems it would not be very profitable either as therapy or as a contribution to knowledge.

The second history is quite different.

Kambi was captured at the estimated age of nine months and reared constantly in the company of other females of her own age. From eighteen months of age onward, she was one of the group of four—Alpha, Kambi, Bula, Bimba. Morphine addiction was briefly established at the age of eight (Spragg, 1940). She showed almost none of the usual sex play before menarche (at age nine) and copulated once only after it—although she showed the physical signs of coming into heat periodically, with the menstrual cycle. She was spayed at the age of twelve for experimental purposes, with no apparent change in over-all personality.

To summarize Kambi's behavioral disturbance first in clinically intelligible language, she gave the impression from early childhood of being introverted, with a very strong preference for human company, and subject to periods of depression. During adolescence, the depression when it occurred was extreme. The attacks continued after maturity and often lasted for months at a time. Her depression was sometimes initiated by a somatic illness; when it did begin so, it did not clear up with the illness but continued long after.*

The actual evidence of depression is as follows. Ordinarily Kambi was easily annoyed by failure to get something she wanted, but she was always responsive to (and acted in a way that was likely to get) attention from the human staff; definitely more interested in such attention than in food, but ordinarily getting enough to eat. But then for a period up to six or eight months in length she would sit day after day with her back hunched up against the wall of her cage, never seeking attention and rarely responding to human overtures, and almost totally uninterested in food so that if she were not caged alone she might have starved: definitely a different animal.

Once more the case shows a Freudian element, in Kambi's

---

* I am indebted, for some of the observations in this summary, to Dr. Henry W. Nissen, who knew Kambi thoroughly in her infancy and at maturity. It was he who obtained her in Africa and brought her to the Yerkes colony with Bimba and a number of other young animals, and later had personal charge of their rearing. I should emphasize that the description is a convenient way of reporting *behavior* and does not necessarily imply anything about conscious states. Kambi in short acted as a depressed introverted human might act.

lack of sexual motivation (which has, however, been observed in other animals at the Yerkes laboratories, with no sign of psychotic involvement). But no traumatic sexual event can be adduced to account for this. The one copulation that was observed was quite normal, and Kambi's lack of sexual responsiveness had appeared much earlier. Disturbed ideas about sex are common in human mental illness, but so are disturbances of eating and sleep, and there is usually no evidence to show that sexual conflict occurs first and is the cause of the more profound disturbance of which it is part. In Kambi's case there was no evidence of sexual conflict at all—simply a complete lack of apparent interest.

The emphasis in these two histories of chimpanzee psychosis, or neurosis, is on the absence of any particular experience to which the behavioral breakdown can be ascribed. But I do not suggest for a moment that experience is not a factor; I shall urge later that experience is a factor in almost any emotional breakdown. The point here is that if it was the main factor, in these two cases, it must have operated in a way that we do not at present understand at all, and quite unlike the mechanism of the "experimental neurosis."

The fact to be kept in mind is that we have two chimpanzees as control subjects (in an unplanned experiment, since no one foresaw the later course of development in Alpha and Kambi, but still an excellent experiment). After capture, Bimba had the same general experiences as Kambi (both captured at the estimated age of nine or ten months), in every respect that our present knowledge would suggest is important. There is no basis for postulating some special trauma for Kambi before she came under psychological observation, for the diaries of the two animals show that for the first three years of captivity it was Bimba, not Kambi, that was less well adapted to her environment: more fearful, less trusting, less cooperative in an experiment—until the age of four, when the roles were gradually reversed.

Again, Alpha and Bula were both born in captivity; and though Bula was left with her mother until the age of fourteen months whereas Alpha was removed at birth, there is little sign in the diaries of the subsequent four or five years to show that this had any effect on their later adjustments.

Experience, and experience alone, may have been the decisive factor in the breakdown of two of these four animals at maturity; but, if so, it operated in some way that is quite mysterious in the light of our present knowledge of behavior. Freudian theory has the credit of recognizing the existence of a kind of learning that causes, apparently, no immediate emotional disturbance and yet may contribute to one much later. Such learning undoubtedly occurs, and may well have been involved in Alpha's or Kambi's illness, but if this is to be postulated we must find some way of incorporating it into other learning theory—not as an *ad hoc* assumption specially made to deal with mental illness.

MECHANISMS OF EMOTIONAL RESPONSE

What I believe to be the mechanisms of primary emotional disturbance have been discussed in preceding chapters, together with a mechanism of emotional learning. It remains to pull the earlier discussions together and to try to show how a mechanism of learning might transform emotional disturbance, as a breakdown of adaptation, into the adaptive responses of attack, flight, and so on: that is, how anger or fear might develop out of an undifferentiated emotional disturbance, and how a failure to develop an adaptive mode of response might constitute neurosis.

The aspects of emotional disturbance that mainly determine this treatment of the problem can be summarized as follows: (1) the great variety of causes of disturbance, ranging from an unfamiliar combination of familiar things (fear of the strange) or an interruption of sleep, to hunger, nutritional deficiency, or withdrawal of a drug from the addict; (2) the fact that a single cause may produce anger, fear, or nausea and faintness, in the same subject at different times, or in different subjects; (3) the great variety of expression even of a single emotion; and (4) the different ways in which the expression of emotion changes, as the subject is habituated to the stimulating conditions.

To account for item 1, it has been assumed that the emotion is a disturbance in the timing of thalamo-cortical firing—a disruption of the phase sequence when the subject is awake, of the intrinsic organization of cerebral activity when he is asleep. The disruption may be slight and brief, in this hypothesis, or extensive and prolonged; it may be produced by a conflict of phase sequences, by a lack of sensory support for the phase sequence, or by metabolic changes.

Now the question is, how far a second assumption can account for items 2, 3, and 4, listed above. This assumption was made earlier (p. 150), to account for the learning by a rat to choose a lighter door and avoid a darker one, in discrimination training. It is, in short, that a disruption of thalamo-cortical timing tends to prevent the recurrence of the phase sequence that led up to that disruption on previous occasions, because of the cyclical (anticipatory and recurrent) organization of the phase sequence. This is a mechanism of learning, and it is proposed now that it would account for the adaptive features of rage (emotional disturbance plus attack) or fear (the same thing plus avoidance), as learned behavior that is determined by the accompanying emotional disturbance. Particularly, it would account for the variability of the behavior and for the marked tendency of the emotional element itself to disappear as the originally disturbing situation is repeated.

Above and beyond the question of the intrinsic plausibility of the idea that flight, in fear, is a learned response (it may not be as implausible as it seems at first glance), is the apparent necessity of my first assumption, that emotional disturbance is a disruption of cerebral timing. If this is necessary, we must then find *some* way of accounting for the other aspects of emotional behavior. Let us look again, then, at the causes of emotional disturbance, which may be arranged in three classes.

Class I. Take as a starting point the infant chimpanzee's fear of the strange. It has already been seen that this is not innate, not a fear of what is totally strange, since the animal reared in darkness does not show it until vision in general has begun to have some "meaning" for him (until it arouses phase sequences). Consider further that a familiar attendant A, wearing the equally familiar coat B of another attendant, may arouse the fear just as a complete stranger would. A causes no disturbance; B causes none; A and B together cause a violent emotional reaction. It is this sort of fact that makes it necessary to suppose that two phase sequences may interfere with one another. The first class of emotional disturbance thus is one caused by a conflict (which may be extended to the disruptive effect of pain stimuli and other "unpleasant" sensory events).

Class II. Now a second case. It was for long heresy to suppose that there could be a fear of darkness. Darkness is a lack of stimulation (at least after the first few seconds in the dark); how can it arouse an emotional response? Fear of the dark is not likely to appear until the age of three or later in human children (Jersild and Holmes, 1935) and so the skeptic who thought that *his* child developed the fear without cause could be answered by the old appeal to ignorance: how can he be certain, with the varied unsupervised experiences a child must have in a three-year period? However, the violent avoidance of solitude by young chimpanzees (Köhler, 1925) is at least as marked as the human fear of the dark, and can be shown to be due only to the *lack* of the perception of companions. This then implies a second class of emotional disturbance: fear of the dark, fear of solitude, fear aroused by loss of support, and the emotional changes observed by Ramsdell * following prolonged absence of the normal auditory stimulation. It would comprise also emotional disturbance due to contact with a dead body (which lacks warmth and the usual responsiveness); anger at the lack of social response in another person ("inattentiveness"), or a monkey's anger at not finding the particular kind of food reward he expected (Tinklepaugh, 1928); grief; homesickness, and so on.

* Personal communication from Dr. Donald A. Ramsdell, who was concerned to understand the high frequency of marked emotional changes which he observed in veterans following traumatic loss of hearing. He arranged experimentally to deafen himself, effectively eliminating airborne sounds for a period of three days. The results are described by Dr. Ramsdell as follows, particularly with regard to the question whether the deafness would contribute to any neurotic or psychotic tendency:

"In my experience there was a definite increase of irritability and a desire to either withdraw from the field or, if held in the field, to 'charge' into it. This would be comparable to being irritated with a friend, and either withdrawing without saying anything or 'letting him have it.' Such behavior would not be characterized by ideas of persecution nor suspicion of the friend. However, you might say that the desire to 'charge' into a situation is such stuff as paranoia is made of, but for a true paranoid idea of

That a conflict of phase sequences, or a lack of sensory support for the phase sequence, should produce any extensive disruption in the timing of cortical action is not a logically inescapable deduction from the schema of neural action presented in Chapters 4 and 5. What the schematizing actually did was suggest the possibility, as something that would account for a similar effect of two so dissimilar causes and make the relationship between perception and emotional disturbance intelligible. The idea then seemed to gain strong support when it drew attention to another set of facts that is usually forgotten in discussing emotional theory. These facts concern the relationship of emotional disturbance to metabolic changes.

Class III. The third class of the causes of fear, rage, and so on, though it was actually arrived at last in formulating these ideas, comes nearer than either of the others to being a necessary consequence of the neural schema. To the earlier discussion of the effects of chemical changes in the nutrient fluids that bathe the neural cell (p. 196), showing that a disturbance of timing must result, I need add only that a large intracranial tumor, compressing blood vessels and interfering with blood flow, obviously could have similar effects; and also that asthma, or vascular disease, or an antigen acting to produce vascular spasm in intracranial vessels—any of these—might produce emotional disturbance directly, by affecting the amount of oxygen in the blood or the amount of blood that is supplied to neural tissues. Emotional changes are in fact frequently associated

persecution, the capacity for interpersonal relationship must be so weak that real suspicion can develop. Assuming then interpersonal relationships to be secure, I would say that deafness is accompanied by a feeling of perplexity and disorientation analogous to the fear of the dark or fear of solitude. Such a disorientation in one's social milieu need not necessarily involve paranoid disturbances any more than being in the dark would induce one to hear footsteps at his back. In my opinion, the feelings of personal inadequacies (impairment of the body image); irritability, and an exaggerated response to stimuli; and the wish to leave the field or, if held in the field, to 'charge' into it, characterize the experience of deafness."

I should like to draw attention also to Dr. Ramsdell's suggestion that the emotional condition might lead to more than one overt pattern of response. This is relevant to the later discussion of the way in which different "emotions" might develop from the same primitive disturbance.

with all such conditions; and the one assumption that seems to provide a common ground for such varied sources of disturbance (including not only the metabolic changes in Class III but also the perceptual conflicts and perceptual deficits of Classes I and II) is the assumption that emotional disturbance is in the first place a disruption of the timing of neuronal activity in the cerebrum. This also accounts directly for the incoordinations of emotion. Until some better guess is made, we must see what can be done with the assumption; and this imposes the burden of accounting for the integrated and coordinated aspects of emotional behavior (Leeper, 1948).

Now this coordinated part of the behavior, in the unpleasant emotions, has one constant function. It is always such as to tend to put an end to the original stimulation (in the pleasant emotions, of course, this tendency is reversed). *Aggression,* in rage, tends to change the irritating behavior of another animal—by cowing, driving off, or killing the annoyer. *Flight,* in fear, tends to prevent or terminate noxious stimulation. *Avoidance*—turning the head away from an unpleasant sight, covering the ears, holding the nose, or withdrawing the hand, as well as actually running away—tends to stop the stimulation that arouses either an irrational fear of some inert object or the practically equivalent disgust. *Fawning* may be a manifestation of fear as much as flight, and so may the *desperate attack* of a cornered animal: and each is a possible way of putting an end to the emotion-arousing behavior of another organism.

Failure to respond, in shame, is a special case, in which one's own behavior is the emotion-provoking stimulus; the effect of the emotional disturbance is negative, preventing the recurrence of that behavior, but this is also in line with the present thesis, namely: All these effects may be achieved because *strong emotional disturbance tends to prevent the repetition of any line of thought that leads up to it,* and to eliminate the corresponding behavior. In some situations, a primitive, undifferentiated disturbance would develop into fear, where withdrawal is the only thing that ends the disturbance; in others, anger, when attack is the only effective behavior; in still others, either fear or anger might result, when either behavior would be effective, and which result happens would be determined by the animal's past experience as well as by his own inherited peculiarities. But in some situations, and for some subjects, no behavior might be discovered that would abolish the emotional disturbance; and the effect of learning in this case might be to reinforce the visceral disturbance and the incoordinations of the skeletal musculature, and—above all—the disorganization of the phase sequence, which is a disorganization of thought.

This is the point at which neurosis and psychosis enter the theoretical structure: they are (1) conditions of chronic emotional disturbance, or (2) ones in which emotional disturbance, in the past, has effected a lasting modification of the thought process (see footnote, p. 259).

The first objection that might be made to such an approach is this. As the hypothesis has been presented so far, it might suggest that aggression, in anger, appears only by default—only because other forms of behavior have been eliminated—and to common sense this is not reasonable. Aggression appears to have a much more intimate and necessary relation to the emotional disturbance of anger. And so with avoidance, in fear. My first answer is that this may be perfectly true, in the adult; even in the four-year-old. But this proves nothing about the origin of the relationship. Emotional disturbance and the aggression may seem inseparable to us for exactly the same reason that nodding the head and Yes are inseparable—in this culture: because the two have been tied in together by long practice and experience.

It is instructive to observe just what happens in emotional learning, when we do have a chance to observe it. Bridges (cited by Jones, 1933) has shown that children's emotional patterns develop out of a primitive undifferentiated excitation. This fact may not be crucial, for the change may depend on physical maturation and not on a learning process. But when chimpanzees are exposed for the first time to certain emotion-provoking situations, the first effect again appears not to be a specific pattern of adaptation but a generalized excitation. When Alfalfa, one of the chimpanzees reared in darkness by Riesen (1947), was brought out into the light she did not show any emotional disturbance at the sight of strangers; as I have already pointed out, the emotion requires a certain amount of visual experience before it occurs. When signs of the disturbance appeared some time later, they seemed completely unspecific: a raising of the general level of excitation, with signs of autonomic action and undirected movements. I have remarked elsewhere (Hebb, 1946b) on the lack of a consistent mode of response of some adult chimpanzees at the first exposure to a disguised person, wearing a mask and acting in an aggressive manner which they were not used to encountering in human beings; and also on the *gradual* emergence of a consistent mode of emotional response, but different in form for different animals.

The implication of my hypothesis, then, is that adult introspection cannot be an argument against its validity, since the essential learning would be thoroughly established in early infancy.

Observe further the conditions in which the adaptive behavior of adult emotion occurs. Apart from the spinal reflexes aroused by noxious stimulation, a fully coordinated emotional response appears always to be a response to premonitory cues, not in themselves disruptive, but associated with disruptive stimulation. When the primitively disruptive event occurs suddenly, without any warning, the response is never a smooth and economical cooperation of effector organs but is likely to involve startle, trembling, sweating, vocalization, vascular change, and so on, and is then followed by a coordinated response which differs according to the subject's perception of the total situation. If the adaptive behavior of fear (that is, avoidance) is indeed a response to events that are not directly disruptive but premonitory cues associated with disruption, the behavior is by definition a learned response. It is then intelligible why there is usually less emotional activity at maturity. As experience increases, rage and fear would tend to disappear in the familiar environment, for the utilization of premonitory cues, to avoid disturbance that is foreseen but not yet in existence, would become more and more efficient. The integrative part of emotional behavior and the disintegrative are inversely related: as one increases, the other decreases.

The objection that we have just considered is that the connection between aggression and emotional disturbance, in rage, is not an accidental one—established merely by association or by the elimination of alternative modes of reaction. The objection may be taken further. It cannot really be a matter of chance whether fear or anger will result, even in situations in which either avoidance or attack would have the same effect of changing a disruptive stimulation. Characteristically, some situations evoke rage, others fear, and so on. The objection carries weight, and must be considered: I should say at once that I do not believe that it is sufficiently answered by what follows, and there are, with reasonable certainty, important constitutional factors determining the mode of emotional response which I cannot deal with. It is also possible that milder degrees of disruption innately tend to lead to aggression, stronger ones to avoidance.

In addition, however, factors of learning are present that should not be overlooked. One thing that determines whether fear or anger will result when the phase sequence is disrupted may be the particular phase sequence itself, and the effect of earlier learning in similar situations, which determines what alternative sequences are available to take over when the disrupted sequence leaves the field open. With this in mind, observe that anger is characteristically aroused *by the behavior of others* (*i.e.*, by social stimulation) when the behavior is not consistent with what one is proposing to do, when one expects resistance in having the behavior changed, and finally when one thinks one may be able to change it.

It is a humiliating fact that one tends not to get angry at prize-fighters, or at the criticism of the higher-up whose praise or approval is important. This is far from being absolutely true, but it seems that anger is most easily aroused by opposition where one thinks one could prevail by force: where the opponent ought to see that you can get your own way, and give in gracefully.

I believe it is also true that, the more authoritarian the regime in which a child grows up, and the more frequent and severe the punishment he suffers for disobedience, the less likely he is, as an adult, to get angry at higher authority and the more likely to be angered by insubordination. If so, it means that anger does not occur in situations where disruptive stimulation has *regularly* broken up the phase sequence that determines aggression; that it does occur where aggressive behavior has not usually been disrupted before. (That such evidence should have to be resorted to—I know of none apart from such folklore—is the best indication of a lack of scientific knowledge, on a very important topic in psychology, which is due to the difficulty of experimenting with any but the mildest of human emotions.)

Now a final objection to the hypothesis that learning is what mainly differentiates the various emotions. Nothing has been said so far to provide for the exceptional vigor that an emotional response is apt to have. This I believe is the greatest defect in the hypothesis. Several things might be suggested to remedy it. One possibility is that when disorganization occurs it leaves transmission units in the cerebrum ready to fire with any subsequent activity. These units would ordinarily be involved in the assembly action that is now prevented; they may then tend to be recruited by whatever assemblies do act subsequently: increasing the strength of the facilitation delivered to motor centers but also tending to make the motor response less precise (since the recruitment of extra cells would tend to change the frequency properties of the individual assembly). This might also be applied to the pleasurable activity, discussed in the preceding chapter, that depends on first arousing apprehension, then dispelling it. It may offer some cue also to the nature of laughter, which may be most efficiently aroused, perhaps, when there is a combination of phase sequences that produces a minor disturbance of timing immediately followed by a further combination of assemblies that have *no* conflict. There would still remain the fragments, so to speak, of assemblies that were disrupted, which tend to induce *some* motor activity. In some cases this may induce anger or fear or embarrassment, if the disruption is extensive; but in other cases a cortically controlled overactivation of the breathing mechanisms may serve to pick up the fragments—which appears as laughter. First a minor conflict, incongruity or apprehension, then a new perception of the situation that leaves no need of avoidance, nothing to be changed in the behavior of other persons or in the total situation, but still leaves a condition of excitation that must issue in one form of behavior or another.

THE NATURE OF MENTAL ILLNESS

It has already been proposed that mental illness consists either of a chronic disturbance of time relations in the cerebrum, or a lasting distortion of the thought process from such a disturbance at an earlier time.* This is a rather general proposition, and we must now consider the theoretical problems of mental illness in more detail. The general approach that has been proposed may have value only in helping to maintain a point of view that is hard to maintain, and yet essential. The point of view is this: neurosis or psychosis is a product neither of experience nor of constitution, but a joint product of both.

Tradition, once more, is the villain of the piece. In this field we are still dominated by the old dichotomy: is the illness mental or physical, functional or organic, and now, under new names, is it psychosomatic, or just somatic?

It may make sense to ask whether a breakdown is primarily experiential, implying that with an ordinary degree of strain it would not have occurred, or primarily constitutional, implying that the mildest of strains would have caused the breakdown, that the patient's ability to withstand strain was low. But this cannot give us two *kinds* of mental illness, any more than, in a completely parallel situation, there are two kinds of tuberculosis.

If there are not two kinds of mental illness, we have no basis for dismissing the mental illness that goes with pellagra or some glandular dysfunction as not being a "true" psychosis; no basis for thinking of a special category of chronic emotional disturbance, of which experience is the sole cause, and psychotherapy in some form the sole method of cure. Logic and the whole clinical literature require that we remember the role of the con-

* This distinction is not further elaborated in the text. It is primarily based on theoretical considerations, but it seems to agree with the fact that the neurotic or psychotic frequently appears to have found a way of thinking and acting that obviates emotional disturbance. The illness is perhaps either (1) a continued emotional disturbance, with anxiety or the like, or (2) changes in thought (new phase sequences) that are not characteristic of the majority of the population but which avoid some conflict that makes for major disruption of assembly or phase sequence.

stitution in any mental illness, just as we must remember the role of experience. It is hard to avoid going to extremes when this topic is discussed; it is very hard to keep from thinking in terms of the old dichotomy; but I believe we must keep a middle way. Until quite recently, the task of the psychologist and psychiatrist was to keep the medical world from thinking of mental illness as always due to some lesion of the central nervous system—a lesion that usually could not be found. Now the pendulum has swung to the other extreme, and the medical world may be in some danger of overestimating the role of psychological causation in both mental illness and illnesses that used to be called physical. The task is still to find a middle way.

I believe there is no longer a danger that psychological factors in illness will not be recognized: there is hardly a popular journal in the western hemisphere that does not publish articles explaining how illness may be due to worry or to a desire to get out of some sort of trouble. In medical practice it may happen that failure to make a definite diagnosis can automatically determine that the patient is psychoneurotic. This tendency has been protested against by physicians concerned with the welfare of the patient (Bowman, 1946; Wilson and Rupp, 1947). But it also represents a mode of thinking by the psychologist or psychiatrist himself that may hinder the development of theory. It is as much incumbent on the psychologist to demonstrate the limits of psychological influence in illness as to demonstrate its extent; as matters stand today, the first need for research in the field may be to ask what we do *not* know about psychological influence.

Psychology's ignorance about a number of these matters is bad, but it is worse when we substitute dogmatism for scientific knowledge. We still need an Ajax to stand up and defy the lightning and ask, What is the evidence? when some authority informs the public that believing in Santa Claus is bad for children, that comic books lead to psychological degeneracy, that asthma is due to a hidden mental illness, or that a child's bed-wetting must be treated by psychoanalysis, and psychoanalysis alone, instead of the simple and effective method of conditioning described by Mowrer and Mowrer (1938).

Let me then present four propositions for serious considera-

tion, even though they may sound ridiculous: (1) that there is
no separate class of mental illness caused by psychological factors alone—by what was seen and heard in childhood; (2) that
we know little about "mental hygiene" or how to achieve it; (3)
that it has not been shown that worry or the like can by itself
cause any bodily condition such as asthma or stomach ulcers,
though it aggravates such conditions; and (4) that it has not
been shown that any specialized psychotherapy, such as psychoanalysis, has any special value in mental illness. The first of
these I think is logically inescapable; propositions 2, 3, and 4
may not be as absurd as they appear. What I am talking about
is *proof;* one may know that psychoanalysis is of value and yet
not have the evidence in a form that would establish this as a
scientific fact. Obviously, in a scientific argument one must
accept the scientific canons; and putting the evidence in logical
shape should ultimately lead to improved medical procedures as
well as more precise theory.

If we are to improve therapy, or if prophylaxis is to be possible at all, we must improve theory first and know more exactly
what leads to what. As long as such questions as those raised
above are answered on *a priori* opinion alone, theory will get
nowhere, for the experiments necessary to it will not be done.
*Evidently the current development of psychological ideas in
medicine has a profound necessity behind it: let us see what
kind of solid factual evidence we need in order to keep this
development on the rails and to extend its influence,* not only in
the clinical but also in the social and educational fields.

MENTAL ILLNESS AS A FUNCTION OF THE
CONSTITUTION

The first question raised was whether there is any class of
mental illness that is due to experience alone. My point of view
here has already been stated: that such a class does not exist,
since any behavioral condition must be a function both of experience and of the constitution that does the experiencing. We
may take it, however, that the relative importance of experience
and constitution may vary in mental illness. At one extreme, it
might be assumed that there is no human constitution that will

not break down when emotional disturbance is sufficiently severe and prolonged (Swank and Marchand, 1946); at the other, that metabolic changes alone may produce emotional disturbance that will persist as long as metabolic factors remain variable and unstable. But the theory that has been developed indicates that the essential nature of the resulting condition may be the same in both cases. There have been an increasing number of reports in the literature showing that trained diagnosticians have not been able to distinguish mental illness precipitated by a physiological disturbance from the mental illness for which no such cause can be discovered, and reports as well showing that the characteristic "functional" disturbance is accompanied, to a more than chance extent, by constitutional deviations.

Typical neurotic or psychotic disorder may be found in brucellosis (Harris, 1944); in pancreatic disorder (Romano and Coon, 1942); in adrenal disorder (Allen and Broster, 1945; Greene, Paterson, and Pile, 1945); in pernicious anemia (Bowman, 1935; Ferraro, Arieti, and English, 1945); in rheumatic brain disease, following rheumatic fever (Bruetsch, 1947); in hypochloremia (Saphir, 1945); in vitamin-B deficiencies (Williams, Mason, and Smith, 1939, cited by Jolliffe; Jolliffe, 1942; Matthews, 1938; Egaña *et al.*, 1942; Spies, Aring, Gelperin, and Bean, 1938). Certain types of neurosis are associated to a more than chance degree with inherited vascular abnormality (Hauptmann, 1946; Cobb, Cohen, and Badal, 1946). Dewan and Owen (1945) have reported twelve from a much larger number of cases of schizophrenia, manic state, depression, psychoneurosis, and so on, which were so representative of the usual picture of mental illness that no physiological or pathological source was even suspected; but the causes eventually were found to include brain tumor, diabetes, uremia, and so on: in all cases, a major cause in the "organic" class.

It may be impossible to distinguish neurosis following head injury from other neurosis (Gillespie, 1944). It is common, as soon as some such "organic" cause is found, to reclassify the illness; but such reports as those cited make it impossible to consider that there is any real psychological discontinuity between organic and functional ills, as these terms are commonly used. This first point is made both on logical grounds and on the basis of the actual clinical facts. It is further reinforced by the factual evidence and discussion of Cobb (1944), Hoagland (1947), Landis (1947), and Bellak and Willson (1947).

Secondly, these considerations make it possible that a contributing organic cause will be found for all those cases that are now called purely functional. The history of psychiatric knowledge shows one syndrome after another being removed from the functional class, as pathological and physiological knowledge has increased. There are still gaps in our knowledge of the complex chain of events in the nutrition of the neural cell; and it is still possible that all well-defined cases of mental disorder will eventually be found to depend, to a major extent, on a predisposing constitutional condition—hereditary or acquired.

Consider for example Kallman's work, the main results of which have been summarized by Garrison (1947). Among other statistics are the following: among the relatives of patients with schizophrenia, the incidence of schizophrenia for brothers and sisters is 14.3 per cent; for fraternal twins, with the same constitutional similarity as any brother or sister, 14.7 per cent; *for identical twins, 85.8 per cent.* For stepbrothers and sisters, growing up in the same home, the figure is 1.8 per cent. There is no apparent way in which these data can be reconciled with the idea that mental illness is unrelated to heredity, that it is due alone to the way a child is brought up. One can argue that two children of different ages have different environments though they are brought up in the same home. An oldest child certainly has a different social environment from that of a youngest child, and of course any one child in a family may have some bad experience that another does not. This might explain why an ordinary sibling of the schizophrenic (born at a separate time) is less likely to have schizophrenia than a twin. But—this difference, predicted by the environmentalist hypothesis, is not observed: siblings and fraternal twins have the same frequency, exactly as would be expected on the genetic hypothesis. And there seems to be no way at all of accounting for the difference between the figures of 14 per cent for fraternal twins, and 85 per cent for identical twins. As we shall see in the following chapter, the data from twin studies have not shown a great deal about the relation of heredity to the IQ; but they could hardly be much clearer as far as schizophrenia is concerned.

There is, however, still the other side of the coin. Eighty-five per cent is not perfect coincidence; it does not make heredity the sole determinant even of schizophrenia, and still less the sole determinant of some other mental ills. A paper by Hobbs (1941) makes the point perfectly: one of a pair of identical twins, brought up with very strict moral standards, broke training as an adult and a psychotic episode followed. The other twin showed no ill effects; heredity provided only a susceptible constitution and did not alone determine that the psychosis would occur. A similar case is referred to by Bellak and Willson (1947).

The same conclusion can be drawn from the very significant experiments of Pavlov (1928), Gantt (1944), Liddell (1938), Masserman (1943), and others on the "conditioned neurosis" or "experimental neurosis." I have suggested (Hebb, 1947) that we should be cautious in identifying this with a full-fledged neurosis in man, since the experimental neurosis is apparently specific to the situation in which it was established. But there can be no doubt that this work is very important for the understanding of clinical neurosis, showing how anxiety (at the least) can be established in a way that would not otherwise have been suspected, since no actual injury or threat may be involved. Anxiety is one source of mental illness, and Pavlov showed that this chronic emotional disturbance can be created in some dogs much more readily than in others: apparently, a constitutional difference between dogs (Gantt, 1938). But here, again, there is cooperation between constitution and experience, for it takes a very special experience indeed to produce the emotional breakdown in most animals, even when they are definitely susceptible.

THE PRESENT SIGNIFICANCE OF MENTAL HYGIENE

The second point of our present ignorance about mental illness is the way in which early experience may be related to a disorder at maturity. The mental-hygiene conception was established some years ago, when it was possible to think of mental illness as simply a set of bad emotional habits. It seemed then that if one could avoid such habits in childhood one could be sure of mental health at maturity, whatever the constitution one may have inherited.

Now this may still be partly true; the unfortunate fact, however, is that we do not have any good basis for being sure how children should be brought up, in order to minimize their chances of getting into a state hospital. The necessary experiments have not been done. What may be necessary to decide the question is to bring up some children in one way, some in others, and see what leads to what. One cannot assert that too much coddling produces mental illness at maturity, or that too little does. For all we know, a lot of spanking, or unsympathetic parents, may only help to prepare the child for the trials of maturity. It cannot be assumed that what produces emotional disturbance in the infant is bad—nor that it is good: the long-term effects may be the same as the short-term, unrelated, or opposed. One must make some decision when a practical problem has to be dealt with, and in these circumstances the only thing to do is make the best guess one can; but opinions should be presented as opinion, and not as scientifically established fact.

In such matters, our ignorance is virtually complete and vitally in need of being replaced by definite knowledge. We do *not* know whether sexy comic books at the age of ten have any deleterious effect at twenty; we do *not* know that play with toy guns and soldiers makes a war-loving nation; we do *not* know that juvenile delinquency, associated with broken homes, is due to the home environment and not just as much to the inheritance of the same emotional instability that broke up the home.

It has sometimes seemed that answers to such questions might be found by anthropological study; when different primitive peoples treat their children differently, what are the effects at maturity? In one tribe, for example, the children are treated generously and the adults are found to be easy-going and friendly; in another, child training is harsh, and the adults are found to be full of hostilities. But, as Klineberg (1940, p. 434) has pointed out, one cannot single out cause and effect here, any more than in the case of the broken home. Heredity, in the two tribes, may differ significantly, producing different adult personalities; or some other variable such as the history of the tribe may be the source of the differences—and the reported facts may mean only that emotionally stable people treat their children well. *

The mental-hygiene program first needs research, then more research, so that we can find out how to rear children to make them as healthy as possible, emotionally, at maturity. It is important to apply what knowledge we have now as best we can; it is equally important to remember how incomplete the knowledge is. We are not now in a position to do more than apply the conceptions of one or other theory of mental illness, that becomes insufficient as soon as one tests it by facts. I have already cited the cases of Alpha and Kambi, chimpanzees of the Yerkes colony, to show that, if early experience is a main cause of mental illness at maturity, we have no real information as to how it works. The theory that has been presented here is much too vague, or general, to provide any useful guide in the practical problems of child education; it may be useful, however, if it leads to more of the obviously necessary research.

PSYCHOSOMATICS AND PSYCHOTHERAPY

The third and fourth points of ignorance that have been listed can be considered together: the questions are whether worry or the like can produce bodily lesions, and whether psychotherapy can cure mental illness. Though the questions may sound ridiculous, I think it may be of some value to consider them seriously and ask oneself just what factual evidence one could cite to justify one's answers.

Just where can one look for the specific evidence on which to base the psychosomatic thesis? Clearly, it is not enough to show that neurotic disturbance and pathological changes in the body go together, † or even that when the first clears up the second

---

* *I.e.*, reverse the statements above: "In one tribe the adults are easygoing, and so children are treated well; in another the adults are aggressive, and children are treated harshly"—as one might expect.

† Obviously, it is also not enough to show that emotion is accompanied by transient somatic changes in normal or psychopathic persons. The very important studies of Wolff (1943) and Wolf and Wolff (1946), for example,

does also—*unless* the recovery is due to psychotherapy. If some metabolic disorder contributed to the neurosis, it may have determined the pathological changes also. Then mental and physical difficulties would appear together, and disappear together. If one could show that asthma, or stomach ulcers, or skin lesions could be cured by talking to the patient—that is, by psychotherapy—then we would have the desired proof. But, as we shall see shortly, there are great difficulties in the way of showing that psychotherapy is effective (chiefly, the difficulty of showing that it produces more cures than are accounted for by spontaneous remission). Despite its general acceptance, in which I concur, the hypothesis that psychological factors affect the recovery of the body from any physical illness has not been established scientifically. It may appear to the reader that it is not necessary to do so; but there must be much that should be found out about the psychological influence—in what conditions it operates best, what its limits are, and so on; and these things will never be discovered until we start examining our assumptions, and start the slow, plodding process of building up a solid body of facts, separate from opinion, upon which the theory of treatment can be firmly established.

Not all cases in which a "psychosomatic" relationship is seen are ones in which the original trouble was emotional. The following case of early asthma offered an exceptional opportunity for separating cause and effect. It is rare that one can have an effective control of asthma, and banish it or not, at will—but when this is possible, new light is cast on the disease.

A child of twenty-one months developed acute, severe attacks of asthma after having had a head cold some months earlier and a persistent nasal infection. The attacks became less frequent several months later, during the summer, but recurred with increasing severity and frequency as winter set in. Eventually it

do not show that chronic gastric and cardiac lesions result from emotional disturbance alone, without contribution from a preceding physiological disorder, although, if it is assumed that "normal" emotion has such effects, these studies help to show us how the lesions are established. It should be clear that what is discussed in the text is the question of scientific proof, not of reasonable belief. Belief in the psychosomatic thesis is reasonable, perhaps inevitable; but the very importance and value of that thesis require that its foundations be inspected and tested rigorously—and periodically.

appeared that a running nose preceded each attack, and it occurred to the physician in charge that a nasal infection might be
the source of the allergen. He found a heavy chronic bacillary
infection, and recommended chemotherapy. The results were
dramatic. The asthma disappeared completely, and a remarkable change took place in the child's behavior. During an attack,
the child had been almost completely incapacitated; but between
attacks, there had been no difficulty in breathing and the child
appeared quite normal—except that she was always emotionally
unstable, easily giving way to tears and being rather hard to deal
with. Actually, this behavior had developed so gradually during the period of illness, and was so constant, that the parents
had not realized that there was any connection between the
emotional picture and the intermittent asthma. Now the patient
became a different child.

Two further observations made the interpretation of these
facts even clearer. It was expected that the allergic sensitivity
would gradually disappear as the child grew older; so on two
subsequent occasions when a nasal infection began the treatment
was omitted at first, in the hope that asthma would not develop.
On each occasion the same sequence of events was observed.
The first symptom of disturbance was circulatory—the child's
hands and feet became very cold. This was followed by the
same emotional disturbance that had been chronic earlier, at
least a day before the first symptoms of difficulty in breathing;
and finally, a definite asthma appeared. This and the emotional
changes were then promptly (in six to twelve hours) banished
by chemotherapy. Such a sequence of events can only mean
that the allergen affected the vascular system *first*—the cold
hands and feet were not due to lung congestion and decrease of
oxygen in the blood stream. On one of the two occasions on
which treatment was withheld, moreover, a placebo was used.
This served as a control of the effects of suggestion, showing
that it was in fact the action of the drug which, when it was
actually used, produced the recovery from asthma and the disappearance of whining, crying, and the need of continual attention. Only one conclusion seems possible: that the allergen
acted more or less directly on the vasculature, including the
cerebral vasculature, or on the central nervous system, thus caus-

ing both emotional and physical symptoms. Ordinarily, with multitudinous sensitivities and no possibility of such cleancut "experimental" manipulation of allergens, cause and effect cannot be separated. The case described might have been a typical psychosomatic picture: first emotional disturbance is evident, then physical symptoms follow. So the first must cause the second. But in this case such an interpretation is not possible.

Because asthma and emotional disturbances go together, or even because an emotional disturbance can precipitate an attack of asthma, it does not follow either that emotion caused the original difficulty, or that psychotherapy can do more than alleviate an illness that may have quite a different basis. It is still possible that some cases of asthma, or some other bodily illness, are psychogenic and can be cured by psychotherapy; but evidence of this has not yet been provided in a form in which it can be evaluated. Future research may well show that the causal relationships in the case I have described are the exception and not the rule (*i.e.*, may show that allergies are usually psychogenic). But this research has not yet been done.

It is implied throughout this discussion that, if psychotherapy can be shown to be an effective treatment of asthma or mental illness, the argument above would be reversed. It seems generally believed that the validity of psychoanalytic theory, for example, is well established by the fact that it has led to curing mental illnesses that would not otherwise have been cured.

If one looks for the evidence, however, one cannot find it. There is no meaning in the fact that a particular patient was psychoanalyzed, and recovered. We do not know that he would not have recovered without the treatment.

The point is clear when it is recalled how difficult it was to show that the insulin-shock method had any value. Psychiatrists and physicians in general were skeptical. Why? Because some not-very-exactly-determined proportion of psychotic patients recover without treatment—perhaps 30, 35, or 40 per cent. The figure varies widely from one series of patients to another; and it took five to ten years of work, by a large number of investigators, to finally establish the fact that insulin therapy significantly increases the proportion of patients that recover from schizophrenia. A few patients recovering after lobotomy would mean nothing: Freeman and Watts' (1942) triumph was in being able to report not only 63 per cent good results in a long series of chronic cases of mental illness, but much higher percentages with certain types of case. These figures had an immediate meaning, since the research on shock treatments had already made known what the spontaneous recovery rate would be, roughly, in such cases. No such data, so far as I can discover, have ever been provided as a test of any form of psychotherapy— that is, the frequency of recovery in an adequately chosen, untreated control group is not available to compare with the frequency after psychotherapy is applied. The one exception to this statement is the paper by Denker (1946), and his conclusions do not show any special value in formal psychotherapy.

Denker's paper is based on admittedly unsatisfactory data, and obviously is not a final answer to the question it has raised; yet it stands as a very important paper, simply because it is the only one, apparently, that has attempted an essential task.

The data reported by Denker are the rates of recovery in a series of 500 patients with severe incapacitating neurotic disorder, treated by general practitioners throughout the United States. These patients were all receiving disability payments from an insurance company—a fact that might delay recovery, at least as compared with the recovery of patients who were paying for treatment. At the end of five years, the recovery rate was 90 per cent. Denker also reviewed the reported recovery rates under more specialized treatment. The average rate of recovery under psychoanalysis is roughly 62 per cent; under psychiatric treatment (which may have included psychoanalysis), roughly 70 per cent. These rates are markedly lower than that obtained by the general practitioner. However, if we assume that the results by specialized treatment are for a shorter period, perhaps two years, we find that the general practitioner's results are about the same: 72 per cent. The conclusion is that rest, sedation when necessary, reassurance, and time are what produce recovery from neurotic disorder—when recovery occurs.

Obviously, this conclusion is not final. We do not know that the patients treated by psychoanalyst, psychiatrist, and general practitioner, in Denker's analysis, were really comparable (however, the one respect in which it is certain that they were not

comparable—the economic factor—is such as to strengthen Denker's argument). Denker's conclusions may be quite wrong; but
the real point is that his are the only data * we have by which
to evaluate psychotherapy.

Such a result cries for research; if nothing else has induced the
psychoanalyst to give us some control data, some evidence for
the validity of his theory and treatment of mental illness, this
should do so. In the meantime, there is no body of fact to show
that psychotherapy is valuable; there are no data to prove that
psychotherapy can cure lesions of the gastrointestinal tract, der-
matitis, and so on; and none to prove that there is a class of
"functional" mental illness that is produced by emotional disturbance alone and susceptible of cure only by talking to the
patient or allowing the patient to talk. I think any psychologist
(or physician) must believe that psychotherapy is important, as
an adjunct of other treatment, and even by itself; but *if we are
to increase its efficiency, we must learn more about it,* and the
first thing to establish is the definite fact that it works at all.

SHOCK TREATMENT AND LOBOTOMY

The final concern of this chapter is a rationale for the shock
and surgical treatments that revolutionized the field of psychiatry.

Lobotomy, a surgical operation that severs most of the connections between the frontal pole and the rest of the brain, and

* An earlier discussion by Landis, however, based in part on the same
data, has clearly led to the same conclusion and must be regarded as reinforcing Denker's conclusions (C. Landis, A statistical evaluation of psy-
chotherapeutic methods, *in* L. E. Hinsie, *Concepts and problems of psychotherapy*, New York: Columbia Univ. Press, 1937, pp. 155–169). Landis
first determined the reported rate of recovery from psychoneurosis, apart
from specialized methods of treatment, as varying around a central figure
of about 68 per cent. Speaking of another such figure (for all mental illnesses), he went on to say that, although the figures given were not strictly
speaking those for spontaneous remission, "still any therapeutic method must
show an appreciably greater size than this to be seriously considered."
Finally, he reported a figure of 58 per cent for psychoanalytic treatment of
the neuroses. The inference, not made explicit by Landis, is the same as
Denker's.

electroshock treatment, in which an electric current passed through the skull induces a brief convulsion, both appear to work best with patients suffering from emotional depression, and both frequently have the effect of banishing the depression. In trying to understand how a cure is effected, the first question might be, What do such different procedures have in common?

The surgical treatment (Freeman and Watts, 1942, 1946) severs a large number of connecting fibers in the brain and leads to retrograde degeneration of a particular nucleus in the thalamus (the *nucleus medialis dorsalis*). A number of investigators have expressed the opinion that it is the loss of this tissue that decreases the strength of the patient's emotion and allows him to recover. But no such gross destruction of tissue results from the passage of the electric current through the head. Is there any other effect of the surgery that might produce emotional changes?

A suggestion comes from the study of frontal lobe removals. A comparatively common operation, prefrontal lobectomy, is usually done so that it severs the same connections that are severed in lobotomy—but severs all other connections of the same area, and actually removes the tissue. In these operations, consequently, the medial dorsal nucleus of the thalamus must degenerate. But the kind of emotional picture drawn by Freeman and Watts (1942), as representing the results of frontal lobotomy, is sometimes definitely not present (Nichols and Hunt, 1940; Mixter, Tillotson, and Wies, 1941; Hebb and Penfield, 1940). On the basis of this fact it was suggested (Hebb, 1945*b*) that the effect of lobotomy might be due not to a simple loss of some function resident in the frontal lobes but to a physiological disturbance set up in that area by an operation that cannot help but be scar-producing. This would account for the fact, also, that the recovery from depression, in lobotomy, is reversible—although the degeneration of the thalamo-frontal connections and of the medial dorsal nucleus is not reversible.

A physiological disturbance in the cerebrum is usually detected in the electroencephalogram, or EEG, by the presence of large potentials (hypersynchrony). My proposal, therefore, amounted to this: that in those patients that recover from depression following lobotomy the EEG will show a hypersynchrony; and that if relapse occurs the hypersynchrony will have disappeared or decreased. Cohn (1945) has reported persistent disturbances in the EEG "in most subjects" of Freeman and Watts' series, and delta waves in ten out of fifteen in one group of patients examined four to six years after operation. This is almost exactly the reported frequency (63 per cent) of chronic recovery from depression. Unfortunately, I have not been able to discover whether those with "bad" EEG's were ones with good clinical results (*i.e.*, lasting recovery), as my hypothesis would predict.

However, a direct confirmation of the hypothesis, up to a certain point, has been provided by Hoagland, Malamud, Kaufman, and Pincus (1946). They report a lowered incidence of fast waves (14 per second or faster) in patients showing remission from depression following electroshock treatment, and the return of fast waves at the time of relapse. This is directly in the line with the hypothesis; although it may be a strain on the term "hypersynchrony" to say that it may appear in a statistical decrease of fast waves, the change is actually in the same direction as if delta waves had been observed.

If the hypothesis should be further confirmed, the effects of electroshock and lobotomy both could be understood on the following basis. It has been proposed here that emotional disturbance consists of a disorganized firing of cerebral neurons. The establishment of hypersynchrony, due to *any* cause, would provide a pacemaker, as it were, that would tend to pick up any neurons that are not incorporated in assembly activities and so substitute the "intrinsic" organization of cortical activity for the diffuse organization of the normal adult waking state. The presence of the hypersynchrony would tend to interfere with the assembly and to lower intellectual competence at the same time that it decreases emotional disturbance. Further, this would account for the lowered pain sensitivity, and the value of lobotomy in cases of intractable pain (Watts and Freeman, 1946). It will be recalled that pain was treated (in Chapter 8) as the equivalent of a local emotional disturbance, in the somesthetic system, and so can be regarded as being affected in the same way by a focus of hypersynchrony.

It is not necessarily implied that scar formation is what produces the hypersynchrony in lobotomy. The effect of deafferenting an extensive cortical region would be to permit it to go into spontaneous hypersynchrony (Adrian, 1934). This, or this plus any effect of scar formation, may be the source of the recovery from mental depression.

11. The Growth and Decline of Intelligence

This discussion began originally, in Chapter 1, with the puzzle of the high intelligence-test scores that are sometimes found after a surgeon has destroyed a large part of the human brain. A tentative explanation was suggested, that these scores are due to a conceptual development which brain damage does not easily reverse. The chapters that followed have tried to make this intelligible physiologically (besides showing what the implications are for other problems). "Conceptual development," "insight," "thought," and so on, have been given a physiological meaning, and a possible basis has been provided for seeing how capacities could be retained, once developed, despite brain injury which if it had occurred in infancy would have prevented the development. This chapter returns to the original problem of the effects of brain operations on intelligence. It presents an interpretation which fundamentally concerns the nature of intelligence, its normal development, and its later decline with old age.

This chapter will be concerned also with certain problems of method. Clinical research on intelligence has difficulties as a blackberry-bush has thorns, and yet is an important source of information for the psychologist, and can be expected to become more important. If the difficulties are to be surmounted, we must know what they are. These matters of method will be taken up first.

IDENTIFYING INTELLECTUAL DETERIORATION

We feel, most of us, that we can make a reasonably good estimate of another's intellectual ability by conversation with him;

and we are apt to feel, too, that we have in general a fairly good idea of what sort of problem can be solved by the healthy, "average," "normal" people in our own communities. Both convictions are frequently misleading. The first point on method is that the detection of intellectual defect, following brain injury, requires the test procedure and (in some form or other) the use of a control group.

Ordinarily, the person who is clear in conversation, quick to understand what is said to him, and coherent in his reply, is "intelligent": that is, conversational ability is correlated with other abilities, and is not a bad basis of prediction. But these correlations sometimes break down with pathological changes in the brain, and then the prediction may be false. Also, one is apt to judge capacity by the patient's alertness and manner, apart from what he says. The physician is familiar with deterioration in the form of unresponsiveness, apathy, slowness, or inconstancy of purpose. Accordingly, when such signs are absent the physician may feel certain that intelligence is not impaired.

It is reasonably sure that this has been a major source of the disagreement about intellectual impairment in aphasia. Because the aphasic always tries to respond, is fully attentive, and gives the *impression* of being quite clear mentally, it is easy to conclude that he has lost nothing but the power of verbal recognition and expression. There are cases on record in which it has been "proved" that aphasia does not affect intelligence, on the ground that the patient nodded and smiled when the physician greeted him, that he knew whether it was morning or afternoon, or that he was able to let an attendant know when he needed the bedpan.

Tests, on the other hand, show that the aphasic usually cannot fit blocks together to make a simple pattern, that he does not recognize absurdities in pictures, cannot make a simple drawing—even though he clearly knows what he is to do. In such performances the aphasic is almost certain to be at a much lower level than a normal individual of the same background and original ability (Weisenburg and McBride, 1935; Hebb, 1942a). The aphasic patient is apt to have trouble in finding his way about, even in a familiar region, and to have trouble in manipulating simple mechanical contrivances. There is no sense in arguing over terminology, and each writer can define that equivocal term "intelligence" to suit himself (though one might expect some consistency in its subsequent use); but because the aphasic is alert, and persistent in trying to discover what 2 and 2 add up to, or to discover what is missing in a picture of a dog with three legs, it does not follow that he has lost only the capacity for communication. There is also a change in what would usually be called intelligence.

To detect deterioration, one cannot depend on impression alone but must also use test methods; and this requires a normal control group. It is most dangerous to assume knowledge of what the "average" person knows and can do. Let me give some examples, based on data obtained in the standardization of some adult tests (Hebb, 1942b; Hebb and Morton, 1943). Somewhere in the neighborhood of half the adult English-speaking population cannot complete the analogy *foot* is to *ankle* as *hand* is to *what?* or *under* : *over—down* : ? (though almost everyone can do *dog* : *bark—cat* : ?). About half the adult population think that *priceless* means "of no value"; nearly the same number are unaware that *brunette* refers to a dark complexion, and many think it a synonym for "blonde"—meaning, any lively young woman. Figure 19 shows some simple problems—apparently simple—that cannot be solved by some fraction, between 10 and 25 per cent, of the adult population (Hebb, 1945b).

The subjects in these tests were able to earn a living and conduct their own affairs with ordinary prudence, and would not be classed as anything but normal in the clinic. If such a person happened to have a brain injury, and the examiner did not know what other persons of the same class would do with such tests, he would be bound to conclude that the brain injury was the reason for the subject's incompetence. No matter how simple one's tests may seem to be, the brain-injured patient's performance must be interpreted in the light of the scores of a normal control group. The professional man's idea of the average intelligence is colored by his preoccupation with the abstract and academic, and by the fact that his intimacy is mainly with others in the professional community whose preoccupations, interests, and abilities are of the same kind as his own.

How is a normal control group to be chosen? Despite some recent discussion making this an esoteric question, almost impos-

FIGURE 19.   Problems from a performance test (top line) and attempted solutions (bottom line) by a person not in any way classed as feebleminded. A pattern in cardboard was placed before the subject, and left there while he tried to duplicate it, using two or more identical wooden triangles. Each of the hatched diagrams shows a subject's placing of the blocks in an attempt to duplicate the pattern immediately above (by B.G., female, 30 years of age, a "normal control subject" convalescent after appendicitis). A fairly large proportion of the adult population will make such errors, and have difficulty in seeing how to change the placing of the blocks when told that the solution is not correct.

sible to understand, the desiderata are comparatively simple. There might be no need of a control group if one could compare the patient's scores after brain operation with his scores before anything was wrong with his brain; all one can get, however, is a pre- and post-operative comparison, which must be a different matter. The condition for which he is being operated on must itself affect his scores, and in fact the operation quite often causes a *rise* in score. The purpose of the control group, then, is to let us know as far as possible what the brain-operated patient would have done if his brain had remained healthy and undamaged. This tells us what to look for in a control group. The object is to find persons who are like the patients being studied in every way that, as far as one knows, affects intelligence-test scores, except in the one respect, that the normal control subjects have undamaged brains.

Now test scores are related to education, social background, and occupation—a concatenation that can be summarized as the factor of sophistication. Scores are also affected by age, rising to a peak in the teens and declining (for almost all tests) after the twenties. These are the correlates of intelligence in normal persons, as far as they are known at present; if they are controlled, one can estimate, by comparing clinical and control groups, the degree and kind of impairment that results from brain damage; but if they are not controlled this is not possible. It is not possible to show that brain damage affects intelligence, by the use of a control group that is made up of hospital employees, or college students, or clerical workers, when the clinical group includes truckdrivers, farmers, and unskilled laborers—persons who are apt to have been long away from clerical work, with a lower average level of education. It is not possible to compare a man who went to high school ten years ago with a student now in high school. If the clinical subjects are older adults, or less sophisticated, they are bound to have lower scores than the normal subjects.

These considerations are what should determine the nature of the *normal* control group. One must then go farther, and use *clinical* controls, if one wishes to know not only that a certain kind of injury produces intellectual defects but also whether it produces more defect than some other kind of injury. If one wanted to show that frontal-lobe damage is more serious than damage elsewhere in the brain, one would use two groups, a frontal-lobe group and a parietal, temporal, occipital group. But note this: everything that was said above about making the normal group equivalent to the clinical group is equally necessary in the comparison of two clinical groups. They must be the same in age, in sophistication, and, in addition, in the size and type of lesion.

Halstead (1947) has criticized Rylander (1939) on the ground that his normal control group was not a clinical control group, and me (Hebb, 1945*b*) for being taken in by Rylander. Actually, Rylander's normal control group was an excellent one, the only good one that has been used in the study of the frontal lobe. His first object was to show that frontal-lobe damage produces intellectual defects, and he showed this clearly. (Whether the defects are greater than with parietal lesions, or whether they are due to the surgical lesion or to an accompanying dysfunction, would be another question.) Halstead's control data, both normal and clinical, do not meet the elementary requirements set forth above: his normal group was younger (the average was 26 years) than either of his clinical groups and had a high proportion of persons with clerical and academic sophistication. His parietal, temporal, occipital group (33 years) was younger than his frontal-lobe group (40 years), the data supplied as to the relative extent of frontal and nonfrontal brain damage (direct or indirect) are insufficient, and so too are the data as to occupation or sophistication (the designation "housewife" should be supplemented either by educational level or husband's occupation).

For some reason, frontal-lobe patients in the clinic sometimes tend to be older than others and may have a larger total destruction when the effects of pressure in the rest of the brain are considered. This may be because the first signs of a frontal-lobe tumor are less specific than those of a tumor elsewhere, so the patient does not seek treatment as promptly. Frontal tumors tend also to produce bilateral damage of corresponding structures, by pressure, more than other tumors do. Consequently, it is very difficult indeed to find cases in which there is, for example, comparable damage of one frontal and one temporal lobe, or of both frontal and both temporal lobes.

There is nothing mysterious about the logic of the control-group method. If one wants to estimate the pre-operative intelligence of a group of barbers with frontal-lobe injury, or of high-school teachers, one would look for a group of barbers or high-school teachers of about the same age and education, and preferably from the same part of the country, since occupational standards vary. The trouble of course is that man is a suspicious, sensitive, and uncooperative animal who objects to having his intelligence tested and is not usually interested in helping a scientific investigation at such a price. To obtain test data for a good sample of the general population, even if only a sample of fifty or sixty subjects, is a very large undertaking (Weisenburg, Roe, and McBride, 1936).

The problem of normal control data has been reviewed elsewhere (Hebb, 1945*b*). The conclusions arrived at can be stated again: Only two studies have utilized an adequate normal control group in psychological study of the effect of brain damage: Rylander (1939) and Weisenburg and McBride (1935). These two consequently are of outstanding importance (though they are defective in not having adequate anatomical data, and one cannot be quite sure that the defects were due to a simple loss of tissue). Rylander's norms, of course, since they are for another culture, are not applicable directly to English-speaking patients; but Weisenburg, Roe, and McBride's (1936) careful, though apparently little-known, analysis of intelligence in a representative group of adult English-speaking subjects still stands as the best basis for the study of intellectual defect. With caution, their data may still be used if one cannot undertake the tremendous task of obtaining new normal-control data for each new study of brain damage.

Dr. Morton and I have also supplemented their test battery with some new tests designed especially for adult use (Hebb, 1942*b;* Hebb and Morton, 1943).* Such norms, however, become less and less accurate with the passage of time, and as more individual tests, of the homogeneous type, become available it would be desirable for someone to attempt a new standardization of a battery of homogeneous tests, each one measuring a single kind of ability and so making it more possible to analyze the intellectual changes that occur in cases of brain damage.

ANATOMICAL AND PATHOLOGICAL DATA

The second major aspect of the problem of method in such studies is the difficulty of getting satisfactory anatomical and physiological data. In an animal study, the only data one trusts

---

* A recent restandardization of one of these tests, in a short form that is more convenient for clinical use, has been done by W. A. Hunt, E. G. French, and I. N. Mensh. An abbreviated form of the McGill Verbal Situation Test, *J. Clin. Psychol.,* 1948, *4,* 406–411.

concerning the locus and extent of lesion are obtained by killing the animal and removing the brain for anatomical study. Human patients, after brain operation, have a regrettable way of living on indefinitely—instead of first making a good recovery, to permit thorough testing, instructing their relatives to permit an autopsy, and then dying of pneumonia.

So one is obliged to make the best guess one can, instead of having exact data. It is not possible at operation to know exactly what tissue is destroyed, particularly when the operation is for a tumor which displaces the brain—as tumors must—and in displacing it is more than likely to produce a diffuse damage throughout parts that may be at some distance from the scene of operation. In operations for tumor, actually, one is practically always dealing with two kinds of lesion: the clean surgical lesion that can often be accurately described, and the diffuse, irregular lesions that result from pressure and have no clearcut boundary. Brain operations seemed to open a new era in the study of the localization of function, as they became common about 1920. Why? Because the effect of pathological lesions is almost impossible to interpret. One cannot say where the diffuse lesion begins and where it ends; attempting to interpret such data, between 1870 and 1920, had led to an endless series of arguments. But this difficulty applies equally to interpreting the effect of a brain operation *plus* a pathological lesion, so in most cases of tumor the fact that the brain has been operated on does not actually make the case suitable for the localization of function.

Such a point would mean little if the effect of the added pathological lesion were slight. But it has been discovered that a comparatively small region of pathological change, producing hypersynchrony, may have a much more deteriorating effect on behavior than a complete loss of the tissue concerned. An idea of this sort was proposed by Jefferson (1937) and Stookey, Scarff, and Teitelbaum (1941). A direct demonstration on the point has been provided in two cases in which the removal of frontal-lobe tissue, in an area of scarring, changed a marked deterioration into behavior indistinguishable from the normal (Hebb and Penfield, 1940; Mixter, Tillotson, and Wies, 1941). A region in which the blood supply is interfered with, but not entirely shut off, usually shows some loss of cells and a number of remaining cells whose staining properties are changed. This indicates a change in the chemical properties of the cell, which in turn implies a change in frequency properties and obviously may account for the existence of a hypersynchrony which interferes with the functioning of the cell-assembly. A focus of hypersynchrony must act as a pacemaker that tends to wean transmission units away from the assembly. When hypersynchrony is not great, it would allow some assemblies to function (particularly those that are long established: p. 197) but would tend to interfere with recent memory, decrease responsiveness, and interfere with complex intellectual activities. When it is more extensive, it would prevent all higher functions.

Hypersynchrony thus extends the influence of a pathological lesion beyond the borders of the lesion itself and may make it impossible to draw any conclusion about the localization of the functions that are affected after a frontal pole, for example, has been removed. When one is interested in an attempt at localization of function, the question must always be asked whether the sequelae of operation are due (1) to the surgical removal; (2) to permanent damage in the remaining parts of the brain; (3) to the transient physiological disturbance that always occurs along the margins of the surgical lesion, that may take from one to six months to subside, and that, since it is reversible, has deceived more than one worker into thinking that recovery is an evidence of vicarious functioning; or (4) to a chronic physiological disturbance, from scar formation or from diffuse pathological lesions throughout the rest of the brain. If a loss of function is due to the surgical lesion, the function depends on the tissue that was removed; if due to dysfunction, it depends on tissue that still remains. All this makes the question of localization complex indeed. It explains why we are little farther forward in the localization of function, in the human brain, than Broca and Jackson were—the "experiments of nature" are poorly designed, and produce disturbance, as well as a simple loss, of function.

The EEG may be a relatively crude index of what is going on in the cerebrum, with no direct relation to the firing of the individual cell; but it is a practical index of the physiological status of the different parts of the brain, and as such it has the greatest importance in any attempt to study localization of function from a patient's behavior after recovery from brain operation. For such a purpose, electroencephalographic report is not merely desirable but essential. With it, one has at least some chance of knowing when defects of behavior can be attributed to a surgical lesion and not to a pathological dysfunction instead.

Animal experiments, anatomical studies, and studies in which the brain of the fully conscious human patient is stimulated electrically have clearly localized a number of sensory and motor areas. But, because of the difficulties of method that have just been considered, about the only localization of a higher function that has so far been achieved is that of the so-called speech area: the middle regions of one hemisphere, usually the "dominant" one (the left hemisphere in a right-handed person), appear to have some sort of executive and organizing role that is essential to speech and some other higher functions. No other localization of function in the human cerebrum has been established. I am aware that this statement is not in accord with much of the literature, but critical evaluation of the evidence presented in support of the various claims concerning localization permits no other conclusion, so far as I can see.

A paper by Klebanoff (1945), very useful as a review and bibliography of most of the psychological work in this field up to 1941, did not sufficiently consider the twin problems of normal control data, and anatomical and pathological data. Failure to solve one or both of these problems tends to invalidate the papers that try to prove that some higher function is resident in some particular part of the human cortex, in the work reviewed by Klebanoff. If one considers the normal control data used in these studies, or the anatomical data, with the same critical eye that would be turned at once on an animal experiment, one will find none of them justifying more than an opinion, a guess, concerning the relation of higher functions to the cerebrum.

Even with regard to the speech area, it is none too clear either what the boundaries are, or that a *limited* surgical lesion in any part of the region will disturb speech. Aphasia may be produced only by a hypersynchrony whose focus is strategically placed here, in a position to disturb function throughout the whole hemisphere. We have no evidence on this, for the surgeon naturally declines to touch this area if he can help doing so; if he must, he disturbs as little of it as possible. However, the case of left hemidecortication reported by Zollinger (1935) shows that a clean surgical extirpation can produce aphasia. Again, anterior lesions in the speech area *may* produce more difficulty in speaking and writing, posterior lesions more difficulty in understanding speech and printed matter; but no real anatomical evidence to this effect seems to exist, and Weisenburg and McBride's (1935) cautious distinction between a predominantly expressive and a predominantly receptive aphasia should not be extended into a sharp dichotomy of "motor" and "sensory" aphasias, since it seems highly likely that both aspects of the disorder are always present.

A number of clinical writers have disagreed with this conclusion, arrived at by Weisenburg and McBride, Head, and others; but they seem never to have established satisfactory evidence. An important paper by Kennedy and Wolf (1936), for example, reports a "pure alexia" and a pure motor aphasia, with no other involvement. But the case reports are typically incomplete: to show that alexia is aphasic, it should be shown that there is sufficient acuity for reading, and that the perception of other (nonsymbolic) visual patterns is undisturbed—else one has simply a loss of vision or a visual agnosia. In the second case of motor "aphasia," what is reported by Kennedy and Wolf is a loss of the capacity for drawing, with no disturbance of anything related to speech: a rare and valuable observation, but not apparently relevant to the question of aphasia. Again, Kennedy and Wolf have provided no details of sensory and motor tests, and these details *must* be given if it is to be shown that such a thing as a pure alexia or agraphia can exist. Neither, certainly, has yet been shown to result from damage to any limited part of the speech area. It is hardly likely that they will be; such conceptions arise from an older type of theory, no longer entertained in psychological thought, and it is highly probable that such questions (concerning what peculiar contribution each part of the cortex makes to behavior) will remain unanswered until we can find out how to ask better questions.

There have been a great many interesting and important observations showing a relation of complex functions to the parietal and temporal lobes in man; but in all the reported cases, of various agnosias, disturbances of the body image, and so on, there is presumptive evidence of the presence of pathological dysfunction as well as of a simple loss of tissue, and we are not yet in a position to interpret such data as far as the localization of function is concerned. Von Monakow wrote that he did not know of a single case in which a purely traumatic lesion in the occipital lobes of an otherwise sound brain had resulted in a persistent visual agnosia.* This, implying that agnosia is an effect of dysfunction and not of an uncomplicated loss of cells, is directly in line with the present discussion (though it should be noted that a traumatic lesion, accompanied by scar formation, may also produce chronic dysfunction). There is little that can be definitely concluded at present concerning localization of the functions disturbed in agnosia, and so on, until the disturbance is found to be produced by a clean surgical lesion, unaccompanied by delta waves in the EEG.

Only one thing need be added: although the frontal lobe is the favorite place in which to localize higher functions when one is speculating about these matters, it is still true that there is no *proof* that any single higher function depends on this part of the brain (Hebb, 1945b). At least as good a case might be made out for the parietal and temporal lobes as the seat of man's distinctive psychological characteristics—if these in fact depend on one part of the brain more than another (see, for example, Kubitschek, 1928; Keschner, Bender, and Strauss, 1938).

Because of the enormous amount of space that has been devoted to the effort to show that the prefrontal lobe is the seat and habitation of some higher function or other (there are few mental processes that have not been ascribed to it), the basis of these negative conclusions must be made more detailed. Doing so will also illustrate other points dealt with in the preceding pages and make them more specific.

---

* Personal communication from Dr. K. S. Lashley. My interpretation of this observation is based on the fact that a traumatic lesion is less likely to produce chronic dysfunction than a tumor or abscess.

The first and most effective piece of evidence is the history of a patient both of whose prefrontal lobes were removed by Dr. Wilder Penfield, with results that radically changed the possibilities of surgical therapy in the frontal area. Before this time, it was universally accepted that loss of both frontal poles must be followed by gross deterioration of personality and intellect. Dr. Penfield's patient completely reversed the prediction, by being psychotic before operation (when the damage was relatively small) and quite indistinguishable from a normal person afterward (when the total destruction was increased in size—with the simultaneous removal of a source of physiological disturbance).

The history is that of a boy of sixteen whose skull was fractured, with damage to both frontal lobes, and who in the following ten years developed severe epilepsy and became (much of the time) an irresponsible and rather dangerous charge. The condition varied, not only with the occurrence of attacks but also between attacks—apparently owing to subclinical seizures: the IQ, on the basis of an uncompleted testing on one day, was estimated to be below 70; next day a completed test gave an IQ of 84. After operation, the IQ was consistently close to 96, no evidence of intellectual loss could be found in any one test or in the pattern of test scores as a whole, and the psychotic behavior completely disappeared. Clinically and socially he was "normal" and was able to take full control of his own affairs: on the last examination he had been doing so for more than five years. He enlisted in the army and served satisfactorily overseas for ten months until he had another fit—at which time the medical officers caught up with him and he was discharged. In his subsequent behavior it is possible that there were deficiencies in planning for the distant future, but it is certain that he had more initiative and planned foresight than many persons with frontal lobes intact.

There must of course have been some loss of function in this patient. Logically, it seems impossible to suppose that behavior can be unchanged after bilateral loss of any area of the brain. My conclusion is not that the frontal lobes have no function, but either (1) that we have not yet guessed at the real nature of this function—have not asked the proper questions in such investigations, or (2) that once the *development* of behavior has been completed the prefrontal lobes have no great further importance. Surely it is the first of these, 1, that is the answer, not 2; but there is nothing in the evidence at present that justifies the idea that the frontal lobes have some special relation to higher functions in human behavior.

This general conclusion does not actually rest on the one case that I have described but can also be established independently. The evidence that has been supposed to show the importance of the frontal lobes does not withstand scrutiny (it has been reviewed in detail elsewhere—Hebb, 1945b). What the Penfield case did was, first, to demonstrate conclusively that an area in which there is dysfunction (the area of scarring that produced both epilepsy and deterioration of behavior) can be far more deteriorating than complete removal of the area; and, second, it raised the question, How are we to account for the astonishing difference between this case and other, apparently similar, cases, in which, however, profound deterioration remained after surgical operation on the frontal lobes?

Examination of the other case reports at once showed strong reason to believe that the deterioration they described was due to dysfunction, or diffuse destruction in the rest of the brain resulting from the earlier pressure of a tumor, or both. It thus appeared that the behavior changes were *not* due to the surgical injury, and therefore that such cases are not suitable for studying the localization of function. The extent of the total lesion in each case was not known, and the loss of tissue was complicated by additional factors. Dysfunction is to be expected also in frontal lobotomy (p. 272), and so cases of lobotomy also are not a source of interpretable data for the localization of function, especially since we do not know at all what the effect would be of a similar bilateral incision in other regions of the brain.

This line of argument then obtained confirmation from the reports of bilateral prefrontal lobectomy by Mixter, Tillotson, and Wies (1941) and Heath and Pool (1948). Equally important, it now appears that monkey or chimpanzee may lose both frontal poles without evident impairment, though earlier work seemed to have established the contrary.*

We have at present, then, no reason to think that a clean surgical removal of both frontal association areas is necessarily followed by observable, clinically evident defects of behavior; nor have we as yet any real understanding of the functions of this part of the brain.

DIFFERENCES BETWEEN EARLY AND LATE BRAIN INJURY

The study of brain operations in human patients has not so far provided the data that would allow one to be very definite about the way in which higher functions are related to special parts of the cerebral cortex; but it has raised one problem that gives us a valuable lead concerning the nature of intelligence. The problem has been referred to already—it arises from the discovery that an IQ of 160 or higher is possible after the removal of one prefrontal lobe (Hebb, 1939) or an IQ of 115 after hemidecortication (Rowe, 1937), and from the frequency with which above-average scores are reported after cortical injury in any except the speech area. It appears possible, however, that similar damage to the infant brain has a much greater effect on the subsequent IQ. This possibility suggests a clue to the nature of adult intelligence and suggests a distinction between two quite different meanings of the term "intelligence"—a distinction that may help to resolve current theoretical disagreements.

The average IQ after brain operation, in all cases in which an IQ was reported up to the end of 1941, was 108—at least 8 points above the normal adult average, which is probably well below 100 according to the U. S. Army data of 1917 and Weisenburg, Roe, and McBride's (1936) data. When brain damage is traumatic or pathological, instead of surgical, there are also frequent indications that on certain kinds of test (on which the Stanford Binet IQ is mainly based) the patient's score is not much lower than it would have been had the brain damage not occurred. These data are given in more detail elsewhere (Hebb, 1942a).

* See T. Spaet and H. F. Harlow, *J. Exp. Psychol.*, 1943, 32, 424–434; R. A. Blum, *Amer. Psychol.*, 1948, 3, 237–238.

But in practically all such cases the use of other tests shows that there is a definite intellectual loss. That is, some tests such as the Stanford Binet show little sign of a loss of intelligence, others show much greater loss. There are then two kinds of test material, or two extremes in test content that shade into one another. The same picture appears when older adult subjects are examined: some (Binet type) tests show no deterioration due to advancing age; others show a marked deterioration; and most tests fall somewhere between the two extremes (Jones and Conrad, 1933; Wechsler, 1939).

The Binet IQ is determined by the use of a composite test, and it amounts to an average level of performance in a miscellany of tasks. It is mainly verbal, however, and mainly involves a kind of problem to which the answer is rather obvious, to the subject who can solve it at all. Tests of intelligence may also consist of nonverbal tasks, and puzzle-like tasks—ones that require an effort and have to be worked out logically. Analysis of the test scores made after brain operation, when aphasia is not present, indicates that it is the first of these two kinds of task that is little affected by brain damage, the second that is much affected (Weisenburg and McBride, 1935; Rylander, 1939; Hebb, 1942a). The IQ shows little effect of brain damage outside the speech areas because it is mainly based on "Binet type" tasks. These consist particularly of tests of vocabulary, information, digit repetition, digits backward, understanding of the meaning of fables or proverbs, and certain problems of a familiar kind, dependent usually on common sense (in the form of a cultural sophistication).

Now, for normal persons, vocabulary and information tests are among the most valid tests of intelligence, and the Binet-type test in general is what best predicts the subject's level of problem-solving outside the laboratory or clinic, in a wide range of situations. This is what presents us with our problem: how can they also be the ones that show the least effect of brain operation, and the degenerative changes of senescence?

But we must consider at once a further fact: that *in certain essential respects, "intelligence" does not decrease after the age of twenty or thirty, and the brain-operated patient very frequently demonstrates an unimpaired level of functioning in his daily occupations.* The patient with an IQ of 160 after prefrontal lobectomy (Hebb, 1939) graduated with honors in his arts course and went on to do well in medical school; the patients with half the cortex removed (Dandy, 1933; Rowe, 1937; Karnosh and Gardner, 1941) *clearly did not act in any respect like the feebleminded,* in their daily affairs. Certain intellectual capacities *are* well retained by the patient; in some respects, the prediction made by the Binet-type test *is* valid. The puzzle is not why the Binet suddenly loses its diagnostic value, after brain injury: but why an important part of intelligence is little affected by the injury. The fact that it is not, at once suggests that this part of intelligence is not directly correlated with the integrity of the brain; and, since the problems in which "intelligence" is unimpaired are in general those with which the patient is familiar, a further suggestion is that part of intelligence is a product of experience.

An idea of this sort led to the examination of the effects of early brain injury (with the help of Dr. Heinz Werner); the results, in short, indicated that any damage to the infant brain would affect later performance on vocabulary tests, information, and the like at least as much as performance on other tests (Hebb, 1942a). The situation apparently is this. Unless every known case of large damage to the infant cortex is a case of speech-area damage (a most improbable situation), destruction of tissue outside the speech areas will prevent the development of verbal abilities, but the same destruction may not greatly affect these abilities once development has occurred.

The evidence for this interpretation is not perfect, but it is rather strong. The one flaw appears to be the possibility that the known cortical-type birth-injury population is made up predominantly or entirely of patients with speech-area lesions. It is conceivable that when palsy is not present only speech-area cases are detected—that all the "exogenous" cases of mental deficiency (Werner and Strauss, 1939) are discovered because of damage to this particular cortical area alone. But against this possibility is the fact that cases of palsy, presumably detected because of it, also have the low verbal test scores characteristic of other birth-injury cases. The twelve cases reported by Doll, Phelps, and Melcher (1932) showed marked vocabulary retardation. The low vocabulary score of the birth-injured is not due to deficient opportunity to learn the meaning of words (Hebb, 1942*a*)—a conclusion supported by the almost identical retardations of vocabulary and digit-repetition scores reported by Doll, Phelps, and Melcher. Further, Doll (1933) reported that there is no correlation of speech defect and IQ in the birth-injured.

It appears, therefore, that an early injury may prevent the development of some intellectual capacities that an equally extensive injury, at maturity, would not have destroyed. To complete the picture, it should be said again that this relationship does not hold—at least not to the same degree—for all intellectual capacities; and sensory and motor capacities after damage to the infant brain tend to reach a higher level than that attained after destruction of the same regions at maturity.

How are we to understand the first type of capacity in the adult, the one that is not greatly affected by brain damage at maturity? Psychologically, the matter might be put this way. The actual modifications of behavior that occur in intellectual development are from one point of view qualitative: faced with a complex situation, the more intelligent subject sees it in a different way, and makes a different response—not more responses, or responses that take more effort. The chief intellectual effort, in such behavior, is demanded on the *first* occasion on which the new way of seeing the situation occurs. Learning to solve a problem usually demands more effort than solving other problems of the same kind on later occasions when one has discovered the principle involved. The same is often true of perception, whether one is solving a formal problem or not; once one has seen a certain relationship in a picture, or heard it in music, it may take no effort to find it again in similar pictures or music. This perception of relationships is essential in problem-solving, and one would steadily accumulate an increasing stock of such ways of seeing and attacking problem situations, as age advances; so, in a familiar field, the fifty-year-old may be definitely more "intelligent" (as defined by the problems he can solve) than a twenty-year-old. At the same time, the problem that requires a radically new approach, new ways of perceiving, is not likely to be solved by the older man with his shrunken brain. The difference in the demands that are made by different professions, or different fields of investigation, would account for the fact that some fields are characteristically the domain of young men, others of the middle-aged. We cannot simply generalize, and say that intellectual capacity, objectively defined, decreases from the age of twenty-five onward. Some capacities do; others do not.

Physiologically, the matter may be put as follows: some types of behavior that require a large amount of brain tissue for their first establishment can then persist when the amount of available tissue has been decreased. This of course is consistent with the theory of cell-assemblies that has been presented in this monograph. It has been postulated that, with the enlargement of synaptic knobs, the number of fibers necessary for transmission at the synapse decreases (p. 66). In the first establishment of an assembly, then, more fibers are necessary than for its later functioning.

Also, it has been said that there is a possibility of "short-circuiting" in the phase sequence (p. 228) so that, after a phase sequence has been well established, some assemblies may no longer be necessary to it. If brain injury occurs in a limited region of the brain, it would presumably remove a small number of transmission paths from each of a very large number of assemblies. These assemblies might still function, though they would have smaller safety margins (p. 197) and therefore would function less reliably. In other assemblies, the loss might be great enough to prevent any functioning; but a phase sequence in which some of these assemblies were originally essential might later short-circuit them, and produce the same ultimate insight or understanding of the situation, though some of the steps of inference would have been omitted.

Visual stimulation may have been involved in the formation of some concept, and yet not be necessary to its later arousal (p. 128). Thus the congenitally blind would be incapable of insights and understanding possessed by those who have become blind after having had vision. In the same way, an area-18 lesion might prevent certain "visual" assemblies from functioning. These may have been originally necessary, as a connecting link, in the establishment of connections between other assemblies, constituting a particular conceptual activity; but once the connections are established, the connecting link may not be needed any longer. The same area-18 lesion in infancy thus might prevent a conceptual development but not destroy it at maturity.

THE TWO MEANINGS OF "INTELLIGENCE"

The clinical evidence has indicated, in effect, that there are two components in intelligence-test performance and in any intelligent behavior. One is diminished immediately by damage to the brain, and amounts to a factor of heredity; one is related more to experience, consisting of permanent changes in the organization of pathways in the cerebrum (in the present theory, these changes are the establishment first of assemblies of cells, and secondly of interfacilitation between assemblies). The hereditary factor is essentially the capacity for elaborating perceptions and conceptual activities; the experiential factor is the degree to which such elaboration has occurred (and particularly, when we speak of intelligence, the conceptual elaboration that is not specific to one occupation or situation, but that enters into many human activities; concepts of number, of causal relations, of common human behavior, and so on).

From this point of view it appears that the word "intelligence" has *two* valuable meanings. One is (A) an *innate potential*, the capacity for development, a fully innate property that amounts to the possession of a good brain and a good neural metabolism. The second is (B) the functioning of a brain in which development has gone on, determining an *average level of performance or comprehension* by the partly grown or mature person. Neither, of course, is observed directly; but *intelligence B*, a hypothetical level of development in brain function, is a much more direct inference from behavior than *intelligence A*, the original potential. (I emphasize that these are not two parallel kinds of intelligence, coexistent, but two different meanings of "intelligence.") It is true that estimating intelligence B requires a summation of observations of behavior in many different situations, at different times; however, if we assume that such an estimate is possible, what we actually know about an intelligence-test score is that it is primarily related to intelligence *B* rather than intelligence *A*. The relationship to *A* is less direct. Most of the disagreement in recent years over the nature of "intelligence" concerns the relation of *A*, innate potential, to *B*, the estimated level of functioning at maturity. If *A* determines *B* fully, "intelligence" is a matter of heredity and maturation only; the IQ is not dependent on experience. But if intelligence *A* is only one of the conditions of intelligence *B*, not the sole determinant, what then? Intelligence *A* is still hereditary, and it would not be true to say that "intelligence" (without qualification) is influenced by experience: only intelligence *B* is so affected.

The dispute in the current literature has arisen, I believe, partly because of the double reference of the term "intelligence" and partly because it has not been realized that if the effects of early experience are more or less generalized and permanent one can concede a major effect of experience on the IQ, and still leave the IQ its constancy and validity as an index of future performance.

An innate potential for development is not logically a guarantee that the development will occur. There is in fact an overwhelming body of evidence to show that experience is essential to the development (the original potentiality is of course equally essential). Binet himself assumed the necessity of adequate experience in the subject to be examined by his method; the content of intelligence tests still makes this a necessary precondition; and all psychologists recognize that one cannot compare the innate intelligence of subjects from two different cultures: experience affects their IQ's to an unknown degree. Why then should we object to the idea that enriching an inadequate environment will raise the IQ, as Stoddard and Wellman (1940) and others have urged?

Some of the objection, certainly, may be occasioned by a faulty use of evidence and be due to the impression that the case for an environmental influence on the IQ has been overstated. But the roots of the objection, I believe, are to be found in certain ideas about the nature of learning. It is apt to be assumed that learning is more or less specific to particular situations; that what is learned can always be forgotten; or that if something can be learned in infancy it can also be learned at maturity. Assuming the truth of such propositions, one might then think as follows:

"If the IQ has any great dependence on learning it must fluctuate easily; it might be raised from 100 to 150 in the adult, or might fall from 100 to 70 if a child is removed from school and other stimulating influences. But the IQ does not in fact behave so—therefore learning does not contribute to it. It must be hereditary, because it is so stable."

However, there are definite limits to the "constancy" of the IQ; and most of the facts that seem to show that it is hereditarily determined would be accounted for if we assume that heredity only sets a *limit* to the IQ, and assume also that early learning tends to be permanent, that it has generalized transfer effects, and that it is not specific to particular situations. That early learning has such properties has already been suggested, in the first part of Chapter 6. I wish now to report some preliminary experiments with the rat, which seem to show that some aspects of this animal's intelligence at maturity are a function of his early experience. If this principle can be established by means of animal experiment, we can then see how it would be applied to the known facts of human intelligence and intelligence-test performance.

EXPERIMENT: INFANT EXPERIENCE AND ADULT PROBLEM-SOLVING

When we test human intelligence, we always assume that the subject has had a certain body of experience common to all "normal" children in the community, the experience whose *lack* may invalidate comparison of the innate potential of subjects from different communities. Apart entirely from controversy about the effect of special experiences on the IQ, we are all agreed, in this sense, on the effect of a certain kind of experience (which is not, however, well defined).

One purpose of the experimental work briefly described here was to find out more about how the ordinary experience of infancy affects mature behavior. It was not certain that such effects could be found in rat behavior, even if they exist for man;

but if one could find some trace of them in rat behavior their nature could be investigated much more easily in a species that reaches maturity in three months than in one that takes fifteen years. Also, the clinical evidence reviewed in this chapter has indicated that the effect of early experience is not found equally in all forms of behavior. Accordingly, these were exploratory experiments, with the main object of establishing the existence of some lasting effect of early experience on the later problem-solving of the rat. The first explorations gave wholly negative results, but they have the value of showing that some behavior is *not* affected by early experience; that is, they serve to delimit the effect.

In the first part of the study, one group of 7 animals were blinded in infancy, and a group of 7 littermates were blinded at maturity. Both groups were handled frequently, and were allowed daily to run outside their cages in a large space in which there were a number of objects. The question asked was this. Would the group with vision during growth learn something about finding their way around that they would retain after being blinded at maturity? Would this affect their behavior permanently, in other situations than those in which their visual experience occurred?

At the age of five months—two months after the second group were blinded—the rats were trained to find food in one of four containers in an open field. Two hundred trials were given, and the learning was not complete for most of the animals in this time—so this presumably is to be classed as rote learning rather than insightful. A second period of training in a similar task also appeared to give rote learning, and in neither could any significant difference be found between the two groups, early- and late-blinded.

At this point, however, a chance observation suggested the possibility that an "intelligence test" for the rat (Hebb and Williams, 1946) might reveal differences between the groups. Although the test had been meant for normal animals, it might work with the blind as well.

The test showed a clear difference between the groups. By this time the experiment was being done with only 3 late-blinded animals and 4 early-blinded, a small number for statistical significance. However, there was no overlap of scores in the two groups—all 3 late-blinded were better than all 4 early-blinded, which is certainly significant.*

Before repeating and confirming this result, it appeared profitable to explore further. The effect of vision during development, on the behavior of rats after being blinded at maturity, was great; would other variations of experience also have effects that could be detected by this—apparently sensitive—method of testing? The obvious experiment was to compare rats reared in ordinary small cages with others that had had the run of a wider environment. Two litters were taken home to be reared as pets,† a first group of 3 (after 1 mortality at home) and a second group of 4. They were out of their cages a good deal of the time and running about the house. While this was being done, 25 cage-reared rats from the same colony were tested.

When the pet group were tested, all 7 scored in the top third of the total distribution for cage-reared and pets. More important still, the pets improved their relative standing in the last 10 days of testing, following 10 days of preliminary training, and 11 days of testing (a total of 21 tests was used). One explanation of the better scores of the pets is just that they were tamer, more used to handling, and less disturbed by testing. But, if this were so, the longer the cage-reared animals were worked with the closer they would come to the pet group, as the cage-reared became tamer with prolonged handling. On the contrary, the pets improved more than the cage-reared. This means that *the richer experience of the pet group during development made*

---

* The experiments described in this section are now being repeated and carried further by B. Hymovitch and H. Lansdell, and will be reported in detail later. The method has been considerably improved since the first report of Hebb and Williams; it will be described in detail in a separate publication. The essential features of the method are: (1) 10 to 14 days' preliminary training gets the animal used to handling, to the test situation, and to daily changes in the route he must take to food, and teaches him where the food is to be found (its position is constant throughout); (2) the test itself is a series of 20 to 24 separate problems, each relatively easy for the seeing rat; he is given between 6 and 10 trials with each, and his score is the total number of entries into error zones (see figure 17, p. 137).

† Grateful acknowledgments are due to the Misses Jane and Ellen Hebb, ages seven and five, for their enthusiastic assistance in the investigation.

them better able to profit by new experiences at maturity—one of the characteristics of the "intelligent" human being. Furthermore, a measure of motivation and tameness in the cage-reared was available, and the correlation of this with the test score was negligible (0.13 ± 0.19).

These results show a permanent effect of early experience on problem-solving at maturity: "permanent," because, in the first experiment with early- and late-blinded, visual experience that ended at three months of age had marked effects at eight months of age (a long period in the life of a rat); and because, in the second experiment, the pet group improved its standing compared to the others as experience increased. Differences of early experience can produce differences in adult problem-solving that further experience does not erase.

These preliminary results are already being confirmed by more elaborate experiments now going on, and a principle is established that, first, is fully in accord with other evidence showing lasting and generalized effects of early experience (Chapter 6) and, secondly, clarifies the interpretation of existing data concerning human intelligence-test performance.

THE NATURE AND NURTURE OF INTELLIGENCE

Actually, some of the data on normal human intelligence (as well as the clinical data) allow only one interpretation, namely, that there is a major effect of experience on the IQ. One difficulty in accepting this interpretation is that it may seem to deny the validity of the intelligence-test method. But, if the principle of a lasting and generalized effect of early learning is accepted, not only on the IQ but also on the everyday problem-solving of the adult, the validity of the intelligence-test method may be extended, not reduced. It is common to say that an intelligence test is not valid when given to a foreigner or a Negro. Not valid in what sense? as an estimate of innate potentiality, of intelligence A. It may be quite valid, on a purely empirical footing, for estimating intelligence B—the actual level of comprehension, learning, and problem-solving *in this culture*. Separating these two meanings of "intelligence" allows one to show where the test is valid, as well as where it is invalid.

Look closer at this question of the relationship between test score and culture. It is agreed by psychologists that the IQ's of different peoples should not be compared, since intelligence tests are culture-loaded and not equally fair to subjects from different cultures. Now it is quite clear from the context of such discussion that the "unfairness" lies in estimating a subject's hereditary endowment. Negroes living in the United States make lower average scores on intelligence tests than whites do, but we cannot conclude that the Negro has a poorer brain than the white. Why? Negro and white speak the same language, are taught in the same curriculum and sometimes in the same schools, work at the same plants, and on the whole intermingle very freely. Why then does the Negro's IQ not have the same meaning as a white man's? Because Negro and white do not have the opportunity to learn to speak the language with equal range and accuracy, are not usually taught in equally good schools, and do not have equally good jobs or equal exposure to cultural influences that usually require a fairly good income.

All this we can accept; but when we do so we must recognize that we have completely undermined the argument that differences of IQ among white, native Americans are determined by heredity.

In what respect does the argument, concerning the Negro's IQ and his innate endowment, differ for the poor white in the South and the white tenement dweller in the North? *They* do not have opportunity to acquire the same vocabulary, are often taught in poor schools, do not get good jobs or have good salaries. The extent of this influence of experience is quite unknown; conceivably, it is small; but one cannot argue that Negro and white IQ's cannot be compared, and at the same time that those of white and white can be, when the white subjects have different social backgrounds. The IQ can be trusted as an index of intelligence *A* only when the social backgrounds of the subjects compared are identical; and this adds up to the proposition that we cannot in any rigorous sense measure a subject's innate endowment, for no two social backgrounds are identical and we do not know what the important environmental variables are in the development of intellectual functions. Intelligence *A* may sometimes be estimated, but it cannot be measured (Hebb and Morton, 1944).

Intelligence in sense *B* is a different matter. We know, beyond dispute, that the adolescent with generally low intelligence-test scores, whether Negro, poor white American, or foreigner, is a poor prospect for college training, or training as a mechanic, or Army officer, or dress designer. The inability to determine intelligence *A* from a test score should not blind us to the fact that a foreigner's intelligence *B* can be estimated, as far as its operation in this culture is concerned.

To be a bank manager, an airplane pilot, a mathematician, a secretary, or a surgeon requires a certain common conceptual development that must occur in this or a closely related culture, and in childhood mainly; and intelligence tests on the whole can provide a rather good index of the extent to which that development has occurred. No other interpretation seems possible of the differences, *both in educability and in intelligence-test scores,* of first- and second-generation immigrants. Supposing that both have an adequate nutrition, father and son must have on the average the same intelligence *A;* the son very often has a much higher intelligence *B.*

The nature of the cultural environment that is necessary to this conceptual development cannot be described accurately. It does not necessarily consist of a formal schooling, and it may be present in spite of poverty. In general, one might guess, it consists of an exposure to ideas, to books, and to intelligent conversation; the opportunity to acquire common technical knowledge and skills; and exposure to persons with social skills, who are good at getting along with other persons. Besides being a guess, of course, such a statement is pretty vague and shows rather clearly how much we cannot say about the matter. Also, we have no way of knowing what ceiling there is on this environmental influence, at what age it is greatest, and so on. Such questions can be answered only by further research.

Our information at present is scanty, almost entirely naturalistic rather than experimental in origin. Neff's (1938) review will show the interested reader how definite the evidence is that environment has a major effect on the IQ. Identical-twin data, for example, are commonly supposed to have shown that heredity is the only major determinant of "intelligence." In none of the studied pairs, however, was one twin brought up in an entirely favorable environment, one in an entirely unfavorable environment; usually they were brought up in about the same stratum of society, so that similar IQ's may be the result of similar environment, a similar heredity, or both.

What we really want, as evidence on this point, is one twin brought up in a good home, with books, toys, kindergarten training, and plenty of exposure to intelligent adults; the other brought up by illiterate, poverty-stricken, anti-social mountaineers with low IQ's: *then* test their intelligences at maturity, and try making doctors, or politicians, of both twins. When this is done, and when it has been shown that the twin with a poor environment (for the first fifteen years of life) can with time become as good a diagnostician or committeeman as his genetically identical brother, it will then be in order to say that the factual evidence shows that "intelligence" and the IQ are without any major effect from experience; not before.

If the Iowa studies (Stoddard and Wellman, 1940) are distrusted, the studies of Gordon, Asher, and Jordan, among others reviewed by Neff, all tell the same story. The constancy of the IQ is the main argument for its being determined by heredity; but the fact is that the IQ is not constant—it is stable, and changes slowly, and more and more slowly as maturity is approached (Anderson, 1939), so that the IQ *of the adult* may be constant (though there are few data on long-term comparisons even here). But prediction of the adult IQ, in infancy, is more accurate on the basis of the parents' IQ's than on that of the infant himself; from an IQ at the age of five, prediction of the IQ at twelve is about 20 per cent better than chance prediction, very little better than can be done from knowing what kind of home the child is growing up in.

There are then two determinants of intellectual growth: a *completely necessary* innate potential (intelligence *A*), and a *completely necessary* stimulating environment. It is not to the point to ask which is more important; hypothetically, we might suppose that intelligence will rise to the limit set by heredity *or* environment, whichever is lower. Given a perfect environment, the inherited constitution will set the pace; given the heredity of a genius, the environment will do so. The essentials of this environmental influence cannot be specified. Though we know that wealth, prolonged schooling, or "intelligent" parents (that is, with intelligence B) are not essential, these things all may contribute. Since the guess has been made that the essential is exposure to intelligence B, it is presumably true that the child must either have intelligent parents or intelligent acquaintances and teachers. Schooling also is becoming more and more necessary to an understanding of adult problems in this society; and a certain amount of wealth, of freedom from economic pressure, may be quite necessary to full intellectual development. The fact is, however, that we know almost nothing specific about the matter. The country may be full of potential geniuses, for all we know, and it should be a pressing concern for psychology to discover the conditions that will develop whatever potentialities a child may have.

Bibliography

Adams, D. K. 1929. Experimental studies of adaptive behavior in cats. *Comp. Psychol. Monog.*, *6*, No. 1.

Adrian, E. D. 1931. Potential changes in the isolated nervous system of *Dytiscus marginalis*. *J. Physiol.*, *72*, 132–151.

Adrian, E. D. 1934. Electrical activity of the nervous system. *Arch. Neurol. Psychiat.*, *32*, 1125–1136.

Adrian, E. D., and Buytendijk, F. J. J. 1931. Potential changes in the isolated brain stem of the goldfish. *J. Physiol.*, *71*, 121–135.

Adrian, E. D., and Matthews, B. H. C. 1934. The interpretation of potential waves in the cortex. *J. Physiol.*, *81*, 440–471.

Allen, C., and Broster, L. R. 1945. A further case of paranoid psychosis successfully treated by adrenalectomy. *Brit. Med. J.*, No. 4402, 696–698.

Allport, G. W. 1946. Effect: a secondary principle of learning. *Psychol. Rev.*, *53*, 335–347.

Anderson, J. E. 1939. The limitations of infant and preschool tests in the measurement of intelligence. *J. Psychol.*, *8*, 351–379.

Arvanitaki, A. 1942. Effects evoked in an axon by the activity of a contiguous one. *J. Neurophysiol.*, *5*, 89–108.

Bard, P. 1934. On emotional expression after decortication with some remarks on certain theoretical views. *Psychol. Rev.*, *41*, 309–329.

Bard, P. 1942. Neural mechanisms in emotional and sexual behavior. *Psychosom. Med.*, *4*, 171–172.

Bartley, S. H., and Bishop, G. H. 1933. Factors determining the form of the electrical response from the optic cortex of the rabbit. *Amer. J. Physiol.*, *103*, 173–184.

Bartley, S. H., and Chute, E. 1947. *Fatigue and impairment in man.* New York: McGraw-Hill.

Beach, F. A. 1937. The neural basis of innate behavior. I. Effects of cortical lesions upon the maternal behavior pattern in the rat. *J. Comp. Psychol.*, *24*, 393–439.

Beach, F. A. 1939. The neural basis of innate behavior. III. Comparison of learning ability and instinctive behavior in the rat. *J. Comp. Psychol.*, *28*, 225–262.

Beach, F. A. 1942. Analysis of factors involved in the arousal, maintenance and manifestation of sexual excitement in male animals. *Psychosom. Med.*, *4*, 173–198.

Beach, F. A. 1947a. A review of physiological and psychological studies of sexual behavior in mammals. *Physiol. Rev.*, *27*, 240–307.

Beach, F. A. 1947*b*. Evolutionary changes in the physiological control of mating behavior in mammals. *Psychol. Rev.*, *54*, 297–315.

Beach, F. A. 1948. *Hormones and behavior*. New York: Hoeber.

Bellak, L., and Willson, E. 1947. On the etiology of dementia praecox · · · . *J. Nerv. Ment. Dis.*, *105*, 1–24.

Bellows, R. T. 1939. Time factors in water drinking in dogs. *Amer. J. Physiol.*, *125*, 87–97.

Birch, H. G. 1945. The relation of previous experience to insightful problem-solving. *J. Comp. Psychol.*, *38*, 367–383.

Bishop, G. H. 1946. Nerve and synaptic conduction. *Ann. Rev. Physiol.*, *8*, 355–374.

v. Bonin, G., Garol, H. W., and McCulloch, W. S. 1942. The functional organization of the occipital lobe. *In* Klüver, H., *Visual mechanisms. Biol. Symp.*, *7*, 165–192.

Boring, E. G. 1916. Cutaneous sensation after nerve-division. *Quart. J. Exp. Physiol.*, *10*, 1–95.

Boring, E. G. 1930. A new ambiguous figure. *Amer. J. Psychol.*, *42*, 444–445.

Boring, E. G. 1933. *The physical dimensions of consciousness*. New York: Century.

Boring, E. G. 1946. Mind and mechanism. *Amer. J. Psychol.*, *59*, 173–192.

Bousfield, W. A. 1935. Quantitative indices of the effects of fasting on eating-behavior. *J. Genet. Psychol.*, *46*, 476–479.

Bowman, K. M. 1935. Psychoses with pernicious anemia. *Amer. J. Psychiat.*, *92*, 371–396.

Bowman, K. M. 1946. Modern concept of the neuroses. *J. Amer. Med. Assoc.*, *132*, 555–557.

Bridgman, C. S., and Smith, K. U. 1945. Bilateral neural integration in visual perception after section of the corpus callosum. *J. Comp. Neurol.*, *83*, 57–68.

Bronk, D. W. 1939. Synaptic mechanisms in sympathetic ganglia. *J. Neurophysiol.*, *2*, 380–401.

Brown, Warner. 1932. Spatial integrations in a human maze. *Univ. Calif. Publ. Psychol.*, *5*, 123–134.

Bruetsch, W. L. 1947. Rheumatic brain disease: late sequel of rheumatic fever. *J. Amer. Med. Assoc.*, *134*, 450–454.

Carlson, A. J. 1916. *The control of hunger in health and disease*. Chicago: Univ. Chic. Press.

Carmichael, L., Hogan, H. P., and Walter, A. A. 1932. An experimental study of the effect of language on the reproduction of visually perceived form. *J. Exp. Psychol.*, *15*, 73–86.

Chandler, A. R. 1934. *Beauty and human nature*. New York: Appleton-Century.

Clark, G., and Lashley, K. S. 1947. Visual disturbances following frontal ablations in the monkey. *Anat. Rec.*, *97*, 326.

Cobb, S. 1944. Personality as affected by lesions of the brain. *In* Hunt, J. McV., *Personality and the behavior disorders*. New York: Ronald, Vol. I, pp. 550–581.

Cobb, S., Cohen, M. E., and Badal, D. W. 1946. Capillaries of the nail fold in patients with neurocirculatory asthenia (effort syndrome, anxiety neurosis). *Arch. Neurol. Psychiat., 56,* 643–650.

Cohn, R. 1945. Electroencephalographic study of prefrontal lobotomy. *Arch. Neurol. Psychiat., 53,* 283–288.

Cowles, J. T., and Nissen, H. W. 1937. Reward-expectancy in delayed responses of chimpanzees. *J. Comp. Psychol., 24,* 345–358.

Dandy, W. E. 1933. Physiologic studies following extirpation of the right cerebral hemisphere in man. *Bull. Johns Hopkins Hosp., 53,* 31–51.

Daniel, R. S., and Smith, K. U. 1947. The sea-approach behavior of the neonate loggerhead turtle. *J. Comp. Physiol. Psychol., 40,* 413–420.

Dashiell, J. F. 1928. Are there any native emotions? *Psychol. Rev., 35,* 319–327.

Davison, C., and Demuth, E. L. 1945. Disturbances in sleep mechanism: a clinico-pathologic study. II. Lesions at the corticodiencephalic level. *Arch. Neurol. Psychiat., 54,* 241–255.

Denker, P. G. 1946. Results of treatment of psychoneuroses by the general practitioner: a follow-up study of 500 cases. *N. Y. State J. Med., 46,* 2164–2166.

Dennis, W. 1934. Congenital cataract and unlearned behavior. *J. Genet. Psychol., 44,* 340–350.

Dennis, W. 1940. Infant reaction to restraint: an evaluation of Watson's theory. *Trans. N. Y. Acad. Sci.,* Ser. 2., *2,* No. 8, 202–218.

Denny-Brown, D. 1932. Theoretical deductions from the physiology of the cerebral cortex. *J. Neurol. Psychopathol., 13,* 52–67.

Dewan, J. G., and Owen, T. 1945. Mental illness and the principles of medicine. *Canad. Med. Ass. J., 52,* 349–357.

Doll, E. A. 1933. Psychological significance of cerebral birth lesions. *Amer. J. Psychol., 45,* 444–452.

Doll, E. A., Phelps, W. M., and Melcher, R. T. 1932. *Mental deficiency due to birth injuries.* New York: Macmillan.

Drew, G. C. 1938. The function of punishment in learning. *J. Genet. Psychol., 52,* 257–267.

Dubner, H. H., and Gerard, R. W. 1939. Factors controlling brain potentials in the cat. *J. Neurophysiol., 2,* 142–152.

Dunlap, K. 1932. *Habits: their making and remaking.* New York: Liveright.

Editors, Nutrition Reviews. 1944. Self-selection of diets. *Nutrition Rev., 2,* 199–203.

Egaña, E., Johnson, R. E., Bloomfield, R., Brouha, L., *et al.* 1942. The effects of a diet deficient in the vitamin B complex on sedentary men. *Amer. J. Physiol., 137,* 731–741.

Erlanger, J. 1939. The initiation of impulses in axons. *J. Neurophysiol.,* 2, 370–379.

Ferraro, A., Arieti, S., and English, W. H. 1945. Cerebral changes in the course of pernicious anemia and their relationship to psychic symptoms. *J. Neuropathol. Exp. Neurol.,* 4, 217–239.

Fields, P. E. 1932. Studies in concept formation. I. *Comp. Psychol. Monog.,* 9, No. 2.

Forbes, A. 1939. Problems of synaptic function. *J. Neurophysiol.,* 2, 465–472.

Freeman, G. L. 1934. *Introduction to physiological psychology.* New York: Ronald.

Freeman, W., and Watts, J. W. 1942. *Psychosurgery: intelligence, emotion and social behavior following prefrontal lobotomy for mental disorders.* Springfield: Thomas.

Freeman, W., and Watts, J. W. 1946. Psychosurgery. *In* Spiegel, E. A., *Progress in neurology and psychiatry: an annual review.* New York: Grune and Stratton, pp. 649–661.

Fuchs, W. 1920. Untersuchungen über das Sehen der Hemianopiker und Hemiamblyopiker: II. *In* Gelb, A., and Goldstein, K., *Psychologischen Analysen hirnpathologischer Fälle.* Leipzig: Barth, pp. 419–561.

Fulton, J. F. 1943. *Physiology of the nervous system.* 2nd Ed., New York: Oxford Univ. Press.

Gantt, W. H. 1938. Extension of a conflict based upon food to other physiological systems and its reciprocal relations with sexual functions. *Amer. J. Physiol.,* 123, 73–74.

Gantt, W. H. 1944. Experimental basis for neurotic behavior: origin and development of artificially produced disturbances of behavior in dogs. *Psychosom. Med. Monog.,* 3, Nos. 3 and 4.

Garrison, M. 1947. The genetics of schizophrenia. *J. Abn. Soc. Psychol.,* 42, 122–124.

Gasser, H. S. 1937. The control of excitation in the nervous system. *Harvey Lect.,* pp. 169–193.

Gellerman, L. W. 1933. Form discrimination in chimpanzees and two-year-old children: I. Form (triangularity) *per se. J. Genet. Psychol.,* 42, 3–27.

Gibbs, F. A. 1945. Electrical activity of the brain. *Ann. Rev. Physiol.,* 7, 427–454.

Gibson, J. J. 1929. The reproduction of visually perceived forms. *J. Exp. Psychol.,* 12, 1–39.

Gibson, J. J. 1941. A critical review of the concept of set in contemporary experimental psychology. *Psychol. Bull.,* 38, 781–817.

Gibson, J. J., and Crooks, L. E. 1938. A theoretical field-analysis of automobile driving. *Amer. J. Psychol.,* 51, 453–471.

Gillespie, W. H. 1944. The psychoneuroses. *J. Ment. Sci.,* 90, 287–306.

Goodenough, F. L. 1931. *Anger in young children.* Minneapolis: Univ. Minnesota Press.

Greene, R., Paterson, A. S., and Pile, G. C. S. 1945. Hypertrichosis with mental changes: the effect of adrenalectomy. *Brit. Med. J.*, No. 4402, 698–699.

Guthrie, E. R. 1946. Psychological facts and psychological theory. *Psychol. Bull.*, *43*, 1–20.

Halstead, W. C. 1947. *Brain and intelligence.* Chicago: Univ. Chic. Press.

Hanawalt, N. G. 1937. Memory trace for figures in recall and recognition. *Arch. Psychol.*, No. 216, 1–89.

Harris, H. J. 1944. Brucellosis: a case report illustrating a psychosomatic problem. *Psychosom. Med.*, *6*, 334–335.

Hauptman, A. 1946. Capillaries in the finger nail fold in patients with neurosis, epilepsy, and migraine. *Arch. Neurol. Psychiat.*, *56*, 631–642.

Head, H. 1920. *Studies in neurology.* London: Frowde, Hodder and Stoughton.

Heath, R. G., and Pool, J. L. 1948. Bilateral fractional resection of frontal cortex for the treatment of psychoses. *J. Nerv. Ment. Dis.*, *107*, 411–429.

Hebb, D. O. 1937a. The innate organization of visual activity: I. Perception of figures by rats reared in total darkness. *J. Genet. Psychol.*, *51*, 101–126.

Hebb, D. O. 1937b. The innate organization of visual activity: II. Transfer of response in the discrimination of brightness and size by rats reared in total darkness. *J. Comp. Psychol.*, *24*, 277–299.

Hebb, D. O. 1938a. Studies of the organization of behavior: I. Behavior of the rat in a field orientation. *J. Comp. Psychol.*, *25*, 333–352.

Hebb, D. O. 1938b. Studies of the organization of behavior: II. Changes in the field orientation of the rat after cortical destruction. *J. Comp. Psychol.*, *26*, 427–444.

Hebb, D. O. 1939. Intelligence in man after large removals of cerebral tissue: report of four left frontal lobe cases. *J. Gen. Psychol.*, *21*, 73–87.

Hebb, D. O. 1942a. The effect of early and late brain injury upon test scores, and the nature of normal adult intelligence. *Proc. Amer. Phil. Soc.*, *85*, 275–292.

Hebb, D. O. 1942b. Verbal test material independent of special vocabulary difficulty. *J. Educ. Psychol.*, *33*, 691–696.

Hebb, D. O. 1945a. The forms and conditions of chimpanzee anger. *Bull. Canad. Psychol. Ass.*, *5*, 32–35.

Hebb, D. O. 1945b. Man's frontal lobes: A critical review. *Arch. Neurol. Psychiat.*, *54*, 10–24.

Hebb, D. O. 1946a. Emotion in man and animal: an analysis of the intuitive processes of recognition. *Psychol. Rev.*, *53*, 88–106.

Hebb, D. O. 1946b. On the nature of fear. *Psychol. Rev.*, *53*, 259–276.

Hebb, D. O. 1947. Spontaneous neurosis in chimpanzees: theoretical relations with clinical and experimental phenomena. *Psychosom. Med.*, *9*, 3–16.

Hebb, D. O., and Foord, E. N. 1945. Errors of visual recognition and the nature of the trace. *J. Exp. Psychol.*, *35*, 335–348.

Hebb, D. O., and Morton, N. W. 1943. The McGill Adult Comprehension Examination: "Verbal Situation" and "Picture Anomaly" Series. *J. Educ. Psychol.*, *34*, 16–25.

Hebb, D. O., and Morton, N. W. 1944. Note on the measurement of adult intelligence. *J. Gen. Psychol.*, *30*, 217–223.

Hebb, D. O., and Penfield, W. 1940. Human behavior after extensive bilateral removal from the frontal lobes. *Arch. Neurol. Psychiat.*, *44*, 421–438.

Hebb, D. O., and Riesen, A. H. 1943. The genesis of irrational fears. *Bull. Canad. Psychol. Ass.*, *3*, 49–50.

Hebb, D. O., and Williams, K. 1941. Experimental control of cues determining the rat's orientation. *Bull. Canad. Psychol. Ass.*, *1*, 22–23.

Hebb, D. O., and Williams, K. 1946. A method of rating animal intelligence. *J. Gen. Psychol.*, *34*, 59–65.

Herrick, C. J. 1929. *The thinking machine.* Chicago: Univ. Chic. Press.

Hilgard, E. R., and Marquis, D. G. 1940. *Conditioning and learning.* New York: Appleton-Century.

Hoagland, H. 1947. Enzyme kinetics and the dynamics of behavior. *J. Comp. Physiol. Psychol.*, *40*, 107–127.

Hoagland, H., Malamud, W., Kaufman, I. C., and Pincus, G. 1946. Changes in the electroencephalogram and in the excretion of 17-ketosteroids accompanying electro-shock therapy of agitated depression. *Psychosom. Med.*, *8*, 246–251.

Hobbs, G. E. 1941. Mental disorder in one of a pair of identical twins. *Amer. J. Psychiat.*, *98*, 447–450.

Hobhouse, L. T. 1915. *Mind in evolution.* 2nd Ed. London: Macmillan.

Hovland, C. I. 1936. "Inhibition of reinforcement" and phenomena of experimental extinction. *Proc. Nat. Acad. Sci., Wash.*, *22*, 430–433. (Quoted by Hilgard and Marquis, 1940, p. 146.)

Hovland, C. I. 1937. The generalization of conditioned responses. II. The sensory generalization of conditioned responses with varying intensities of tone. *J. Genet. Psychol.*, *51*, 279–291.

Hull, C. L. 1934. The concept of the habit-family hierarchy and maze learning. *Psychol. Rev.*, *41*, 33–54; 134–152.

Hull, C. L. 1943. *Principles of behavior: an introduction to behavior theory.* New York: Appleton-Century.

Hull, C. L. 1945. The discrimination of stimulus configurations and the hypothesis of afferent neural interaction. *Psychol. Rev.*, *52*, 133–142.

Humphrey, G. 1940. The problem of the direction of thought. *Brit. J. Psychol.*, *30*, 183–196.

Hunt, J. McV. 1941. The effects of infant feeding-frustration upon adult hoarding in the albino rat. *J. Abn. Soc. Psychol.*, *36*, 338–360.

Hunter, W. S. 1934. Learning: IV. Experimental studies of learning. *In* Murchison, C., *Handbook of general experimental psychology.* Worcester, Mass.: Clark Univ. Press, pp. 497–570.

Jackson, T. A. 1942. Use of the stick as a tool by young chimpanzees. *J. Comp. Psychol., 34,* 223–235.

Jacobsen, C. F., Jacobsen, M. M., and Yoshioka, J. G. 1932. Development of an infant chimpanzee during her first year. *Comp. Psychol. Monog., 9,* 1–94.

James, W. 1910. *Principles of psychology.* New York: Holt.

Jasper, H. H. 1937. Electrical signs of cortical activity. *Psychol. Bull., 34,* 411–481.

Jasper, H. H. 1941. Electroencephalography. *In* Penfield, W., and Erickson, T. C., *Epilepsy and cerebral localization.* Springfield: Thomas, pp. 380–454.

Jasper, H. H., and Fortuyn, J. D. 1946. Experimental studies on the functional anatomy of petit mal epilepsy. *Publ. Ass. Res. Nerv. Ment. Dis., 26,* 272–298.

Jefferson, G. 1937. Removal of right or left frontal lobes in man. *Brit. Med. J., 2,* 199–206.

Jersild, A. T., and Holmes, F. B. 1935. *Children's fears.* New York: Teach. Coll. Bur. Publ.

Jolliffe, N. 1942. The neuropsychiatric manifestations of vitamin deficiencies. *J. Mt. Sinai Hosp., 8,* 658–667.

Jones, H. E., and Conrad, H. S. 1933. The growth and decline of intelligence: a study of a homogeneous group between the ages of ten and sixty. *Genet. Psychol. Monog., 13,* No. 3.

Jones, H. E., and Jones, M. C. 1928. A study of fear. *Childhood Educ., 5,* 136–143.

Jones, M. C. 1933. Emotional development. *In* Murchison, C., *A handbook of child psychology.* 2nd Ed. Worcester, Mass.: Clark Univ. Press, pp. 271–302.

Kappers, C. U. A., Huber, G. C., and Crosby, E. C. 1936. *The comparative anatomy of the nervous system of vertebrates, including man.* New York: Macmillan, Vol. I.

Karnosh, L. J., and Gardner, W. J. 1941. An evaluation of the physical and mental capabilities following removal of the right cerebral hemisphere. *Cleveland Clin. Quart., 8,* 94–106.

Kennard, M. A. 1939. Alterations in response to visual stimuli following lesions of frontal lobe in monkeys. *Arch. Neurol. Psychiat., 41,* 1153–1165.

Kennard, M. A., and Ectors, L. 1938. Forced circling in monkeys following lesions of the frontal lobes. *J. Neurophysiol., 1,* 45–54.

Kennedy, F., and Wolf, A. 1936. The relationship of intellect to speech defect in aphasic patients. *J. Nerv. Ment. Dis., 84,* 125–145; 293–311.

Keschner, M., Bender, M., and Strauss, I. 1938. Mental symptoms associated with brain tumor: a study of 530 verified cases. *J. Amer. Med. Ass.*, *110*, 714–718.

Kinder, E. F.   1927.   A study of the nest-building activity of the albino rat. *J. Exp. Zool.*, *47*, 117–161.

Kinsey, A. C., Pomeroy, W. B., and Martin, C. E.   1948.   *Sexual behavior in the human male.* Philadelphia: Saunders.

Klebanoff, S. G.   1945.   Psychological changes in organic brain lesions and ablations. *Psychol. Bull.*, *42*, 585–623.

Kleitman, N.   1939.   *Sleep and wakefulness.* Chicago: Univ. Chic. Press.

Klineberg, O.   1940.   *Social psychology.* New York: Holt.

Koffka, K.   1924.   *The growth of the mind.* New York: Harcourt, Brace.

Koffka, K.   1935.   *Principles of Gestalt psychology.* New York: Harcourt, Brace.

Köhler, W.   1925.   *The mentality of apes.* New York: Harcourt, Brace.

Köhler, W.   1929.   *Gestalt psychology.* New York: Liveright.

Köhler, W.   1940.   *Dynamics in psychology.* New York: Liveright.

Köhler, W., and Wallach, H.   1944.   Figural after-effects: an investigation of visual processes. *Proc. Amer. Phil. Soc.*, *88*, 269–357.

Krechevsky, I.   1932.   "Hypotheses" versus "chance" in the pre-solution period in sensory discrimination-learning. *Univ. Calif. Publ. Psychol.*, *6*, 27–44.

Krechevsky, I.   1938.   An experimental investigation of the principle of proximity in the visual perception of the rat. *J. Exp. Psychol.*, *22*, 497–523.

Kubitschek, P. E.   1928.   The symptomatology of tumors of the frontal lobe based on a series of twenty-two cases. *Arch. Neurol. Psychiat.*, *20*, 559–579.

Landis, C.   1947.   A modern dynamic psychology. *J. Comp. Physiol. Psychol.*, *40*, 135–141.

Landis, C., and Hunt, W. A.   1932.   Adrenalin and emotion. *Psychol. Rev.*, *39*, 467–485.

Lashley, K. S.   1929*a*.   *Brain mechanisms and intelligence: a quantitative study of injuries to the brain.* Chicago: Univ. Chic. Press.

Lashley, K. S.   1929*b*.   Nervous mechanisms in learning. *In* Murchison, C., *The foundations of experimental psychology.* Worcester: Clark Univ. Press, pp. 524–563.

Lashley, K. S.   1930.   Basic neural mechanisms in behavior. *Psychol. Rev.*, *37*, 1–24.

Lashley, K. S.   1934.   The mechanism of vision. VIII. The projection of the retina upon the cerebral cortex of the rat. *J. Comp. Neurol.*, *60*, 57–79.

Lashley, K. S.   1937.   Functional determinants of cerebral localization. *Arch. Neurol. Psychiat.*, *38*, 371–387.

Lashley, K. S.   1938*a*.   Experimental analysis of instinctive behavior. *Psychol. Rev.*, *45*, 445–471.

Lashley, K. S. 1938b. The mechanism of vision: XV. Preliminary studies of the rat's capacity for detail vision. *J. Gen. Psychol.*, *18*, 123–193.

Lashley, K. S. 1938c. The thalamus and emotion. *Psychol. Rev.*, *45*, 42–61.

Lashley, K. S. 1941. Patterns of cerebral integration indicated by the scotomas of migraine. *Arch. Neurol. Psychiat.*, *46*, 331–339.

Lashley, K. S. 1942a. The problem of cerebral organization in vision. *In* Klüver, H., *Visual mechanisms*. *Biol. Sympos.*, *7*, 301–322.

Lashley, K. S. 1942b. An examination of the "continuity theory" as applied to discrimination learning. *J. Gen. Psychol.*, *26*, 241–265.

Lashley, K. S. 1944. Studies of cerebral function in learning: XIII. Apparent absence of transcortical association in maze learning. *J. Comp. Neurol.*, *80*, 257–281.

Lashley, K. S., and Clark, G. 1946. The cytoarchitecture of the cerebral cortex of *Ateles:* a critical examination of architectonic studies. *J. Comp. Neurol.*, *85*, 223–306.

Lashley, K. S., and Wade, M. 1946. The Pavlovian theory of generalization. *Psychol. Rev.*, *53*, 72–87.

Leeper, R. W. 1935. A study of a neglected portion of the field of learning—the development of sensory organization. *J. Genet. Psychol.*, *46*, 41–75.

Leeper, R. W. 1948. A motivational theory of emotion to replace "Emotion as disorganized response." *Psychol. Rev.*, *55*, 5–21.

Lehmann, J. E. 1937a. The effect of changes in the potassium-calcium balance on the action of mammalian A nerve fibers. *Amer. J. Physiol.*, *118*, 613–619.

Lehmann, J. E. 1937b. The effect of changes in pH on the action of mammalian A nerve fibers. *Amer. J. Physiol.*, *118*, 600–612.

Levine, J. 1945a. Studies in the interrelations of central nervous structures in binocular vision: I. The lack of bilateral transfer of visual discriminative habits acquired monocularly by the pigeon. *J. Genet. Psychol.*, *67*, 105–129.

Levine, J. 1945b. Studies in the interrelations of central nervous structures in binocular vision: II. The conditions under which interocular transfer of discriminative habits takes place in the pigeon. *J. Genet. Psychol.*, *67*, 131–142.

Lewin, K. 1938. Will and needs. *In* Ellis, W. D., *A source book of Gestalt psychology*. London: Kegan Paul, Trench, Trubner, pp. 283–299.

Libet, B., and Gerard, R. W. 1939. Control of the potential rhythm of the isolated frog brain. *J. Neurophysiol.*, *2*, 153–169.

Liddell, H. S. 1938. The experimental neurosis and the problem of mental disorder. *Amer. J. Psychiat.*, *94*, 1035–1041.

Liddell, H. S. 1944. Animal behavior studies bearing on the problem of pain. *Psychosom. Med.*, *6*, 261–263.

Lorente de Nó, R. 1938a. Synaptic stimulation of motoneurons as a local process. *J. Neurophysiol.*, *1*, 195–206.

Lorente de Nó, R. 1938*b*. Analysis of the activity of the chains of internuncial neurons. *J. Neurophysiol.*, *1*, 207–244.

Lorente de Nó, R. 1939. Transmission of impulses through cranial motor nuclei. *J. Neurophysiol.*, *2*, 402–464.

Lorente de Nó, R. 1943. Cerebral cortex: architecture. *In* Fulton, J. F., *Physiology of the nervous system.* 2nd Ed. New York: Oxford Univ. Press, pp. 274–301.

Lorenz, K. 1935. Der Kumpan in der Umwelt des Vogels. *J. Ornith.*, *83*, 137–213; 289–413.

Loucks, R. B. 1935. Experimental delimitation of neural structures essential for learning: The attempt to condition striped muscle responses with faradization of the sigmoid gyri. *J. Psychol.*, *1*, 5–44.

Loucks, R. B. 1938. Studies of neural structures essential for learning. II. The conditioning of salivary and striped muscle responses to faradization of cortical sensory elements, and the action of sleep upon such mechanisms. *J. Comp. Psychol.*, *25*, 315–332.

Luckhardt, A. B., and Carlson, A. J. 1915. Contributions to the physiology of the stomach. XVII. On the chemical control of the gastric hunger mechanism. *Amer. J. Physiol.*, *36*, 37–46.

McBride, A. F., and Hebb, D. O. 1948. Behavior of the captive bottlenose dolphin, *Tursiops truncatus. J. Comp. Physiol. Psychol.*, *41*, 111–123.

McCulloch, T. L., and Haslerud, G. M. 1939. Affective responses of an infant chimpanzee reared in isolation from its kind. *J. Comp. Psychol.*, *28*, 437–445.

McCulloch, W. S. 1944*a*. Cortico-cortical connections. *In* Bucy, P., *The precentral motor cortex.* Urbana, Ill.: Univ. Illinois Press, pp. 213–242.

McCulloch, W. S. 1944*b*. The functional organization of the cerebral cortex. *Physiol. Rev.*, *24*, 390–407.

McGeoch, J. A. 1942. *The psychology of human learning.* New York: Longmans, Green.

Maier, N. R. F., and Schneirla, T. C. 1935. *Principles of animal psychology.* New York: McGraw-Hill.

Marshall, W. H., and Talbot, S. A. 1942. Recent evidence for neural mechanisms in vision leading to a general theory of sensory acuity. *In* Klüver, H., *Visual mechanisms. Biol. Symp.*, *7*, 117–164.

Masserman, J. H. 1942. The hypothalamus in psychiatry. *Amer. J. Psychiat.*, *98*, 633–637.

Masserman, J. H. 1943. *Behavior and neurosis: An experimental psychoanalytic approach to psychobiologic principles.* Chicago: Univ. Chic. Press.

Matthews, R. S. 1938. Pellagra and nicotinic acid. *J. Amer. Med. Ass.*, *111*, 1148–1153.

Miller, G. A. 1947. The masking of speech. *Psychol. Bull.*, *44*, 105–129.

Miner, J. B. 1905. A case of vision acquired in adult life. *Psychol. Rev. Monog. Suppl.*, *6*, No. 5, 103–118.

Mixter, W. J., Tillotson, K. J., and Wies, D. 1941. Reports of partial frontal lobectomy and frontal lobotomy performed on three patients: one chronic epileptic and two cases of chronic agitated depression. *Psychosom. Med., 3*, 26–37.

Morgan, C. T. 1943. *Physiological psychology.* New York: McGraw-Hill.

Morison, R. S., and Dempsey, E. W. 1943. Mechanism of thalamocortical augmentation and repetition. *Amer. J. Physiol., 138*, 297–308.

Moss, F. A. (Ed.). 1942. *Comparative psychology.* Rev. Ed. New York: Prentice-Hall.

Mowrer, O. H. 1941. Motivation and learning in relation to the national emergency. *Psychol. Bull., 38*, 421–431.

Mowrer, O. H., and Mowrer, W. M. 1938. Enuresis—a method for its study and treatment. *Amer. J. Orthopsychiat., 8*, 436–459.

Muenzinger, K. F. 1934. Motivation in learning. I. Electric shock for correct response in the visual discrimination habit. *J. Comp. Psychol., 17*, 267–277.

Murphy, J. P., and Gellhorn, E. 1945. Further investigations on diencephalic-cortical relations and their significance for the problem of emotion. *J. Neurophysiol., 8*, 431–447.

Nafe, J. P. 1934. The pressure, pain, and temperature senses. *In* Murchison, C., *Handbook of general experimental psychology.* Worcester, Mass.: Clark Univ. Press, pp. 1037–1087.

Nauta, W. J. H. 1946. Hypothalamic regulation of sleep in rats: An experimental study. *J. Neurophysiol., 9*, 285–316.

Neet, C. C. 1933. Visual pattern discrimination in the *Macacus rhesus* monkey. *J. Genet. Psychol., 43*, 163–196.

Neff, Walter S. 1938. Socioeconomic status and intelligence: a critical survey. *Psychol. Bull., 35*, 727–757.

Nichols, I., and Hunt, J. McV. 1940. A case of partial bilateral frontal lobectomy: a psychopathological study. *Amer. J. Psychiat., 96*, 1063–1083.

Nissen, H. W., Machover, S., and Kinder, E. F. 1935. A study of performance tests given to a group of native African negro children. *Brit. J. Psychol., 25*, 308–355.

Pavlov, I. P. 1927. *Conditioned reflexes.* Oxford: Humphrey Milford.

Pavlov, I. P. 1928. *Lectures on conditioned reflexes.* New York: International.

Pavlov, I. P. 1932. The reply of a physiologist to psychologists. *Psychol. Rev., 39*, 91–126.

Penfield, W., and Jasper, H. 1946. Highest level seizures. *Res. Publ. Ass. Nerv. Ment. Dis., 26*, 252–271.

Pennington, L. A. 1938. The function of the brain in auditory localization. IV. Method of training and control experiments. *J. Comp. Psychol., 25*, 195–211.

Pilgrim, F. J., and Patton, R. A. 1947. Patterns of self-selection of purified dietary components by the rat. *J. Comp. Physiol. Psychol.*, *40*, 343–348.

Pillsbury, W. B. 1913. "Fluctuations of attention" and the refractory period. *J. Phil. Psychol. Sci. Meth.*, *10*, 181–185.

Polyak, S. L. 1941. *The retina.* Chicago: Univ. Chic. Press.

Postman, L. 1947. The history and present status of the law of effect. *Psychol. Bull.*, *44*, 489–563.

Pratt, C. C. 1939. *The logic of modern psychology.* New York: Macmillan.

Prentice, W. C. H. 1946. Operationism and psychological theory: a note. *Psychol. Rev.*, *53*, 247–249.

Prosser, C. L. 1934. Action potentials in the nervous system of the crayfish: I. Spontaneous impulses. *J. Cell. Comp. Physiol.*, *4*, 185–209.

Richter, C. P., Holt, L. E., and Barelare, B. 1938. Nutritional requirements for normal growth and reproduction in rats studied by the self-selection method. *Amer. J. Physiol.*, *122*, 734–744.

Riddoch, G. 1941. Phantom limbs and body shape. *Brain*, *64*, 197–222.

Riesen, A. H. 1947. The development of visual perception in man and chimpanzee. *Science*, *106*, 107–108.

Riesen, A. H., and Nissen, H. W. 1942. Non-spatial delayed response by the matching technique. *J. Comp. Psychol.*, *34*, 307–313.

Roethlisburger, F. J., and Dickson, W. J. 1939. *Management and the worker.* Cambridge: Harvard Univ. Press.

Romano, J., and Coon, G. P. 1942. Physiologic and psychologic studies in spontaneous hypoglycemia. *Psychosom. Med.*, *4*, 283–300.

Rowe, S. N. 1937. Mental changes following the removal of the right cerebral hemisphere for brain tumor. *Amer. J. Psychiat.*, *94*, 605–614.

Rubin, E. 1921. *Visuell wahrgenommene Figuren: Studien in psychologischer Analyse.* Teil I. Berlin: Gyldendalske Boghandel.

Rylander, G. 1939. *Personality changes after operations on the frontal lobes: a clinical study of 32 cases.* London: Humphrey Milford.

Saphir, W. 1945. Chronic hypochloremia simulating psychoneurosis. *J. Amer. Med. Ass.*, *129*, 510–512.

Schneirla, T. C. 1948. Psychology, comparative. *Encycl. Brit.*

Scott, W. W., Scott, C. C., and Luckhardt, A. B. 1938. Observations on the blood sugar level before, during, and after hunger periods in humans. *Amer. J. Physiol.*, *123*, 243–247.

Senden, M. v. 1932. *Raum- und Gestaltauffassung bei operierten Blindgeborenen vor und nach der Operation.* Leipzig: Barth.

Sherrington, C. S. 1906. *Integrative action of the nervous system.* New York: Scribner.

Sherrington, C. S. 1925. Remarks on some aspects of reflex inhibition. *Proc. Roy. Soc.*, *97B*, 519–545.

Sherrington, C. S. 1941. *Man on his nature.* New York: Macmillan.

Skinner, B. F. 1938. *The behavior of organisms: an experimental analysis.* New York: Appleton-Century.

Smith, D. E. 1939. Cerebral localization in somesthetic discrimination in the rat. *J. Comp. Psychol.*, 28, 161–188.

Smith, K. U. 1936. Visual discrimination in the cat: III. The relative effect of paired and unpaired stimuli in the discriminative behavior of the cat. *J. Genet. Psychol.*, 48, 29–57.

Smith, W. K. 1945. The functional significance of the rostral cingular gyrus as revealed by its responses to electrical excitation. *J. Neurophysiol.*, 8, 241–255.

Spearman, C. 1927. *The abilities of man.* New York: Macmillan.

Spence, K. W. 1938. Gradual versus sudden solution of discrimination problems by chimpanzees. *J. Comp. Psychol.*, 25, 213–224.

Spence, K. W. 1940. Continuous versus non-continuous interpretations of discrimination learning. *Psychol. Rev.*, 47, 271–288.

Sperry, R. W. 1943. Visuomotor coordination in the newt (*Triturus viridescens*) after regeneration of the optic nerve. *J. Comp. Neurol.*, 79, 33–55.

Sperry, R. W. 1947. Effect of crossing nerves to antagonistic limb muscles in the monkey. *Arch. Neurol. Psychiat.*, 58, 452–473.

Spiegel, E. A., Miller, H. R., and Oppenheimer, M. J. 1940. Forebrain and rage reactions. *J. Neurophysiol.*, 3, 539–548.

Spies, T. D., Aring, C. D., Gelperin, J., and Bean, W. B. 1938. The mental symptoms of pellagra: Their relief with nicotinic acid. *Amer. J. Med. Sci.*, 196, 461–475.

Spragg, S. D. S. 1940. Morphine addiction in chimpanzees. *Comp. Psychol. Monog.*, 15, No. 7.

Stoddard, G. D., and Wellman, B. L. 1940. Environment and the IQ. *Yearb. Nat. Soc. Stud. Educ.*, 39 (I), 405–442.

Stookey, B., Scarff, J., and Teitelbaum, M. 1941. Frontal lobectomy in the treatment of brain tumors. *Ann. Surg.*, 113, 161–169.

Swank, R. L., and Marchand, W. E. 1946. Combat neuroses: development of combat exhaustion. *Arch. Neurol. Psychiat.*, 55, 236–247.

Thorndike, E. L. 1931. *Human learning.* New York: Century.

Thurstone, L. L. 1935. *The vectors of mind.* Chicago: Univ. Chic. Press.

Tinbergen, N. 1942. An objectivistic study of the innate behavior of animals. *Bibl. Biotheoret.*, Leiden, 1, 39–98.

Tinklepaugh, O. L. 1928. An experimental study of representative factors in monkeys. *J. Comp. Psychol.*, 8, 197–236.

Titchener, E. B. 1920. Notes from the psychological laboratory of Cornell University. *Amer. J. Psychol.*, 31, 212–214.

Tolman, E. C. 1932. *Purposive behavior in animals and men.* New York: Century.

Tryon, R. C. 1939. Studies in individual differences in maze learning: VI. Disproof of sensory components: experimental effects of stimulus variation. *J. Comp. Psychol.*, 28, 361–415.

Valentine, C. W. 1930. The innate bases of fear. *J. Genet. Psychol.*, 37, 394–419.

Walker, A. E., and Weaver, T. A. 1940. Ocular movements from the occipital lobe in the monkey. *J. Neurophysiol.*, *3*, 353–357.

Watson, J. B. 1924. *Behaviorism.* New York: Norton.

Watts, J. W., and Freeman, W. 1946. Psychosurgery for the relief of intractable pain. *J. Int. Coll. Surg.*, *9*, 679–683.

Wechsler, D. 1939. *The measurement of adult intelligence.* Baltimore: Williams and Wilkins.

Weddel, G., Sinclair, D. C., and Feindel, W. H. 1948. An anatomical basis for alterations in quality of pain sensibility. *J. Neurophysiol.*, *11*, 99–109.

Weisenburg, T., and McBride, K. E. 1935. *Aphasia: a clinical and psychological study.* New York: Commonwealth Fund.

Weisenburg, T., Roe, A., and McBride, K. E. 1936. *Adult intelligence: a psychological study of test performances.* New York: Commonwealth Fund.

Weiss, P. 1941a. Autonomous versus reflexogenous activity of the central nervous system. *Proc. Amer. Phil. Soc.*, *84*, 53–64.

Weiss, P. 1941b. Nerve patterns: The mechanics of nerve growth. *Growth (Third Growth Symposium), 5,* 163–203.

Werner, H., and Strauss, A. 1939. Types of visuo-motor activity in their relation to low and high performance ages. *Proc. Amer. Ass. Ment. Defic.*, *44*, 163–168.

Wilson, G., and Rupp, C. 1947. Present trends in the practice of neurology. *J. Amer. Med. Ass.*, *133*, 509–511.

Wolf, E., and Zerrahn-Wolf, G. 1937. Flicker and the reactions of bees to flowers. *J. Gen. Physiol.*, *20*, 511–518.

Wolf, G. A., and Wolff, H. G. 1946. Studies on the nature of certain symptoms associated with cardiovascular disorders. *Psychosom. Med.*, *8*, 293–319.

Wolff, H. G. 1943. Emotions and gastric function. *Science*, *98*, 481–484.

Wolff, H. G., and Hardy, J. D. 1947. On the nature of pain. *Physiol. Rev.*, *27*, 167–199.

Woodrow, H. 1927. The effect of type of training on transference. *J. Educ. Psychol.*, *18*, 160–171.

Woodworth, R. S. 1921. *Psychology.* New York: Holt.

Woodworth, R. S. 1938. *Experimental psychology.* New York: Holt.

Wortis, H., Stein, M. H., and Jolliffe, N. 1942. Fiber dissociation in peripheral neuropathy. *Arch. Int. Med.*, *69*, 222–237.

Yerkes, R. M. 1916. The mental life of monkeys and apes: a study of ideational behavior. *Behavior Monog.*, *3*, No. 1.

Young, P. T. 1941. The experimental analysis of appetite. *Psychol. Bull.*, *38*, 129–164.

Young, P. T. 1944. Studies of food preference, appetite and dietary habit. I. Running activity and dietary habit of the rat in relation to food preference. *J. Comp. Psychol.*, *37*, 327–370.

Zangwill, O. L. 1937. A study of the significance of attitude in recognition. *Brit. J. Psychol., 28,* 12–17.

Zener, K. 1937. The significance of behavior accompanying conditioned salivary secretion for theories of the conditioned response. *Amer. J. Psychol., 50,* 384–403.

Zollinger, R. 1935. Removal of left cerebral hemisphere: report of a case. *Arch. Neurol. Psychiat., 34,* 1055–1064.

Index